THE AMERICAN FRONTIER

Our Unique Heritage

BOOKS BY NELSON BEECHER KEYES

The American Frontier: Our Unique Heritage

Hope of the Nation

THE AMERICAN FRONTIER

Our Unique Heritage

Nelson Beecher Keyes

HANOVER HOUSE

Garden City, N.Y.

Contents

6 *Contents*

THE AMERICAN FRONTIER

Our Unique Heritage

Introduction

> The frontier with its continuous influence is the most American thing in all America. In future generations we may perhaps become an amalgam of the European races and lose the advantages of a fresh continent, but we shall still possess and be shaped by a unique heritage.—Frederic L. Paxson, *History of the American Frontier*.

I T W A S within the lifetime of older generations still with us today that one of our leading historians, Frederick Jackson Turner, professor of history at the University of Wisconsin, and at Harvard, came to a striking conclusion. It was his contention in a paper which he read before the American Historical Association in 1893 that the American frontier held the key to the interpretation of our history. Surprisingly enough, however, he began his learned thesis by reading the obituary notice of the frontier on which his attention was focused.

Such a notice had appeared from no less authoritative a source than the bulletin of the Superintendent of the Census of 1890, in which that official had stated:

Up to and including 1880 the country had a frontier of settlement, but at the present the unsettled area has been so broken into . . . that there can hardly be said to be a frontier line. In the discussion of its extent, its western movement, etc., it cannot, therefore, any longer have a place in census reports.

Sometime during the decade between 1880 and 1890 the traditional frontier, which one of Dr. Turner's willing followers has called in the quotation at the head of this introduction "the most American thing in all America," had peacefully expired in good old age. In the welter of preoccupations in our rapidly growing country, it had been laid away in an unmarked grave. When the realization of what had transpired struck home to the good doctor, he rose to the occasion and pronounced a fitting requiem. His words of eulogy, titled *The Frontier in American History* can be found in almost any library, and are worthy of careful reading, for they explain in full this unique and abundant heritage that is unmistakably ours.

Exactly what was it that had lived so full a life and, despite its potent influences, been crowded from the national scene? What does the term "frontier" call to mind, and specifically the *American* frontier? To round out our answer we had best go back to Europe at the time when men first began to speculate on just what might lie to the west of them over the unknown ocean. In their homelands a frontier was a fortified boundary between two countries, running customarily through settled and fairly well populated areas. Such lines of demarcation might be crossed peaceably for trade, but not infrequently were they crossed in a quite different spirit in time of war. By and large European frontiers were restrictive barriers.

When the adventurous first came to these shores, they were in a sense extending the frontiers of their homelands, and the footholds gained on beaches and riverbanks were European outposts. They brought the cultures of native lands, and sought to establish and maintain experienced ways of life at great distances and under heavily altered circumstances from those under which their habits had been acquired. Many of the early defeats of settlement on this side of the ocean stem from attempts to transplant manners, methods, and ways of thought ill adapted to the "fresh continent."

The American frontier from the outset exercised a powerful influence, impartially culling out the incompetent and demanding of those to whom it permitted any degree of security marked revision of their thinking and their attitudes. And there is abundant evidence that it continued to exert a huge influence upon American development during the ensuing centuries, and is still a vital legacy, with certain values worthy of perpetuation.

In the earliest days it had many of the vestiges of European frontiers, in that a right to occupy new territory had to be bought—in goods, or in blood. But even where penetration was relatively peaceful, this new and untamed land levied other burdens upon those who would make it their own.

Beyond the initial clash between civilization and savagery there was another that was often even more costly between hungry stomachs and a reluctant nature. The wilderness, if it was to be won, imposed its own discipline upon those who entered it, and had its own heartless ways of making them more tractable with respect to its demands.

Life may have been a struggle back home in Europe, but in America it was primitive, and along the frontiers often violent, godless, and near to savagery. Yet it had its compensations. Many who came here did so under pressure of one sort or other, and in an age that was primarily agricultural they were almost without exception land-hungry. For more than two hundred fifty years after people in some numbers began to reach our shores, there was almost always just beyond the farthest cabin in the last village or hamlet *free* land. This was the magic impulse that drained men and women from Europe, and later on from the eastern colonies and states, and filled in America from one ocean to the other at a pace undreamed of by even its most sanguine early promoters.

Beyond the initial contests for possession of the land, and that with unwilling nature, the frontier set up another struggle which was to have wholesome effects upon Americans and American affairs and managed to stir men to their great benefit across much of the world. Men sought the frontiers here not only for land, but also for freedom. As long as one's neighbors' chimneys were not too close, individualism could grow to be pretty rugged. Men and women thrown largely upon their own resources learned to be self-sufficing as well as self-sustaining, and in some instances might carry such sufficiency to rather unfortunate ends. But with frequent threats from the displaced natives close at hand, or from a capricious nature overhanging their efforts, there was almost always present some call for co-operative action. There were times when neighbors either stood together and both weathered the storm, or they ran the rather certain risk of perishing separately.

The permanent settlements along the Atlantic seaboard from Maine to Georgia were at first predominantly English. Although the colonists clustered about them were forced to adjust to conditions at the edge of a wilderness, these tidewater communities changed less rapidly than did the more resolute, which soon began to press back into the interior. Communication was difficult and hazardous during the seventeenth and most of the eighteenth century, so that contact with the coastal areas was relatively infrequent. A trip to Boston from the Connecticut River settlements, or to Charles Towne from above the Fall Line in the Carolinas was an event of a lifetime, if ever experienced, for the great majority. The more remote communities were generally under the necessity of working out their own problems and settling their own affairs, with the result that the people in them were soon on the way to becoming Americans rather than just neo-Europeans.

As the disinherited of other nations began to arrive and in many instances headed quickly for the frontier, slowly but constantly shifting further inland, there was a forced mingling of diverse backgrounds, out of which came a selection of characteristics best adapted to the rigorous life to be faced. By the time this frontier was piercing the Appalachians at the onset of the Revolution, it was breeding a race of men with an inherent sense of democratic ways. Their numbers increased rapidly as we moved into the next century, and they were soon influencing thought throughout the land, and in Europe as well. The realistic schooling in individualism on the one hand, and the willingness to co-operate for group benefits on the other, were two of the frontier's great contributions in the formation of American character.

Had we continued as colonies, and the proclamation of George III given in 1763, limiting western expansion to the headwaters of rivers flowing into the Atlantic, been enforceable, our history would have been far different. The limited frontiers would have soon been overtaken, have been absorbed by and become integral parts of the populous coastal areas, and their inhabitants remained British, or at least markedly European, in spirit. But one of the unique features of our heritage is the continuing influence of the frontier as it recurred time after time, and in area after area across the broad waist of North America. It was more than a "melting pot," and actually a long series of refiner's furnaces, burning the dross from older cultures and transmuting the remainder into a bright new metal with excellent characteristics. It was in the white heat of the frontier that American character was patterned and formed.

Although it was some sixty years ago that Dr. Turner observed its influences upon us in the following words, we would hesitate to alter his estimate in any major respect today, and might well wish that although the frontier based largely upon land in a fresh continent has passed, there are other frontiers before us, with power to further mold us for our continuing good. Said this great master of his subject:

From the conditions of frontier life came intellectual traits of profound importance. The works of travelers along each frontier from colonial days onward describe certain common traits, and these traits have, while softening down, still persisted as survivals in the place of their origin, even when a higher social organization succeeded. The result is that to the frontier the American intellect owes its striking characteristics. That coarseness and strength combined with acuteness and inquisitiveness; that practical, inventive turn of mind, quick to find expedients; that masterful grasp of material things, lacking in the artistic, but powerful to effect great ends; that restless, nervous energy; that dominant individualism, working for good or evil, and withal that buoyancy and exuberance which comes with freedom—these are the traits of the frontier, or traits called out elsewhere because of the existence of the frontier. Since the days when the fleet of Columbus sailed into the waters of the New World, America has been another name for opportunity, and the people of the United States have taken their tone from the incessant expansion which has not only been open but has ever been forced upon them. He would be a rash prophet who would assert that the expansive character of American life has now entirely ceased. Movement has been its dominant fact, and, unless this training has no effect upon a people, the American energy will continually demand a wider field for its exercise.

Ours is indeed a unique heritage, and one with which we need be more familiar. Much happened along the American frontier from the days when the first Norseman pointed his *knorr* westward until the yesterday in which this older type of frontier passed from the scene through natural causes. It can perhaps best be visited by examining typical and often unusual incidents which occurred along it, and by a concise look at their causes and consequences, which we will do in the pages that follow.

I

America is Discovered

They sailed. They sailed. Then spake the mate:
"This mad sea shows his teeth tonight.
He curls his lips, he lies in wait,
He lifts his teeth as if to bite!
Brave Adm'r'l, say but one good word:
What shall we do when hope is gone?"
The words leapt like a leaping sword:
"Sail on! sail on! sail on! and on!"

—Joaquin Miller, *Columbus.*

CHRIS PIGEON, as his neighbors knew him as a boy in north Italy, grew up to be a determined, persevering, and resourceful man. Also he was under the spell of an all-pervading idea. It was his unshakable belief that if you sailed west, instead of east as custom dictated, you would not plunge over the outer edge of a flat earth and into certain destruction in a watery abyss, but instead you would very likely discover land, and possibly a shorter, less obstructed route to the Spice Islands off the coast of Asia. If that could be accomplished, fortune was certain to smile on you, for you could then break the monopoly in the profitable trade that originated there.

In the days before artificial refrigeration, spices were very much a necessity, needed to keep food palatable until it could be eaten up. The lucrative commerce in them had long been in the hands of the Saracens, a Moslem people, who brought these condiments into the eastern Mediterranean, whence they were distributed through much of Europe by the merchants of Venice. Naturally those who profited so handsomely from this trade carefully guarded the Red Sea approaches to its point of origin.

One division of these Moslem peoples, the Moors, had brought a remarkable civilization across from North Africa into the Spanish peninsula, nurturing and perfecting it there for several centuries. But they stood in the way of an ambitious husband and wife team attempting to seize control in this southwestern corner of Europe. Thus it happened that these Moors were in the process of being exterminated at the very time our navigator with the novel belief sought backing from this busy king and queen.

He had pleaded his case with many others among the powerful and wealthy, but without avail, and had come to the conclusion his best hopes lay with these joint rulers, Ferdinand of Aragon and Isabella of Castile.

With a major enterprise claiming their attention, his suit made little progress. But the man was patient, and by now penniless, and he had little choice but to wait. He employed his time exploiting his project among the members of the court, and succeeded in building up sufficient opposition in certain quarters that he barely escaped falling into the lethal clutches of the Inquisition.

Yet his persistence ultimately paid off, and Christopher Columbus not only obtained the necessary backing, but managed to secure an agreement which promised him huge benefits. The undertaking was a gamble, and Columbus surely realized how great a one. It was not that he doubted the basic idea, for of that he was certain. But there was a broad, uncertain, and at times vindictive ocean to cross, in none too seaworthy vessels, manned by crews hagridden by nonsensical fears, and officered by men whose loyalty in all cases might not be beyond question. But he made a skillful presentation of his case, giving it the appearance of a well-calculated risk to his royal backers. And once the agreement was signed, he hurried through the preparations and set out to give his hazardous enterprise a trial on the gaming board of geography.

What had built into this Genoese navigator and adventurer the assurance that his ideas were sound? Here he was prepared to risk his life on uncharted seas, or his neck in a noose, if he returned empty-handed from a wild-goose chase beyond the horizon. What made him sufficiently certain his scheme would work? And was it original with him, and completely untested? To these latter queries even he would have had to reply with a qualified "Hardly!"

EARLY NAVIGATION AND NAVIGATORS

Men had been sailing about the seas since time immemorial. They had hugged the shores at first, then, being now and again blown far off course by a contrary wind, had made new discoveries and developed the courage to start island-hopping. In the long, long ago Solomon was sending ships, built at his own yards at Ezion-geber on an arm of the Red Sea, as far down Africa's eastern shores as Madagascar, and also to India and Ceylon. Tarshish, to which he and Hiram of Tyre sent fleets, was probably outside the Gates of Hercules on the Atlantic coast of Spain; while it is thought Hiram's ships even brought tin from the mines in the Cornwall hills of Britain for use in the cosmetics trade in Egypt nearly three thousand years ago.

By the time Alexander the Great was striding with a heavy heel across the Near East as far as India, another navigator whose home port was in the Mediterranean seems to have slipped up as far as the northern tip of Scotland and been encouraged there to go on to Iceland. His name was Pytheas.

Then as the Christian centuries began to drift by, navigation over wider areas was no longer confined to the sailors of the Mediterranean basin. Up about the Baltic and North seas were hardy tribes, known to us as the Norsemen. Quite frankly they were pirates —not entirely an ignoble profession in those days—and in early raids they attacked and subdued Slavish settlements in what is now Russia. Driving up the rivers there that flowed toward the west, they conquered as they went, and then either hauled their boats overland or built new, and descended eastbound streams that carried them to the Black and Caspian seas. Even then their unbounded energy was far from spent, and they came near to capturing the great trading city and center of empire Constantinople.

Next they turned their attention down the Atlantic shores, overran the British islands, wrested half his kingdom from Alfred the Great in 886, and within a hundred years had control of both England and Norman France. These archplunderers were well on the road to the acquisition of an empire. But while they were without the political competence to achieve lasting dominion over other lands, their ability in navigation and the handling of ships was destined to take them over unsailed waters and into unknown lands.

Heading west from Norway some seven hundred miles over open ocean, they came to Iceland about the end of the ninth century, only to find the Irish there ahead of them. But the latter were for the most part priests, who had fled to this chilly island for retreat, refuge, and new fields of missionary endeavor. Since they gave little opposition, the Norse began colonizing, and by the early 900s their Iceland settlements boasted a population of nearly fifty thousand.

Astonishingly enough a fair share of these settlers had come, or been brought there, from the British Isles. Thus we begin to realize that the North Atlantic was not at all unused to ships, and long before Columbus sailed that August day in 1492.

The life in this Iceland outpost was sanguine and virile, and men not infrequently killed other men—but sometimes too many, or those with too much influence. Eric, the redheaded son of one Thorvald Asvaldsson, became involved in one of these unfortunate affairs, and, being no longer a trustworthy asset to the community, was banished for three years. Making a virtue of necessity, he decided upon a voyage in the hope of tracking down an interesting rumor.

Someone had reported small, low-lying islands to the west, so off he went in search of them, and roamed far enough to encounter a real find, a huge glacier-clad land mass. He looked it over thoroughly during most of three years, and then sailed home to exploit his discovery. With the ingenuity of a realtor promoting a new subdivision, he had the temerity to call this bleak and icy waste Greenland.

The tall tales he told back home in Iceland not only won him forgiveness, but soon headed him back to Greenland, about 985, in command of fourteen ships bearing some five hundred people and their creatures and belongings, bent upon establishing colonies. Eric the Red had managed to open up and take a limited look beyond the closely drawn curtains which the awe-inspiring waters of the broad Atlantic had long draped to the west of Europe. Soon some of his kinsmen would have a more extensive view behind this obscure backdrop.

THE FINDING OF VINLAND THE GOOD

In the early summer of the year 1000 the Norse king, Olaf Tryggvason, bid farewell to three palace guests who had been with him for some months. Although the former rulers and their people in this land had stoutly resisted Christianity, it had at last been embraced, and the king had succeeded in converting these three young chieftains, who were now returning to their respective colonies as missionaries.

One of them was Leif Ericsson, from Greenland, son of the redoubtable Eric. On his inbound voyage he had attempted to come direct, but had touched at the Hebrides. The return trip he determined to make without a stop. But a storm wind caught hold of his knorr, and together with the Greenland and Labrador currents, drove the vessel and its occupants far, far to the southwest.

Where did he finally manage a safe landing? Where was it that he saw *mausur* or maple trees, from which he cut logs, and native fields of grain—probably wild rice—as well as the grapes which he eventually took home to his colony on Davis Strait? At least six states would like to feel that he found a haven on their coasts, but Massachusetts seems to have been favored by his visit. However, he had a considerable mission to perform at home. So after but a brief stay he took off for the northeast, and being a capable navigator, arrived safely at his destination and soon had Greenland Christianized.

But the grapes which he brought home, either in their natural state or made into wine, and the tales Leif continued to tell made some of his hearers restless. By 1003 an extensive party composed of his relatives and their retainers set off for Vinland the Good. The old Norse sagas which contain our only preserved records of this journey are not too considerate of details, but the several vessels and their occupants apparently dropped south to the forbidding coasts of Labrador, where they found little but desolate rocky headlands, and so they named it Flagstone Land. Skirting along its grim shores, these folk from treeless Greenland must have been very gratified when they found timber at the mighty peninsula's southeast corner, which they named Markland.

Swinging into the Gulf of St. Lawrence, they seem to have followed up this waterway, perhaps to the Point du Monts, where they may have become conscious they were ascending a great river valley. Feeling their way back to the east along its southern shores, and probably near the tip of the Gaspé coast, they chanced upon a rather startling find. It was the rotting keel of a ship, and in a land where the native peoples did not build keelboats. What European, possibly before Leif Ericsson's visit here, had been first in America but had not lived to tell the tale of his exploits?

How far did these Greenlanders get? They reported seeing *Skraelings,* or inferior people, a term they used for the Eskimos. But the description given of these natives in the sagas better fits the Indians. Finally they did reach an area which fitted the accounts Leif had given of the country to which he had been driven. For a time they had hopes of establishing a colony, only to encounter sufficient trouble with the natives that they abandoned the idea and sailed for their homes in Greenland. At what spot was their settlement to have been located? An enterprising schoolteacher, who had given the matter intensive study, spent a profitable vacation several years ago. At Bass Hole, near Yarmouth on Cape Cod, he found evidence which seemed to point conclusively to a lengthy Norse visitation.

What had been achieved? The scholarly Dr. Edward Channing of Harvard long maintained that our history would have been exactly what it is now had Leif Ericsson never been born, and if no Norseman had ever turned the prow of his knorr west of Iceland. This assumption can well be subject to some qualification, as another too little known Norse deed of daring may help to indicate. It was lost sight of for more than five hundred years, and might have lodged in oblivion, had not an enterprising farmer cut down a tree and found that its roots held in their tight clutch an important bit of stone.

When this stone was extracted from the tree's firm embrace and dusted off, it was found to be covered with strange graven characters. These were pronounced to be *runes,* an ancient form of Scandinavian writing. Those who first examined it soon after its finding in 1898 insisted it was spurious. But the incident it recorded was so unusual and fraught with drama that it set off many years of serious research. That narrative which it climaxed is briefly as follows.

THE STORY OF THE KENSINGTON RUNESTONE

The year was 1355, and Norway, like most of Europe, had suffered heavily from the Black Death. There had been other catastrophes as well, both in the homeland and in Iceland. The times were confused and the future so highly uncertain that the great landowner and judge, Paul Knutson, who had just strode from the castle at Bergen, was convinced that the king's orders to him stemmed from sheer madness. But he was in no position to refuse His Majesty's commands, and hoisting himself into the saddle, he set off in company with a young priest for the western harbor where ships were being readied for this dubious mission. As their horses plodded along over the rugged trail, the older man discussed the project with his companion.

There had been little or no word from the "western," or second and more distant of the two settlements in Greenland for several years, and then the report that it had disappeared. Had it been wiped out by the plague, as had so many communities? Had it abandoned Christianity, planted there so long ago by Eric the Red, and joined with the Skraelings, the Eskimos, and gone off to their haunts to live in sin beyond the control of their sovereign; or been butchered by them? Or had it moved on to a more favorable climate, perhaps to the storied Vinland?

It was Paul Knutson's duty to investigate the situation, and whatever the conditions, right them. King Magnus' shrill words still rang in his ears, "We will not let the colony perish in our days. You must find it, even its remnants, and bring it back to Christian thoughts and ways. Your task is before you, and whatever it costs in time, in effort, even in lives, you must not return empty-handed!"

By the end of the three-day journey to where the ships lay, the Christian zeal of the young priest had altered Knutson's pessimism at least to tolerance. The leader quickly inspected the ships, men, and equipment. Surely the king had not been niggardly; and since preparations were complete and spring was well advanced, the little fleet was headed down the fiord and out into the Atlantic's broad waters.

But a violent storm hurled the ships far off their course to the north, and it was many days before they could get the pole star firmly over their starboard gunnels and their prows pointing toward their objective. As it was they hit the mighty headland far up along its eastern shores, and spent precious days, and made sizable inroads on their provisions before they crept around its southern cape.

A good Catholic himself, and under the constant tutelage of this resolute priest, Knutson had become appalled by the thought of men and women turning from their Savior and selling their souls to the evil one. As they crept up the rugged western coast his fervor for the task ahead mounted, never to abate.

Then came a day late in the summer fast slipping behind them when the sinking afternoon sun brilliantly lighted up a green fringe at the inner end of a deep fiord. This was unmistakably their destination. But the day was surely too far spent for them to hope of reaching a landing there before dark. So they hove to, and through the dark hours tried to console themselves that it was lights they could see, and not just reflections from the brilliant stars overhead.

As they moved up the channel in the receding shadows of early morning, the sharpest-eyed lookouts were posted above. Could they perhaps make out smoke from the town's chimneys? Were there no boats headed down the fiord to welcome them? To all such questions there were only negative answers. Could this mean there was to be a struggle ahead? Arms were made ready and fresh lookouts sent aloft. Or had they perhaps mistaken the fiord?

After tense moments the lookout on the mast of the knorr in the lead cried out, "I see no houses even! And no signs of men, women, or creatures!"

More discouraging minutes crept by, and at last they were at the mooring stones, but not one of the colony's vessels was in sight. The knorr stood off until the men from the smaller boats were ashore. Then her plank was thrust out and Paul Knutson clambered onto the rocks and led thirty picked men up the slope to where there should have been a village of many homes, in which a thousand or more people had formerly lived.

In the hush of expectancy hardly a word was spoken. Against the south wall of a reef of rocks lay a tangled heap of whitened bones. The men examined them carefully, spreading them about with their spear points. But they were definitely not human, thank heavens. The larger ones were unmistakably the remains of cows, the smaller those of sheep.

Hurrying on, they came to the end of what had once been the main street of this western settlement. It was marked off by heaps of stone and sod now well leveled and spread about by savage winter frost and winds. But search among these ruins as they would, there was not a plank, not a tool, not a shred of anything man-made left behind. There were graves, but none seemed to be too recent, and there were no remains of human bodies aboveground. There were no indications that either Black Death or savage carnage had visited this remote outpost. Still every man, woman, and child of a once populous settlement nearly three hundred years old had vanished into the already crisp Arctic air, without a trace of the reason, or of a possible destination.

The harbor about the cluster of once much used mooring stones was equally barren of clues, as was the countryside for as far as it could be seen from the top of the rocky ridge behind the village site. Questions piled up as the search continued, but they soon began to group about three possibilities. Had the Skraelings—in this case the neighboring Eskimos—done away with the people, and then carried off all that had belonged to them? But there was little or nothing to indicate that this had happened. Could it be then that they had voluntarily joined with the once detested heathen natives at some distant rendezvous? Such a move could not be reconciled. Or was it that, numbed in body and spirit by this savage climate, they had transferred to Markland, or more probably to the traditionally more clement and better favored Vinland the Good far to the south? Ah! Had they indeed?

This was not the time or the place for conjecture, for the daylight hours were growing shorter and the lengthening nights were by now biting-cold. A hasty conference aboard the knorr decided their next step. They would search for these renegades along the shores of Markland, and then of Vinland, since to do so was distinctly within the spirit of the king's orders. Thus the lines were cast off, the mooring pins withdrawn from the stones to which the ships had been lashed, and they headed down toward the mouth of the fiord, there swinging toward the southwest into icy waters.

A LONG JOURNEY INTO THE UNKNOWN

From here on certain assumptions must of necessity enter into the telling of a heroic tale. The first is that they sought their quarry in more temperate lands that traditionally lay to the west and south, and it seems most probable that they did. The south-flowing current in the strait before them, into which the setting sun dipped, would have carried them to and along the rugged Labrador coast, and through the narrow Belle Isle passage between it and Newfoundland. Along the now timbered shores, which harbored game for sustenance, but more probably further on at some point in the Gulf of St. Lawrence, they no doubt beached their craft and hastily arranged winter shelter for themselves.

With the onset of spring they quite likely started their search, and the lower reaches of this great river are so vast that anything like thorough exploration of them should have exhausted a full season.

It is safe to believe they later moved out around the great headland to the south, and down the coast, carefully checking the shores of Nova Scotia, of Maine, even of New England or beyond. There are a number of years to account for, but a rugged, heavily broken shore line, with bays, sounds, and river outlets, might have consumed long periods if they were fully investigated. In the next cove, or along the banks of the next navigable river, might be the settlement of those they so avidly sought. By now they were completely dedicated to their task. The abandoned townsite in Greenland had raised questions that must be answered. Their reputations, possibly their lives, were at stake. They could not go home empty-handed!

There may have been another reason, too, for the long continuation of what must at times have seemed a most fruitless proceeding. The consoling thought can well have dawned upon them that there might be commercial possibilities in this great "island" on the other side of the sea, for they took it to be only an island, albeit a large one. Almost unbelievable tales were filtering into all the capitals of Europe of the wealth and wonders that had been discovered in lands far, far to the east by Marco Polo, by Friar John, by William Rubruquis. Under such stimulus there would surely be the hope that they, too, might come upon equally astonishing things in this New World over the ocean to the west.

Four years could have been spent quite handily along the eastern seaboard. Then perhaps came the compelling wish to get this arduous assignment completed and sail for home. They had not found the other side of the island onto which they had blundered, and which appeared to grow ever larger. At least there seemed no way around it toward the south. Could it be that the Greenland folk had reached its western shores by using a northerly route? A northwest passage to the Orient would be very much in the minds of Europeans during the next one hundred fifty years, and such a possibility could easily have occurred to this group. A search for it may well have sent them back up the coast, where they patiently made their way along repelling shores, and into the tremendous sea that splits northern Canada. If an intrepid Englishman in the employ of Dutch merchants could accomplish the feat a century and a half later and give his name to Hudson Bay, surely these dauntless Norsemen did not lack the courage to make a similar attempt.

Once in this huge bay, they would find but few rivers of any size along its eastern shores. In fact there would be none to compare with the St. Lawrence they had recently visited until they came, on its western coast, to the mouth of the Nelson. This mighty stream, equal to or larger than any in Europe, draws its waters from far below the present Canadian border. Considering their purpose, it would surely deserve to be explored.

Leaving their larger ships under guard at its outlet, these impatient men may well have reasoned that they could find a point where its headwaters, and those of the St. Lawrence, or other of the larger streams encountered in Vinland, would be separated only by a narrow height of land. Had not their forefathers crossed Russia from the Baltic to the Black and Caspian seas in this very manner five centuries before?

They were not above poling heavy craft through rushing rapids, or portaging them across country by means of log rolls beneath their keels if sufficient inducement lay ahead. It is said that the other early explorers of our Middle West heard stories from the Indians of a people whom their forefathers had once encountered and their descendants still spoke of as "wooden boat men." Thus there must have been contacts with the natives, from whom they may well have learned the benefits of their much lighter skin boats, or canoes, by means of which exploration of inland waterways would have been a far less exhausting task.

Fifty of the original party were apparently still alive, and ten of them, having been given detailed instructions, were left to guard whatever was left of the little fleet that had sailed from the homeland so long before. The remaining forty, presumably with Paul Knutson at their head, set off up the Nelson River.

What a thrill they may well have had as that stream suddenly widened. Had it not been for the freshness of its waters, they could at first have taken Lake Winnipeg for an arm of the sea, even the western sea which they sought. Its eastern shores would have been searched hopefully for a river leading back toward Vinland, or for traces of the displaced Greenlanders. Surely there would have been disappointment as they finally came to its southern end and found there the somewhat smaller Red River, pouring out from a trackless wilderness. Yet there was still hope, and up this stream they evidently worked their way, ever anticipating some discovery of consequence.

MINNESOTA IN 1362

It was now 1362, and seven years since they had sailed from their homeland. The summer was advancing, and the thought of another winter, another year, maybe longer, away from home began to sap their remaining enthusiasm heavily. This smaller river up which they struggled was anything but promising, and each stretch of shoal water, each more frequent need to portage their craft added to their growing discouragement.

Then suddenly the nature of the country changed. Where their course had for countless miles been over virtually treeless plains, they began to skirt heavy forest land stretching away to the east. There had been Indians along their route, but in open country they could be avoided. Now they encountered more frequent signs of these red people, and they not only seemed more savage, but appeared from and disappeared back into the forest lands in far greater numbers. Once or twice they had missed an attack by overwhelming numbers only by the narrowest margin.

A change in the direction of the river made it advisable for them to shift over into what was taken to be a great chain of lakes, which were either interconnected, or had but short, easy portages between them. Food, too, had been something of a concern, and finding the fishing good in one of the larger of these lakes, a camp was established at its northern end. The hot sun and the air free from moisture made it an ideal spot in which to dry their daily catch, which might stand them in good stead in the uncertain days ahead. With the exception of a sufficient number left to guard and maintain the camp, usually about two thirds of the men were set to fishing. Those who remained behind cleaned the day's catch, built light racks, and set the split fish out to dry.

The south end of their chosen lake proved the most fruitful spot, and the skin boats now being used customarily gathered there over a deep hole, just out of sight of the camp, which was hidden from them by a long sliver of land. The boats were well loaded as they headed home late one afternoon, and there was the customary hallooing and calling as they moved up the lake, but today surprisingly no response. This seemed rather strange, for the breeze had gone down and the water surface was like glass.

As the distance shortened and still no reply was forthcoming, paddles dug a little deeper and there was an extra thrust as the craft sped along. Soon the camp was in full view, but not a man stirred anywhere about it.

Only the lightest weapons had been taken on the fishing trip, and these were caught up quickly as the boats touched shore and the men sprang out. A few quick bounds and they were up the hillside and in the camp, which was a shambles. The ten who had been left behind were strewn about, their bodies red with blood from the gaping wounds where their scalps had been slit and torn away. A quick search showed that most of the arms, tools, and gear had been carried off, and there was ample evidence that the attack had been carried out by fully a hundred warriors.

It was a staggering blow, made doubly heavy by the fact that Paul Knutson was among the dead, an arrow driven clean through his neck. From among the thirty still alive, guards were posted, others collected what was left of the scattered gear and stowed it in the small boats, while the remainder fell to digging one grave suf-

ficiently large to hold the ten bodies. It was dark before the gruesome task of burial was completed; and waiting no further, the
dispirited remnant slipped out onto the lake and spent the night on
the larger of the two skerries, or small islands, which lay a mile or so
offshore.

By the crack of dawn they were headed south, in the opposite
direction from which their attackers had left, moving as rapidly as
they could from one lake to another by connecting streams and
hurried portages. It was a feverish day, and so was the next; but by
the end of the third, and after what seemed a comfortable number
of miles between them and their enemies, they came to a tiny lake
having a little skerry in it from which a fair view could be had in all
directions.

Here they settled down to catch their breath, and also to finally
decide what best to do. They had lost all count of time, but one
among the thirty survivors, the young priest who had left the castle
with Knutson that fateful day now so long, long ago, was certain the
following would be the Lord's Day. There had been but the briefest
prayers said beside the common grave of the ten who had perished,
and no proper requiem. So in the evening he and two others sought
out a spot for an altar.

By the edge of the plot carpeted with the buffalo grass on which
they had chosen to sleep was a slab of stone about as long as a man's
arm, half as wide, and not too thick. Flat and smooth on one of its
larger faces, it was set upon a cairn of smaller stones, and the priest
agreed it would do admirably. And so it was that, as they awoke at
sunrise, the good father stepped before his rude altar and sang a
Mass for their departed comrades, adding a litany for their own pres-
ervation.

As they were rising from their knees, he asked of their new
leader, "Should we not set this altar slab up as a memorial to them?"
It was quickly agreed, and a boatman with chisel and maul assigned
to him to carve an inscription.

Picking bits of charcoal from the ashes of the fire of the past
night, the priest laboriously sketched the runes, and they were cut
into the stone one by one as he drew them. But this piece of native
graywacke was granite-hard, and the more than two hundred characters took the remainder of that day, and part of the next. At last
finished, the inscription was read aloud several times to the satisfaction of all. A shallow hole had been dug to receive it, into which one
end was tipped, and it was firmly tamped in place with smaller stones.

It was toward sundown when all was finished, and the priest had pronounced a benediction over it.

And then those that remained of this gallant party seem to have disappeared quite as thoroughly and completely as the Greenlanders they had sought. Tools and weapons presumably theirs have come to light, but the most convincing bit of evidence of their visit to western Minnesota nearly six hundred years ago lies in the stone memorial which turned up just before the advent of the present century. It had been found on what had once been an island in a small lake; and experts agree that it reads:

> (We are) 8 Goths and 22 Norwegians on (an)
> exploration-journey from Vinland (across)
> the West. (We) had a camp by (a lake with)
> 2 skerries one *days-journey* north from this
> stone. We were out and fished one day. After
> we came home found 10 (of our) men red with
> blood and dead. AV(e) M(aria)! Save (us)
> from evil! (We) have 10 of (our men) by the
> *sea* to look after our ship(s) 14 *days-journey*
> from this island. Year 1362.

Two questions quite logically present themselves at this point, the first being dual: Is there no trace of these survivors; and did their companions left to guard their ships find their way home? Some believe that those who left this memorial stone were absorbed by the tribe of Mandan Indians, but there is little to substantiate such a theory. As to those not engaged in this brush with the Indians, it is quite certain they did return either to Iceland or Norway. But the journey had resulted in failure, the silent years were descending on the homeland, and sagas recording great exploits were no longer written.

The second question then follows naturally: How can this effort, great as it may have been, have in any way influenced Columbus and his achievement?

In the years before he won the consent and backing of Ferdinand and Isabella, Columbus served his apprenticeship at sea. It is known that he visited England, and there is some reason to believe that he touched at Iceland. It would be folly to believe that he did not improve each and every opportunity to learn all that he could about journeys to Greenland and beyond. And any who have been at sea know the loquacious tendencies of most old salts and their almost inexhaustible fund of sea lore reaching back through the ages.

Long before Columbus was born there are reported to have been charts indicating a large island lying in the Atlantic well to the west of Ireland, which had been given the name Brazil. The Cabots sailing out of Bristol, England, but five years after Columbus' first voyage were in search of it, and it is claimed that others out of this same port had sought for it during many years.

The navigators and seafaring men of that distant day were neither scholars nor budding authors in search of a publisher. But when in port, and warmed by a mug of grog, many of them could recount thrilling and highly illuminating experiences. Without thought of disparagement of Columbus, his inquiring tendencies can well have uncovered pretty convincing evidence that a voyage to the west from Spain had well above an even chance of depositing him on land. With reasonable reservations, he may have had a personal conviction that it would be a New World. For his immediate purposes it may have been more prudent to predict it would be the Indies.

But with or without Norse thrusts to the west, it was his caravels that sailed, and it was through his efforts that America was made known to a restless world. Within a few years his successors were ashore on the mainland, bent on conquest; and with some of them we will have a firsthand look at a portion of what is today our "native land."

II

Coronado Enters Our Southwest

Spanish expansion owed much to the work of the missionaries, who gave up everything for the faith and who incidentally spread the seeds of Hispanic civilization. The Spaniards, led as a rule by the Jesuits, the Franciscans, and the Dominicans, penetrated farther and farther inland. The missionaries' intense religious fervor and disregard for their own safety or personal advantage became a powerful force in European expansion.—Boak, Hyma and Slosson, *The Growth of Western Civilization.*

ALTHOUGH Columbus received little in the way of tangible returns from his voyages of discovery, the Spanish crown was astute enough to realize there was a probable potential involved that deserved protecting. So it was that within a year of the "admiral's" leaving on his second trip west, the Treaty of Tordesillas was entered into with Portugal dividing the spheres of influence of the two countries along a north and south line drawn 370 leagues west of the Cape Verde and Azores Islands. Portugal was to have title to all new lands lying east of this boundary, and Spain those discovered to the west.

There were uncertain years as Ferdinand and Isabella were consolidating their gains at home, and especially after the death of the former in 1516. But during those years Cuba and Puerto Rico were subdued and made ready as bases for operations on the mainland. Ponce de León did land in Florida in 1513, and claimed that area for his sovereigns, but a well-placed Indian arrow quickly terminated his occupation.

It was while Charles, the Hapsburg grandson of Ferdinand, was solidifying his hold on his forebear's throne that Hernando Cortés attacked Mexico. Within three years the doughty conquistador had full control of that land, was shipping galleons of gold from its glittering Aztec capital to the homeland, and made that city the headquarters of the viceroyalty of New Spain, with himself its captain-general and governor.

The strongly religious Isabella had been swayed in supporting Columbus' ventures by the hope that Christianity might flow through Spanish means to heathen peoples beyond the seas. That intent and purpose was never fully erased from Spain's colonial endeavors. But the golden loot from Mexico, followed after Pizarro's conquest of Peru in 1533 by a literal torrent of the yellow metal flowing into the coffers in Madrid, gave both the Spanish crown and its favorites an insatiable thirst for plunder. The result was that Christian charity and pagan greed marched hand in hand onto the American continent.

THE SEARCH FOR THE SEVEN GOLDEN CITIES

Unquestionably it was this hope of quick, easy riches that had taken another Spanish nobleman into Florida. There Cabeza de Vaca had been frustrated in his search, and he and a handful of survivors suffered a long series of hair-raising experiences as they struggled to make their way back along the Gulf coast to Mexico. Several years were spent among the Indians in Texas as medicine men.

Finally breaking away from their captors, De Vaca and three others, including a swaggering Negro, Estavan, wandered across the Texas plains, through New Mexico, and eventually appeared in Compostela in western Mexico in 1536, more dead than alive, and very likely a bit deranged after what they had been through. As they recuperated, they spun a web of fantastic tales of what they had seen and experienced, including one describing seven fabulous Indian cities. These were filled with houses five or more stories high, whose walls were sheathed in glistening gold. Since there was a probable limit to the portable wealth that could be seized and shipped off home from either Mexico or Peru, this news of new sources was of transcendent import.

When the accounts were related to Don Antonio Mendoza, the king's viceroy in Mexico City, this top man in Spanish America realized they should be investigated, and with dispatch. Since De Vaca had sailed for home, and was not available to provide further details, His Excellency chose a priest, Fray Marcos de Niza, provided him with an escort party, including the slave Estavan, and hurried him to the north to verify the reports.

Estavan and some sixty others were sent on ahead to make

peace with the Indians. But the Negro managed only to antagonize the natives, was slain by them, and the remainder streaked back to meet the good padre and his associates. Whether Fray Marcos managed to get closer to the Seven Cities of Cíbola than the point one hundred fifty miles away where this meeting took place is not clear. But within the year he was back in the capital again, giving blanket endorsement to De Vaca's reports, no doubt taking the word of those who had fled after Estavan had been murdered.

The good father's optimistic confirmation set fire to smoldering ambitions. With covetousness goading him on, the viceroy made plans worthy of the occasion and set them in motion with a dispatch quite uncommon in Spanish affairs in the latter years of their colonial efforts on this side of the ocean.

He had brought out with him from Spain, some four years before, a young nobleman, Francisco Vásquez de Coronado, whom he had recently installed as governor of the west coast province of New Galicia. Although but thirty years old, Coronado had already been well seasoned in both the arts of war and of administration, and was the very person to head this expedition. So great were its probable rewards that the flower of Spanish aristocracy then gathered in Mexico bid against one another for the privilege of taking part.

The rallying point was Compostela, seat of government in Coronado's domain; and there, following Mass on Sunday, February 22, 1540, Mendoza held a grand review and inspection. By his side stood a notary, who carefully drew a muster roll of men, steeds, and armor. The soldiery was almost without exception of high birth; and 230 among the near three hundred such were mounted. Among them they had 552 horses, all but two of which were *caballos*, or spirited stallions.

The remainder of the men were formed into infantry companies, and preserved records indicate the manner in which each of them, and the horsemen above, were accoutered. Such was the care with which Spain kept account of her colonial activities.

Beside Coronado there was an ensign-general, the second-in-command; an army master, whose rashness brought his death within the first few days; a captain of artillery; and one of infantry. These, with their charges, together with their commander in chief appeared one by one before the viceroy, and with a hand upon a missal held by a Franciscan father, swore by God and His Majesty, the king, to obey commands and fulfill their duties to the very best of their knowledge and understanding.

In addition to this select group, there were some eight hundred Mexican Indian allies, together with the personal servants of the nobles, and their Negro bearers, lackeys, grooms, and herders, to the total number of something above eleven hundred souls. But by no means least among this sizable party were the four Franciscan friars and two oblates making up the religious contingent, headed by none other than Fray Marcos, whose substantiating report the previous year had activated this bold undertaking. What a pity that he could not have remained behind.

On Monday morning, the twenty-third, the imposing army, banners fluttering and armor bright, marched bravely out of Compostela, and were soon to learn that northwestern Mexico at its very best is far from being a hospitable land. This fact, plus the failure to make contact with supply ships sent up along the eastern shore of the Gulf of California, added to their difficulties. So, too, did some of the less friendly Indians along the line of march.

Still the spirits of these would-be conquerors were not too badly shaken, and their hopes were still high when some weeks later they crept up the San Pedro Valley, swung away from the stream that flowed through it, crossed into what is today United States territory, and headed north past the later site of Fort Grant. Now in the midst of true desert country, they suffered heavily, and not a few perished in the blazing stretch below the Gila River.

Fording its nearly dry bed, they soon came to another whose flowing waters are the color of blood, and which they promptly named *Colorado*, the Spanish for crimson. Pressing on along this Little Colorado, they took its north fork and entered New Mexico and the Zuñi country. It was on July 7 that the advance party came to Hawikuh in this area, having negotiated nearly a thousand arduous miles in 135 days. The bulk of the army, left behind, was to join this spearhead later on at a more leisurely pace.

To his everlasting credit let it be said that in his first contact with the Indians in our Southwest, Coronado did his utmost to keep relations peaceful. But the independent and freedom-loving Zuñis, whom he had encountered some miles west of the supposed site of the fabled golden cities of Cíbola, turned a deaf ear to his earnest approaches. His patience in the matter far outlasted that of the religious members of his party, and finally, nettled by a comment of Fray Marcos, he reluctantly gave the order to attack.

Any who have ever driven across New Mexico in the late afternoon and seen the deception which the setting sun's lingering shafts work on the clay walls of a pueblo can readily understand how De Vaca and his men may well have been deluded. Their tawny unbroken surfaces turn so readily to a shimmering gold that they can easily set ablaze man's native greed.

Perhaps our hopeful plunderers now found their own moment of disillusionment, for having smashed their way through to them, the "seven cities" proved to be nothing more than so many unimposing pueblo villages, scattered across some fifteen or more miles. The largest consisted of perhaps two hundred houses, the smaller ones of from thirty to sixty, or not more than six hundred in all.

An assault was made upon the largest, Coronado leading the troops in his golden armor, his helmet brave with plumes. But the Zuñis were totally ignorant of the niceties of European warfare, and insisted upon hurling huge stones from the upper walls onto their besiegers, much to the discomfort of the latter. The commander himself was felled twice during the fray, as he would live to recall. Many others were knocked senseless, although fortunately none were killed.

The Indians were finally driven out and the "city" searched for plunder. But the wealth which it contained probably did not equal the damage done to Coronado's glittering armor alone. These Zuñi dwellings, while not squalid, were furnished and adorned with monastic severity. Wealth, or anything approaching it, was nonexistent in the whole locality.

The hope of great gain from these "seven golden cities" evaporated as does a mirage; but there was, of course, that other phase of all expeditions under Spanish auspices. With true zeal, the friars began to press for peace, and for converts. The terrified natives, however, fled en masse to the shelter of neighboring Thunder Mountain.

Thorough search of the now deserted pueblos confirmed Coronado's growing fears. Fray Marcos was summoned, and pointedly questioned. He made a valiant try at justifying this lack of plunderable wealth, and the bad judgment of his favorable report the previous year, but to no avail. Much humiliated, he was summarily ordered back to far-off Mexico City.

Word of the Zuñis' defeat spread rapidly among their neighbors, and emissaries from other possible victims of attack sought the conquerors without delay. Among early arrivals was one Rigotes, or "Long Whiskers," whose heavy beard was a great oddity among Indians. He came from Cicuye not far from present-day Santa Fe, bearing a most unusual gift—buffalo hides.

Interchange of thought being dependent almost entirely upon descriptive gestures, he of the thatched chin must have had quite a task convincing Spaniards, totally unaware of such a beast, that countless numbers of these great, humpbacked cows roamed the everlasting prairies, often in herds so large they reached to the horizon in all directions. The disillusionment in connection with golden cities would tend to make them wary. But when it was understood the animals could be eaten, and with relish, that put a different light on the matter; and may have hastened the departure of Don Alvarado, captain of artillery, with a party headed toward the east, and primarily to prepare a camp to accommodate the main army yet to arrive.

THE ADVANCE INTO TEXAS

At his first halting place, the Don came upon another and even more startling character, held slave by inhabitants of a nearby Indian village. Although this creature was unmistakably an Indian himself, and probably from tribes far to the east, he was thought to look like a Turk, and was at once so called by the Spaniards to whom he was released. He had perhaps more fluid gestures than the bearded one, and in an ingratiating manner began to describe such wondrous prospects ahead that Alvarado and the advance party set off on a reconnaissance while waiting for the main column to catch up with it.

Piloted by this glib, imaginative "Turk," its members hastened to the upper reaches of the Canadian River and followed that stream down over the staked plains where it breaks out into what is today the Texas Panhandle. Here, as their eyes fairly popped from their sockets, they beheld buffaloes, thousands upon thousands of the creatures. And what a treat their steaks were when barbecued over a pit fire!

The Turk was a subtle one, and as this rich diet revived Spanish hopes, he began to unfold exciting stories about Quivira, those incredible Indian cities lying far to the north across the plains. Set in a beautiful, level country, they bordered a river two leagues wide, filled with fish as big as horses. Over its surface sped great canoes with twenty rowers to a side, the tribal sachems taking their ease under canopies sheltering raised decks at the rear.

While bolting down thick, juicy slabs of buffalo flesh, the Spaniards listened attentively as the weaver of tales described the lord of this country, who took his afternoon nap beneath trees hung with golden bells which, when stirred by the breeze, lulled him to sleep. Why, even the dishes and water jugs of the common folk were of solid gold!

His fascinated hearers, their physical appetites at last satiated, now unleashed their venal appetites. They recalled their first doubts as the captive had told about the humpbacked cows. But here they were gorging themselves on luscious steaks from the beasts. This Turk had proven his reliability. Soon Quivira would turn out to be all he had claimed for it. Why it must be these cities of Quivira, rather than of Cíbola, that they really sought! Hopes flamed up anew, and they hurried back to enlighten their commander in chief.

While they had been sampling the wonders of the Texas plains, the main army had joined Coronado at the camp in New Mexico. The first snows were beginning to fall, and the shivering host sought more commodious quarters, finally found at Tiguex, a pueblo standing on both sides of the Rio Grande River near the present site of Bernalillo. From it, its Indian tenants were ruthlessly driven to find shelter as best they could. And it was here, after Alvarado's return, that Coronado had ample time during the winter of 1540–41 to absorb the arousing tales of the Turk.

But there were other employments as well, for the dispossessed Indians and their mistreated neighbors revolted. Driven to desperation at the loss of their homes and stored food, they became warlike, and a great massacre of them finally occurred at Arenal. This was a grave mistake, and would ultimately prove a costly one. The native remnant took refuge at Mohi, which pueblo was under siege for some fifty days.

As a last resort, their women and children were released to the Spanish on the assurance of the priests that they would not be killed. The remaining natives then fought on to the last man. By the end of that severe winter and the coming of milder weather in the spring of 1541, Indian resistance had been subdued in central New Mexico; but the Spanish had earned a reputation for ruthlessness that would live on to haunt them in their attempts at colonization in the next century.

THE FIRST WHITE MEN IN KANSAS

In late April the army left the Rio Grande and, with the Turk as its guide, headed for certain riches and glory to be reaped from the opulent inhabitants of Quivira, somewhere in the great beyond. Nine days of marching brought them to the buffalo country, and among still more hostile tribes of Indians. Then for forty additional days they wandered about on the limitless plains, eating their fill of buffalo meat, but with little other food left.

The Turk's stories were not checking with the facts, and that hapless wretch was finally clapped into a cage, put under heavy guard, and prohibited from communicating with any except his appointed interrogators. As the food situation worsened, and the plains, bare of all except buffalo grass and the everlasting grazing or stampeding herds, seemed to have no end, Coronado ordered the main army to turn back. In his own mind hopes were growing dim; but just in case, he selected thirty picked men and forged ahead, trundling the caged Turk along with him.

For another forty days they beat their way across the flat grassland, the monotony of which began to clutch at their sanity. They were confident the Turk was in league with the devil, but stubbornly drove themselves forward.

Then suddenly in what is now central Kansas, somewhere in the vicinity of Rice, or perhaps Dickinson County, they had a moment of exhilaration. Ahead were human habitations, and they hurried their weary way toward them. It was indeed Quivira, but what a letdown, what mean, unlovely clumps of grass-thatched huts! The avarice which had driven them on suddenly clotted, choking their hearts and spirits, and their disappointment knew no bounds.

Although the inhabitants of these squalid dwellings were not wealthy, they were at least hospitable and peaceably disposed. But before learning more about this goal of their fruitless quest, there was a pressing task to be carried out. The Turk's cage was beset, and the boastful one, now cringing before them, had to confess that his sole purpose had been to draw them and their army out onto the great plains to perish. That he was promptly and most unceremoniously strangled to death was slight compensation for their outraged pride.

Lest there be riches suddenly hidden from view on their approach, Coronado and his party remained for twenty-five days among these benighted Quivira Indians in their wattle and grass villages. But neither fame nor fortune was to be found here, and now reasonably rested, the party began to retrace its steps.

The fall of 1541 was well advanced before its members were back with the main forces on the Rio Grande. New recruits, fired with the zeal the veterans had known in the spring of the previous year, had arrived from Mexico City in Coronado's absence. These latter were for pushing the search even further, and at once. But the second winter that suddenly descended upon them cooled their ardor markedly.

While it was in no way as severe as the former had been, the frosty days and nights dragged on and on, and discontent simmered. The more seasoned troops and their commander in chief, with two major miscarriages behind them, were for calling it a day and returning to their homes and the remains of their fortunes. The newcomers continued to be in determined opposition. But when news seeped through that their supply base in northern Mexico had been destroyed, Coronado's own mind was unalterably made up.

It was on one of the milder winter days that he and Captain don Rodrigo Maldonado had had their mounts saddled and sought relief from the tedium of the camp. As they cantered along, Maldonado, stimulated by the bracing air, proposed a race. As an answer, Coronado clapped spurs to his horse, and they were off, he being slightly in the lead.

They were hardly at a full gallop, however, when the commandant's saddle girth parted, hurling him backward over his horse's rump and directly beneath the cruel hoofs of his companion's spirited steed. The badly injured man hung for several days between life and death, and was in critical condition during the remainder of the winter. Division of sentiment, influenced by this sad accident, grew more and more marked. The camp seethed with charges and countercharges, plots and counterplots. The ailing Coronado from his sickbed tried his best to poll opinions; but he ached not only from his recent wounds, but from those suffered at Cíbola the year before. Yet it could be that the greater hurt came from his deflated vanity. He was not destined to be another Cortés, another Pizarro. That fact had become painfully clear to him.

By spring he was on his feet again, and preparations were begun for the return. Opposition to this move was sternly quelled, and a broken and sadly dejected remnant of the once proud army at last moved off to the south, homeward bound. It was late summer before the advance party could report to the viceroy, who had still maintained his hopes, despite the forced return of Fray Marcos with discouraging news the previous year. And while Mendoza stoically accepted Coronado's report and explanations, and even returned him to his post as governor in New Galicia, he perhaps began to realize that inflated Spanish hopes in the New World were about to shrink markedly.

While it failed to show the way to continued plunder on a huge scale, the expedition was not, however, without its rewards. Father Juan de Padilla, fully as enterprising, if not quite as gullible as Fray Marcos de Niza, had accompanied Coronado all the way to Quivira. Incidentally, too, he had been one of the small party that had made the side trip into Arizona, during which its members gazed upon the vast reaches of the Grand Canyon. He was thus totally undeceived as to the nature of the country or its inhabitants. Better still, he had no ambition to sudden riches in his stout heart, but his soul did sorrow for the Indian peoples he had encountered.

In the following year, 1542, he made the long journey of nearly fifteen hundred miles back to Quivira to labor there among its people.

Here it was that he was later slain, reportedly because they were jealous of his leaving them to work among other tribes. Thus he became the first Christian martyr within what is now the United States, and one of the first, too, of that long line of dedicated friars who, at the risk of life and limb, brought Christianity to the natives of our Southwest and Pacific coast. It was not gold, but the souls of men, which challenged them to cross mountains and deserts to far places in those early days.

While Coronado was still in New Mexico, other Spanish adventurers were making preliminary explorations of the California coast. But for some years activities in what is our Southwest would be restricted, for South and Central America would occupy most of Spain's efforts on this side of the Atlantic.

For forty years the New Mexico country would lie fallow, while recollections of the ruthlessness of the Coronado party slowly died out. Then De Espejo made a peaceful penetration, followed in 1598 by a colony established at San Gabriel by De Oñate. In 1610 Don Pedro de Peralta was designated governor, and a capitol building, designed in Madrid, was erected in Santa Fe, and remains today as the oldest public building in the United States. There was peace for a few years, and by 1633 the industrious padres had built no fewer than ninety churches in the area, many of which missions still stand and are in daily use.

Then the Spaniards were driven out during a rebellion in 1680, only to return in 1692 to enlarge the communities in the Rio Grande

Valley we will later visit, as Americans began to look with marked interest at that Spanish province. Finally, in 1846, the Stars and Stripes would be unfurled over this area which Coronado had first visited more than three hundred years before.

III

The Contest for Foutholds in America

The evocation of Iberian Christian energy by the stimulus of pressure from the Moors is attested by the fact that this energy gave out as soon as the Moorish pressure ceased to be exerted. In the seventeenth century the Portuguese and Castilians were supplanted in the new world that they had called into existence by interlopers—Dutch, English, and French—from the Transpyrenæan parts of Western Christendom, and this discomfiture overseas coincided in date with the removal of the historic stimulus at home through the extirpation, by massacre, expulsion, or forcible conversion, of the remaining "Moriscos" of the Peninsula.—Arnold J. Toynbee, *A Study of History.*

FOR more than eight centuries the people of Spain had lived shoulder to shoulder with the infidel Saracen "Moriscos" in an atmosphere that had bred freedom of action and individual initiative. These intruders were then liquidated within a generation or two. But they had built up a momentum in the land that was turned to the outfitting of ships and armies, beginning early in the 1500s. During the next three generations the flower of Spanish youth was drained off into activities overseas, while energy at home was depleted by the flow of wealth from the New World and initiative was dried up by an authoritarian and despotic government. The seeds of her rapid decay were thus sown at the very moment her great opportunity was opening before her, still for nearly a century Spain would be in position to discourage any very serious attempts to contest her hold on America.

The French king would facetiously ask to see Adam's will, by which Spain had seemingly laid claim to the huge areas appearing out of the mists of the western ocean. But for a time he would do very little by way of open challenge beyond sending an Italian navigator to sail along the coast, drop into a number of its larger bays, and make a precarious claim of the whole area in the name of France. Ten years later he would dispatch one of his own capable sailors to the West, but Jacques Cartier's explorations would be confined to a latitude well north of immediate Spanish interests.

However, a frontier was opening up on this side of the ocean, and one in which Dutch, English, and French "interlopers," as Toynbee calls them, would soon be prepared to hurl the gauntlet into the lists. Although they were as yet not prepared to do so openly, it was actually the French who first drew blood in this struggle for empire. Even though Cartier had purportedly been searching for a northwest passage to China and India, his activities had been known to and had nettled the Spanish, placing them on guard against other probable encroachments.

ANOTHER RELIGIOUS PHASE OF AMERICAN COLONIZATION

The two countries separated by the Pyrenees Mountains were quite in contrast to one another. The Spanish were somewhat dour and the consolidation of the monarchy had resulted in a stultifying absolutism that now pervaded most of Spanish life. Even with more and more cargoes of gold coming in from the West, its streets were rapidly filling with beggars, for enterprise at home had been driven into hiding.

To the north over the mountains, the French were a vigorous, even lusty, but somewhat discordant people, among whom heresy, stamped out in Spain by the Inquisition, was on the increase, despite rigorous efforts of the clergy to curb its growth.

This heretical Huguenot element, receiving its inspiration from nearby Geneva, worked underground, and was rapidly enlisting more and more men of influence and daring. Although Francis of Guise, the French king, professed to be a willing burner of the heterdox, the Huguenots had managed to organize and dispatch an ill-fated expedition to the coast of Brazil in 1555. Three years later the zealous Portuguese wiped out the stain on their orthodoxy brought about by this "Antarctic France."

By 1562 the heavy clouds of religious strife had settled over France and asylum was in pressing need. A second expedition was organized under the command of Jean Ribaut of Dieppe, and through connivance that must have reached into court circles, managed to sail from Havre for the coasts of Florida.

The two small, high-decked vessels hove to off the mouth of the St. Johns River on the first day of May, and gave the name River of May to that stream. The natives on shore appeared friendly, and so proved to be, but a further search of the coast before a settlement was established seemed in order.

Some two hundred miles to the north the broad bay on which the Marine Corps base at Parris Island stands caught their fancy, and here, at Port Royal, they decided to cast their lot. A fort seemed to be the first essential, and they set to work upon it to the utter disregard of less martial but still more essential needs. Ribaut, seeing the party well started on this enterprise, sailed back to France for further supplies and man power, having given absolute assurance to them of his prompt return.

But religious wars that were well under way at the time of his arrival in the homeland made this impossible. Those he had left behind were outright adventurers rather than determined settlers, warriors rather than farmers and husbandmen, with the consequence they were rather quickly on short rations. Empty stomachs and the monotony of camp life bred boredom and then internal strife. The end which ultimately came was too sordid to recount here, except to say it involved cannibalism, but Charlesfort, the first Protestant attempt at settlement in North America, terminated most ignominiously in 1562. It was but another of many such faltering steps that would be made, but all of which in one way or another were in some degree a contribution to the eventual winning of the continent.

On the twenty-first of the following June, another French fleet, this time of three larger vessels, was at the mouth of the River of May, but again filled with adventurers, restless soldiers, and discontented small tradesmen. There was not a true colonist among them. They were, of course, Huguenots, fleeing persecution in their native land, and this time under the command of one René de Laudonnière.

As before, the Indians were friendly, and the St. Johns being acceptable, they at once began construction of Fort Carolina on the north shore at its mouth. To enhance their security, they made a solemn treaty with Satouriona, "lord of all that country," as the ancient records style him. While these relations would be strained at times, they would stand the French in good stead during trying days ahead.

But once again improvidence and ultimate dependence upon the Indians led to difficulties. The members of this group, like the first, were in search of adventure and easy plunder; and being denied both, the uneventful days and their but partly satisfied hunger soon brought discontent and finally conspiracy such as had wrecked the Charlesfort settlement at Port Royal.

Nonetheless, word of their trespass was soon winging its way over the ocean to Spain, some said via French priests close to court circles. It might quite as well have been by way of the West Indies. There one of the vessels which had stolen away from Port Royal had turned up bent on piracy.

Conditions at Fort Carolina had by now advanced through conspiracy to mutiny, and the end might have come sooner and less dramatically had not a huge fleet suddenly appeared off shore, led by a stately ship. Fear mingled in equal parts with their joy, and the immediate question was whether the armada was French or Spanish. Strangely enough it turned out to be English, and under command of the redoubtable Sir John Hawkins, father of the English slave trade, en route through the Spanish Main disposing of its human cargo. His appearance and generosity in supplies gave the disorganized colony stability to carry on for another month, until a French fleet under Ribaut hove in sight. The future now seemed better secured.

THE SPANISH TAKE FIRM POSSESSION IN FLORIDA

But the word of French encroachment had swept through Spain and set fire to patriotism and religious zeal, particularly that of one of its foremost noblemen, Pedro Menéndez de Avilés. He had wielded a sword since childhood, had amassed a fortune in the Indies, but was sufficiently in need of resumption of royal favor so that he petitioned the king for permission to drive the heretical intruders from Florida at his own expense.

Roused by this great burst of ardor, Philip gave his royal sanction, and Menéndez raised and spent a million ducats—some two and a half million dollars—outfitting a punitive expedition of no mean proportions. The king's concern was sufficient to warrant his adding men and equipment; and since this vexatious intrusion was complicated by rank heresy, the undertaking began to assume the flavor of a holy war.

Thus preparations were pressed with such vigor that the expedition sailed from Cadiz on the twenty-ninth of June, 1565. The thirty-four vessels bore no fewer than 2,646 persons, for the most part

picked soldiers. Menéndez had been invested with well nigh absolute power over Florida, which, by his commission, encompassed
all of North America from Mexico to Labrador. With him were
twelve Franciscans and eight Jesuits, beside other religious, including one Fray Mendoza, who left for us a detailed account of this
crusade.

Sailing by way of Dominica and Puerto Rico, storms, alternating
with breathless calms, separated the vessels of the vast armada, and
it was the fourth of September before the flagship and its attendants
were abreast of the north Florida coast. Its lookouts in the afternoon
watch of that day made out ships at anchor in the mouth of the St.
Johns, which soon proved to be Ribaut's far smaller squadron, which
had arrived barely a week before. Once it was unmistakably identi-
fied, Menéndez gave thanks to heaven for having brought him to
this spot at this very hour. Then orders were promptly relayed to
those ships of his own fleet which had kept up with him, and the
formidable group was prepared for battle.

But unfortunately a thunderstorm blew up just as he came
abreast of the French. Time was then required to reform and position
his ships, and it was not until past midnight that the crisp notes of a
Spanish trumpet sounding a call to parley sped across the water.
The French answered this summons, and Menéndez inquired in
tones of labored courtesy, "Gentlemen, from what country is your
fleet?"

"From France," was the brisk answer.

"What is your purpose here?" demanded the Spanish commander.

"We have brought men and supplies for a fort which His Majesty,
the king of France, has in this land, and for a host of others soon
to follow."

There was the briefest pause as this bold assertion was weighed;
and then Menéndez, his voice fairly dripping insolence, made the
somewhat surprising demand, "Are you Catholic or Lutheran?" (To
the Spanish, all wanderers from the faith were known by this latter
term.)

Over the darkened waters came his answer in a resounding
chorus, "Lutherans!"

Again there was a pause. Then Menéndez crisply disclosed his
identity, explained his commission from the king, his purpose in being there, and ended by informing them that, come daylight, he
would board their ships and slay every heretic among them!

In jeering tones the same chorus of voices screamed back at him, "If you are indeed a brave man, you will not wait for daylight! Come aboard now and see what awaits you!" Taunted into a rage, Menéndez headed toward the three rather small French ships.

For this ready acceptance of their rash challenge, Ribaut was hardly prepared. The bulk of his soldiers were ashore at Fort Carolina, and discretion being the better part of valor, he slipped his cables, hoisted every possible inch of sail, and prepared for flight. With cunning, ready-witted sailors aboard, he managed to run the gauntlet of enemy fire and gain the open sea.

While a part of the Spanish fleet was ordered to give chase, Menéndez brought his flagship in before the French fort. But by the time this maneuver had been completed, the enemy ashore was prepared to receive him. Not daring to assume the risk alone, the Spanish commander swung about, stood out to sea, and made his way down the coast. Turning into the next sizable inlet, he was gratified to find that three of his ships had arrived there before him and were unloading stores. The place seemed ideal for a post, and on the eighth day of September, 1565, the *adelantado,* to the chanting of the *Te Deum Laudamus,* took formal possession and named the place *San Agustin.* Thus the oldest continuously occupied town on the continent had its birth. Gangs of Negro slaves were soon busy throwing up entrenchments and ramparts, and a stout base of operations would be established there.

EUROPEAN BLOOD STAINS THE FLORIDA BEACHES

After eluding his Spanish pursuers, Ribaut swung his ships about and stole back to Fort Carolina. There Laudonnière, displaced as commandant, lay ill with a high fever, and the camp was in turmoil. It was at his bedside, however, that three plans of action were discussed. That of Ribaut, a most competent seaman, won out; and on the tenth of that same fateful month the troops were loaded aboard his ships and the dejected remnant left behind watched them sail away and turn to the south along the coast. The strategy decided upon was to attack the Spanish before they were too firmly dug in at St. Augustine. To carry it out, the French fort had been stripped of all but a few serviceable weapons and virtually all effective manpower, but was burdened with women, children, and a goodly number of worthless camp followers, which the ships had recently brought from the homeland.

The following day Ribaut was at the bar just beyond the entrance to St. Augustine Bay, his decks black with armed men, when a sudden squall struck. It rose rapidly to a whole gale, forcing the French fleet to hurry out from the shoal waters. This evil weather advanced quickly to a tropical storm of hurricane proportions not uncommon in that area at the beginning of autumn.

In the meanwhile a bold plan had been forming, too, in the mind of Menéndez, and the forced exit of the ships, plus the oncoming storm, persuaded him to put it into action at once. With five hundred chosen men, he would set off overland to capture and destroy Fort Carolina, leaving behind what he judged to be sufficient forces to at least hold the French at bay, if they attempted to strike at his new base.

This sizable party left on the morning of the seventeenth with the adelantado at their head and two Indians and a renegade Frenchman as guides. But they were soon plunged into a perfect hell of quagmires, swollen streams, stabbing yucca thickets, and tangled jungle growth, through which they had to stumble forward hour after terrible hour. Only the importance of the heretic hunt on which they were bent, continually dinned into their ears by their commandant, kept them to their purpose. How in two days they managed to negotiate this forty miles of endless hazards drenched by a continual downpour will never be known. But do it they did, and late in the evening of Wednesday the nineteenth they were close to their goal.

The night outside was so wild that the French felt safe in abandoning their usual guard contingent, so that all might catch a little sleep. But they paid for their folly when, at the first faint traces of dawn, they were awakened by the terrorizing enemy war cry, "Santiago! Santiago!"

Such as could bear arms jumped to the little fort's defense, but they were completely overwhelmed, and before the bloody day drew to a close no less than a hundred forty-two French bodies, many of them hacked to bits, had been piled along the river's bank. It is said that Menéndez had a placard placed by one ghastly heap reading, "I do this not as to Frenchmen, but as to Lutherans."

There were perhaps fifty among those entrapped at Fort Carolina who managed their escape in two of the ship's boats that Ribaut had left behind. After a frightful crossing of the broad ocean, during which many of them perished, one of these tiny crafts landed in La Rochelle, while the other made Swansea in Wales. By the stories of these survivors were the Spanish accounts of this gory day further substantiated.

With their master gone off to the north on this dangerous venture, the Spanish detachment left behind at St. Augustine kept fearful watch for Ribaut's certain return. Even after a messenger had stumbled from the brush, followed shortly afterward by the adelantado and his party to confirm the good news of Fort Carolina's destruction, there was some measure of tension. Four days elapsed, and then an Indian runner brought word of a French ship wrecked down the coast, and of a party of its survivors huddled in a camp on the ocean front near by.

Certain that his luck still held, Menéndez quickly selected a group of sixty men and set off to reconnoiter. The party rowed down the waterway behind Anastasia Island, debarking on the latter where that long strip of land narrows, and crossed over to the ocean side. Marching briskly along the hard-packed beach, with now and then a stretch of marsh to wade through, they came late at night upon lights at some little distance that were surely from campfires. Although it was about the hour of greatest darkness, the vengeful Spaniard would have set his men upon the castaways then and there. Unhappily it was soon discovered a broad inlet lay between them and the ill-fated Frenchmen. Today this stretch of water still bears the name *Matanzas,* the Spanish word for slaughter, prophetic of what might soon take place by its shores.

With the coming of daylight, Menéndez proved himself both an archdissembler, and altogether a deceitful wretch. He offered the French an opportunity to surrender, and some two hundred of them promptly agreed to do so. The adelantado had addressed them in words which, among men with any sense of justice, would have been taken as a pledge of life and safety.

As further assurance of good intents, it was explained to the prisoners that their hands were being bound behind their backs by way of token, and only incidentally as greater protection to their captors. Then they were marched off ten at a time toward the north.

Some distance away in the direction of the Spanish fort at St. Augustine was a low bluff. As soon as its shelter was achieved, out of sight and hearing, each group was stopped and confronted with the ominous question, "Are you Catholics or Lutherans?" Frank avowal to being the latter sealed their doom. They were struck down in cold blood, and only a mere handful escaped the sword.

A second crimson harvest was soon reaped, and the adelantado earned himself the well-deserved title of "the pious butcher of Spain." By the reckoning of his own followers, three hundred fifty Frenchmen were slain, in part for trespass, but in larger part, it might well appear, because of their misplaced zeal.

But Florida was firmly in Spanish hands, and would remain so, with an interlude of a few years under British dominion, until permanently ceded to the United States in 1819.

I V

England Seeks a Foothold in America

The only able Tudor was Queen Elizabeth. She built up the British navy by doing nothing for it. She told her sea captains to act on their own authority, and at their own cost. She wouldn't even pay for the powder and lead they used to defend England against the Spanish Armada. Her plan was to do *no* planning. With great firmness of character and consistency of purpose she always decided to decide *nothing*. By this highly intelligent means she let her subjects found the British Empire.—Henry Grady Weaver, *Mainspring*.

DID that sudden but fortunate appearance of Sir John Hawkins and his fleet of slave ships at the French Fort Carolina in 1564 mean that he was in search of additional markets for his wares, that he was taking the precautions of spying on this enterprise of England's cross-channel neighbors, or was he making a reconnaissance of the coast of this New World? The English had visited our Atlantic shores only six years after Columbus' first voyage to the west, when the Cabots ranged along them in search of "Brazil wood" used in dyeing cloth. There is reason to believe that there were quite a few other, albeit brief, visits here through the years, conveniently unrecorded, or by now long forgotten.

England during much of the sixteenth century was in considerable turmoil. Surely it was true while Henry VIII reigned, and Weaver comments in connection with the quotation above that the land was so completely disorganized it required all of his daughter's wit and energy just to hold on to her throne. But it would appear that her subjects were willing to employ their individual initiative, even to tempting and baiting the Spanish in America. In 1584 Queen Bess sanctioned Raleigh's endeavor to found a colony in what is now North Carolina, to which area Spain firmly claimed title.

That the attempt foundered is true, but in that connection it is interesting to speculate as to whether it was pure coincidence that another robust English sailor, Sir Francis Drake, casually happened by, and was thus on hand to return the disgruntled settlers to their homeland.

As Raleigh's second attempt was being made in 1587, the Spaniards were preparing to dampen any and all growing ambitions of the English, and in the following year sent their supposedly invincible armada to wreak havoc on the British Isles. But a rare combination of English courage and most inclement weather sent the bulk of this invading fleet to the bottom of the ocean. From that moment the people in the "right little, tight little island" were in better position to appear in the Western Hemisphere, and elsewhere across the seven seas as "interlopers."

It was a group of merchants banded together in the London Company, and not the British Government, that sent out three ships and about a hundred twenty colonists in 1606–7 and founded the first permanent settlement in America on the banks of the James River in Virginia. It was a competitive attempt by another merchant company that landed a second party at the mouth of the Kennebec River in Maine that same year. There was religious dissension boiling up at home, and also a small army of free men recently released from the last vestiges of serfdom in search of land they might call their own. England needed elbowroom, badly needed an outlet for pent-up energies, and America seemed ready-made to her purposes.

Jamestown had its romantic trappings, in the fabled exploits of John Smith, the abduction of the desirable Pocahontas by Captain Argall, and other similar incidents. But in reality the early years there were one long story of hardship and disappointment. The colony faltered, slowly stabilized, knew better times, was shaken to its foundations by a rebellion, then prospered, and by the time of the Revolution was the most populous of the thirteen.

Massachusetts would begin to fill in before the Virginians had any near neighbors. These latter came in 1634 as the Calvert colonists, who founded St. Mary's at the mouth of the Potomac in the Baltimore grant, called Maryland.

There would be transitory attempts in the tidewater lands to the south, but no permanent settlement between Virginia and St. Augustine until 1670, when Charles Towne was started on the lower bank of the Ashley River toward the southern edge of a huge royal grant from which the Carolinas developed.

While the Stuarts, who succeeded to the throne following Elizabeth's death, were committed to belief in the divine right of kings and sought to get firmer control of the overseas colonies, the frontier developing in Virginia and Carolina managed to win and retain a very considerable degree of self-determination. The former found its security in tobacco, which became the principal cash crop, and even influenced the social structure of the colony.

In the latter, rice, and then indigo, were soon in successful cultivation, and that colony began to increase in importance following the turn into the 1700s. As in the Virginia colony, expansion would set up tension with the natives and there would be even more continuous strife in that direction in Carolina than in the colony to the north. Still Indian trouble would be a characteristic of virtually every American frontier opened up during most of the next two centuries. However, growing commerce from the port of Charles Towne, and from other colonial ports, would develop another situation which, although we do not customarily associate it with the frontier, was definitely one of its vestiges. While it is not commonly thought of as a particular menace in connection with colonization, yet for a time it was a decided concern along the Carolina coast, and even as far north as New England. This threat to life, liberty, and the pursuit of profit came from the pirates.

PIRACY IN AMERICAN WATERS

Piracy, most simply defined as robbery on the seas, is probably as old as man's activities on navigable waters, and thus antedates history. It had thrived in ancient times, and Europe had suffered grievously from it, especially at the hands of the roving Vikings, whose sons were not thought to have achieved manhood until they had made at least one plundering raid on neighboring coasts.

The pattern was thus well established, and when golden cargoes began to move toward Spain from the New World in the early 1500s, the Caribbean Sea soon became the rendezvous for the freebooters of all Europe. Restrictive laws in connection with wool and cloth had made of Merrie England "a piece of land entirely surrounded by smugglers," and this gentry, together with others of their kind from French and Dutch ports, swarmed the coasts of the Spanish Main, plundering Spanish ships and raiding the mainland.

While England long had had harsh laws aimed at piracy, the seas were alive with her own privateers, Hawkins and Drake among them, frankly commissioned to prey upon Spanish commerce. The line between piracy and privateering was thus wavy and indistinct, not only in these earlier days, but quite as much so when Americans chose to engage in sea-roving under the latter designation to better by-pass the restraints of the Navigation Acts.

As the take from ships and settlements in and about the Caribbean began to fall off, new hunting grounds were prospected. The Bahama Channel off the eastern shores of Florida proved for some years a promising locale, and New Providence, occupying the present site of Nassau, took over the distinction of being the pirate headquarters. As its buccaneering population grew, toward the end of the 1600s, some of its abler frequenters shifted their shore bases into the sheltered sounds along the North Carolina shore line. These ample but secluded hideaways were reasonably close to the happy hunting grounds to the south, and soon proved even more conveniently located to care for the increasing shipping from colonial ports.

As long as the primary business activities of this skull-and-crossbones set were confined to the warmer West Indies waters, they were not only tolerated but even welcomed in ports as far north as New England. As they returned from ministering to enemy shipping the sea robbers were lavish spenders, not only for entertainment, but for the reoutfitting of their ships. Many coastal harbors catered to them, and during those years when the Caribbean was the focal point of their efforts, the hard money in circulation in the colonies was principally the gold and silver coins brought in by pirates and privateers.

In addition there was plunder to be disposed of, and goods could be bought from the ships flying the black flag far below the exorbitant prices demanded by English merchants for similar necessities and luxuries. There is thus abundant evidence to indicate that in these earlier years the friendliest relations obtained between colonists and pirates, and that by one means or another virtually every colony was not only affording them asylum, but even encouragement.

Then, as the 1700s were reached, the situation, and these favorable relations, altered. Worth-while prizes from the West Indies and the mainland beyond were rapidly decreasing, while there was markedly better hunting on up the coast. The birds of prey followed it, and were soon infesting harbors from Charles Towne to Boston, but now with their claws bared. Their friendliness swung quickly to complete insolence, and within a few years South Carolina particularly was in most distressing straits. The big-name brigands were not only stifling its commerce, but even threatening to sack Charles Towne and put it under tribute.

One among them—Thatch, Teach, Drummond, or whatever his

real name may have been, but perhaps more readily recognized as Black Beard—had long maintained a secure hide-out at Ocracoke Island, the sandspit slanting to the southwest from Cape Hatteras. Not only had he enjoyed the sustained good will of the thinly scattered population along the bleak coast and its many inlets, but he had achieved very cordial and convenient relations with both the appointed governor and the secretary of the North Carolina colony.

Riding at anchor in his secure base, and encouraged by his substantial backing, he began to lay plans to work his will on thriving Charles Towne, hardly more than a day's sail before a fair breeze down the coast. While Indian involvements were distracting attention inland, he struck, and his rapid and rather brilliant, but devastating, exploits off the entrance to this important port made him a marked man.

The colony was stunned, for it was unable to resist him out of its own resources, and was called upon to enlist the aid of Governor Spotswood of Virginia. This gentleman realized that his own domains might soon be similarly threatened, and he promptly outfitted a suitable force and sent it to track down this demon of the waves. The Virginians managed to surprise the evildoer in his snug harbor, blow him and his cutthroat crew out of the water, and then sailed away home with Black Beard's ugly head lashed to the bowsprit of one of their sloops. His long career was thus summarily terminated.

Still piracy up and down the coast was hardly at an end, and had been so close to the fringe of decency that it had recruited to the profession some most unexpected practitioners.

"THIS HUMOR TO GO A-PYRATING"

Black Beard's origin is shrouded in mystery, but not so that of an erstwhile associate, whose ambition it was to take his tutor's place after the Virginians had terminated his activities. By his own words he had been seized with this "humor to go a-pyrating," not as a beardless boy, but well along in middle life, and after having served with distinction in the army in Barbados.

His name was Stede Bonnet, and he was from an excellent family, possessed of considerable wealth, had enjoyed a reasonable education and achieved the rank of major. He should thus have been quite content to live out his declining years in peace and comfort, but such was not his intent. His friends defended him by saying he was mentally affected, yet subsequent events tended to disprove this. There is also the more charitable suggestion that his strange "humor" may have stemmed from a broken home life.

Pouring his money into the outfitting of a fine sloop mounting ten guns, which he named the *Revenge,* he sailed from Bridgetown, port city of his home island, early in 1717, and headed north. He began his exploits off the Virginia capes, and there, and on up to New England waters, left clear indications of his determination, if not of finished craftsmanship. His training had all been as a soldier, rather than as sailor and navigator. His crew soon realized his short-comings, grew sullen and rebellious, and had to be kept to their duties at pistol point.

Charles Towne's shipping drew him like a magnet, and he achieved a seizure of the harbor mouth. The hull of the *Revenge* was stripped and burned at some point up the coast; and as soon as damage to this prize was repaired, he slipped off to the Bay of Honduras, presumed a likely point at the moment in which to employ his growing talents. There it was that he fell in with Black Beard, who had not yet met his desserts, and a deal was made between them to undertake a joint sortie.

The enterprise was hardly under way before the more experienced freebooter recognized Bonnet's complete lack of seamanship. Forthwith he demoted him from command of the sloop and took him aboard his own ship in a subordinate but completely safe capacity. Since old Black Beard's crew were utterly loyal to their chief, and quite as contemptuous of this interloper as his own men had been, the soldier-turned-pirate had no choice but to suffer his lot and fume in silence at the humility to which he was subjected.

Thatch, or Teach, took the first prize of the cruise off Jamaica, reconverted it, and sailed off, bent on further exploits at the head of a three-ship squadron. It was at that point in his lively career that he hove to off Charles Towne Harbor, and while managing to terrorize the city, still sealed his doom.

The next stop was at Top Sail Inlet, North Carolina, where joint activities were summarily terminated. Bonnet again gained command of his own vessel, and still smarting from his experiences, pulled away quickly, and thus for the time being saved his hide.

He did not put out to sea, however, until he had appeared before Charles Eden, the unsavory governor of the North Carolina province, and, taking advantage of the king's standing offer of pardon, sworn a false oath of his intents to reform. He then asked for, and quite readily obtained, a commission to operate as a privateer against the

Spanish operating from the West Indies island of St. Thomas. This adroit maneuver prepared him to re-enter his adopted trade under better circumstances, and with perhaps sanction equal to that of any practitioner of the craft since the notorious Captain Kidd had departed England with the special blessings and backing of King William.

An apt scholar, Bonnet had rapidly acquired the rudiments of seamanship under a master tutor; and being a fearless, capable, and determined fighter, he soon had the confidence and loyalty of his revised crew. As a bit of mockery aimed at the English ruling house, he rechristened his sloop the *Royal James,* and altered his own designation to "Captain Thomas."

Finally at sea, he disclosed his real purposes to his men, and to test their metal, managed two captures off the Virginia capes, followed shortly by two more exceptionally valuable prizes in Delaware Bay. Freighted with the plunder, he put back into the Cape Fear River in August 1718 for repairs. There being need for haste, so he might take advantage of the increased outbound traffic in the fall, he seized a small shallop locally, breaking it up for its timbers.

This crass and arrogant act sparked enough antagonism so that word quickly spread that a harried pirate was holed up near the dividing line between the two Carolinas. The news was received at Charles Towne with misgivings, since the rice and indigo crops and other desirable cargoes would soon begin to flow from that port to England. Once a friendly outfitting place for the sea robbers, majority opinion now set up a clamor for aggressive action.

But once again the provincial government was in such sorry state financially that it could not outfit an expedition. By good fortune, though, the public spirited Colonel William Rhett of the city was not only able to assume the costs, but eager to lead a force against this intruder.

Two sloops were speedily chartered. The *Henry,* under Captain Masters, mounted eight guns, and was chosen by Rhett as his flagship. The somewhat smaller *Sea Nymph* mounted the same number of guns, yet could carry but sixty men, rather than the seventy which the *Henry* accommodated. By the tenth of September, the ships were moved across the harbor to Sullivans Island for final preparations before sailing. There the report that another pirate was operating close at hand took them on a wild-goose chase through the waterways that coil along the shores immediately to the south, and consumed ten precious days.

Thus it was the twentieth before Rhett and his ships stood out to sea and headed up toward Cape Fear. A storm, or perhaps contrary winds, must have now beset him, for he was six days negotiating about a hundred twenty miles. But sighting the great headland off the river's entrance on the evening of the twenty-sixth, he pushed on in, and spied the topmasts of the pirate sloop and the prizes, visible over the higher land upstream. In his anxiety to be at the foe at a spot in which he might well be trapped, Rhett miscalculated the channel, and was soon hard aground. There, at the harbor's mouth, he had to remain, for the tide would not be high enough to free him until long after dark, if then. And with him stayed the other smaller vessel, also lying in shoal water.

Bonnet, or "Captain Thomas" as he now preferred to be styled, had prudently set lookouts; and word of his pursuers was relayed to him perhaps before they, in turn, had seen his masts. Deciding upon his best course, he chose the *Royal James,* and braced himself and his crew, expecting immediate attack. But when the ships still lay downstream at sunset, he dispatched two ship's boats for a closer look. Learning their plight, he realized there was little choice for either side but to await the return of day. However, preparations for impending battle went on through the dark hours, their sounds clearly audible between the contestants.

As the sky began to gray on the morning of Saturday, September 27, 1718, there was a long moment of silence heavy with apprehension. Who would make the first move? Then, as the light increased, creaking tackle and whining windlasses upriver indicated the caged bird was about to take wing. This was confirmed by the sound of anchors being brought inboard, and the flapping sails, soon filled by the land breeze, swung the pirate sloop out into the stream and fuller view. Almost dead ahead of this light wind, it began to charge down toward the two attackers, afloat again, and at anchor. Bonnet's plan was quite evident—run the gauntlet if possible, and escape to the open sea. Rhett, sensing it, lost no time, drew his own anchors, upped sails, and headed in to meet the quarry and attempt to force him aground.

Dangerous at best, this was a highly hazardous maneuver even in well-charted waters. But the situation was sufficient to justify the risk, and the *Henry* in the lead, followed by the *Sea Nymph,* soon gathered headway and bore down on the runaway as though they intended to ram the pirate full on his quarter. So threatening was this attack that the *Royal James* swung to avoid probable impact, and soon drove its bow hard ashore at the edge of the channel. Almost at the same moment the *Henry* gave a shudder and ground to a sudden halt, its keel fast on a hidden bar. There the two opposing craft lay helpless, barely a long pistol shot distant from one another. But before either of them realized their predicament the *Sea Nymph* also grounded, yet sufficiently far off, and in so awkward a position, that she could be of little assistance through the critical hours ahead.

The tide was now running out swiftly, causing the opposed ships to list rapidly. And fortune seemed to favor the *Royal James,* for her deck was slanted away from the *Henry,* while the latter's lay exposed before the guns of her advisary. Realizing his advantage, "Captain Thomas" started to rake the other craft with a deadly fire, hoping to drive the gunners from their posts. So confident was his crew of easy victory that his bloodthirsty followers began to taunt and jeer, begging the enemy to board them, and then with mock concern suggesting that they run down their flag before being blown to bits. But neither Rhett nor his men were easily scared.

Realizing they were now in a fight to the finish, they stood their ground, manned their guns with astonishing coolness, and slugged it out. As the hours dragged on and the wounded began to mount on both sides, there was a common realization that the outcome depended not alone on bravery and staying power. Nature might well cast the die, for the first ship to gain buoyancy would be in better position to make the kill.

As afternoon shadows began to lengthen, this sense of expectancy became almost unbearable. Both because of fatigue and apprehension, the conflict seemed to lessen. The tide had turned and was now running into the river again, and the idling minutes stretched out. Then, almost imperceptibly at first, but more certainly with each heartbeat, the *Henry* seemed to feel life along her keel. The men could barely restrain a rousing shout as she began to right herself inch by inch. But their repression paid off, for they were virtually afloat before the pirate crew was fully aware that the once exposed deck was no longer an open target.

As the sloop from the south at last shook herself free from the sandy embrace her badly torn sails caught sufficient wind and she bore in on the still marooned pirate ship. Slowly Rhett was in a position where a well-placed shot might fire the seabooter's magazine. The South Carolinians, now rejuvenated men by this stroke of fortune, were in better shape to press along side and board. The *Sea Nymph* seemed to be righting too. Definitely the jig was up, and the pirate host set up a cry for immediate surrender. Bonnet, however, expecting no quarter, refused to give in and threatened to blow up his ship and all aboard.

Black Beard had been known to galvanize mutinous crews to ready obedience by such threats, but Bonnet's resolution was not sufficient to this occasion. As the *Henry* edged in with the unmistakable purpose of boarding, a flag of truce was hurriedly run up; and ship, crew, and skipper were surrendered unconditionally.

It took three days to get the little South Carolina fleet and its prize seaworthy enough to make the short trip to Charles Towne. When Rhett landed there on October 3, the townspeople gave him and those of his brave companions who had lived to return a rousing ovation, and capped it off by clapping thirty of the pirate crew in jail under heavy guard. Their leader, however, together with his sailing master and the boatswain, were put in custody of the town marshal and lodged in the latter's home.

While majority sentiment still ran heavily against these pirates, there were quite a few, with a goodly number of influential people among them, who were favorably disposed, particularly toward a man with such gentlemanly antecedents as those of their principal prisoner. Pressure was exerted in his behalf with the governor, and the people terrorized by threats of what might befall them if he were not freed. But Bonnet and his crew remained captives.

Then another approach was tried by the dissident faction, and quick results were obtained when a little ready cash was distributed among the guards that patrolled about the marshal's house during the night. Bonnet and his sailing master promptly disappeared to parts unknown, leaving the boatswain behind, now prepared to turn state's evidence. Although the government at once posted a reward of seven hundred pounds, hope of recovering the fugitives was slim indeed.

Lest the crew be allowed to escape, its members were promptly brought to trial. These proceedings were near a satisfactory termination when word filtered in that it might not be amiss to have a searching party examine Sullivans Island, within sight across the harbor. Rhett at once gathered another picked band, hurried over, and began to beat the thickets of myrtle scrub which then covered the northern end of this bit of land. After several hours they flushed a covey of desperate men. There was an exchange of shots, in which, among others, the sailing master was killed, but Bonnet was taken alive.

Friends had placed him on a small vessel to be returned to his fastness on the Cape Fear River, but adverse winds had turned the party back and deposited it at a convenient point for capture.

Ferried over to the town, the pirate chief was this time unceremoniously clapped into jail and placed under dependable guard. There, two days later, he could listen as his condemned crew were led out in a body to be hanged, and to find a common grave in the nearby marshland. In still another two days, he, too, stood before the Admiralty Court and, despite a last show of bravado, heard himself condemned and the date of December 10 set for his execution. In the short time that now remained to him, his bold front quickly melted away, and when the fatal moment arrived, he had to be dragged to the gibbet.

These events in the fall of 1718, coupled with Black Beard's sudden demise, tolled the death knell of piracy on the Carolina coast. These desperadoes did not disappear completely or at once; but the great among them had now fallen, and the activities of lesser members of the breed grew rapidly fewer until piracy was cleared from our shores.

The Southwest in later years would have its Sam Bass, its Billy the Kid, California its Black Bart, the Middle West its James Boys, and Montana its Henry Plummer. These knights of the road may have been brothers beneath the skin, members, as it were, of the same fraternity. But by their time there was a somewhat firmer moral line between right and wrong, and these bandits knew no period when they were tolerated, let alone being treated to friendliness and encouragement. Pirating was something of a strange phenomenon in this respect, and when it disappeared from the American frontier in the early 1700s its like did not recur.

V

The Search for Freedom

In many cases they regarded their congregations as theocracies and their structure and government as functions of their faith. That Roger Williams, the prophet of liberty of conscience, should be outlawed, that Quakers should be mutilated or tortured or killed, that every man and woman who held different beliefs regarding human nature and human destiny should be horribly penalized for those beliefs was long a matter of course to Massachusetts Puritans and their peers elsewhere on the continent. The "freedom to worship God" which they are said to have sought on New England's "stern and rock-bound coast" was freedom for themselves from others, not freedom for others from themselves.—Horace M. Kallen, *The Education of Free Men.*

SOME captious person has said that there were but two tangible benefits from Raleigh's attempts at colonization: the potato was added to Britain's diet, and tobacco to the other demoralizing influences in all Europe. But as a later promoter of colonization in America contended, in any worth-while structure some of the stones are lost to view in the building of the foundations.

Mace, who made a trip to the Hatteras region in 1602 to look for traces of the Raleigh colonists, brought back a shipload of trading commodities; and in that same year Gosnold and Gilbert also headed west. After a reasonably short voyage, they sighted Cape Elizabeth on the Maine coast, visited York Harbor, and edged their way down to Cape Cod and neighboring islands in Massachusetts. What they found was reassuring, and had some of the members been a bit more intrepid and willing to hazard the commander's safe return to England for supplies and a reappearance the following spring, the first permanent colony planted by Englishmen might well have dated from 1602 and been located on Martha's Vineyard, on Nantucket, or the nearby mainland shores.

In 1605, Captain George Weymouth also set his course due west along the 40th parallel, and in six weeks was investigating the "gallant" islands, coves, and river mouths of the Maine shore line. Finding the Indians particularly friendly, he encouraged several of them to return to England with him, where he added his favorable report to that of Gosnold and Gilbert.

Tensions and pressures within the homeland, coupled with the hopes for sudden and substantial profits through discovery or trade, were bringing this New World into sharper focus and widespread interest. While profit was the compelling motive in the minds of merchant groups that began to shape up plans, it would be principally the religiously dissatisfied and the economically disinherited who would furnish the man power to carry them out.

Strong endorsements stemming from the visitations above resulted in the formation of two organizations. The first, the London Company, was chartered by "divers knights, gentlemen, merchants, and others" of that area, with its leading light none other than Sir John Popham, lord chief justice of the realm. The second was fostered by a similar group in the western cities of Bristol, Exeter, and Plymouth, took the name of the Plymouth Company, and was largely the creation of Sir Ferdinando Gorges. Between them they would erect two highly important milestones in America, in 1607 and 1620 respectively. The first was at Jamestown, and is well known. But that there was a second attempt made under the same auspices, and at that same time, which did not yield such favorable results is less widely known. Since it amply illustrates the hazards of colonization, and the rigors faced as the American frontier was opened up, it deserves brief attention.

The charters of the two companies had been granted in 1606, and by common agreement between Popham and Gorges each was to send out a ship to attempt a plantation in the region given endorsement by Weymouth. But Gorges' ship, captained by Chalons, violated instructions, sailed south to benefit by the favorable westerly trade winds, and so made its first landfall at Puerto Rico, where it was promptly seized by a Spanish fleet homeward bound from Havana.

Martin Pring, Popham's sailing master, moved out of the Severn River on what was his second voyage west, and took the northern route. When he failed to find Chalons at an appointed meeting place, he made an exact survey of the northeastern coast, yet hesitated to leave either settlers or supplies, and took his information back to Sir John.

ANOTHER ENGLISH COLONY FOUNDERS

The chief justice was experienced in colonization activities, having planted colonies of Scots in Northern Ireland. Also he had perfected his plans for a plantation on the Chesapeake, and by December of this same 1606 his Jamestown expedition managed to sail, but was held in English waters by foul weather and did not get to sea until after the turn of the year.

By May of 1607, Popham had two more ships outfitted, provisioned, and filled with more than a hundred men who had professed ambition to become planters in the New World. The expedition was placed under command of a kinsman, George Popham. It sailed on two craft, the *Mary and John,* which had as its skipper Raleigh Gilbert, who had accompanied Gosnold, and a lesser ship, known as the *Gift of God.* It was shortly after the landing had been made at Jamestown that the two craft bravely headed from Plymouth Harbor and on past Land's End into the open ocean.

Despite the fact that their compass was somewhat amiss, when a sounding was taken on July 27 and showed but twenty fathoms of water beneath their keels, they knew that land must lay but a short distance beyond. So they anchored briefly, and in two hours caught all the cod they could use.

Pressing on again, they soon sighted land and hove to for a night in the lee of what is now called Monhegan Island. Hardly was it light when they had a bad fright. A Spanish shallop was heading toward them. Was it possible the jealous Spaniards were on hand to receive them? But the tiny craft proved to be filled with Indians, who may well have acquired the craft from Basque fishermen who had long frequented these shores. Three of its occupants consented to come aboard the *Mary and John,* and finally spent the night there.

After the departure of their unusual guests the following morning, the first landing was made and the ship-bound men reveled in the gooseberries, strawberries, raspberries, and *hurts,* or huckleberries, with which the island abounded. Several days were spent in exploration, turning up, among other interesting finds, two of the natives who had accompanied Weymouth to England and had been returned to their homes on this coast.

The party's objective was the Sagadahoc, now known as the Kennebec River, and on August 14 both ships anchored in its mouth. Three days later they went ashore again and selected a site for their forts and base. Some claim it to have been on Sabino peninsula, others that it was on what later was known as Porter's Island.

The members were assembled to hear a stirring sermon by their preacher, Richard Seymour. Then they listened attentively to the reading of the commission of their president, George Popham, and to the laws which were to govern them. Next they chose and swore in the five who were to serve as the president's assistants. These preliminary organizational affairs cared for, the men were quickly assigned tasks, the majority being put to digging entrenchments and raising walls for the fort and attached storehouses. As these structures were completed, fifty rude cabins, and finally a church, were added.

The carpenters, however, were set to building a pinnace, which, when finished, has the distinction of being the first seagoing vessel built in New England, if not in all America.

In the meanwhile, Gilbert had cruised to the west, rediscovering Cape Elizabeth and Casco Bay, and returned from his trip fairly glowing with enthusiasm for all he had seen.

The fall passed from September into October, and on into November, the days being put to good use in the completion of Fort St. George. While there had been one brief moment of concern in an upriver contact with the Indians, the settlers' intercourse with the savages had on the whole been quite satisfactory, and the future seemed secure.

As winter began to threaten, it was suddenly decided to send the *Gift of God* back to England with a glowing report calculated to assure that a goodly supply of stores and additional man power would be on hand early in the coming year. Among other letters borne home was one from President Popham to King James, assuring the monarch that his virtue, ability, and justice had been fully expounded to the natives. But perhaps of greater moment in the years that lay ahead was his report on the abundance of fine naval pine available.

Hardly had the *Gift of God* passed from sight beyond the horizon, when winter set in with a vengeance, its severity that year being as evident in Europe as on the rock-bound coast of Maine. The excessive frost found its way to the very marrow of the colonists' bones. And as if this were not enough, the Indians grew restless and became a trying concern. Next the storehouse at the fort burned, destroying a part of their provisions and putting on short rations men already becoming restless and discontented. Visions of easy riches had been replaced by the reality of hard toil. A search for mines to work had been without results; and their president, leader, and source of cheer and encouragement, George Popham, had died.

Spring lingered in 1608, but at last the promised ship arrived. It brought supplies, but also the distressing word that Sir John Popham, the chief justice and mainstay of the enterprise, had passed on. Raleigh Gilbert, who had assumed leadership at George Popham's death, would have made an admirable successor, but he received word of a brother's death back home, which had provided him a sizable estate, in connection with which his presence was badly needed.

When looked back at today, these unfavorable factors seem to have been heavily outweighed by others of much promise. The fort had been put in order, its provisions replenished, there was a "goodly store" of sarsaparilla and furs ready for shipment, and there had been but the one death among them. By contrast with the first year at Jamestown, and later at Plymouth, this group had made excellent progress.

But the weather had been severe enough that "all former hopes were frozen to death." With one accord the hundred odd "plantation builders" trooped aboard the supply ship and their own small pinnace, the *Virginia*, and upped sail for home. Were they accused on arrival of being quitters? Seemingly so, for the old records attest that they "did coyne many excuses" to save face. The colony on the Sagadahoc thus came to an untimely and rather inglorious end, much to the chagrin of Gorges and other colonial promoters.

The experiences which had attended the two Huguenot settlements attempted in Carolina and in Florida had in some measure been repeated in Maine, building up ample evidence that something more than a spirit of adventure was needed to gain a lasting hold on this frontier. There were no doubt many men anxious to escape tedium, poverty, or temporary difficulty at home; but so long as they could pull up stakes and return there when the going on this side of the ocean made that the easier course, permanent settlement would be hard to come by. The New England area received a bad name back home, and might have fallen under the sway of the French, had not the folk at Jamestown stamped out an early attempt.

France had established a stout fortress at Port Royal on the Nova Scotia coast. No doubt this post had been aware of the arrival, and also of the departure, of the Popham colonists, for it was not long after their disappearance from the mouth of the Kennebec that a mission post was founded a little to the north on Mount Desert Island by two priests, Fathers Baird and Masse. There, at St. Saviour, they ministered for some five years among the local Indians.

But in this same year, 1608, the spirited Captain Samuel Argall, later governor of the Jamestown colony, sailed up the coast and paid a visit to the Maine shores. Whether it was to explore the wonders of upper Virginia, which reached then from Florida to an indistinct line in the neighborhood of the Bay of Fundy, or to make a contact with the settlement presumed to be at St. George, but now vacated, or merely in search of codfish, is not known. But at least he spotted the French intrusion, and while his own ship was lost, he managed to get back to his home in the south bearing the upsetting news of Frenchmen as interlopers on what, to his way of thinking, was undeniably English territory.

It was some five years before he was in position to return, but in 1613 he led a small fleet of thirteen fishing smacks up the coast bearing a fair number of armed men. Descending upon St. Saviour, he captured it and took its inhabitants prisoners. Father Masse and a portion of Frenchmen who had joined the padres there were callously set adrift in open boats. But a kind providence guided them safely to a point off the Nova Scotia coast, where friendly ships returning to France took this benighted group aboard. The remainder, including Father Baird, Argall carried home to Jamestown. Thus a contest between England and France in the New World was launched, and would continue during the next century and a half.

But the following year the rather fabulous John Smith, late governor of the Virginia colony, visited the northern coast on what he termed a private adventure of "four merchants of London and himself." He employed his time well, and made an excellent map of the stretch from Cape Cod to the Penobscot Bay, which was later welcomed by the Plymouth colonists, although they turned down an offer of his personal services.

There were two ships in this quite legitimate enterprise. But after they had headed home, Thomas Hunt, master of the second vessel, absconded, turned pirate, and kidnaped a large number of Indians, whom he disposed of as slaves among the Spaniards. Yet out of this evil deed came a small scrap of good fortune. One of the poor creatures managed to escape from his captors, turned up in London, was returned to his home shores, and was on hand to act as interpreter for English settlers soon to follow.

And there would be further settlers, and in this New England region, too. Smith helped to repair the damage done it by the default of the Popham group; and chicanery between the merchant backers of the Pilgrims and the captain of the *Mayflower,* sent that substantial contingent of colonists into this area rather than further south. In fact the intense activity would be in this section in the half century just ahead.

While there had been little religious motivation behind the Jamestown settlement, it would be definitely present in providing its nearest neighbor, St. Mary's in Maryland, and a controlling factor in bringing Plymouth and the rash of towns in the Massachusetts Bay colony into being.

Since many of the country's leading historians of the last century were New Englanders, that section's early struggles, even its bigotry and unfortunate excesses, received much attention and are widely known. By today's standards, the temper of life was pretty stolid and stodgy in these first communities that were opened up from Cape Cod to Cape Ann, and Dr. Kallen characterizes them very aptly in the quotation at the beginning of this section. The men and women who made them up came here in search of freedom, but freedom limited as to form and purpose, as he points out. They had zeal, but it required, and would receive, modification and mitigation along a whole series of frontiers, of which this was but the first.

Nonetheless, these people had the priceless ingredient of persistence. Also they had a strong moral sense, which some of the other settlers coming to this same vicinity did not possess. Plymouth and the Bay towns may appear narrow and even vindictive as they got under way. But let us take a look at another neighboring enterprise of radically different stripe, and in the decided contrast judge what type of impulses, and whether zeal or zest separately, gave greater promise of resolving the America we know and love along this and the frontiers to follow during the next two and three quarter centuries.

THE PLYMOUTH COLONY'S NEIGHBORS

Tested as they were almost to the utmost extent of human endurance that first frightful winter, the Plymouth colony, too, might well have failed. But its men and women were under the necessity of remaining here and making a go of their endeavor. Also, for the most part, they were inspired by a militant faith in their mission in this New World, and despite their adversities they persisted.

There is a prevalent impression from our school histories that for the next ten years they were very much alone on these shores, with precious little in the way of human contacts other than the neighboring savages, but this is hardly the case. Rather quickly after their advent here, others began to drift into the country immediately to the north, gaining footholds as individuals or small groups.

This penetration without fatal consequences at the hands of the natives was due to the fact that the Indians' numbers had been severely reduced some years before by an epidemic, possibly spread among them by European sailors immune to the disease of which they were carriers. The savages had been struck down in such great numbers that even virile little Miles Standish had found an "army" of eight men sufficient at the outset to afford protection to the village rising behind Plymouth Rock. And there would be white men, quite as well as red men, to put this fireball of a man to the test.

Those in England backing colonization sought means to enjoy exclusive rights within the territories granted to them, and to this end wheedled a royal proclamation in 1622 which forbade all persons to trade with or have dealings among the Indians except under license from the Council for New England. To implement this edict, an agent was dispatched here the same year, but he was derelict in his duties, and was replaced the following year by Robert, the son of Sir Ferdinando Gorges. This young man, too, soon gave up the unequal struggle of chasing down intruders and departed for home, leaving the preserves of his backers wide open to poachers.

English immigration to America was getting under way, and during the following five years a wide array of fishing stages and trading posts spotted the shore from Plymouth to present-day Gloucester. Some were on islands, but most of them were along the mainland, with quite a nest cropping up in the vicinity of what would one day soon be Boston and its environs. They were inhabited principally by rugged, self-sustaining, and thoroughly independent souls. Yet one among them was far more colorful than the rest, and his type would reappear, with minor variations, at the edge of many another wilderness as the line of settlement marched slowly westward toward the Pacific.

Since he had occasion to write a history of his exploits, we know him with some degree of intimacy. His name was Thomas Morton, and to maintain a status befitting his ultimate intentions, he carefully added "of Clifford's Inne, Gent." This would indicate he was an attorney, and thus a person of some education, and parts. For this volume to which he applied his rather venomous pen, he chose the satirical title *New English Canaan*, a gibe at the colonial fathers, who would ultimately dissuade him from his picaresque activities.

He claimed to have arrived in these parts and quite likely did, for the first time in June of 1622, with "thirty servants, and provisions of all sorts fit for a plantation." This was no doubt as an associate of one Andrew Weston, who set up a trading post at Wessagusset on the south side of Massachusetts Bay, about twenty-five miles above Plymouth. This enterprise ran the full gamut of dishonesty, thriftlessness, folly, and the final retreat of its survivors to England.

In 1623, a Captain Wollaston formed a partnership to establish a plantation at a site not far from the above, and near present-day Quincy. He sent over a number of indentured servants to man it; but neither they nor this type of operation was suitable to local conditions, and a portion of them were shipped to Virginia, and there sold into further servitude. More of these unfortunate creatures were to be shipped down to the colony to the south, when Morton suddenly appeared on the scene.

He was one of the partners in the scheme, had a legal background, and was both quick-witted and resourceful, as well as a promoter somewhat ahead of his time. Sizing up the situation, he took sides with the bond servants, drew them to his leadership, and drove Wollaston's deputy from the settlement. The plantation was then altered to a trading post, and accorded the jubilant and enticing name of Merry Mount.

If Weston and his profligates had given staid Plymouth concern, Thomas Morton and his knot of boon companions would soon flare up as a galling source of irritation and alarm. The Indians were by then recovering somewhat from the scourge which had left them dead in heaps and unburied nearly ten years before; and by his gross mistreatment of the red men, Weston had placed the Pilgrims in growing jeopardy. Standish had had to use stern measures among the natives, too stern, some thought. But this fellow Morton! He was erring in quite the opposite direction.

There were no two ways about it, the man was downright immoral. Undeniably you should treat all men, even the lowly natives, as brothers, but not necessarily clasp them to your bosom in unabashed surrender. And as though that were not enough in itself, his merry trading post was becoming a despicable place of refuge, a "Vale of Hinnom." This Philistine was not only attracting the riffraff and discontented bond servants, but many formerly irreproachable settlers had begun to frequent the place to pamper the strictly human side of their natures. To the strait-laced Governor Bradford now in charge in Plymouth the goings on at Ma-re Mount, as Morton preferred to spell it, smacked decidedly of the evil one. Why report had it that as much as "ten pounds' worth of strong liquor had been downed there in a single morning."

No gainsaying the fact, Thomas Morton, Gent., took quite a different view of life than did his neighbors to the south of him. They may have approached it with *zeal*, while he embraced it with *zest*, and had a particular fondness for roaming the woods and shore line with dog and gun, or sailing about the Bay, as fancy dictated, sampling the sporting qualities of its fish. But "sport" that he was, he had another side to him, which encompassed a ready eye for business.

The Indians fairly cherished him because he utterly refused to peer down his nose at them. He knew them, trusted them, and even respected them for what they were—savages—and they loved him for this complete understanding. As a consequence he had the choice of their furs in his trading with them, and it was at this point that he began to tread on doubtful ground, which ultimately led to his undoing.

He primed them with lusty liquor, and of all things he sold them guns, powder, and shot. He may have justified this in the belief firearms would aid their hunting and his take in furs, from which he managed several hundred per cent profit. But more responsible and farsighted men saw in such traffic the beginning of trouble, which came a half century later with the onset of King Philip's War.

His trade was of sufficient volume to maintain him and a coterie of hangers-on in continuous, idle revelry, and to permit the opportunist host of Ma-re Mount to play fast and loose with colonial security. Not only Indians, but any white man willing to risk his reputation could find an abundance of good cheer at Morton's rendezvous. And that term should be remembered, for it forecasts similar spring revels undertaken in the Rocky Mountains by the fur trade two hundred years later.

Much of what transpired at this notorious post had a decidedly frowsy taint. Some leavening of the rather sodden Puritan loaf may have been called for, but here, close at hand, were excesses which, in the long run, were highly detrimental. Left to his own devices, this former London barrister would have developed a situation which, in all probability, would have defeated the world of good intents and purposes put to work in the Bay area.

One spring, as the snows of March and April disappeared and the

Indians were due from the back country with the winter's catch, something more than the usual preparations for conviviality seemed in order, and he and his cohort rose to the occasion. By Morton's own words, "A goodly pine tree of 80 foote longe was reared up, with a pair of bucks horns nayled on somewhere neare unto the top of it: where it stoode, a faire sea marke for directions how to find the way out to mine host of Ma-re Mount."

While its prime purpose was a beacon, it turned out to be a most welcome Maypole; and the vernal celebration which centered about it made up in gusto whatever it lacked in decorousness. Morton composed a mock classical poem which ran strongly to the ribald, and tacked it to the tall pine shaft. This rollicking chanty, said mine host, "was sung with a Corus, every man bearing his part; which they performed in a daunce, hand in hand about the Maypole."

Trader Morton's archenemy, the governor at Plymouth, writes that for many days they had "Indean women for their consorts, dancing and frisking togither like fairies, or rather furies." His intents were, no doubt, that the fur trade might be made even more profitable, and perhaps it was, and he garnered more than his share of the pelts which were an important item in the commerce of all the colonies for years to come. The man was nothing if not resourceful, and the profit motive may have blotted out the religious motive in the unfavorable reaction that began to mount rapidly among his neighbors.

It would be unfair, however, to overlook another and perhaps the principal cause in this increasing opposition. He had founded a rifle range on which to improve the Indian's skill with firearms, and this act no doubt precipitated the warmth that descended upon mine host. All the scattered settlements southward from Maine, so it is said, combined in requesting the most populous community among them, Plymouth, to subdue this daring, unorthodox, and rather fey spirit. Summary action was called for.

When Standish, in quelling a threatening Indian uprising four years before, had killed two natives lest his own life be taken, one of the Pilgrims' backers in Holland had lamented, "How happy it had been had you converted some before you killed any." So it was perhaps with this stern admonition still fresh in mind that Governor Bradford resorted first to friendly reproof, hoping Morton would be won from his loose ways to more becoming conduct. But even a second more pointed protest glanced ineffectively off this man's adamant hide. His love of freedom was a consuming fire, and totally without the protective qualities of a sense of responsibility.

But the Pilgrims were unmistakably thorough, and Miles Standish, at the moment not otherwise employed, was ordered to Merry Mount, together with a group from other settlements, to arrest this brazen fellow. Sending that particular gentleman at the head of this mission was like adding insult to injury, for to Morton Standish was "Captaine Shrimp, a quondam drummer." Still the captain and his posse either appeared at mine host's place of business quite unexpectedly, or certainly at a most inopportune time, for the hangers-on there were far gone in liquor, and in no fit condition to offer concerted resistance.

There was a one-sided brawl, Morton made a few pointed remarks which he thought appropriate to the occasion, but nonetheless was brought back to Plymouth, and from there shipped off to England—and good riddance to him!

But at a distance from the frontier in which they had been committed, his sins did not seem quite so cardinal. So the Council in London was very lenient, and Morton was soon back on this side of the ocean. Liquor once again flowed freely at the mount of merriment, and his other former threats to probity and security were renewed.

Governor Endecott had by now come to this country as advance agent of the proposed Bay colony, and took strong exception to this defiant, lone-wolf operator. At first, however, he tried to take over Morton and his operations. Then, failing in this, the Maypole was leveled, mine host had his fine house at Mount Wollaston burned before his eyes, he was thrown into fetters, and when a convenient ship arrived, returned to England a second time.

There he at once joined the ranks of the enemies of the Massachusetts Bay colony promoters, wrote his animated and informative book, and bided his time. He had florid dreams of returning in power and glory to take control of the colony in the name of the king. But circumstances were against him. It was a full ten years before he found his way to New England for the last time, his fire and enthusiasm by then pretty well burned out. Treated courteously at Plymouth, he managed to run afoul of and fall into the hands of authorities in the Bay colony, now very much a going concern. They quickly stripped him of his remaining property, and penniless and broken in spirit, he stole away, to live out his few remaining years at York in Maine.

The flowering of New England involved many and diverse types of people, but none quite the equal in spirited waywardness of Thomas Morton, Gent.

VI

The Swedes Made a Contribution to the American Frontier

The first (tour) was to Old Historic Salem. Here the Pioneer Village was visited, a historically accurate reproduction of the first settlement in Salem. The first surprise was that there were *no* log cabins. "What! no log cabins! Why every history I studied as a youngster showed pictures of Pilgrims and Puritans with log cabins." Thus, it was possible to point out that the English in America (at the outset) reproduced what they knew in England, and in England they did not know the log cabin.—Franklin C. Roberts, *Third Dimensional History*, in American Heritage Series.

DESPITE the heavy hand of Spain, which for years had rested on their land, the frugal, energetic Dutch merchants of Holland and Zeeland had prospered and achieved a trading supremacy which was to continue through the 1600s. When a Spanish truce was concluded in 1609, their East India Company was already at work, and at the same moment Henry Hudson, an English navigator in their employ, was cruising the shores of North America, trying to ferret out a northwest passage to the Orient. While such a convenience was not available, he did manage to discover a river which penetrated a considerable distance into the interior of a countryside offering strong inducements to settlement and trade.

But glory in the minds of the Hollanders lay in profits rather than discovery, and since they were heavily involved at the moment, even the profit possibilities of this promising area lay fallow for several years. Finally a group of Amsterdam traders founded in 1621 the Dutch West India Company, with the privilege of exploiting the huge stretch of land between Maryland and the eastern tip of Maine. Thus they became potential interlopers, not only in a section which the Spanish had claimed as a part of Florida, but in one in which British activity was mounting rapidly.

However, it was several years before a settlement was attempted. The first contingent sent over consisted of some thirty families of religious outcasts, who scattered rapidly in all directions, out onto Long Island, up the Hudson as far as present-day Albany, and even to the South River, in what was to become the Philadelphia area. But it proved a fortunate beginning, particularly since the vessel which had brought these colonists carried home a cargo of furs valued at twenty-five thousand guilders. This fact had quite an impact, and soon the authorities were trading about twenty-four dollars' worth of trinkets to the Canarsie Indians for possession of a long narrow island at the mouth of their North River for a base, only to find shortly after the deal was completed that it must be repurchased from its rightful owners, the Manhatoes.

Additional settlers seeped in very slowly, and to speed them up the patroon system was inaugurated in 1629. By it any company member who transported a colony of as many as fifty adults was named a patroon and made its virtual master. It was strongly feudal in spirit, and the English lords-proprietors attempted a similar scheme a half century later in Carolina. In connection with this Dutch enterprise it worked most successfully, for the wealthy in the homeland came hurrying over with colonies of their sponsorship, bent upon becoming aristocrats in this "New Netherlands."

The French, then the English, and now the Dutch were contesting Spain's title to the Atlantic coast line. Soon the Dutch, even if somewhat obliquely, would be aiding and abetting a fourth nation to enter the competition. We come to its entry into the area by way of tough-minded old Peter Minuit, who had taken charge of the activities of the Hollanders in 1626 and become the first real governor in their newest colony. He may have been a bit crochety and inclined to self-seeking, but he was an able organizer, and soon tidied up the whole colonial enterprise to the exacting standards of Dutch orderliness.

But company members back at headquarters felt he was too partial to some of the patroons. So he was called home, divested of his responsibilities, and an archblockhead installed in his place. Minuit was naturally pretty disgruntled, and began to cast furtive glances over the dikes in his native land in the hope some other nation might wish to avail itself of his knowledge of the American frontier. Beyond the shores of the North Sea he was soon to find an interested customer.

SWEDEN DECIDES TO TAKE A RISK

Sweden, which occupied an important place in European affairs at the beginning of the seventeenth century, came to lean years during the reign of Christina. The exchequer needed replenishing, and it appeared essential that foreign trade, which had fallen off markedly, be revived. America, if colonies could be planted there, seemed to offer live possibilities; and to resolve the matter, the Swedes deposited their problems squarely in old Peter Minuit's lap. As a necessary mechanism by which to achieve their hopes, he, in association with a few other disaffected Dutchmen, set up the New Sweden Company, and focused its attention on the country along the South, or Delaware, River.

Under its auspices the first of three somewhat desultory expeditions set out late in 1637. As a beginning, a fort was erected on the present site of Wilmington, Delaware. The second party came in 1640, and the third a year later. The settlers had been rather carefully screened, were of a hardy variety, and being land-hungry, soon scattered out along the river to the extent that they might have been easy prey for the Dutch, had not that people been fully employed at the moment making themselves secure from the Indians further to the north.

To stabilize the project, the fourth and most ambitious expedition was sent out in 1643 under command of Colonel Johan Printz, one of the most remarkable and little known of the many picturesque characters destined to leave their impress upon our colonial affairs. He was in size and strength a Hercules. He had been a cavalry officer in the European wars, heading groups of Finnish troopers, that land being then subservient to Sweden. Since he weighed more than four hundred pounds, all the horses of Europe must have breathed a sigh of relief when he headed west over the ocean. Although well educated, and cultured after a fashion, he was a rough, tough, violent, headstrong creature when aroused, and at all times overbearing, arrogant, and completely arbitrary.

For his personal headquarters, he took over Tinicum Island, south and west along the river from present-day Philadelphia, and there set up the first permanent colony and seat of government in what is now the state of Pennsylvania. From his mansion, Printzhof, he ruled the small group of Swedes and Finns in his colony with a rod of iron, held the Dutch at bay, cut heavily into their trade, and for a time threatened to drive them from this area rich in ultimate possibilities.

Short-lived New Sweden reached its zenith during Printz's residence here, and came to an abrupt end when it fell to the Dutch within two years after his return to the homeland in 1653. But brief as was its existence, this colony provided us with one of our most effective pioneering tools, and a sentimental symbol of our formative years. What follows, while essentially fact, has had to be decked in a bit of fancy with respect to characters and incidents so it may better tell a story which deserves to be widely known.

HOW WE CAME TO HAVE LOG CABINS

As the huge Printz, with his distorted nose and jutting chin, stepped ashore that bleak February day in 1643, the retinue which he had brought with him almost totaled those already settled upon the land. The briefing he had received in advance, plus his own subsequent observations while on a hurried inspection of his domain from Cape Henlopen to the falls near present Trenton, showed him clearly that what he lacked in man power must be compensated for in bravado, strategy, stubbornness, and in making every man in the colony as fully productive as possible. The Dutch were perhaps merely biding their time.

So his first efforts went toward extending fortifications that might add to the Hollanders' hesitancy. Also there was this recent English settlement on the east side of the river filling in with people from the New Haven colony seeking a milder climate. A fort was set up to overawe them and keep uppermost in their minds the promise exacted of them to respect Swedish authority. This outward show accomplished, the Swedish Goliath began to make plans for his own comfort, security, and aggrandizement.

Tinicum Island, in the midst of a large marshy area, was set off from the land rising slowly to the westward merely by a lazy main creek and its smaller side branch. At its southern point, by means of forced labor, Printz erected first a fort and storehouse, and then his own residence, constructed of selected hemlock tree trunks, neatly squared and laid horizontal, the overlapping logs fitted snugly together by well-cut notches, where they formed corners.

Ruder cabins employing this basic log construction had already been erected by his countrymen, and had caught the fancy of the few Dutch and English families in the vicinity. This first interest, though, had been rather casual. Now as this almost palatial home took form, the merits of log walls became more marked, particularly the speed with which sound, lasting shelter could be achieved. Word of them began to leak out to both the north and the south.

His own and the general needs of the tiny colony in hand, Printz began to give some thought to those of its backers at home, to which the fur trade was the key. While the local Leni-Lenape Indians provided some skins, by far the better ones—beaver and otter—flowed in from the Minquas, a tribe living in the Susquehanna Valley, whence they had beaten a well-marked trail to the trading posts set up by both the Dutch and the Swedes along the Delaware. The settlers, too, were soon using this Indian path for excursions into the back country.

Having heard repeatedly of a small waterfall near where this trail crossed the east branch of the creek whose lower meandering course set apart his island domain, Printz finally caused his great bulk to be lowered into a canoe, and was paddled up the creek for a firsthand inspection. Finding a convenient place to sit and contemplate these falls, a scheme for their employment suddenly came to him. The site would ideally adapt itself to a small gristmill. It could sit upon stilts on the flat rocks where the creek below fell over a low stone reef. A hasty but sufficient survey convinced him of its complete feasibility, and orders for its erection were given forthwith.

By 1646 it was in operation, a tiny log cabin housing the millstones, the upper of which was rotated by a vertical shaft, taking its power from an undershot wheel set on the horizontal, and fed water through a plank flume from the pond above the falls. Crude though it was, it operated for well over one hundred years, and the relief afforded from the toil of hand-grinding was widely appreciated. Even the Englishmen in the settlement at Salem, miles away across the Delaware, gladly patronized it.

It was perhaps in the fall of 1648 that two youngish men set out from this latter place in a canoe heavy with sacks of shelled maize, bound for the mill at Mölndal. For want of a real name, we will call one of them Benjamin Stokes, already a householder at Salem. The other might have been, say, Edward Beach, a courier from far-off New Haven in the Connecticut colony, bearing dispatches to and fetching word back from those trying to establish themselves at this outpost on the Delaware. Quite likely they were cousins, or of kin, and Beach had come along on the journey to the mill for a closer look at the country and its settlers.

Once out of Varkens Creek, on which Salem stood, a favorable breeze had helped them up the big river. They had slipped by Tinicum and watchful eyes there in the half-light of evening, taking shelter in Bow Creek, the smaller of the streams which set off the large island from the mainland, and which joined the Delaware and the Muckruton, or Darby Creek, above the latter's real mouth. There they spent a rather sleepless night, fighting off mosquitoes. It was perhaps largely because of these pests that they were on their way up the Muckruton when the sky was still faintly gray, and not too long after sunup they were at the mill itself. A Finlander who manned the place together with his grown son arriving at about the same time, their grain was soon milled, the mill charge paid in flour, and the remainder stowed in their sacks. By that time the two Englishmen had every detail of the mill and its operation firmly in their minds.

Beach, who had been billeted with Swedish and Finnish troops for a time on the Continent before shipping to New England, had enough skill in the languages to keep a conversation alive. And there being no other customers at hand, the mill was shut down and the four repaired to the shore on the west branch of the creek for a frugal meal and a little conversation.

The blond-headed, blue-eyed miller and his son proved much less reticent than was customary, and the Englishmen were soon plying them with questions. Printz's harsh rule seemed to be the burden of their concern.

"And what do you propose to do about it?" queried Beach.

"Well," admitted the elder Finn, "we do not as yet have our roots down, as it were. We have no farm made, which might tend to hold us. The Dutch invite us continually to their New Amsterdam, but we fear their Governor Stuyvesant might be just another Colonel Printz. Some of the English people have slipped across from the bay they call the Chesapeake and made promises, and some of our people have stolen away with them. Then there are other Englishmen who make their way up the river from the colony in Jamestown. They offer us passage and good land there, but we hear they are in serious trouble with the Indians, like the New Netherland Dutch. Yet some have gone there; and if this Printz remains, maybe we, too, and many others will leave these parts."

Above their conversation and the noise of the creek came the sound of gunfire at some distance to the west. The Englishmen turned quickly toward the echoes, but the two Finns showed little concern, saying, "It is no doubt one of the Polsson boys. They passed by yesterday, going out to build a house on the main branch of the creek, perhaps two miles from here."

At once Beach was all attention. He would like nothing better than to see the actual construction of one of these log structures and learn how the logs were chosen, trimmed, notched, and laid up. In a few minutes' conversation with the others arrangements were made, and he, Stokes, and the young Finn set out along the trail, the father staying behind to watch the mill.

It still lacked an hour and a half of midday as they made their way over the crest of the first long gentle hill and down into the valley of the main branch of the creek. The trail then wound up along its banks for a mile through handsome stands of evergreens, oaks, and a few maples. Walking rapidly in anticipation another two miles over the fine trail brought them to a point where they were welcomed by the crashing of a felled tree in a small meadow-like clearing by the side of the creek. Greetings were exchanged, and they made their way over the stream on convenient stepping stones, and up to a log crib about twelve or fourteen feet square, and already three logs high. To one side, skinned, slit, and hung to bleed, was a deer carcass, the result of the single shot that had brought them there.

Acquaintance was soon established all around, and since the two strangers seemed not only fully acceptable, but willing to lend a hand, it was agreed they would spend the night there, and perhaps escape the worst of the mosquitoes that lurked along the river. The young Finn from the mill promised to secure their flour and canoe, and soon took his leave, certain they would have no trouble finding their way back on the morrow.

There being a third ax, and four trunks already on the ground and needing attention, Beach seized the ax and fell to with the Polsson boys lopping off branches, while his cousin carried them away to a rapidly growing pile. Carefully he watched the boys as they judged trees for size and the manner in which the logs would best fit together. Then he began to pick up the technique by which the corner notches were positioned and chopped. When the bark, under which destructive borers lurked, was peeled off, the logs were laid up and any high spots axed down for the closest possible fit so the chinking between would be held to a minimum.

Proud of their craft, the two young Polssons willingly gave the Englishmen a rigorous schooling during the long afternoon. Time was not even taken to clean and cut up the deer, still pretty green, for there were other provisions on hand. Slabs of fresh pork spitted over a fire, and a corn cake larded with apple butter sticky with boiled cider was downed with relish. Shortly afterward the four were sound asleep and snoring lustily, bedded down in a pile of hemlock tips.

Staying on in the morning to breakfast and to fit three more logs to a crib now almost shoulder-high, the two Englishmen at last somewhat reluctantly took their leave. At the mill, they packed their flour sacks in the waiting canoe, bid farewell to the miller and his son, and started downstream. More boldly this time they kept along the main creek, within fair sight of Printzhof, which was passed without incident, and they were back at Salem by sundown.

It had been an exhilarating experience, and two days later Edward Beach set out for Cape May, at the southern tip of Jersey, there to make contact with an English trading smack which would return him to New Haven. From this latter place it was but a dozen miles to his father's home in Milford.

Men such as he may well have carried the knowledge of the useful log cabin, which began to appear in ever greater numbers in the newer settlements in Connecticut and Massachusetts by the beginning of King Philip's War. The Dutch, too, started it on its way up the Hudson, and other visitors, or quite likely Swedes and Finns who stole away from the rigorous hand of Printz, took it to Maryland and Virginia. It pushed fairly early into the Carolinas, Boone took it into Kentucky, and long before the Revolution it was in wide use. Perhaps America would have become the America we know without it, perhaps not. It was indeed a quickly built, weather-tight, and long-lasting type of shelter, and while Scandinavian in origin, multiplied until it became completely American frontier.

There were perhaps no Edward Beach, no Benjamin Stokes, no Polsson boys—at least by those names, or in the places in which they have been put. Yet there stands to this very day by the banks of Darby Creek in the township of Upper Darby, Pennsylvania, a log house built in the years between 1638 and 1655 when the area was a part of New Sweden. And it is still in use! By the same token there was a small mill built in 1646 in the east fork of this same creek. This branch is now called Cobbs Creek, and forms the western border of the city of Philadelphia. Records show that until late in the 1700s people continued to carry grain on horseback for twenty or more miles to have it ground there.

In 1655 the Dutch from New Amsterdam under Stuyvesant ended Swedish hopes in America; and by 1674 the Hollanders themselves ceded their own colonies here to England. The struggle for empire was already launched, and would last another hundred years.

While Sweden was a tenant in the Delaware Valley but seventeen years, she succeeded in making a contribution out of all proportion to her own benefits from colonial effort here in America. Our mental picture of the frontier life from which we draw so rich a heritage would suffer markedly if, as we try to imagine the birthplace of some of our patriots, or we visualize a suitable home for the men and women who tamed and won us this marvelous homeland, we were deprived the satisfaction of centering in it a log cabin, with a whisp of smoke curling from its stubby chimney.

VII

Colonial Activity along the Gulf Coast

The interest of France in the Mississippi Valley extended over nearly two centuries. There is a striking continuity in her efforts to unite the fortunes of the province of Louisiana and to control the Mississippi Valley. This she desired to do as a bar to the advance of England; and as a means of supplying the French West Indies; (and later) as a lever by which to compel the United States to serve the interests of France; and as a means of promoting French ascendency over Spanish America.—Frederick Jackson Turner, *The Significance of Sections in American History.*

SOME say its name originated in an exclamation of astonishment as the great beaklike headland rose from the north shore of the St. Lawrence above the small ships of the early adventurers pushing their way up that stately stream. Others claim it stemmed from an Indian term meaning "narrowing of the waters." Both help indicate why Samuel de Champlain, in 1608, established a base at the foot of its steep cliffs, which he named Quebec; yet it was what lay about it and far beyond in the trackless wilderness that patterned its destiny and made it the anchor of French hopes of empire in America. Before the seventeenth century had run its course, intrepid explorers from there, and from the smaller settlement at the foot of Mount Royal further upstream, had pushed west to the great lakes and discovered a shore line stretching on and on, like that of the Atlantic coast and the gulf of Mexico, which furnished ready access to the boundless interior of the continent.

From the far shores of the fourth of these Great Lakes, they had discovered a long narrow bay slanting to the south and west, into the lower end of which flowed a rather lazy river readily navigated. By the briefest of portages at its headwaters, they had come to a second river flowing in the opposite direction, down which they made their way through the Wisconsin country to the upper reaches of the Father of Waters, winding down a gigantic valley to North America's southern ocean front. If they could gain and maintain control of this almost unbroken waterway, they could control the great American heartland. And the plans to this end discussed before cheering fires on the hearths of Quebec's solid homes during long winter evenings must have been sweeping, stirring, and perhaps a bit grandiose.

Contact with the homeland was reasonably frequent, and these schemes and hopes born of a knowledge of the wilderness and its huge potential were rehearsed by the hearths of chateaux back in France, from which they made their way to the drawing rooms of the French court. On the assumption that, if they were painted vividly enough and poured into the right ears, these aspirations would be understood, approved, and implemented, French Canada's sons pressed their case assiduously. For greater motivation they stressed the threat that Spain, well entrenched in Mexico and the West Indies, might very soon press to the east along the Gulf coast and seize the lower end of the great Mississippi Valley, and thereby control the natural outlet of this mighty inland domain. Possession of the mouth of the Mississippi was the key to dominion. It must be firmly in the hands of France. What did the king and his ministers propose to do about the matter?

It took further exploration on this side of the ocean, and added agitation back home, to sell America's possibilities. The times, too, had not been fortunate. Then the signing of the Peace of Ryswick in 1697 gave war-taut Europe a breathing space. Hardly was the ink dry when Louis XIV began to show lively interest in the expanding contest for footholds in the New World. And quite as though they had long anticipated this new concern, the king's ministers promptly offered him a Canadian-born champion, eager to enter the lists for France.

He was Pierre Lemoyne d'Iberville, whose father, the son of a Dieppe innkeeper, had been among the early settlers in Quebec. There the elder Lemoyne had accumulated a sizable fortune. This permitted his setting aside a tidy estate for each of his several sons. Eldest among them to survive was D'Iberville, who was selected to command an expedition of several ships, which finally left Brest in 1699. Following instructions, a course was laid for the Caribbean, where this party was to search out the elusive mouths of the Mississippi, which had been discovered and then lost track of by the unfortunate La Salle party. When found, a colony was to be planted in the vicinity before the English or the Spaniards accomplished such an enterprise.

Among the members of his party were two of his brothers. Nearer his own age was Sauville, or, as the name is sometimes spelled, Sauvole. Also there was the far younger Jean Baptiste Lemoyne, Sieur de Bienville, at that time a youthful but quite competent naval cadet. Although credit for establishment of the first permanent French colony along the Gulf of Mexico should go to D'Iberville, it was eventually Bienville who became the "father" of Louisiana, and especially of its chief city, New Orleans.

THE FOUNDING OF LOUISIANA

The D'Iberville party entered the Gulf of Mexico and began to reconnoiter the coast, starting at the edge of Florida. As had been feared, they found the Spanish already entrenched at Pensacola, and with sufficient vessels on hand to make any contest for that site too hazardous an undertaking. Their first objective was a harbor sufficient to shelter shipping but close enough to the coast so as not to risk the possibility of their life line stretching back to Europe being cut. This had been the pattern of the settlements along the Atlantic seaboard up to this time, and inherent needs would extend it to other attempts.

Moving on west, their first colony was located at Biloxi. But while he solidified his position there, D'Iberville sent his adventurous younger brother to search out the coast on toward the great river's mouth. When the young midshipman found its outlet, he sailed up its sweeping course, and to his chagrin found an English party there ahead of him. It involved two ships, and was intent on planting a post or fort in the long bend, some distance above the mouth, which is still spoken of as the English Turn.

Ingenious as well as brave, Bienville applied his charm, and heaped such sound reasoning upon the English officer in charge that the latter decided to abandon his project. After bidding these British interlopers good-by, the Frenchman carefully examined the banks along the huge stream for a number of miles, made preliminary plans of his own, and took himself and his survey party back to Biloxi. When D'Iberville departed for France soon afterward, he left Sauville in command. But when this brother died within two years, the still youthful Jean Baptiste assumed charge in his place.

A second colony had been planted at Mobile, but there was suf-

ficient internal strife so that little progress was made either there
or at Biloxi. For some time Bienville had been attempting to found a
third colony on the Mississippi at the point visited some years before.
But while the English managed to be free spirits and largely self-
determining in their activities on this side of the ocean, the French
and Spanish held a taut rein from the homeland, and so curbed individual enterprise and incentive that the contest here was remark-
ably one-sided. Sanction for such a move was withheld year after
year until the whole area fell under control of John Law and his
Mississippi Company, which ultimately blew a huge speculative bubble that burst, and left France on the brink of financial ruin.

In the interim, the former cadet had become a seasoned explorer
and administrator, when, in 1718, he was at last permitted to begin
the building of New Orleans, one hundred ten miles up the Mississippi from the Gulf. For the task, he had the services of an able military engineer, Sieur Le Blond de la Tour. There were in addition a
handful of woodsmen sent down the river from the Illinois country,
some two dozen carpenters, and about an equal number of convicted felons shipped to this country to ease the pressure on French
jails. To this force he was later able to add a number of galley slaves,
and also a few artisans as they could be scraped together.

First task was to erect a levee to restrain the mighty current
surging past their very doors. By the end of two years there were
in addition about a hundred huts, together with several larger structures, fairly rude, including the church, a hospital, a government
building, and a number of storehouses. A well-planned street system
had been mapped, some of the ground had been cleared and leveled,
and the principal streets bravely named for the princes and nobility
of France. But to its three hundred or more inhabitants the townsite
was a dreary, soggy, somewhat uninviting place set in water-logged
surroundings. However, its location had certain distinct advantages,
and authority was given in the summer of 1722 to shift troops, stores,
and the government trappings to this new post. Henceforth New
Orleans would be the capital of the Louisiana province, a scheme
Bienville long had advocated.

But nature seemed to take exception to this move. Hardly was
the installation of the government there completed when an untimely hurricane wreaked havoc, carrying down many of the structures. As though this were not a sufficient rebuke, John Law's
Mississippi Bubble promptly exploded, and distress in faraway
France was severe enough to set up repercussions in its colonies.

The next few years were humble ones indeed. Then better times returned, and with them one of the most colorful happenings in Louisiana's early history, provided by a paternalistic government back home.

The Place d'Armes, now Jackson Square, was the center from which the struggling town radiated. The still rather crude church, reconstructed after the devastating windstorm, occupied the site on which today stands the gracious old St. Louis Cathedral. Next on its right was a small guardhouse, and the indispensable prison. To its other side was the dwelling of the Capuchin fathers, under whose spiritual care came the people here and others thinly scattered up along the river to the Illinois settlements. There was also the government house, not particularly pretentious; and not far from this cluster of structures, and on the corner of what was formerly Arsenal Street, a hospital presided over by a group of Ursuline sisters, who had been sent over to found a girls' school, and to minister to the ailing.

A few among the colonial officials had brought their wives, but their households made up a very inconsiderable fraction of the growing community, which consisted for the most part of hard-bitten soldiers, trappers, woodsmen, miners, galley slaves, and redemptioneers bound to three years' service before their ultimate freedom. Even the French jails had been scoured to provide colonists. With a preponderance of males, this early New Orleans citizenry was a roistering, carousing, heavy-drinking, wayward lot; and many of the women who lived among them a similarly refractory group. As it was then, so it would continue to be a hundred years later, a sort of Babylon on the Bayous. While the town was slowly taking shape architecturally, the need for distinct improvement in its social and moral aspects was painfully apparent. Unmistakably there was a missing ingredient here which must be supplied.

Bienville, filled with plans as ever, but either openly opposed by his provincial council or given indifferent attention by the powers in the homeland, had long sought to take steps suitable to bring order from the near chaos. He did finally manage to have the wholesale importation of vagabonds and criminals shut off. And at last he had been able to fix penalties for gambling, which, although they did not stamp out the evil, made it less open and all-pervasive.

Better still he had been able to bring in a group of stern Jesuits to take in hand the more unruly youths, and to get many of them started in sobering agricultural pursuits. The intense earlier rawness of the town was gradually smoothing out.

Let there be no mistake that most of the male members of the province were wantons and wastrels. There were sober-minded, ambitious men among them, and even among the soldiery, who, by and large, were a venturesome, unsavory group. Many of the latter would willingly, with just a bit of encouragement, have slipped out of their uniforms at the end of their periods of enlistment, and made very worth-while citizens. Some strong encouragement in this direction was called for.

The crying need was for homes, for men with their roots down, and for sons and daughters born into family groups in which they would be encouraged to permanently embrace opportunities opening up in this land of promise beyond the seas. But the sweepings from the gutters of French cities, wayward squaws from neighboring Indian tribes, and the other flotsam and jetsam of a crude river town were hardly the material from among which to choose mothers for a coming generation.

FILLES À LA CASSETTE

The problem had been thrashed out in council, and then relayed to France with certain suggestions. Now a hoped for answer was on the way, and word of its forthcoming arrival had spread quickly through the town. For some days more than customary attention had been given the stretch of river to the south in the hope the expected ship's masts and sails might glide into sight; and not a few of the more pious had implored St. Christopher in their prayers to watch over its precious and priceless cargo.

Then one morning out of a wintry sunrise, her sails well filled with a south breeze, the long-awaited vessel made her way up the great curving arc of the river and lay just off the levee before the Place d'Armes. By the time she had been warped in close to the bank, the coarse grass that covered the square to the west was black with people in holiday mood, cheering, huzzahing, and shouting out needless instructions to the crew.

As the tall ship was at last made fast, the crowd pressed in even closer, elbowing their way to vantage points where the deck could best be seen through the line of willows which had been planted in the hope of strengthening De La Tour's protective earthworks. It was with some difficulty, and only by the use of a squad of soldiers, that a passage was made for the group of Ursuline sisters who had come down from the temporary convent quarters, and two by two made their way through the press, to stand quietly chatting in a group just to the rear of the governor and his welcoming party.

The earlier bawling and shouting had by now subsided as a number of sailors lifted a cleated plank walk from the deck, slid it out over the side and down to waiting hands beneath. As it was made fast by sailors who nimbly ran down it and lashed its lower end, conversation fell to a mere whisper. Every eye was glued to the upper end of this gangway.

There was a bit of stir aboard, and the captain, appearing from his cabin aft, paced across the deck, then stepped over the side, and descended. Governor Bienville rushed forward, and a cordial welcome was extended by him and members of his retinue, the crowd trying to keep track of these proceedings and also maintain a watch on the vessel at the same time.

Now the captain, mildly gesticulating, was in earnest whispered conversation with Bienville, and the result was a crisp command and a noisy remonstrance from those who had crowded in close. They were unceremoniously pushed back by the soldiery, and a sizable space cleared on the top of the levee beside the official party.

When this had been done to the satisfaction of the ship's master, he gave a hand signal to the mate at the rail, and sailors at once began to file across the deck, each bearing on his shoulder a similar *cassette*, or small leather trunk. A rousing cheer went up as the first came to the rail and started down the planking. Then followed five others, each carrying a cassette, which they in turn deposited in a line in the cleared space. Hurrying back aboard, the file soon reappeared, bringing six more to form a second row, and then a third, a fourth, and soon there were ten rows of six each of these almost identical little trunks. Four somewhat different chests were also carried down and piled near the waiting sisters.

As the sailors returning from the last trip ashore took positions down along the gangplank, the spell of expectancy brought another hush. Above the ship's rail appeared the black veils of four Ursuline sisters, who were helped over the side and carefully passed along down, to be taken to the bosoms of the group of their religious comrades waiting on the levee.

And then, in the cabin doorway, and barely visible over the rail, appeared a Paris bonnet, and another, and another. What was beneath them? How the moments seemed to drag as these bits of femininity and their wearers were being assembled on the deck. Then came a lusty shout from the crowd, "There she is!" as the first trim but decidedly bashful "casket girl" was being handed over the side and began to pick her mincing way down the steep plank, handed along from sailor to sailor ranged at intervals on its side. Then followed another, and another—and the mob fairly shouted itself hoarse, and would not cease until the last of the sixty young women had descended.

As they stepped on dry ground, each made the sign of the cross, courtesied before the governor, and then found her way to the casket that bore her name. The sisters moved quickly among them, being introduced by the four who had chaperoned this party on the journey across. When all had been welcomed to the new land, the nuns took this precious contingent in their charge, and with soldiers shouldering the trunks, a way was opened once again through the throng and the procession headed across the Place d'Armes. In the church, a Mass was solemnly celebrated before a far larger crowd than the structure had ever before housed. The first of many consignments of casket girls had arrived.

Who were they? They were young women carefully selected from the hearthstones rather than from the streets of the homeland. They had signified a willingness to leave family and friends to face life in this New World, and there find husbands with the advice and guidance of the nuns, that they might build homes and families in New France.

Their mates would be for the most part soldiers, chosen for good conduct and enterprise, and after a close screening by the Ursuline sisters.

During the years between the arrival of this first contingent in 1728, and the last shipload in the 1750s, many hundreds of resolute young women came under such auspices to Louisiana. Other hundreds had arrived under very similar circumstances in the Jamestown colony a hundred years before. Just past the middle of the century to follow the "Mercer Girls" would be shipped from the east coast around to the Pacific Northwest in the realization you cannot expect a country to grow without women.

In Louisiana, as in Jamestown, and later in our own West, these girls became the cement which gave life at the edge of the wilderness its permanence and lasting bond. Were the marriages which ensued successful? They were bound to be, for they had the proper ingredients—two people with a real need for each other. And many a family today proudly traces its ancestry back to a courageous casket girl, and to a man beside whom she bravely stood and helped build a home along the American frontier.

France, which had become a power in the St. Lawrence basin, would now become a threat to the ambitions of Spain along the Gulf of Mexico, and women played their part in stabilizing the endeavor.

VIII

Mr. Mason and Mr. Dixon Draw the Line

The emigrants to America in colonial times came from different social classes in the Old World, and found their way to the New World by various methods. Broadly speaking, they fell into four general classes. The first included farmers, merchants, and well-to-do people who had money enough to pay their passage, and often enough beside to establish themselves in agriculture, industry, or business . . . The second group embraced emigrants too poor to pay their passage and hence dependent upon others for their transportation. It was customary for shipowners or other capitalists to supply passage money to emigrants in return for their promise, or *bond*, to work a number of years to repay the sum advanced. This system was called bond, or indentured, service. On their arrival bond servants were sold to employers and had to work for their masters for a term ranging from five to seven years. At the end of their indenture they were free. A third class of emigrants was made up of whites who were compelled to come to America against their will. Thousands of men, women, and children were *kidnapped* in the towns of Great Britain, taken forcibly on board ships, carried to the colonies, and bound out to employers. Akin to the kidnapped in their sad plight were many convicts transported to the colonies in lieu of fines and imprisonment. Among them were debtors, petty offenders against harsh laws of England, and *rebels* who had taken part in agitations against the British government. To the class of persons seized and brought to America must be added Negroes imported from Africa and sold as slaves.—Charles A. and Mary R. Beard, *The Making of American Civilization.*

WHILE serfdom did not entirely disappear in France until 1789, it had been largely eradicated in other countries clustered about the English Channel and North Sea by the time the first settlers were departing for this side of the Atlantic. Yet an age-old pattern still obtained in even these more progressive lands— that of living as far as possible from another's efforts. Many a landed estate in the British Isles still kept the retainers born upon it in a most subservient condition, and there were numerous attempts to transplant this way of life to the New World and perpetuate it here. The patroon system established by the Dutch in New Netherland was of this nature. There was the intention of developing Carolina by the imposition of a landed aristocracy. Vestiges of the outmoded system appeared in the Maryland and Pennsylvania colonies, while land schemes in Kentucky and the Ohio Valley just previous to the Revolution had aristocratic tendencies, through the functioning of which it was hoped that huge estates, and thus vast wealth, might be acquired by the few.

It was all a part of a manner of living so well inculcated in Europe that it was taken largely as a matter of course. It had developed there as the people had struggled from beneath the crushing burdens of outright servitude. The land to which the freed men had formerly been inseparably attached from birth, and idle land to care for a slowly increasing population, was let, or granted, to those who would live upon and till it.

But since the grantee was unable to pay any substantial amount to acquire it, he was forced to agree to render to the grantor a continuous annual service, or thing of value, in default of which his rights to occupancy terminated. The service, or payment in cash or in goods, was termed a quitrent, and it was paid in perpetuity—forever and a day—as long as he remained upon the land.

It was through the operation of this system that proprietors of royal grants, Lord Baltimore and William Penn among them, as well as the promoters of the first of the western land companies, hoped to make themselves and their heirs wealthy through generation after generation. By means of such a device the great bulk of the population, still dependent upon agriculture and thus upon the possession of farming lands, could be bound to that land and kept in better control and made to yield substantial returns. It was a pleasant prospect, but one which would prove un-American, although certain aspects of the basic idea prevailed until fairly recent times in the abuses of share cropping.

When Calvert and Penn were moving settlers into their grants, there was little in the ethics of those times to condemn the practice of exacting quitrents. By the members of their class it was considered the height of prudence and exceptionally good business to build an estate upon them. Thus selection of these gentlemen in this instance does not necessarily cast aspersions on either of them, or their families; but the controversy which ensued between them does point up the conditions under which substantial areas along the frontier were opened up, and provides us, too, with the manner in which one of the most famous of our boundaries came into being. The question of "what is mine, and what is thine" would recur frequently in the years ahead, and two able gentlemen would set a high standard for future land surveys, and thus their purposes and activities deserve attention.

THE PENN-BALTIMORE CONTEST

During the sixteenth and seventeenth centuries five European nations attempted to obtain footholds along the Atlantic coast line. Spain had seized and held Florida, the French had taken over the St. Lawrence Valley and the area about the lower reaches of that great river, while the English were for some years competing with the Dutch, incidentally the Swedes, and eventually the French, for the lands between these extremes. But by the time the seventeenth century was three quarters gone, the British grip on the stretch from Maine to Georgia was fairly firm, settlements which she had planted or taken over were expanding, and the newer immigrants were heading back into the interior, and clearing land, in at least one instance near the extremity of an original grant. Border difficulties which had obtained between the several nations at the first would now give place to those involving individual plots granted by the British crown. As the Dutch lost their claim to the lands along the Hudson and Delaware rivers the territory which they had occupied was subject to new allotments, and its assignment was promptly under way.

Maps of the possessions on this side of the ocean were far from accurate in those days, and at a distance, and in comparison with England itself, America seemed almost limitless. Thus it was hard for the king's ministers to realize that grants of open country, as large or even far larger than England itself, could readily develop conflicts with others of similar size. But the second Lord Baltimore, with firsthand knowledge of conditions here, must have watched the reshuffling of neighboring areas with apprehension and misgiving.

He had already experienced some difficulties with his neighbors on down the Chesapeake. His own patent, a wedged-shaped area which had been lopped from the original Virginia grant, had as its southern boundary the *south* bank of the Potomac River, running out along that stream to its "first fountain." This outer limit of the boundary was highly indefinite, but that the long common bound should have been established on the *lower* bank, thus tending to cut the Virginians off from unhampered access to this important waterway, was bound to engender friction.

The northern limits of the Maryland colony had been set at the "fortieth parallel." In its earlier days such encroachments as were made by the Swedes and the Dutch were not then a cause for alarm. But when a new grant of the land taken over from the Hollanders was in order, some questions might arise in connection with this northern boundary. Lord Baltimore's uneasiness soon proved to be well founded.

It was in 1681 that William Penn, pressing for payment of a debt against the British Government in the amount of sixteen thousand pounds which he had inherited from his father, was granted a rectangular block of land lying west of the Delaware River, a portion of which had a few years before been wrested from the Dutch. But when this attractive package was opened and investigated, it proved to have one highly detrimental flaw. It was all *inland* property, no part of it bordering directly upon the ocean. This would never do, for contact with the homeland would be in continual jeopardy. What was needed in this instance was the addition of the Delaware area immediately below what appeared to be the southern limits of his grant. So Penn went after it, peaceably of course, as was his Quaker wont.

Lord Baltimore quite naturally resisted any such encroachment. The land in dispute was unquestionably within the bounds of his own charter. Did not the patent read "to the fortieth parallel"?

But the Duke of York, heir to the throne, summarily disallowed any such claim. Still Lord Baltimore pointed out the figures, set forth so clearly a child could read and understand them. However, he was at a decided disadvantage, being far less in favor at court than even his father had been in his latter years, and for a time there was a stalemate. Delaware's fate as a separate colony and later as a state looked doubtful.

Then His Highness, the duke, seemed for a moment to retract his stand. Although he still would not openly admit Baltimore's claim, he did offer to purchase from him the disputed area. But the Maryland proprietor stood pat and refused to sell; whereupon the duke handed Penn a quitclaim deed to Delaware. Even then the Baltimore interests did not give up their hopes in regard to it, but turned their attention to a more fundamental phase of the issue.

The language used in describing the bounds of Penn's grant was anything but specific. His east-west line was to run for five degrees of longitude, but on what was it to be based? The north-south dimensions were from the "*beginning* of the fortieth degree of Northern Latitude" up to the "three and fortieth." Such loose wording was bound to be questioned, and it was.

Yet to the Penns it seemed crystal-clear. The seventeenth century had begun with the year 1600, yes? And your fortieth year began with your thirty-ninth birthday, was that not so? Then quite obviously the *beginning* of the 40th degree must be at the 39th parallel. Surely that was merely good logic. At least it was the position they took, and well they might. William Penn had planted his "greene countrie towne" right at the 40th degree, and with remarkable accuracy as a later check of Thomas Holme's 1681 survey proved, Philadelphia's southernmost street resting directly upon that parallel in the early days. Thus he was under the necessity of making his contention stick or risking the loss of both the seat of his colonial government and ready access to the open ocean.

Soon there was a blizzard of charges and countercharges between the contending parties that snowed the matter under, and would keep it bogged down for years to come. There were attempts, and not without their earnest moments, to find a satisfactory solution; but there were stumbling blocks, some arrogance, and even bad faith on both sides. Also there were two family fortunes based upon quitrents at stake, and the stakes were high. There were soon many settlers in the contested area, who were not certain to which side they owed allegiance—and rent—with the consequence that uncollected rents and taxes began to pile up and stimulated each of the contestants to fight on and on in the hope that the matter would be resolved in his favor.

The original contenders passed from the scene without either side scoring a decided advantage, unless it was Penn's more active use of the debatable area. Finally in 1732, a half century after the controversy had first flared up, it seemed briefly as though it might be terminated. A basis of adjustment had been set up, with a definite time limit for agreement, and a penalty of five thousand pounds to be levied against the side that malingered and prevented a settlement by a certain date. The alternative to any such clear-cut decision was to drop the matter in the laps of the justices of the British Court of Chancery. This the Penn heirs finally elected to do, and there it bumped and dragged along for fifteen years, from 1735 to 1750, piling up costly litigation fees.

A decision reached in this latter year seemed for a time to offer an equitable solution. At least it brought renewed action. Another survey line—one had been attempted before—was now run across Delaware to the Chesapeake shore to finally establish the southern boundary of the Delaware colony, which had by then been conceded to be a separate entity by the Baltimore heirs. But after it was completed, this bound was not mutually satisfactory. Both sides agreed to disagree further; and the justices had another ten-year bout with this boundary question. Meanwhile both colonies had filled in rapidly, and the stakes had consequently mounted to excessive limits.

OUR FIRST PRECISE ARTIFICIAL BOUNDARY

In August of 1760, almost eighty years after the onset of this drawn out wrangle, commissioners representing both factions were assembled at New Castle, Delaware. With more dispatch than the past experiences would seem to foster, they were soon at work, checking the transpeninsula line which had been run ten years previously, weeding out errors, and running off additional lines to complete the boundary of Delaware, which was assured of a separate and distinct future.

Surprisingly, too, they managed to carry on with reasonable harmony, having come to a point three years later where they were certain they could compromise the small differences which remained. Then news reached them—and rather startling news indeed. The proprietors had engaged the services of a Mr. Charles Mason and a Mr. Jeremiah Dixon, two mathematicians, astronomers, and surveyors, who would soon come over to assist them.

The commissioners brought their activities to a halt, and decided to withhold their proposed report from their principals, at least for the present. How much better to let the responsibility rest, if possible, on the shoulders of this seemingly authoritative pair.

History unfortunately has pretty well emptied her file drawer of material dealing with the personal affairs of these two men whose names were destined to become household words in our land. That they had worked with the astronomer royal of England is known, and also that they had been employed to make observations at the time of an eclipse, being sent to India for the purpose, but actually doing the work in Africa, where shipwreck or similar untoward cir-

cumstances deposited them. Also, while we have no record of a formal agreement or appointment, it is known that the Royal Society
contributed funds and took a keen interest in their determination of
the surface length of a degree of latitude in connection with their
work in America. Interest in precise measurement had multiplied
rapidly in the years since this dispute had gotten under way, and it is
well it had. Now two master surveyors were approaching our shores,
bent on once and for all drawing a line that would end this perennial
feud.

So keenly have certain writers felt the lack of details regarding
this somewhat fabled pair that at least one among them has even
resorted to the dubious practice of handwriting analysis and applied
it to the many signatures of both gentlemen left by them among the
notes written into the *Journal* of their joint endeavors. From his
studies of this sort, we are assured that Mason was "cool, deliberate,
painstaking, and of quiet courage," while the somewhat younger
Dixon was, as if by complement, "active, impatient, and of a nervous
temperament."

Be that as it may, the two very earnest gentlemen, put under
agreement in England in June of 1763, arrived in Philadelphia early
in November of that same year. Immediately they began the first of
an unbroken series of daily entries in their *Journal* which, in at least
one of the three copies still preserved, continued until 1768 and their
departure for the homeland.

The first bit of business was the determination of the exact
latitude of the southernmost point of Philadelphia. With this they
"busied" themselves—and the term is well chosen—during the next
fifty-three days, or until January 7, 1764. The important 40th parallel
was found to intersect the front wall of a house standing on the lower
side of Cedar, or, as it is now called, South Street, then the lower
edge of Penn's rapidly growing town, but now one of the limits of
the heart of the city. Had the Baltimores been able to extend their
claim to such a point, both the history of the Quaker colony, and
possibly of our United States in its formative years, might have read
differently.

The measurement established to their satisfaction, they set
out for the forks of the Brandywine Creek, thirty odd miles to the
west. There they set up a station from which to determine another
key point along the same parallel. Their intents and purposes were
equally serious and thoroughgoing out here in the countryside, and

they spent more than three months, or until April 22, locating this important intersection point.

Bent on high accuracy, they spent ten days running a line fifteen miles due south from the Brandywine station. Not satisfied with results, they remeasured and reworked this same line during two more full months. When a little later they ran a tangent line, extending it for many miles, only to find it had a deviation at its end of twenty-six inches, they spent seven weeks bringing their work to complete rectitude. The ground was deep in snow before they were ready to terminate this year of effort.

Then on April 4, 1765, came the great day. A careful check of previous work made it appear sound enough to build on, and it was then they started to run the great east-west border line which has since been associated with their names. Beginning at a point a trifle beyond the present northeast corner of Maryland, and at the end of the circular boundary arched above New Castle, they headed toward the west, their first principal objective the eastern bank of the Susquehanna River just above, twenty miles away. They reached it on May 27.

After a session with the representatives of the proprietors, they were back at the river crossing again in late June, and had extended their survey on west 117 miles to the foot of North Mountain by the end of October. Then, as they slowly worked their way back along it, they carefully located the offsets by which this long border becomes the gentle curve of a meridian of latitude rather than a straight line. The stones to permanently mark it were set during the winter months.

In the spring of 1766 this dividing border was extended to Savage Mountain, while a wide swath, or vista, was cut along its entire length back to the starting point, which work consumed the seasonable months of a third year. There was an attempt to press on west in the early summer of 1767, but the work was heavily curtailed through the unwillingness of the Indians of the Six Nations to see the Europeans advance beyond the Allegheny front of the Blue Ridge. By fall arrangements had been made so that the line might be extended, and the northwestern corner of the Maryland grant was passed, and a portion run along the then common border of Virginia and Pennsylvania.

Finally, when a certain war path of the natives was reached, they protested so vehemently that the work ceased at that point. There, for the time being, it was to terminate, some two hundred thirty miles west of where it began. Yet this monumental surveying job ended more than three quarters of a century of strife.

The drawn plans of their enterprise were delivered on the 29th of January, 1768, on which day they made the last entry in that copy of the *Journal* which remained in the possession of the Penn heirs and the Pennsylvania province. Returning to England later that same year, they presented their bill, vouchers for which are still in existence. Those who care to total them will find that the survey cost the proprietors of the two colonies fully seventy-five thousand dollars, which was approximately the amount of the debt paid by England when Penn was given his grant. How much the Penn and Baltimore families expended between them through the years on lawyers' and commissioners' fees is beyond calculation, but it was certainly a princely sum.

Charles Mason returned to this country a few years later, bringing along his wife and eight children, and died and was buried here in 1787. Jeremiah Dixon completed his days in England, dying some years earlier.

But what of the Penn and Baltimore heirs, now three generations removed from the original warring principals? They were at long last in peaceful possession of their precisely determined domains, with decided advantages on the part of the Penns. But the enjoyment on both sides was short-lived, for the Revolutionary War terminated absentee landlordism. The remnants of this older and now dispossessed proprietary class, together with the Tories expelled during the war, filed claims for their confiscated properties, and their unsatisfied demands were a bone of contention between the new nation and Britain until after the War of 1812.

There were those still in the newly formed states with proprietary ambitions, whose land-speculation activities in the postwar period and early 1800s were in many instances somewhat unsavory. Many of the newly formed states became landed proprietors by the seizure of unoccupied lands, and entertained something of the proprietor's point of view. Colonial proprietary aspiration began to spread, and the clash with the land-hungry was carried over into the Union and colored the politics in both the states and the federal government.

Out of this variance of interests developed the rights of the squatter. As in the case of the Penns and the Baltimores, large parcels of land had been transferred without preliminary survey, and there were no exact locations of metes and bounds until some settler took up residence and blazed a series of trees, or in similar manner indicated what he considered to be the extent of his claim. He might one day be forced to negotiate with someone for a deed to it, but if it was unoccupied land when he took it over, his very occupancy gave him strong precedence in a claim to it. In the frontier sense of justice —and the words of Colley Cibber—"Possession is eleven points in the law," and the frontiersman was prepared to contest on this basis with proprietors, large owners, and grantees, and even the state itself.

But the Mason-Dixon enterprise had set a precedent, and also a pattern, and as a public domain was organized with the establishment of the Northwest Territory, the land was surveyed with reasonable care in advance of its opening to settlement.

As to the Mason-Dixon Line itself, it went undisturbed until toward the end of 1785. Work was then started by other men, who extended it to the Ohio River. In the following year a line was run from this extension north to Lake Erie, to determine the western limits of Pennsylvania and the eastern boundary of the Northwest Territory.

There would still be slipshod surveys made as more and more of the West was opened up—too many of them in fact. Great areas, it is said, were at first laid out by no more exact means than driving a team across country in as straight a line as the horses could be guided, and determining distances by counting the revolutions of a wagon wheel. In later years such methods caused confusion and controversy when land values increased, and especially where oil and mineral rights were at stake. But there were whole armies of worthy practitioners of the craft who would work along the frontier, carrying forward the precise methods first displayed by Messrs. Mason and Dixon, until this fine heritage would come to rest securely in the hands of our unsurpassed Coast and Geodetic Survey.

IX

Freedom of the Press, and of Trial by Jury

The prinsaple knowledge nesecary for a free man to have is obtained by the Libberty of the press or publick newspapers. But this kind of knowledge is almost ruened of late by the doings of the few . . . But the few, being closely combined & determined to destroy our Government, find it necessary to destroy the Liberty of the press first . . . To efect this they imploy no printers but those that will adhear strictly to their vuies and interests.—William Manning (1747–1814), *The Key of Libberty.*

SURELY there is not a school child in America but has been given a lasting picture of the seventeen-year-old Ben Franklin on his arrival in Philadelphia, strolling up the High Street from the riverbank wharves, a baker's penny loaf tucked under each arm, and munching upon another, seeking an employer. Why was he there? Principally because his elder brother, to whom he had been apprenticed, was in hot water with the authorities in Boston as the result of a newspaper he had sought to publish. Young Ben had stopped briefly in New York, found the prospects rather restricted in that province, and promptly pushed on to Pennsylvania, already earning the reputation of being a more radical colony, where an atmosphere of greater freedom promised larger opportunities.

Printing had first appeared in the English colonies when a press was established in 1639 in Cambridge as an adjunct of Harvard College, just coming into being. During its early years it was an integral part of the New England Puritan "theocracy," and after it ceased operation in 1692 and other presses appeared, there and in colonial centers to the south, they were customarily operated by royal, or official printers, and more or less under strict censorship. By this same token, the earliest presses in Philadelphia had been conducted under the stern eyes of the Quaker fathers, still the diverse nationalities which soon began to enter America through that port made it a more liberal community than New York or Boston. While Puritan fanaticism had been much diluted by the early 1700s, the Massachusetts colony was being closely scrutinized from London, and was in the hands of men who brooked no interference with their ideas or acts. One still had to mind one's words, especially in the public prints. And in New York, where the strong admixture of Dutch tended to promote more liberal viewpoints in certain respects, there was a royal governor in residence, and the spirit of government was the enforcement of obedience.

During the 1600s such American presses as there were issued principally religious books and tracts, government documents, and handbills. Newspapers were springing up in Europe, and in 1690 the first of them to appear in the colonies—*Publick Occurences*—was launched in Boston. In the eyes of local authorities such an endeavor was highly "controversial," and when this first paper had the temerity to publish an article expressing political opinion, it was promptly suppressed.

It was fourteen years before it had a successor, the Boston *News-Letter*, which began publication in 1704. It had a strong Tory bias, and by carefully refraining from criticism of the authorities in power, managed to stay alive until the onset of the Revolution. During its first seventeen years there was none to challenge its expressed views.

Then, in 1721, James Franklin began his New England *Courant*, primarily to appeal to the growing liberal element in the colony, and probably in hope of profiting by contention, which seems to be the lifeblood of most newspapers. But the powers-that-be gave him short shrift when their acts were held in question, put him permanently out of business, and incidentally hastened the younger brother, Ben, off on a search for a milder political climate.

However, the newspaper was a badly needed mechanism for the rapidly increasing number of patriots and even the more conservative element, who also realized that British blundering in colonial administration sorely needed pointing up and correction. As Manning says in the quote at the outset of this section, here was a means to "knowledge nesecary for a free man." Still it would be fifty years before there were twenty-five newspapers regularly printed throughout the colonies, and of that number appearing in 1771, many were recent ventures. The heavy restrictions were lifted slowly, and largely by reason of a victory won in one of the greatest battles over our basic liberties ever fought—and not with guns, but with ideas.

THE TRIAL OF JOHN PETER ZENGER

The companies of English merchants and the proprietors who had hoped to make themselves wealthy overnight were finding their American enterprises either not sufficiently profitable or too involved to be manageable across three thousand miles of ocean. One by one the colonies, growing in size and importance, were passing under control of the crown. While governance under trading company and proprietary direction had been far from what it should have been, that dispensed by the great majority of royal appointees now being sent over to these shores was, if anything, much worse.

In the New York colony alone there was a procession of these incumbents, involving among them such dissolute and also ludicrous characters as Sir Edward Hyde, who frequently chose to parade about dressed in women's finery. By contrast, there was the genial but not too able Robert Hunter, and then again the money-mad, power-hungry Colonel William Cosby. This latter overbearing satrap appeared upon the scene in August of 1732, and one of his first acts clearly indicated his cast of mind and method of operation.

Rip van Dam, the senior member of the provincial council, had served temporarily as governor until the colonel could arrive from England and take over his post. No sooner had he landed than he accosted Van Dam and demanded one half of the man's salary during the period he had held the office. The able burgher, of Dutch ancestry, countered with a proposition of his own. He would meet Cosby's demands if the latter would yield to him one half the perquisites, or side money, which the office would nominally have yielded during this same period.

This deal was vehemently thrust aside by Cosby, who at once entered suit against his predecessor. When the chief justice of the province, Lewis Morris, Sr., "pronounced the proceeding illegal," the new governor had this able justice removed from office and replaced with a more pliant reed, James De Lancey. With a favorable verdict assured from this new appointee, Cosby felt himself equipped to sweep aside opposition to both his own interpretation of the existing laws, or his personal whims. It looked very much as though the colony henceforth was to be ruled by men rather than by law.

In a land where liberty and freedom were becoming consuming ambitions, this was bound to court resistance. Although newspapers were still few, their power among the people, more and more of whom could read, was becoming very apparent. There was a newspaper in New York operated by William Bradford, the public printer. But the man owed his living and existence to the work he did for the colony, and it would hardly be expected he would purposely drop his bread butter side down by attacking the clique in power. He had set up his press as early as 1693, but it was not until 1725 that he summoned the courage to start his New York *Gazette*.

Obviously he had heard of the rough handling that Franklin had had at the hands of the Massachusetts authorities, and he had no wish either to have his own paper stopped or risk losing the colonial printing. No doubt he was frequently approached to open his sheet to contrary opinions, but he was most circumspect in this matter, and the aggrieved would have to be content with oral protest.

New York, too, was growing, and its influence spread into Connecticut on the one hand, and over into the sister colony of New Jersey, gathering population across the Hudson. Had the time arrived when a second paper, which did not hew quite so close to the Cosby line, might find sufficient support? There were evidently enough able men in the province who would not only contribute to its pages, but would do what they could to bring an opposition paper into being.

Bradford had had in his employ for several years an able, willing, enterprising young German. He had served a very satisfactory apprenticeship, and been taken into the business as a partner. And having a much more liberal outlook than the senior member of the firm, was widely and favorably known among men of consequence in this community, then numbering close to ten thousand souls. Many of these latter had already had their toes benumbed by Cosby's resolute and vindictive tread, among them the Lewis Morrises, the ex-chief justice and his son, William Smith and James Alexander, able legal lights, and Dr. Cadwallader Colden. Their outraged feelings began to clamor for expression which would carry beyond the range of their individual voices.

It soon occurred to them that Bradford's partner, John Peter Zenger, was ideally suited to their purposes; and under their encouragement Zenger separated himself from the security of his past connections and launched out in competition with the publication of his New York *Weekly Journal*. Its first issue was dated November 5, 1733. The still aggrieved Van Dam, so it is claimed, was the financial backer, while the five gentlemen named above were in the forefront of its spiritual godfathers, writing most of the articles which appeared in its columns, albeit without appending their names to their compositions.

Written cautiously in the earliest editions, these articles quickly became but slightly fogged attacks upon Governor Cosby and his "bully boys" in the province. Since their words were carefully and purposely whetted to a keen edge by a resolute honing with hard facts, their rapier-like thrusts began to cut deeply. The indifference with which they were at first received by the governor and his coterie soon had to be replaced with other more resolute methods of combat.

As this opposition group sharpened their darts, they drew blood, and the new chief justice led off with a guarded attack at the January session of the Supreme Court in 1734, attempting to get the grand jury aroused to action against these disturbers of his peace. But reluctance in that quarter was evident, and particularly so at the opening of the fall session. Meanwhile the weekly appearances of the little paper pointed directly at prevailing corruption, and more and more openly, but ever careful that claims were based in incontrovertible fact.

This unmerciful flailing soon became unbearable to Cosby. It not only pointed up current abuses, but showed that his tyrannical conduct was of the same stripe which had caused him to be removed from his last post in Minorca. Since De Lancey, his handpicked chief justice, was affording him no relief, the governor tried his own hand. He complained to the General Assembly, and with the backing of that body, and his own Council, issued a drastic order. All copies of issues numbered 7, 47, 48, and 49, which seemed most libelous and offensive, were to be collected and turned over to the common hangman to be burned.

Since such a move tended to place a higher value on the *Journal* among the bulk of the thinking populace, who began to give it their open support, it became necessary to descend upon the enterprise in force. On Sunday, November 17, 1734, Zenger was peremptorily seized and lodged in jail, and there he stayed until the following spring.

At a hearing in April his counsel, Messrs. Alexander and Smith, known to be aiders and abettors of this newspaper project, were tidily disbarred by Chief Justice De Lancey. This servile fawner promptly chose succeeding counsel, but most certainly his selection was not such as to favor Zenger. It even took a bit of pressure to get him to set trial for the August term; leaving four months in which the defendant was forced to sit in a cheerless jail, to reflect upon his supposed libelous tendencies.

But there was a stunning surprise in store for the simpering De Lancey in the form of a hard-bitten, elderly gentleman from the second colony to the south.

THE DAYSTAR OF THE REVOLUTION

During the months ahead of the trial, it might be profitable to pay a hurried visit to the province of Pennsylvania, over whose southern boundaries there was still a bit of concern. In the settlement launched by the Swedes, but brought to fruition by the able William Penn, the outstanding and most illustrious name was that of Andrew Hamilton, Esq. He had risen to greatness through sheer ability and integrity of purpose, had held almost every post of importance in this colony, and had the distinction of having been the speaker of the Assembly in the Delaware colony as well. Patron and adviser of young Franklin, by many thought to be the designer as well as the promoter of the province building that later became Independence Hall, he was without doubt the most influential person in all the colonies in the early years of the 1700s.

Although there is reasonable doubt of the exact date of his birth, a pleasant tradition has it that he was near eighty, and in somewhat precarious health, at the time John Peter Zenger was in such dire peril. Fat fees through the years had made him a wealthy man, and he had no need to add further luster to so bright a name. But he was ever willing to joust with any and all who threatened what he believed to be the inherent rights of men.

Cosby, too, had become a threat to affairs in Pennsylvania, and this earlier and unfortunately lesser known of the two great patriots to bear the name of Hamilton rose from his sick bed, and made the then burdensome trip to New York to take over Zenger's defense.

There he faced all the connivance and legal chicanery which could be thought up and set as a stumbling block before him. Chief among the obstacles which he had to circumvent was that in regard to evidence, none being admissible except the fact of publication of defamatory material by Zenger. This was further complicated by the law of that time—truth not constituting a defense in cases of libel in England.

Came at last that historic day, August 4, 1735, and the opening of the court. The attorney general, one Bradley, presented the "information," containing specimens of the published material deemed libelous. Many hours, perhaps even days, might have been consumed by the prosecution hearing witnesses and seeking to prove the fact that this material actually appeared in the public prints. But the elderly barrister from Philadelphia rose and disposed of any such move by boldly and bluntly conceding publication. Then very adroitly he managed to take charge in this perhaps most important trial of pre-Revolutionary days. The cards had been stacked against him, but he was never in better form.

During the opening day and the many others which succeeded it, the deft Hamilton fired salvo after telling salvo in defense of his client, winning for generations of unborn colleagues at the bar the proud encomium of "smart as a Philadelphia lawyer." An able jurist of our own day has said that had De Lancey, who presided, been a more able jurist, he would not have allowed Hamilton to get away with some of the things he did. But he also hastens to add that had De Lancey had the ability which his position demanded he would not have allowed the suit to come to trial in the first place.

Actually, however, this proceeding was no longer merely a trial, it was no longer just a court case, but a revolt against tyranny and double-dealing, and became another in the long series of great forward steps which culminated forty-one years later in the Declaration of Independence.

On the eighteenth, when Mr. Hamilton had summed up, De Lancey began his charge with these words: "Gentlemen of the jury, the great pains Mr. Hamilton has taken to show how little regard juries are to pay to the opinions of judges, and his insisting so much upon the conduct of *some* judges in trials of this kind, is done, no doubt, with the design that you should take but very little notice of what I may say upon this occasion . . ."

The distinct impression which the great lawyer and patriot had made upon them apparently had been sufficient for the jurors to take the justice at his word. They were out but "a small time" when they returned with their verdict and proudly announced, "Not Guilty!" The following day Zenger walked forth from almost a year's imprisonment, a free man.

Our heritage from this famous Zenger case is customarily believed to be limited to the freedom of speech and of the press enjoyed in this country. Had it accomplished no more, Hamilton would still be deserving of an even greater place in our affections than the history books prepare for him. But beyond that mighty contribution, he established freedom of the jury—freedom to reach a verdict unhampered by judicial pressure. He did it singlehanded, and was without doubt the only man in all the colonies at that time capable of the feat.

X

The Birth of a College

Rules and precepts that are observed in (Harvard) college: 1. When any scholar is able to understand Tully, or such like classical Latin author extempore, and make and speak true Latin in verse and prose, And decline perfectly the paradigms of nouns and verbs in the Greek tongue: Let him then and not before be capable of admission into the college . . . Every one shall so exercise himself in reading the Scriptures twice a day, that he shall be ready to give such an account of his proficiency therein, both in theoretical observations of the language, and logic, and in practical and spiritual truths, as his tutor shall require, according to his ability; seeing the entrance of the world giveth light, it giveth understanding to the simple, Psalm 119: 130.—Excerpt from an anonymous letter, dated Boston, September 26, 1642.

WHILE the heat was being applied to Zenger previous to his actual seizure by the New York authorities, there had been an admission in the *Journal's* columns that encouragement had been given to move the paper across the river to the New Jersey province and publish from there. The response to this suggestion had been that such a course "would be leaping out of the frying-pan into the fire," for "we are both under the same governor, and your Assembly have shown with a witness what is to be expected of them."

The year was 1735, and such sentiments were very likely justified at that particular moment. While politics would play but a subordinate part in an interesting incident that would come to culmination in the province to the west of the Hudson a score of years later, it might be illuminating to consider the circumstances that brought it to pass.

Settlements begun by the Dutch and the Swedes in the mid-1600s were not of lasting consequence, and no truly permanent towns occurred in the New Jersey area until late in that century. In 1664 control passed from the Dutch to the English, and under proprietors to whom grants had been made by the Duke of York, a colony was launched at Elizabeth Town. Two years later New Englanders settled Newark, and another group of them soon founded Passaic, these activities taking place in what was then termed East Jersey.

The western division of the grant received attention from the Quakers, but there came a time when ownership there and throughout the province became heavily involved, and its history for a number of years was unsteady and complicated. Finally in 1702 the two divisions, East and West Jersey, were brought together as a crown colony in the time of Queen Anne, yet remaining a dependency of New York until 1738.

Cosby having died the year following the Zenger trial, Lewis Morris, Sr., whom he had removed as chief justice, was restored to favor, managed New Jersey's detachment and separate status, and was appointed its first governor. Despite difficulties in its previous years, the colony now began to grow rapidly in both numbers and in importance.

However, the shifting fortunes which it and its sister colony, New York, had lived through, had tended to discourage certain developments already achieved in New England and in Virginia. As the 1700s moved along, there was increasing need for better educational facilities in these two middle provinces, particularly such as would be suitable to train young aspirants for the ministry.

As early as 1636 John Harvard had taken the steps which assured the establishment of the college in Cambridge which came to bear his name and leave its impress on Massachusetts and beyond. Fifty-seven years later, in 1693, the College of William and Mary in Virginia was granted a charter and opened in Williamsburg. Both these schools concentrated on ministerial training in their earlier years; and it was with a similar purpose in mind that Yale was brought into being in 1701.

The particular Protestant faith then dominant in New Jersey saw its needs better served by either of the New England schools than by William and Mary. Distance, quite as much as theological differences, would have debarred the use of the latter. It was not only five hundred miles away by indifferent roads or irregularly scheduled sailings, but as detached dogmatically as the national churches of England and Scotland. Still another controlling element was the fact that the pious parents whose sons generally received the call to the ministry were as poor as they were respectable. Something in the way of facilities for higher learning closer at home was called for.

Although Pennsylvania under the Penns is generally thought of as being strongly Quaker, the founder's extreme tolerance had encouraged the influx of many other denominations. To care for their needs, such faiths as the Seventh-Day Baptists established the Cloisters at Ephrata in 1732, while the Presbyterians found temporary satisfaction in Tennent's Log College near Hatboro in Bucks County, launched in 1736. This latter institution played its part in fostering a more enduring institution, and deserves brief consideration.

The Reverend William Tennent was one of a number of outstanding ministers of this sect through the middle provinces who were conducting classes in their homes. By such means chosen young men among their own and neighboring congregations were being fitted for the shepherding of flocks in the new communities now mushrooming across the countryside. Another in this group was the Reverend Samuel Blair at Fagg's Manor in the same colony, while the Reverend Samuel Finley operated in a similar manner at Nottingham in Maryland. There were also the Reverend Jonathan Dickinson, and the Reverend Aaron Burr, at Elizabeth Town and at Newark respectively, in New Jersey.

The demands upon Tennent were such that he had to expand his facilities, and the result was his larger but unchartered enterprise, derisively dubbed the "Log College." While the local synod of his own church would one day soon disown this "college," his accomplishments were of an order to set fire to the ambitions of his contemporaries in New Jersey. Among them was one whose acquaintance it might be well to make.

THE OTHER AARON BURR

Mr. Dickinson and Mr. Burr had both been graduated from Yale. Upon one or two others in East Jersey, but perhaps most heavily upon them, fell the responsibility of not only maintaining a parish, but of educating younger men vitally needed for church expansion. What was required was a formal institution, and that was certain.

But to their everlasting credit let it be said that however pressing their primary need, they were sufficiently aware of the other phases of their common life to sense that a denominational training school was far from all that was justified. No, its sole task would not be merely preparation for the ministry, whatever persuasion the graduates might choose to serve. These two dominies had vision, and they realized that the America they hoped to help bring into being would require well-educated men to guide its political and its business affairs, quite as much as to occupy its pulpits.

Burdened as they were, their hopes had found little material form during several years, when an event took place that threw down a challenge. Restrictions placed upon Tennent's log cabin school in Pennsylvania practically terminated the effectiveness of that frontier institution. There was a clarion call for quick action, and it was taken either at the end of 1745 or very early in the following year, when the group of New Jersey divines made bold to approach Governor Morris and ask a charter for their proposed school of higher learning. But there the rub began.

Morris was a staunch Anglican, as well as a gentleman well steeped in legal precedent and niceties. A liberal at the time of the Zenger affair, he now took a somewhat contrary attitude, doing what he could to block this "Presbyterian matter." Such activities were destined to be among his last official acts, for death claimed him that same year.

Although his successor, Acting Governor Hamilton, was of the same faith as his predecessor, age seems to have mellowed him more markedly. Taking the time to assure himself that what the petitioners asked was not restricted to denominational bounds or aspirations, he went out of his way to favor and advance the enterprise. If evidence of this is needed, it is apparent in that he even by-passed the local legislature and the home government in England, handling the matter through his own Council, and the seal of the province was affixed to the approved charter on October 22, 1746. He deserves credit for displaying an abundant amount of liberal-mindedness in an age not especially noted for its employment.

His somewhat shielded action was bound to bring repercussions, however, and there was a considerable faction ready and willing to do its utmost to hamper and delay this worthy activity. Worse still, death again reached its icy hands to the governor's chair, and Mr. Hamilton departed this life toward the middle of the year 1747. His temporary incumbency had already been cared for by the appointment in London of a permanent governor, Jonathan Belcher. Had providence been kind in the choice of a successor?

There was a brief period calling for patience, for Mr. Belcher had been embarrassed in clearing away his obligations in England and securing passage money sufficient to return to the colonies to assume his post. But arrive he did, and not too long after Mr. Hamilton's sad passing. The incorporators were at once encouraged.

The new governor, it appeared, was Massachusetts-born. Also he had graduated from Harvard, had had wide business experience, then later been governor of that province, and thus a member of the board of overseers of its famous college. The future seemed better secured since he took an immediate interest, and perhaps as a tender of his caliber and ability, promised a new and better charter.

However, the first document was already being acted upon. Seven trustees had been named who, beside four ministers including Dickinson and Burr, embraced three prominent laymen, one of the latter being William Smith of New York, a backer of Zenger, and a fair successor to the position in the legal field held by the late Andrew Hamilton. Six of them had been educated at Yale, the other at Harvard, assuring those two schools a place as foster parents of the new college.

Since it was permissible, the first seven to be named had brought in five additional trustees, including William Tennent and his rather hotheaded son Gilbert, of the now defunct Log College. There were also the Reverends Blair and Finley, and one other minister. The trustees' choice of a president fell quite naturally upon Mr. Dickinson, and in May of 1747 the College of New Jersey was scheduled to open its doors in his home in Elizabeth Town.

Even this earlier charter had emphasized the liberal intents of the founders by providing that "no person be debarred any of the privileges of the said college on account of any *speculative* principles of religion; but those of *every religious profession* having equal privileges and advantages of education." With this tolerant proviso as evidence of the breadth of its intents, it was empowered to bestow such degrees as were conferred by British universities. The faculty at the outset would consist of the president and one tutor, Mr. Caleb Smith.

But something more tangible than mere willingness was needed to make of it a going, functioning concern. While the sum might seem a mere pittance today, there had not been the £780 and 260 volumes from a patron, which had been such an aid in the initial endowment of Harvard College. None of the original incorporators of this College of New Jersey, with one possible exception, could have been called wealthy. Defraying organizational expenses had been a drain upon advance contributions, but to operate a college took capital, and it was an immediate need. Education for some reason has usually had to lean heavily upon charity, and that source again had to be tapped. Church collections here and in England gave it its first funds, however meager they were.

Governor Belcher continued to take a sincere interest in Mr. Dickinson and "the affair in which he is concerned." But the affair was soon to have a rude setback, for that reverend gentleman died suddenly in October 1747, of an attack of pleurisy, and the little college in Elizabeth Town rested for the moment on the shoulders of the tutor, Caleb Smith. What now would be its fate?

Belcher had come to speak of the struggling institution as "my adopted daughter," and perhaps by his instigation, or those of the trustees alone, its activities were soon moved to the home of the Reverend Aaron Burr in Newark. He had been conducting his own school for a number of years, had been as active as the late Mr. Dickinson in organizational activities, and being located but a few miles distant, was the logical choice and perhaps the only person capable of weaning this immature infant.

There is no date of the exact transfer, but the student body, now totaling eight, was moved, and the College of New Jersey found its second location in the Burr parsonage. Some of the students had to find board and lodging in nearby homes, but by the records of that day, such accommodations were had at the almost unbelievable sum of eighty cents a week.

Nonetheless, Governor Belcher had far greater plans on the fire. He pressed through a more serviceable charter than the first, and one which made him an ex officio member of a board of trustees, now increased to twenty-three. This extended number brought in other prominent men from neighboring provinces, thus broadening the influence of the institution. Also, the more liberal charter provided that the governor should be the president of this board, although not the head of the college's academic aspects. In addition to such matters, he also used what influence he could in raising funds, even to the proposing of a lottery, although this was not permitted in the Jersey province.

But possibly his most beneficial contribution was the manner in which he headed up the sentiments and desires for college buildings sufficient to command respect for the scholastic efforts being put forth under trying conditions. There was distinct need that the already appreciated institution have a permanent home of its own, and he set to work to see that this was achieved. But where should it be built?

Two localities showed an interest. One was New Brunswick, already a well-established town on the Raritan River in the former East Jersey. The other was Princeton, an up-and-coming border town near the line that had formerly divided the two portions of the province. Princeton being located about midway between New York and Philadelphia, it seemed to be slightly preferable.

Similar propositions were offered both towns. The one chosen would have to subscribe a total of a thousand pounds, give clear title to ten acres suitable for a site for the buildings, plus an added two hundred acres of woodland located no more than three miles distant on the outskirts. Fuel and construction materials were definite considerations.

Princeton was first in meeting these stipulations. A portion of its subscription money was paid in, and this sum, added to collections taken here, in England and Scotland—and not forgetting the proceeds of a lottery drawn in Philadelphia—permitted work to begin. On September 17, 1754, the first cornerstone was laid. This central building was to embody both classrooms and a dormitory. As a token of appreciation of his considerable efforts, it was to have been named for Governor Belcher. But whether through modesty, or perhaps because he realized another well-chosen name might redound to the greater benefit of the school, he refused the honor. As a substitute he suggested it be called Nassau Hall, in honor of the family name of William III, recent king of England.

This move was made by him at the last commencement exercises to be held in Newark at Mr. Burr's residence, the date being September 1756. Work at Princeton had proceeded slowly, but Nassau Hall being sufficiently advanced to be able to accommodate the student body, it was decided to move. However since their number had by now increased to seventy, and some preparation would be required, it was not until early in November that the migration from Newark to Princeton took place. This must have been previous to the thirteenth, for it was then that the first formal exercises were held, President Burr preaching on a text from Psalm 119:64. On that historic day the earth must have seemed to him to be especially filled with the Lord's mercy, since a new, secure, and commodious place had been provided, through His guidance, in which His statutes might be taught.

At last the College of New Jersey was in its permanent quarters, and the president's duties in the ensuing year would be heavy. They encompassed completion of the physical plant, the enlarging of the curriculum, the raising of further funds, and making preparations for a glorious future. To complicate his task and compound his worries, Governor Belcher began to ail in a most distressing and alarming way.

He was put to bed, and made such indifferent response to locally prescribed treatment that a hurried request was dispatched to Dr. Benjamin Franklin in Philadelphia, asking the loan of his somewhat mystical but already widely talked about electrical globes. These were promptly dispatched, and Mr. Burr employed them as directed in an earnest attempt to restore the sinking governor. But despite his arduous efforts, creeping paralysis overtook the college's willing and ardent patron. The aged Jonathan Belcher seemed to be beyond the aid of human ministrations.

As hope of recovery was seemingly lost, Mr. Burr made a hasty journey to Stockbridge in the rugged Berkshire Hills in western Massachusetts. His purpose was to visit his father-in-law, the Reverend Jonathan Edwards, one of the great theologians of colonial days. He had hoped to encourage this gentleman to open a department in his chosen field at the expanding new college.

He had hardly returned from this exhausting trip, however, when he was called to Elizabeth to make a frantic appeal that his scholars be exempted by act of the Assembly from military service in the French and Indian War now boiling up. Then a bit of business in Philadelphia required immediate attention before he could catch his breath from this last endeavor. This added effort brought him home from the Quaker City burning with fever. While he was prostrate at home, word was brought to him of the sad passing of Governor Belcher.

He valiantly pulled himself together to preach a funeral oration over the body of his dear friend. Barely able to finish it, he hoped by immediate return to bed to be recovered sufficiently to carry on during the commencement exercises scheduled a few days ahead. But the efforts of the past weeks, plus the stinging loss of this staunch supporter of what had become his life's work, was too great to be borne. Four days before the first commencement at Nassau Hall, Aaron Burr, Sr., was dead, a comparatively young man of forty-one, although he had now served as president of this college for ten years.

When he had come to Princeton from Newark less than a year before, he had brought his wife and their infant son, who had been named Aaron for his father. This child was to grow to manhood, graduate from this same college in 1772, serve on Washington's staff during the Revolution, and go on to become Vice-President of the still young United States.

But unlike his father and grandfather, both dedicated men of God, this younger Burr was fated to write one of the more sordid and personally defamatory chapters in our history. Every school child manages to encounter him, and to have some knowledge of his later years. Thus, by way of antidote, it is well to recall that there was another—and far worthier—Aaron Burr.

By now the reader must have assumed that the college which he helped bring to fruition was Princeton University, although it was not officially so known until 1896. Fourth among the schools of higher learning to be established in the English colonies, it was soon followed by King's College, ultimately Columbia, in New York, and by the academy which developed into the University of Pennsylvania. As the new nation's area and population began to increase in the nineteenth century, so did its colleges and universities.

XI

The Prelude to Union and to Revolution

In 1754, war with France being apprehended, a congress of commissioners from the different colonies was, by order of the Lord of
Trade, to be assembled at Albany, there to confer with the chiefs
of the Six Nations concerning the means of defending both their country and ours . . . I projected and drew a plan for the union of all
the colonies under one government, so far as might be necessary
for defense, and other important purposes . . . Its fate was singular;
the assemblies did not approve it, as they all thought there was
too much *prerogative* in it, and in England it was judged to have
too much of the *democratic* . . . The colonies, so united, would have
been sufficiently strong to have defended themselves; there would
then have been no need of troops from England; of course, the subsequent pretence for taxing America, and the bloody contest it
occasioned would have been avoided. But such mistakes are not
new; history is full of errors of states and princes. Those who govern,
having much business on their hands, do not generally like to take
the trouble of considering and carrying into execution new projects.
The best public measures are therefore seldom adopted from previous wisdom, but forc'd by the occasion.—Benjamin Franklin, *Au-
tobiography.*

IN THEIR earlier years the thirteen colonies, principally English
in their establishment and in their language, were still highly individual and distinct. The nature of their founding, local conditions, hopes, aspirations, and even religious sentiments tended to
keep their differences clear cut during the 1600s, and the distances
between them at the outset and the lack of regular communication
tended to accentuate their individual characteristics. But as the numbers arriving here increased, and the settlements expanded throughout the tidewater areas and inland up navigable streams and along
Indian trails, traffic and interchange among them became more frequent. There was not only the flow of individuals and family groups,

but on numerous occasions larger contingents abandoned one colony
for another.

Small ships cruising coastal waters bore the bulk of the earlier
flow, but as pack animals gave way to wagons and carts, the better
Indian paths were beaten into roads of sorts. A typical instance of
the latter was the development of a wagon way from the valleys
in central Pennsylvania down through connecting valleys in western
Virginia, which one day would take settlers to the Holston River
area, and Boone to the entrance to the Kentucky country.

Although connecting highways suitable for regular and comfortable travel were not well established until after the Revolution,
movement between one colony and another was sufficient early in
that century so that it was already breaking down the distinctions
that had originally existed. In fact Dr. Alexander Hamilton, who completed an extensive journey in 1744, reported that he found "but
little difference in the manner and character of the people in the
different Provinces I passed thro'. . ."

This was encouraging, for they had a common destiny to face,
and would soon be tested for competency in uniting to make common cause in facing outside pressures. The first real threat, however,
would not come from the homeland beyond the ocean, but from the
French, determined to limit English ambitions to the area east of
the Alleghenies, so they might consolidate their own hold on the great
inland empire beyond the mountains.

Such a contest had been under way for many years, and Virginia
and Massachusetts in particular had long realized the necessity for
some measure of mutual aid. As early as 1684, delegates from these
two colonies, together with agents from New York, had met at Albany to explore problems having to do with their general welfare,
and there had been treaties of commerce and amity between New
York and New England. Virginia would co-operate with the Carolinas in the face of common danger from either the natives or the
pirates, but through the ensuing years there was great reluctance to
engage in joint efforts which might in any way encroach upon individual sovereignty.

There were times when the British Parliament would have
welcomed, and even attempted to foster, greater unity among its
provinces scattered along the Atlantic coast line. But it reportedly
encountered visions of commonwealth status, hopes of self-suffi-
ciency, and growing opposition to regulations formulated in London.
Differences in many respects had been washed away, but the zeal

for self-determination, colony by colony, was still deeply ingrained, as would soon be amply indicated.

THE ALBANY CONGRESS

European intrigues, with their resulting conflicts, managed to transmit shock waves across the ocean and embroil the colonists, and there were four colonial wars during about three quarters of a century which stemmed from primary encounters back in the homelands. The third of these, King George's War, had terminated with the peace treaty signed with France at Aix-la-Chapelle in 1748. Although it had been an English victory as respects American action, it left the French strongly entrenched in Canada, and in no measure dampened their ambitions on this side of the ocean. Thus within a few years their activities among the Indians, and their line of forts being advanced toward the Ohio Valley from the upper St. Lawrence and the Great Lakes, were sufficient to give the northern colonies as well as Virginia deep concern. It was enough of a threat in fact that New Hampshire, Massachusetts, Connecticut, Rhode Island, New York, Pennsylvania, and Maryland needed little persuasion from the British Lords of Trade and Plantations to convene a congress of delegates at Albany in June of 1754. Virginia, too, was indirectly represented, since she had authorized the governor of New York to act in her behalf. Also there was a delegation of chiefs from the potent Six Nations of Indians.

Virtually every school child has made in spirit the arduous journey with the twenty-one-year-old Major Washington from Williamsburg over the mountains to the Forks of the Ohio, and on almost to the shores of Lake Erie to spy out the French activities. His reports on his return early in 1754 had been disconcerting enough to send him back almost at once into the same area at the head of a limited force of militiamen in the hope of convincing these Frenchmen that they were going too far in their trespass. The probability of armed encounter was thus known to the congress as it got down to business, with one ear cocked for word from the wilds of western Pennsylvania.

Its task, as outlined from London, was to adopt measures for protection against the French "interlopers," and also to enter into "articles of union and confederation for the general defense of his Majesty's subjects and interests in North America as well in time of peace as of war." The need for such action was definitely before them, and they pitched in with a will. Benjamin Franklin, appointed nearly two years before postmaster-general in America, was one of the most widely traveled and influential of those present, yet he admits that his own was only one of several plans to effect such a union presented. However, as he says, it "happen'd to be preferr'd, and, with a few amendments, was accordingly reported." It proved to be a well drawn and thoroughgoing federal constitution.

Philadelphia, centrally located as respects all the colonies, was to become the capital of the federation of American provinces. There would be a governor-general, appointed and supported by the British crown, offset by a Congress composed of delegates for three-year terms, selected by the popular assemblies in each province, with representation proportional to the contribution of each to this central government. The governor would appoint the militia officers, and have a veto power. The Congress would appoint civil officers as needed, levy taxes, regulate commerce, and carry on other appropriate governmental functions.

The defeat of the youthful Washington and his little force in the wilds of western Pennsylvania as the deliberations were in progress was seemingly not needed as a goad to its acceptance. The representatives of all but one colony subscribed to it, and it was referred to the assembly in each for ratification. But there it foundered. Jealous of and tenacious in maintaining their individual rights, these colonial legislatures refused to accept the scheme. The consequence was that it was never referred to the crown, and was in reality still-born.

Franklin, writing in his later years, and in view of all that had intervened, commented briefly on the shortsightedness involved. Unconsciously, but positively nonetheless, the die was cast at Albany. While the Revolution was not inevitable as a result of colonial indifference to the press of common problems, the quote at the beginning of this chapter indicates what might have been avoided by a more constructive approach at this time.

Within a year Braddock had met defeat at the hands of the French and gone on to his own death in an encounter near the Forks of the Ohio, which touched off an onslaught that soon embroiled most of the major nations of Europe and spread carnage from the American frontier across that continent and on into Asia on the opposite side of the world. Known in America as the French and Indian War, it was to become a training ground for many who would serve as military leaders in the Revolution. Also, it was to break French power on this side of the ocean, even if it did not completely snuff out that country's ambitions here. When the Treaty of Paris was signed in 1763, England was in a position to toy with the hopes of world empire. She had a firm hold on America from Canada to the tip of Florida, and on all the North American continent, in fact, east of the Mississippi, excepting New Orleans and a small bit of Louisiana, which the treaty had lodged in Spanish hands.

With the French out of the picture, the Indians were quiescent for the time being. Even in the colonies it appeared to be the beginning of an era of great advancement. There was one immediate exception, yet it influenced the thinking of but a few, and was perhaps no immediate or considerable handicap. King George had put a limit on expansion. By proclamation in 1763, a line had been drawn from below the course of the St. Lawrence down along the headwaters of the rivers flowing into the Atlantic, and swinging back to that ocean near present-day Jacksonville. This was the boundary of the thirteen colonies, to the west of which there could be *no* settlements. The country that lay over the Appalachian highlands was to be reserved to the Indians.

Other actions by the home government made a more far-reaching and immediate impress, for London, after years of somewhat indifferent attention, began to look upon her American colonies with a more critical and discerning eye. There were nearly a million and a half people living in them, perhaps as many as one fifth the number then inhabiting the home island. This closer scrutiny brought several impressions into stronger focus. First among them was the feeling that the time had come when the colonies must pick up and carry their share of imperial costs. And there were not a few back home that felt their overseas "cousins" needed to be a trifle less haughty and insolent, not quite so impatient of being ruled, not so disdainful of subjugation, and not so intent upon independence. They had need to be more pliant and submissive like, say, the people of Bengal.

But what they thought back in England made little impression over here, that is, until they actively sought revenue through taxes. Immediately the skies began to cloud in quite perceptibly. First there was a levy on sugar, without so much as a by-your-leave. Then, when that failed, there was one by means of stamps. Irrespective of what color the ink with which these latter were printed, the colonists began to see red.

UNWILLING STAMP COLLECTORS

Soon ships bearing these stamps were dispatched across the ocean, headed for the four principal colonial centers, Boston, New York, Philadelphia, and Charleston. In this latter port, Fort Jackson dominated the harbor, and had been manned by a British garrison since its erection in the early years of the 1700s. Whether the commander of the sloop of war bearing the first consignment of the hated stamps had some misgivings of his possible reception is not known. In any event, he sailed into the bay, swung in just off the fort, and dropped anchor.

Things ashore were pretty feverish, with mobs swarming around the city and noisily protesting this encroachment upon their rights without a word of say in the matter. There had been riots by vindictive crowds directed and led by the wealthy merchant Christopher Gadsden. On one occasion the unruly rabble had swarmed into the town house of another merchant prince, Henry Laurens, and he claims to have recognized many of its members as close friends and the elite of the colony, despite faces smeared with soot and grotesque getups. Such activities were in the nature of dress rehearsals for the later Boston Tea Party. The Sons of Liberty, growing rapidly in numbers, contained enough "persons of consequence" to give the crown officers deep concern. Quite likely the sloop had been signaled to take a berth under the fort's guns until the turmoil ashore subsided.

But the patriots had other plans in mind, and with nightfall began to put them into action. Slipping out along the south shore of the harbor, they managed to infiltrate the fortifications, and soon were in undisputed possession. The guns of the fort were quietly regrouped, loaded, and trained on the vessel riding peacefully at anchor less than a pistol shot away.

When it was light enough to do so without arousing his suspicions, a boat put out and invited the ship's commander ashore. Once inside the walls, he was shown the handiwork of the dark hours just past. Then the gentlemen temporarily in charge gave him a simple choice. Either hoist sail and be on his way back to England or stand to be blown out of the water, ship, stamps, and all.

A careful look at their faces and the determination apparent in their voices was enough. The skipper of the armed sloop did not have to flip a coin to come to a decision. Discretion was for him very much the better part of valor. As soon as he was back aboard, he and his vessel, plus the cargo of stamps, were gone forthwith. And this was but one among many such incidents which permitted the less stubborn of the king's ministers back home to taste the stern resolve of these haughty colonists who disdained subjection.

In no more than a few months, there were groups in localities all up and down the coast banding together to resist enforcement of the hated Stamp Act. Perhaps the first organization for the specific purpose was the Westmoreland Association in Virginia, brought into being by Richard Henry Lee on February 27, 1766. The resolutions which he drafted for the body were quickly ratified, and influenced public opinion in the remainder of the colonies most profoundly. The Patriots were standing up to be counted even this early.

By 1769 tension along this frontier of American liberties had grown sufficiently so that an exchange of indignities between townspeople and British troops touched off the unfortunate Boston Massacre. It was then that the cry "To Arms! To Arms!" first rang out. From the heat this sorry affair generated, and which was kept smoldering by Paul Revere's somber engraving of the melee, the conviction slowly grew that force might ultimately have to be met by force. The next resounding shots would be fired in May of the following year some seven hundred odd miles away.

THE BATTLE OF THE ALAMANCE

The people who had settled in the back country of North Carolina west of the seacoast plains were a pretty resolute and freedom-loving lot. And they had in the person of their governor a man to try their patience to the utmost. The passionate Tryon was a bitter royalist, and a vengeful character, who was certain beyond question his word was law.

The legislation in the colony had been growing progressively more and more oppressive, and to resist it bands of Regulators had been organized, principally to defeat collection of the heavy taxes and imposts. Once these armed bands commenced roaming the countryside, there was near anarchy, and the governor's fingers began to itch to slip a noose about the necks of some of these rebels.

Finally at the head of some four hundred militia, backed up by a few pieces of artillery, he pushed into the country west of Raleigh where this outlaw activity centered. As he pitched camp to wait for reinforcements to catch up, the disturbing word was brought him that his additional troops had been scattered, and that their stores and powder, on which he had counted, had fallen into the hands of his enemies. In the hope of surprising these irregulars before they could consolidate their recent gains, he pressed on, and encountered a stout force of them at the Alamance Creek, a couple of miles west of present-day Burlington, on May 16, 1771.

There was an attempt to parley, perhaps to gain time and advantage at the governor's expense. But when an older man approached bearing a message, accompanied by a flag of truce, the hotheaded Tryon yanked a musket from the hands of one of his militiamen and shot the messenger dead, and just missed picking off the flag-bearer before he regained his companions. At once the battle was on. It was a short, sharp encounter, and cost the lives of nine militiamen and twenty Regulators. But the latter were outnumbered and the victory went to the governor, who a month later hanged six other Regulator sympathizers at Hillsboro in neighboring Orange County.

Consequentially, North Carolina contends a bit with Massachusetts as to whether Alamance Creek or Lexington was the first armed conflict of the Revolution. She takes pride, too, in pointing to the Mecklenburg Resolutions, tacked up during the militia muster at Charlotte soon after the Lexington and Concord affair, as one of the first group expressions of hoped for independence. Also, there was a cluster of small settlements in a mountain valley a hundred fifty miles west of the Alamance affray, to which some of its survivors fled, and which about a year later, as the Watauga Association, adopted its Articles. This document is claimed to be the first written constitution in America of a free and independent people. The area in which it originated was then still a part of the Carolina colony.

The prelude to Revolution involved all the colonies in one way or other, and the next in the series of outstanding incidents took place far to the north.

"ALWAYS CATCH A MAN BEFORE YOU HANG HIM"

England's drive to exact revenue from her American possessions quickly bogged down. Not only were tax laws being flouted, but British goods were being boycotted. This latter brought down the wrath of the powerful merchant class at home, and since lost trade and lost customs duties were in a way tied together, a means of correcting the situation was set in motion. The privateers were active, especially in and out of Narragansett Bay, and the crown commissioners at Boston decided to levy on this sub rosa trade, and at least collect revenue if the trade itself was not discouraged.

To plug this leak, the armed schooner *Gaspé*, under command of Lieutenant Dudingston of the British Navy, was sent to cruise these waters. When the vessel appeared, Governor Wanton, quite within his rights, dispatched the high-sheriff to have a look at the commander's commission papers. But Dudingston had no intention of observing the niceties of the situation, heaped insult and threats on the arm of the law, and sent the sheriff back home in a rage sufficient to set fire to the aggrieved shipping trade along the Providence water front.

As though this were not enough, the Britisher rubbed further salt into wounded feelings by demanding that all shipping passing by his craft dip their colors in salute. In place of any willing gestures of respect, he was merely courting some pointed nose-thumbing. Whether he realized it or not, he was muddying the already roiled waters, and it was not long before the touchy skipper's bluff was certain to be called.

The packet *Hannah* suddenly decided to scud by without laying a hand to the color halyards. When she was well past and her flag had not missed a flutter in the fair breeze, the *Gaspé* came about and started to give chase. But the *Hannah's* helmsman knew the bay waters like the stones in his own hearth at home, and the pursuit came to an abrupt and ignominious end when the revenue cutter went hard aground on a hidden sand bar. There she hung fast, to await the next incoming tide.

The *Hannah* kicked up her heels and lit out for the Providence wharves. The merchant group there were waiting for just such a turn of events. John Brown, the third and most adventurous of the four brothers who would help later on to make history in the East India trade, pitched upon this occasion. Calling a group together in the early evening of June 9, 1772, at the Sabin Tavern, the posthouse of the Boston stage line near his office, he provided the leadership for plans regarding H.M.S. *Gaspé*.

The story goes that the expedition organized consisted of eight boats, each carrying four men, with this party under the command of Abe Whipple. How many more joined with them and rowed down the bay with muffled oars is not known. But there were quite enough for their purposes; and they at last came upon their quarry, still grounded off Bristol.

As they stole in closer, a pistol shot rang out. The bumptious lieutenant had fired the first shot—or that was the stout contention—and a musket ball in return wounded him, so that he had to be rushed below for the attention of the ship's surgeon. The schooner's crew looked out over the dark waters, saw it fairly bobbing with boatloads of men, took a dim view of their chance of resistance, and gave up without a struggle. So the punitive expedition swarmed up over the sides, told the Britishers to fetch their gear, and freighted them all ashore. When the last of them were off, the *Gaspé* was set afire, and when her magazine was ignited, she blew up.

Great Britain screamed bloody murder at this gross affront. Why it was an outright act of piracy! Large rewards were promptly posted, large enough so they would seemingly find the weak spots in the armor of the rebellious. But so faithfully were secrets kept that not one of the participants—known to a host of people in this important commercial town—was ever betrayed. It was a ringing kick in the shins. And this aftermath, as much as the blow itself, smarted British pride. Even when hostilities were later well under way, the insult still rankled in the minds of the officers of His Britannic Majesty's Navy.

In the early days of the Revolution, Captain Abraham Whipple, leader of the boarding party, was heading up a small naval force and doing his best to hamper the British blockade of Narragansett Bay. To his great amusement a note was one day thrust into his hands which read: "You, Abraham Whipple, on the 10th of June in 1772, burned his Majesty's vessel, the *Gaspé* and I will hang you from the yard-arm." It bore the signature of Sir William Wallace, commandant of the force he was now harrassing.

With complete forthrightness, he succinctly replied: "Sir:—Always catch a man before you hang him!—Abraham Whipple."

In December of 1773 came the Boston Tea Party, and by then committees of correspondence were in earnest communication with each other between the various colonies. The barometer was falling, and with a speed that threatened a hurricane. It was becoming a matter of just when and where the storm would break. By September of the following year the First Continental Congress was called in session, for a time in Carpenters' Hall, but soon in the more commodious quarters of the State House in Philadelphia. Franklin's blueprint of twenty years before was being put to work.

The pressure continued to mount as the year 1775 began; and then came that crisp April midnight when hoofbeats rang out along the Medford Road from Charlestown, to be followed soon after daylight by the shot "heard round the world" fired on Lexington Common. Lights hung in the old North Church belfry, signaling to a man over in Charlestown, Massachusetts, had touched off the fuse. But another event at about this time, in another Charleston (Charles Towne), nine hundred miles down the coast, gave a better clue to what the eventual outcome would be.

EXIT LORD WILLIAM

Near the head of Meeting Street, and in those days not too far from the river, stood the huge three-story house built by the famous Huguenot family the Hugers. It had for several years been the home of Lord William Campbell, the crown governor, who had married a local belle, Sarah Izard. Sentiment had by now set in rather strongly against the gentleman for what he represented, and one evening a mob, of the character of those protesting the Stamp Act several years previously in this same city, gathered before his house and staged a noisy and decidedly hostile demonstration.

His Lordship had been deliberating upon the course of events in His Majesty's colony, and this precipitate occurrence was very convincing. The American climate was no longer a congenial one as far as British aspirations were concerned. Stomping into his office, he carefully collected the instrument that best symbolized British power, the Great Seal of the Province. With it carefully tucked under his arm, he made his way out into the garden at the rear. There, with the aid of servants, he mounted into a small boat, and, with muffled oars, was rowed out into the stream and tucked safely aboard H.M.S. *Tamar*.

But a colonial seal was no longer an effective weapon. Britain from now on would maintain herself in this country only by force of arms. There would be a declaration of American intentions for all the world to read early in July of the following year, 1776. The freedom frontier had filled in with enough resolute souls to risk defending it.

XII

Between Lexington and Yorktown

It was through the Declaration of Independence that we Americans acknowledged the *eternal inequality* of man. For by it we abolished a cut-and-dried aristocracy. We had seen little men artificially held up in high places . . . our own justice-loving hearts abhorred this violence to human nature. Therefore we decreed that every man should thenceforth have equal liberty to find his own level. By this very decree we acknowledged and gave freedom to true aristocracy by saying, "Let the best man win, whoever he is."—Owen Wister, *The Virginian.*

I T I S often maintained that several generations of Southerners were weaned, grew up, and passed through school and life without the realization that "damnyankee" was in reality two words. While the forepart of this epithet has long since been discarded, the Yankee portion still obtains, although its origin appears to be a bit cloudy.

Presumably it derived from a noun in the Cherokee Indian dialect, roughly *ee-ank-ee,* which denoted something between, or a combination of, a slave and coward. Tradition has it that the disgusted Virginians thought it a pat designation of the New Englanders who could not quite see their way clear to aiding the Old Dominion in subduing these same Cherokee savages when the French were stimulating them to make trouble early in the 1700s. Thus it became quite a common opprobrium, used when one wanted to castigate a person or group. Any object of scorn was a Yankee.

As such it registered quite forcibly with a Britisher on the staff of General Abercromby previous to the Revolution. He was an army surgeon, Dr. Richard Schuckburgh, and part of the contingent headed up the Hudson Valley to face the French at Fort Ticonderoga during the difficulties in 1758. The troops to which he was attached had paused at Fort Crailo in Rensselaer, across the river from Albany. As beautiful as was the countryside, it quite likely had a depressing influence upon the doctor, for he seems to have been in a frame of mind that would take strong exception to anything American. His dislike may even have been heightened by the stop at this small post to make a junction with groups of local militiamen, who, to the eye of a professional British soldier, were a raw lot indeed.

The limited buildings of the fort would have been highly congested, and he had presumably wandered out in back of them in search of a quiet spot where he might compose a letter to the homeland. When he found himself enveloped by a company of these emergency troops, swarming about, shouting at each other, and wandering off in search of such excitement as the neighboring village would provide, he was perhaps highly vexed. What a pack of plowboys and yokels these rustics were!

Seating himself on the raised curb about the mouth of a well, he set his inkpot, letter case, and quills down, and contemplated the scene before him. Suddenly it began to frame itself in words, and in the form of what seemed a devastatingly funny jingle. Dipping his pen, he started to set it down. To its author, it promised to be a wry bit and a relaxing pastime. So he tried it in one or two forms, and finally came up with what he thought a prime jab at these uncouth bumpkins.

It is probable that in a malicious moment this dilettante showed his verses to one of the militia officers. In some manner it came to the attention of the rank and file—the Yankee-Doodles, and they thought it something very special, fitted it to a convenient tune, took it to their hearts, and it soon became a favorite at training days and rifle frolics. So popular did it become, even in England, that Benjamin Franklin, then agent of Pennsylvania in London, mentions "the tune of 'Yankee Doodle'" in his "Intended Speech" for the King to deliver at the opening of Parliament on November 29, 1774. By the time the Battle of Bunker Hill was fought seven months later it was virtually a paean, and long remained in favor, particularly in the North.

This artless act of a British officer was of itself a small affair; but like other more ponderous moves of men bent on assembling an empire, and who tended to look upon Americans as the underprivileged and the rebellious, fit only to be governed and exploited, it boomeranged. Out of a spirit of contempt came the Revolution's top marching song.

Unhappily Britain's opportunities, born of her signal triumph over France in the war spoken of as the French and Indian, were in large measure lost to her through the corruption and ineptitude that too often follow military victory. The situation was further complicated by the determination of George III to have his way without carefully weighing the consequences. There were hotheads in America, along with many cooler heads as well, but the latter joined hands with the former when conditions were no longer bearable. By the early months of 1775 the tinder was dry enough and piled so high that the shots that rang out at Lexington set it afire. By the middle of the following year there was no turning back. America had outgrown its role of a European frontier and was ready to become a self-determining entity.

During thirty or forty years some of Europe's ablest political thinkers had been forecasting what now took place. Not too long before hostilities were joined, the French ambassador at Constantinople had summed it up in a few words when he observed to an English acquaintance, "She [England] will call upon them to contribute toward the support of burdens they have helped to bring upon her, and they will answer by striking off all dependence."

WE STRIKE OFF DEPENDENCE

What influence had the frontier, which was now to become a distinctly American frontier, upon the action undertaken in the crisis being faced? How were some of the strong national characteristics listed at the end of the introduction to this volume, and already shaping up, expressed, and in what manner? Although there might well be several candidates for a place in the answer to these questions, the choice quite naturally falls to one among them whose name occurs frequently in the era beyond the Revolution.

He was a tall, narrow-shouldered young man, only thirty-three at the time of one of his greatest achievements, and possessed of a most inquisitive and original mind beneath his shock of center-parted, reddish-brown hair. His kindly blue-gray eyes that looked out from a freckled face missed little, and he was not only a man of action, but also an avid reader and student.

His father, of gentlemanly antecedents, was still something of a pioneer, the senior surveyor for the crown, and familiar with western Virginia to the topmost ridge of the Alleghenies when that country was still a howling wilderness. His eldest son was born well out in Albemarle County, and spent his boyhood in the thinly settled area, rubbing shoulders with the sons of other frontier families, and capturing the frontier viewpoint in his most formative years.

Then his scheme of life shifted. He went down into the tidewater country, attended the College of William and Mary, and stayed on in Williamsburg to read law and dip into a host of other subjects as well. He was admitted to the bar, became something of a disciple of the Enlightenment being wafted here from Europe, and from France in particular, played the fiddle, practiced law, and then started back to the hills to build up a considerable plantation, hoping to live close to and from the bounties of the soil. He chose to call his home Monticello, "Little Mountain," which fitted the man equally well.

His name was, of course, Thomas Jefferson. He had been born and reared a gentleman, but the term as applied to him should be divided into its component parts, with equal stress upon each.

It was quite natural that he gravitated into politics, and his liberal tendencies very logically linked him closely with such others in his colony as George Wythe, George Mason, James Madison, and the other long roster of well-known names championing colonial rights.

He was a thorough, meticulous thinker, but despite a well-modulated voice, his thoughts found readier expression in the written than in the spoken word. This is not to say that he was not an engaging conversationalist, but rather that he neither professed nor hoped to be an orator, a common ambition of his time.

His wide reading and range of thought was brought into direct contact with political realities in the House of Burgesses. He seems to have had a clear realization of coming events; and even before his "brethren" of the Bay colony received their baptism of fire, he was most firmly aligned in the forefront of the Patriots. Thus it was to be expected that he would be among the group selected to represent the Old Dominion at the Continental Congress, called into session in Philadelphia, 325 miles, or ten days on horseback, away.

On the second day after taking his place among the delegates came the sobering news of Bunker Hill. And on the very next he and a group of others rode out of the city a short way with Washington, leaving for Massachusetts to take command of the Continental forces. He would be in regular attendance at each of the sessions in the State House on Chestnut Street, in the block between Fifth and Sixth streets. But he took no part in the debates, expending his efforts in committees; for, like Washington and the aging Franklin, prolonged haggling on the floor of the Congress wearied him. Since he was fluent with penned words, he soon had more than his share of paper work.

It was a bit confining, and for exercise he liked to walk out during recesses, especially to a new home being built a block west, and another north of the State House. Keenly interested in construction back at Monticello, he watched progress on this house, which had been started just previous to his arrival. He had noted particularly the fine oak and cherry timbers that had gone into it, watched the brick walls as the alternate red and black courses crept up one, two, three stories. It was being done in most excellent taste for a Mr. Graff; and by the time it was completed in the forepart of 1776, Tom Jefferson had engaged one of the rooms on its second floor.

Then came that momentous day in early June 1776 when Richard Henry Lee of the Virginia delegation rose and moved, in obedience to instructions from down home, that the Congress declare the United Colonies to be free and independent states. There was obviously some debate, but four days later a committee was appointed to prepare a suitable declaration. Its members were Jefferson, John Adams, Dr. Franklin, Roger Sherman, and Robert Livingston. The seventeen days between the appointment of this committee on June eleventh, and its report to Congress on the twenty-eighth, would be busy ones for the Virginian with the facile pen.

In his new quarters in the house at the corner of Seventh and High (Market) streets, the inspired denouncer of George III set to work. This cannot have been new and entirely untrod ground to him. Many of the resounding phrases that would now appear on paper had very likely long been in embryo in his mind, merely awaiting the proper moment to be born. That he had the advice of the other members of his committee is certain. Artists have sketched the group in earnest consultation in Jefferson's quarters, but even the single flight of stairs to reach it could have been a bit of a trial to the elderly Franklin's gouty limbs, which kept him away from Congress during most of June.

By his own words, his purpose was "not to find out new principles, or new arguments, never before thought of, nor merely to say things which had never been said before; but to place before mankind the common sense of the subject, in terms so plain and firm as to command respect." Here was frontier practicality, directness, and the strength of simplicity in effecting great ends.

There may have been a word here, or a phrase there, that had been suggested, principally by Franklin or Adams. Yet the manuscript placed before Congress on June 28 was not only in Jefferson's hand, but very much in his spirit as well. It has been said, and justifiably, too, that "Jefferson revolted at government"—at least at too much government—and so did the frontier. Autocratic power in particular was an abhorrence to him, as it had been to his boyhood neighbors, and that was what he was now attacking.

It was not until July 2 that debate began on the document which he had drawn; and then for three days he perhaps wished himself back in the seclusion of his chamber in Mr. Graff's home. But he sat patiently as his brain child was treated to minor surgery, assenting to such changes as were by common consent thought advisable. Then, on that historic Fourth of July, it was accepted, and started on its way to immortality.

The words had been penned in an upper room of a brand-new house on the High Street in Philadelphia, most populous of the colonial towns. But the vision that guided the moving quill was far broader than the outlook from his second-story windows, and borrowed much from the frontier philosophy and attitudes which he had absorbed as a boy. The Declaration of Independence which he had drafted had been fitted to continuing democratic needs by a man who might easily have been an aristocrat, but whose earliest training and experiences gave him an abiding sense of the dignity and worth of the common man. Destiny had made a shrewd choice.

The six years between Bunker Hill and Yorktown are tightly strung with interesting instances and episodes playing upon the whole range of human emotions. There is also a considerable galaxy of characters, some of them forbiddingly martial in school history books, but completely human, even to their weaknesses, when looked at in full circuit. There were dreary days aplenty during these war years, but there were lighter moments and thoughts as well. Some realization of them might have been had by following the redoubtable John Paul Jones as he walked down the staid streets of Portsmouth, New Hampshire, on his way to the shipyard on a rainy morning beneath his bright red umbrella, and noting that the amorous eyes of many of the town's belles were watching closely but discreetly as they peered through half-opened shutters. The war, by itself, was by no means an all-consuming interest.

In more somber vein, but on the venturesome side, would be exploits such as that undertaken by Nathan Hale in attempting to learn British plans and strength in the New York area for Washington, and which had such an unhappy conclusion. Not so well known perhaps was the ambitious scheme undertaken by John Champe, a Virginian from Loudoun County. By arrangement, this Continental soldier "deserted" and made his way to the British lines, where he enlisted in the traitorous Benedict Arnold's command. His purpose —to capture this turncoat. He did his best, but being unsuccessful, he deserted the British, returned, and rejoined the American troops.

On the more sordid side were the mass desertions which left Washington at times with little more than a skeleton force, and also those farmers in the Valley Forge country who, while hungry men left bloody footprints in the snow, preferred to trade their grain for British gold rather than for Continental paper currency of fleeting value. One might point, too, at the treatment of the Tories, whose displacement and expulsion was in many respects as inhumane as like activities practiced by the Assyrians and Babylonians in Bible times.

There were many of these Empire Loyalists in Boston, New York, Philadelphia, and especially in the South, where the heavy debts of many of the planters, owed to British factors, gave direction to their loyalty. They did much to aid the rapid entry of the Cornwallis expedition into Georgia and the Carolinas, and also brought about conditions that kept most of the resistance in that area on a partisan basis. And thereby hangs a tale, which also gives some indication of the part that women were called upon to play in the winning of our liberties.

MRS. BRATTON STANDS HER GROUND

Dependence upon memory alone would make the Revolution seem to be almost exclusively a male enterprise. It is true, there was Mary Ludwig, who in her later years was awarded a pension for her part in the Battle of Monmouth, New Jersey. That name may be unfamiliar, but it was she who served water to the hard-pressed American forces, and thereby won renown as "Molly Pitcher." While her statue at Carlisle, Pennsylvania, her birthplace, shows her with a cannon swabber in her hands, that bit of tradition is very probably fictional, and a confusion with the contribution of a Mrs. Margaret Corbin who saved the weapon of her wounded husband from capture in another engagement. Wives did follow their husbands to war even in Revolutionary times, and not infrequently right into battle, as these two incidents indicate.

However, that turns up but two heroines, although a little serious searching, particularly in local sources, will disclose many, many more. Largely unsung are the hundreds who ran farms singlehanded, and fought off debt, drought, and Indians while their menfolk were far from home bearing arms. In other cases they lived the thankless existence of camp followers, doing what they could to make life more bearable for husbands called into service. These were the chaste, sober wives who were often thrown in with the riffraff and jetsam that made up the scarlet contingent that followed armies in those days.

The British had encountered heavy going in the North, and by the spring of 1780 were turning their efforts to a section well down the coast which had experienced the war so far but lightly. There had been assurance that the considerable number of Tories scattered from Georgia up through the Carolinas would join with regular British troops and make conquest relatively easy. Savannah soon surrendered. Georgia was quickly subdued. Then Charleston fell with a thud, and with the capture of so many regular Continental troops that the back country was without protection except by partisan bands.

Though he and his brother officers had had but indifferent luck as soon as they moved back from their supply ships at tidewater, Cornwallis now set off inland on what he hoped was to be a whirlwind conquest of the southern colonies. His prospects looked reasonably bright, for about all that stood in his way apparently were the local irregular forces, and Gates and such American militia as he still retained would soon be beaten at Camden. Thus those of the country folk who remained loyal to the cause of freedom were forced to do all they could to stay Cornwallis' proposed thrust up the Catawba River Valley into North Carolina.

It was this threat of invasion that was keeping old Colonel William Bratton, for one, away from home far more than he might have wished. He had served in Braddock's forces up at the Forks of the Ohio some twenty-four years before, and those with French and Indian War experience were being called upon to put it to effective use.

He had a homestead, and a clearing planted to cotton, corn, and a little grain a dozen miles west of the Catawba and some seven miles south of York. Consequently it was not far below the North Carolina line, and right in the area through which the British might well surge. This he had had to leave in charge of his considerably younger wife, hoping she, their two young sons, and the creatures and few slaves would make out. Now that the British regulars combined with the Tories were staging raids in the section, it was particularly disquieting.

The colonel's worst fears were realized when just such a party drew up in front of the Bratton home one day. Sensing quickly what this mixed group of thirty or forty, with red-coated soldiers and officers among them, surely was, his wife Martha stowed the two boys far back in the big fireplace, pulled her courage together, and answered the harsh rapping at the front of the house.

As she partially opened the door, one of the Tories stood before her, with two British officers immediately behind him, Thrusting out with one foot, he pushed it full open and demanded that she step out. This she could not well refuse to do, although she would have preferred to look down at him from the added height of the threshold.

He, it appeared, was to be the spokesman, and his first question was to inquire for her husband. Although she sought to be evasive, she had to admit that he was not at home. Searchers, who had been dispatched to check the rear of the house and outbuildings, just then returned, and since they shook their heads, she had to be believed.

Well, if he was not at home, where was he? Since she did not know, she could be of no help in this direction. For a moment she had felt the British officer, the surly-faced one, was about to enter the questioning, but he resisted the impulse.

There was more sparring back and forth, and when it began to be evident that she neither could nor would provide much in the way of information, the Tory, too, became impatient. But with an effort he quieted his tone, launched into a lengthy harangue on the merits of the Tory cause, and shut off the now glowering Britisher still eager to take over. Finally he came to the peroration of his well-rehearsed address and began to press the good woman to use her influence in shifting the allegiance of her husband, thus saving their property and their lives.

Despite the gravity of the moment and the evil scowl on the red-coated officer's face, she gave this whole proposition a flat and final "No!"

Hardly was this refusal uttered when the Britisher, all restraint now blown to the skies by this "peasant woman's" resolve, pushed the Tory spokesman aside, grabbed Mrs. Bratton, swung her across the narrow porch, pressed her down to her knees, and forced her head against the porch enclosure. Reaching up with his right hand, he snatched a long, curved-blade sickle, or reaping hook, from where it was fastened on one of the porch posts. Whirling it up over his head, he buried its point deep into the rail, where it hung in a razor-like arc above her bare neck.

But this was carrying the matter just a bit too far. There was a scuffle, some pointed words, and the second officer crowded in. Shouldering the other two men aside, he yanked the reaping hook free, hurled it out on to the ground, and assisted the now shaking lady to her feet. Then clicking his heels, he withdrew his plumed hat and bowed low. But without a word of apology, he turned to the others, waved them down the steps ahead of him and out toward the remainder of the party and their waiting horses.

There was a crisp command, and the group moved on down the road toward the south. But they went not more than two hundred yards, then they paused. At this the woman's heart froze within her. Were they going to pay her a return visit? She and the two boys kneeling on the floor peeked cautiously from a side window. But there the raiding party stayed, to be joined in the early afternoon by an even larger group, after which they were soon busy setting up a camp. Yet except that they searched the farm buildings for eggs and the slave quarters for whatever food might be found there, they bothered Mrs. Bratton no more that day. By dark she had gotten her composure back sufficiently so that she and the boys, the doors and window shutters closed fast on this warm July night, tried to snatch a little sleep.

Perhaps it was late when she dropped off, for it was after sunup when she bounded from bed at a sharp crack of musket fire. There was volley after volley, screaming men, riderless horses racing past, and all the noise of a sharp battle. Fortunately it was a short one, although it was some time after the shooting ceased before she peered from the window. Then her heart started to pound as men headed down the road toward the house. But she soon recognized some among them, and they were bearers of good news. They were partisans looking for sheets and other cloth for wrappings for their wounded, and for water from the well. They had surprised the notorious Captain Christian Huck, and killed him and no less than forty others of his raiding, plundering band. They promised they would bring some of their prisoners down for her to identify later on.

When they did come back that afternoon, whom did Martha

Bratton see among the prisoners marked for execution but her erstwhile attacker of the day before. As she stood in her doorway looking
out she could see the reaping hook still lying on the grass before
the porch, but she found herself almost instinctively pleading for this
wretch—and so fervently, too, that his life was spared.

Such were one woman's contributions along the freedom frontier.

THE FRONTIERSMEN STRIKE A TELLING BLOW

In the following month Cornwallis was the victor over Gates at
Camden, and it seemed for a time that his talons were so deeply
sunk into the Southland that he could not be shaken free. He prepared to press on to the north, wiping out the partisan resistance,
so the country could be held by the Tories with a minimum of
support from his regular troops. As part of this sweeping movement,
a debonair Scot, Major Patrick Ferguson, comes briefly into the
limelight.

He was a dashing, swaggering character, the best shot in the
whole British Army, and busy equipping the Tory forces with the
advanced type of breech-loading rifle he had perfected. All that
seemed to stand between him and an easy junction with his superior
in the northern province was a bucolic group of Virginia and Carolina men and boys from the hill country, who, in their turn, did not
seem overly impressed by this lustrous Britisher.

For his own part, he was most contemptuous of this skin-hatted
rabble, and their tomahawks, scalping knives, and long rifles, and
especially of their leaders, Jack Sevier, redheaded Bill Campbell, Ben
Cleveland, and Ike Shelby. To the latter he sent word that he was
on his way over the hills to hang all rebels. The gentleman addressed
ruminated on the matter briefly, and decided he and his moccasin-
clad followers could show their hospitality in no better way than by
meeting the man at least halfway. So they set off.

Ferguson and about a thousand regulars managed to dig themselves in on the bald, boulder-strewn crown of King's Mountain, some
eighteen miles, as the crows winged it, over the rolling hills from
where Mrs. Bratton had made her stand. By his own brash estimate,
"God Almighty could not drive him from the spot." It was here that
about an equal number of the mountain men from the Holston country and the hills of western Virginia came upon him toward midafternoon one October day in 1780. As was their wont, they filtered

in slowly and silently through the woods and brush lower down the mountainside, and soon had the Britishers completely surrounded. Not considering themselves rebels, and with no intention of being hanged, they went to work. Before nightfall these woodsmen, trained in Indian fighting, had either killed, wounded, or captured every last redcoat, with a loss of only twenty-eight killed and sixty wounded on their side. The body of the showy Ferguson was given preferential treatment, being wrapped in a freshly flayed cowhide before it was laid to rest in one of the two common graves dug for the dead. A party of frontier hillbillies had turned the tide against the hopeful Cornwallis.

The Quaker blacksmith from Rhode Island, Nathanael Greene, soon took command of the shattered American forces in the South, and with reinforcements made them into an army. He held the British at Guilford Court House, and other places, and then roundly whipped them at the Cowpens. Soon Cornwallis was dashing north with but one purpose in mind, evacuation by a British fleet in the lower Chesapeake Bay. But instead he swarmed into a trap, faced Washington, and Britain was through in America. Our frontiers were our own, to develop from then on as we saw fit.

XIII

America Crosses the Alleghenies

"Fathers, I desire you may hear me in civilness, if not, we must handle that rod which was laid down for the use of the obstreperous. If you had come in a peaceable manner, like our brothers the English, we should not have been against your trading with us, as they do; but to come, fathers, and build houses upon our lands and to take it by force, is what we cannot submit to. Fathers, both you and the English are white, we live in a country between; therefore the land belongs to neither one nor t'other: But the great Being above allowed it to be a place of residence for us; so, fathers, I desire you to withdraw."—Report of the plea of an Indian chief before a French commandant, George Washington's *Journal* of his expedition to the Ohio, 1754.

T HE term "West" is frequently used in American history, and as a variable, in that it did not for long determine any single area. There were times when the Connecticut Valley might have been so designated by people in the Bay colony, or the Susquehanna Valley by the Philadelphians, the upper Potomac area in Maryland by the Chesapeake towns, or the great valley into which Governor Spotswood of Virginia and his Knights of the Golden Horseshoe penetrated by those on the lower James River. Actually it was this latter section, and the Piedmont belt stretching down into the Carolina grant, that might truly be called our first *West*.

This plateau, which extends from Pennsylvania to Georgia, was largely cut off from the tidewater country in the early days, since it lay beyond the Fall Line of the rivers, above which navigation was broken. Access to it was best afforded from the Great Valley of Pennsylvania, and Scotch-Irish, German, and English pioneers flowed down the trails through the interconnecting valleys, and established settlements and a culture that was quite unlike that along the seacoast. So different were they, in fact, that the colonies, and later the states involved, encountered strong antagonisms between their two well-defined sections. These tensions were prevalent from before the Revolution through the first third of the following century.

It was to a large extent this Piedmont plateau that fed settlers into Kentucky and from there into southern Indiana and Illinois, also into Tennessee, and further south into northern Alabama and Mississippi. The area's economic, political, and social interests, developed in pioneer communities, bred the democratic hopes and aspirations that soon had a profound influence in American affairs. This primitive section helped nurture Jefferson's political philosophy, and from it he drew much of his political strength; while it gave us, through birth and training, such leaders as Jackson, Lincoln, and Polk.

Daniel Boone, whose Berks County birthplace is now a Pennsylvania shrine, had gone south with his family, and later opened up the Kentucky country. Abraham Lincoln's great-great-grandfather's stone home still stands a half dozen miles away. The push of pioneering settlers into the West began in the Pennsylvania colony, and it would be the jumping-off spot for thousands more during, and in the period immediately following, the Revolution.

THE CONTEST FOR THE MISSISSIPPI VALLEY

The peace treaty signed in 1783, in which the United States of America was recognized by Great Britain as independent, was delayed by the fact that our French allies, due to Spanish influence, were reluctant to make boundary concessions west of the mountains. France, England, and Spain all realized that control of this transmountain area and the Mississippi would definitely limit the power of the new nation along the Atlantic seaboard. Attempts by these three countries to exert influence there, and to hamper and hamstring each other's ambitions, made the ten years from 1793 to 1803 a most critical period in our history. The embroilments of Europe would still reach across the ocean to plague us, and especially along the frontier, which had now been pushed over the mountains into the valleys of the streams finding their way to the Mississippi, rather than to the Atlantic.

Although France had been divested of most of her American possessions in 1763, her ambitions here had by no means terminated. It was her intent to limit the United States, which she had fostered by her aid, to the eastern slopes of the Alleghenies, keep her subservient and dependent, and a willing ally. But the press of people into western Pennsylvania and the upper Ohio Valley, then into Kentucky and along the left bank of the Ohio River, and a little later into the Cumberland and Tennessee valleys further south, gave her much concern.

Even while the American Revolution was in progress the twenty-five thousand families on the tributaries of the Ohio above the Scioto sought to be declared a separate state, to be called Westsylvania. The ferment beyond the mountains and the need to deal constructively with that situation, together with the necessity of gaining a firmer control on the lands as far as the Mississippi, pointed up the weakness of the Confederation, and bulked large in the demands for a strong central government. The adoption of the Constitution came none too soon.

FRENCH INTRIGUE IN AMERICA

The French Revolution of 1789 brought Washington's administration face to face with serious foreign problems. Many of the people here felt that we should repay our debt to France by supporting that country, wracked with internal troubles, against the other European powers. But our ability to make war was highly limited, and the President decided upon a course of strict neutrality. In an attempt to circumvent it, the French sent over a new ambassador, Citizen Genêt, well tutored in political connivance. Soon to be involved in a war with both England and Spain, France had needed to drive the Spanish out of the Mississippi Valley, from which she hoped to provide produce and trade to aid her faltering colonies in the West Indies. Spain had shut off the mouth of the great river at New Orleans, and the discontent of the settlers to the west of the mountains was so great that Genêt hoped to turn them from American to French allegiance, raise an army among them to descend the river and seize this key city, and with a minimum of assistance from the homeland return Louisiana to French hands.

Landing in the spring of 1793 at Charleston, Genêt at once contacted Governor Moultrie, the Revolutionary leader, and disclosed to him plans developed in Paris with the aid of Americans residing there. Plagued by Indian attacks stimulated by the Spanish to the south, the Carolina governor lent his aid as the Frenchman busily armed privateers and made other plans for the seizure of Florida. After a short but profitable visit there, Genêt turned north, and

his overland journey to Philadelphia was punctuated by many meetings with democratic admirers of France. Intimations of the new ambassador's intents and purposes had, however, reached the capital
ahead of him, having been received direct from Paris. As a consequence, Washington promptly issued his proclamation of neutrality
toward the belligerent powers. But it was not well received even
by the people of Philadelphia, where rioting threatened. Trouble
with Spain over the Mississippi, and her fomentation of Indian up-
risings in the Southwest, seemed to many to justify our aiding the
French, if not actually combining with them for action against this
menace. Even Jefferson, then Secretary of State, while he paid lip
service to the proclamation, considered it a somewhat timorous move.
He listened attentively to Genêt, although at this first encounter he
remained noncommittal. By and large, the ambassador considered
the over-all situation reasonably promising.

He was, perhaps, a bit over optimistic, and at the very outset
succeeded in completely alienating Washington. When he pressed
for payment on the debt owed by this country to France, which
funds he had been instructed to use in equipping such enterprises as
he could set in motion, he met with impassive resistance. Since the
administration could not seemingly be won over, he shifted to intrigue.

His agents had been at work beyond the mountains, with rather
encouraging results. George Rogers Clark, bitter over the lack of an
open route to market from the Kentucky area, offered his own services, and agreed to raise a regiment of Kentucky riflemen and clear
the river of the Spaniards down to and including New Orleans.
Promptly Genêt commissioned him "Major General of the Independent and Revolutionary Legion of the Mississippi." Soon afterward
he took over André Michaux, whom Jefferson had engaged to make a
transcontinental exploration, purportedly for the benefit of the
American Philosophical Society, and established the botanist in the
Kentucky area as a screen behind which other activities might be
carried on.

Reaching north to the St. Lawrence country, he set fire to slum-
bering French Canadian ambitions, and despite "old Washington,"
who did whatever he could to hinder his progress, the thirty-year-
old conspirator was indeed making time. His contacts among men
prominent in western affairs increased, and as some indication of
what he was preparing reached the Spanish governor of Louisiana
and West Florida, that gentleman was thoroughly alarmed. Spain's

posts were very weak, and could hardly hope to withstand an assault by frontiersmen determined to open a way to market, particularly when supported by French ships.

As his plan and his hopes grew, Genêt was encouraged to turn
his blandishments again upon Jefferson. That formidable Virginian's
support was essential because of his political strength in the West.
Genêt had the discretion to approach him as Mr. Jefferson rather than
as Secretary of State, and disclosed to him his intents and purposes
in detail, even to the text of an address to be made to the Canadians.
He labored to assure the American that he merely wished to free
Louisiana and establish it as an independent state tied to France, but
open to commerce with the United States. The sage of Monticello
listened attentively, took notes, as was his habit, and decided to
ponder the matter well before any extensive commitments. The
scheme was daring, subtle, and intriguing.

Even as a private citizen, Jefferson was clearly aware of its
short-term advantages, as well as its serious implications. He was not
opposed to insurrection in Louisiana, and he made that clear to his
appellant. But he had no wish to see the unhappy Kentuckians slip
a noose about their necks, which they would assuredly do if they
took up arms against a nation at peace with the United States. His
attitude on this point he also made very clear. Still he agreed to give
and did dispatch a letter rather carefully recommending Genêt to
Governor Shelby of Kentucky. On the surface it looked like an ingenious bit of fence straddling, but the gentleman who wrote the
Declaration had a lifelong habit of thinking matters through. Let it
be said to his credit, too, that it would be a dozen or more years,
until there was a substantial and enduring sense of nationalism in
this new land. Even he would not become thoroughly imbued with
it until he achieved the presidency. The moment had not arrived
for final decision.

The young Frenchman, far from discouraged, went on with his
activities. Clark and his associates were busy with advanced preparation out at the Falls of the Ohio (Louisville) for a descent of the
Mississippi. Down the coast privateers and armed contingents were
readied for an attack on St. Augustine. By playing upon divided
sentiments Genêt was working toward a position where he might
not only win back Louisiana, but limit the United States in area and
importance and make this country a vassal of the French. Laboring
at first behind an aura of great disinterestedness, his true purposes
began to show through, and Jefferson, along with the Federalist

supporters of the administration, began to be deeply concerned. If Genêt's insurgents moved, war with England and Spain appeared inevitable.

The answer to the quandary came, however, from France rather than from this side of the ocean. The revolution there was passing into its third phase, and the Jacobins, who now came into power, disavowed and recalled the ambassador whom their predecessors, the Girondists, had sent here for such dubious purposes. In the letter which ordered him home it was pointed out that he had been dispatched to treat with the American *Government,* and not merely with a portion of its people. He was sent here as an ambassador, and not as a proconsul.

While the threat had now passed, it indicated the breach which obtained between the East and the West, and that the peoples beyond the mountains were then not firmly welded to the older sections from which they had sprung. It also emphasized the fact that at least three European nations had a continuing interest in the great Mississippi Valley, and that our hold upon it was thus uncertain in two respects. There was still a third aspect of this situation to be explored, which would involve one of the most colorful of our Revolutionary heroes, and mark the beginning of the United States Army as a well-trained, effective striking force.

BEYOND THE FORKS OF THE OHIO

Along with the agitation to form the state of Westsylvania while the Revolution was still in progress, there had been other tension in regard to western lands, claimed principally by Virginia, Massachusetts, and Connecticut. The Continental Congress had pressed all states having such claims to cede them to the federal government, and this was eventually done. Since the population had increased measurably by the termination of the war, and the lean years which followed had sent the land-hungry in search of new homesteads, the shift to the west necessitated some constructive action in regard to the huge section beyond the Forks of the Ohio.

One of the last, and possibly the most constructive of the acts of the Congress of the Confederation, was the drafting and passage of the Ordinance for the Government of the Lands Northwest of the Ohio River in 1787. With added stability given the area, the years just ahead would witness the flow of great numbers into the Ohio Valley.

By May of 1788 an association centered in New England had colonists establishing Marietta. A land speculator also set up a post on downstream at the mouth of the Miami River, and gave it the resounding and skillfully fabricated name of Losantiville. When the territorial governor, General Arthur St. Clair, arrived the following year to set up Fort Washington near by, he arbitrarily rechristened the growing settlement Cincinnati, honoring the military society of which he and many another Revolutionary officer were members. Bonuses for their services, and those of the enlisted men, had been in land certificates redeemable in this area.

THE INDIAN PROBLEM

While Kentucky, south across the river, was filling in so rapidly that the Indians there would soon be outnumbered, they were still thick in the virgin area to the north. There they had been concentrated by ejection from their former homes at the hands of other tribes or the whites, some of them migrating from as far away as the St. Lawrence Valley, the Atlantic coastal region, Tennessee, and South Carolina. They comprised several major tribes, and their attitude with respect to their hunting grounds was quite the same as had been expressed a generation previously in the quotation which begins this chapter. As flatboat after flatboat dropped more and more settlers ashore on the upper or right-hand bank of the great river, they became very restless.

Although they and their ancestors had accumulated some two hundred years of experience with these white interlopers, they could not yet comprehend or adjust to their white brothers' single-minded insistence on permanent ownership and exclusive rights to land. First the French had intruded upon their preserves, and by sharp dealings had gained certain rights which developed to be not for a season or two, but for all time. Then the French had been succeeded by the British, who were even more demanding. Still they, like their predecessors, had been few; there had been some benefit in trade, and their hunting lands and village sites had not been heavily invaded. But when these Americans had begun to descend upon them in hordes, had talked them into numerous treaties, the proceeds from which were soon consumed, and had made clearings, scattered the game, and even tried to drive them away, the Indians realized the time was at hand when the "rod . . . laid down for the use of the obstreperous" must be put to use.

As if the homesteaders, held fairly close to the bank of the river by Governor St. Clair, were not enough, the entrance of survey gangs running lines far back into the interior was unmistakable evidence that there would be wholesale new evictions. So they began to gird for a struggle ahead.

Their resolve to stay was strengthened by the British. Although they were reported to have made some treaty by which they had given up their "claims" to the area, the men in red coats appeared to be in no hurry to leave. Since they promised assistance in resisting this newer and very threatening influx, the natives cast their lot with them, and with British arms, ammunition, and guidance, took to the warpath. During the years between 1783 and 1790 they massacred no less than fifteen hundred of those who braved the attempt to carve a home from the Ohio country, and probably maimed an additional thousand.

Still the settlers persisted, more and more forged in, and the government tried to hold the situation together with offers of peace and a long procession of solemn treaties. The Indians had now come to thoroughly distrust the latter, and sought the British for more weapons and powder to continue their resistance.

General Josiah Harmar, who had won acclaim for his exploits during the Revolution, was sent with a force to quell them in 1790, but his insufficient, ineffectual contingent was quickly wiped out. St. Clair then took command of the available "army," a motley group, tried to repair the damage done by this defeat, but shortly afterward suffered a similar calamity. Something constructive now had to be done, for we were fast losing face.

THE FIRST AMERICAN LEGION

From the beginning, Congress had been steadfastly set against the establishment of a sound, well-trained, hard-hitting professional army, lest it tempt, or be used to force, the young nation down a militaristic path. But this second disgrace in the Ohio country shifted such sentiment, and a bill was rushed through to increase and improve the military arm. That accomplished, Congress had a political field day over the choice of its commander. Finally, after much haggling, Washington managed, in April of 1792, to get the name of Anthony Wayne, of Revolutionary fame, confirmed by the Senate.

The so-called "Mad" Anthony, former man about town, Beau Brummell, and scion of a well-to-do family, was by now on into middle age, racked by gout, in bad state financially, and, being something of a compromise candidate, not exactly a popular appointee. But he had a natural bent and innate enthusiasm for soldiering, and took his new task with great seriousness. This was evidenced by the fact that he spent his remaining days in Philadelphia in a series of earnest conversations with men who knew the Ohio country intimately. It was something of a left-handed compliment perhaps, but the British, with ambitions of their own in the Northwest, considered him a distinct threat. This was certainly a good augury for what lay ahead of him.

The remnant of the army in the West, lacking discipline, wholly untrained, and now demoralized after two bad drubbings, was evaporating rapidly as its members deserted into the encompassing wilderness. Wayne's presence and firm hand were sorely needed. So, with a quickly gathered cavalry detachment as an escort, he set out over the rugged trail for Pittsburgh. There he found his new command, four lean regiments, some few among them veterans, but mostly raw recruits, and known collectively as the Legion of the United States—an "American Legion." His first task was to make this mediocre body more worthy of its resounding name, and he set to work with a will. A vacillating government back in Philadelphia would afford him the time.

The year was 1792, and Wayne was quite certain there could be no lasting peace until recent scores had been balanced by a decisive contest with the savages. However, the East was in no mood for an extended Indian war, and Secretary Knox of the War Department had his hands full holding his new commander in chief in check.

The West, face to face with the realities of the situation, was of an entirely different disposition. Defiant colonists, especially in western Pennsylvania, were just then testing the mettle of the federal government in a whiskey insurrection. With this unsettled fringe of civilization about him, Wayne was willing to accept instructions he found awaiting his arrival, which ordered delay in any incursions among the natives for at least a year.

Pittsburgh of that day was a robust, lusty, log town; and to get his soldiers away from its sordid distractions, he moved them twenty-two miles to the northwest along the Ohio, and built a new camp, which he christened Legionville. There, in the early days of 1793, he began a rigorous training program calculated to whip his disorganized mob into a commendable striking force. Continued hesitancy by the government back East would extend the monotonous months of preparation. But one day, although he may not have fully realized the part he was destined to play, he would fight a decisive battle with his Legion.

Despite the heavy snows in December, and the fast-frozen river holding up supplies and threatening for a time to make Legion-ville another Valley Forge, the camp did shape up slowly. By Christmas time the men and officers had reasonably snug quarters and the defenses being erected were stout enough to dissuade the Indians. And they had need to be, for scouts brought in word that as soon as the leaves were out, the Shawnees, backed by the English and keen for war, would be upon them.

Why wait? Why not take the offensive and attack first? Wayne dispatched a proposal along these lines to Philadelphia; and while he awaited a reply, he stepped up the already long hours of drill, and on top of them demanded both target practice and still stronger entrenchments. Desperate over the clothing and equipment of his forces, he sent off so biting a demand for new supplies that they were promptly forthcoming. Not only were the new uniforms top quality and well made, but they were outright elegant—almost too gaudy for wilderness use. Reoutfitted in resplendent dress, and already showing the results of relentless drilling, the Legion began to take on new spirit and seemed more formidable.

The condition of their arms and the handling of weapons were next improved. Liberal rations of liquor to the best shots, and to the runners-up, brought noticeable improvements in marksmanship. But the everlasting drilling, and particularly the sham battles, were held in derision, and there was a tidal wave of desertions. However, a ten-dollar bounty paid to any who turned in these truants soon cured this relapse. Hard-driving "Dandy Tony" was something of a martinet, but, like a master workman, he knew the value of good tools. Then as the men began to shape up, the conduct of some of his officers threatened a breach in the armor he was forging. Camp life tended to be demoralizing.

DISLOYALTY PLAGUES WAYNE

Second in command was Brigadier General James Wilkinson, who had been the teen-age hero that day in June 1776 when information he had supplied the still loyal Benedict Arnold had permitted escape from a British trap, saved the American forces from annihilation, and marked perhaps the turning point of the Revolution. Like this eventual traitor, whose aide-de-camp he had been, Wilkinson was even now playing with fire, and ugly rumors that he tried at various times to sell out his nation to both the English and to the Spaniards have always attached themselves to his name. However, at the moment he was far downstream, having been sent on ahead to Fort Washington to make preparations for the troops when, and if, they were permitted to advance. Officer trouble would increase markedly after he and the main Legion were together.

Sanction to move on down the Ohio finally arrived, and on April 30, 1793, the garrison, loaded on a fleet of flatboats, set off. A short distance downstream Fort McIntosh was passed. Here the treaty of 1785 had been signed, giving—falsely the Indians now maintained —the right to make limited settlements in the Northwest Territory. A little further along Wayne hurried past Wheeling's first few cabins. Neighboring Pittsburghers were condemning it as an "outlaw" town. His immediate objective was Marietta, Ohio's first settlement to survive, where more legionnaires awaited him, and supplies had also been laid down.

Pausing there only briefly, he was soon under way again. He did tarry long enough at three-year-old Gallipolis to enjoy a bit of the hospitality extended by its almost exclusively French population, and then was off for Fort Washington, on the site of present-day Cincinnati.

Once there, Wayne and his officers were roundly entertained. However, the still rather dissolute community was not a suitable place for his troops, and he moved out beyond easy reach and set up a new camp, which he called Hobson's Choice. Here he settled down to more drill and target practice, awaiting further instructions from President Washington and Secretary Knox.

The five months' delay gave an opportunity for strong factions to form among the officers, one group loyal to Wayne, the other to the engaging Wilkinson. While Genêt was at the moment working feverishly back in Philadelphia, there is no indication that Wilkinson was directly involved in these particular French machinations. The pause also provided the time to cut a sixty-foot-wide road through the Miami Valley to connect with crude outposts which had already been established. At Fort Jefferson, forty-four miles up this broad swath through the wilderness, Wayne began to lay in supplies.

During this further delay, a council that had been attempted between American envoys and Indian leaders came to naught. By September word reached the commander via Philadelphia that the savages might be expected to strike in about two weeks. But the news had long since been anticipated, and Wayne had already called on Governor Shelby of recently admitted Kentucky, south across the Ohio, to provide fifteen hundred four-month volunteers. Still by the time official word to be on his guard had been received, no more than three hundred sixty Kentuckians had reported for duty, many were disgruntled, and the service period of some had nearly run out.

It was October before this and other complications could be ironed out and he was ready to move north from Hobson's Choice. It was by no means the proper time of year for an attack, for bountiful summer hunting and the fall store of corn, beans, and pumpkins had the Indians well fed and at the peak of their resistance. Still the commander drove his forces ahead up the road into the wilderness hoping for a pitched battle, in which he felt certain he could weaken the enemy.

Arriving at Fort Jefferson, he found the stores he had planned upon had not arrived, and he dared not advance beyond the end of the road, which stopped abruptly six miles north of this post. This late in the year he definitely needed a well-stocked base behind him. Timidity in Philadelphia, and not the enemy, had stalled him. But there seemed no sense in retracing his steps; so while he belabored the army contractors to speed up supplies, he also put the soldiers to work building a new base at the terminus of the road, which he named Greene Ville in honor of Nathanael Greene, who had hamstrung Cornwallis in the South.

There they dug in for the winter, Wayne bedeviled on the one hand by the highly independent contractors, and on the other by the wily, pernicious Wilkinson. Aching from the gout, and subjected to an avalanche of abuse poured upon him back in the War Department by his archdetractor and second-in-command, the once "Dandy Tony," as he had formerly been known to his cronies, spent a most miserable winter at Greene Ville in 1793–94.

Wilkinson finally persuaded the contractors to further slow down the flow of supplies, hoping to so sabotage the proposed spring drive that the strict, two-fisted commander would be recalled and the old free-and-easy days would obtain once again on the frontier.

The officer cliques, too, were sniping at each other, and treachery mounted to the point where Wayne hardly dared trust his own aides. Then the enlisted men's slender pay of three dollars per month was held up. The commander and Wilkinson both knew that it was due to the yellow fever epidemic which had made Philadelphia a

ghost town that summer and fall. Yet the latter furtively spread the
rumor that Wayne had appropriated the funds to line his own pockets. Why the hard-pressed man did not lose his reason during these
bitter months will never be known.

But he was focusing on the spring, and the time when he was
certain the Indians would be least able to withstand the blow he
was preparing. In the dead of winter he pulled himself from a sickbed, and led a party on to the site of St. Clair's earlier defeat, and
there established Fort Recovery. Under flags of truce, he admitted
Indian envoys to Greene Ville, paraded his men before them, emphasized the strength of the post, and implied sore trouble for them
in the days ahead. While matters drifted in Philadelphia, he drove
himself and his men toward ample readiness. Still it was not until
June that a subtly worded dispatch from the War Department dimly
flashed the go-ahead signal.

Almost at the moment of its receipt the Indians made a raid,
stampeded some three hundred sixty horses, drove them off, and
killed fifty quartermaster hostlers transferring them to Fort Recovery. Not content with this easy victory, the two thousand braves
overruled their chiefs and fell upon the fort itself. The garrison with-
stood the onslaught, and this attack set Wayne on the march with
blood in his eye. There were but three days remaining in July of '94
when he was off.

Beyond Recovery the troops plunged at once into the wilderness. Struggling through underbrush, fighting off enormous mosquitoes, and fording innumerable creeks and streams, they were at the
St. Mary's River three days later on August 1. Two days were spent
there throwing up a blockhouse, while scouts probed ahead searching for the enemy. Here, too, Wayne saved his life by jumping from
beneath a falling tree, but managed to add severe injuries to his other
harassments.

However, his mind was still in the clear, and he came up with
a plan that baffled not only his own associates, but the Indians and
their English allies as well. Harmar had followed the dictates of
accepted strategy, made the roundabout march up the St. Mary's
toward the headwaters of the Maumee, and had come by his defeat
at least in part because of this too obvious move. Wayne was determined to be more subtle. So he began spreading varied false rumors
of his intentions among the tribes in the confederation he was facing, leading each to believe he proposed passing through its territory.

Quite as he expected, they at once separated, each to guard

its own home area. As they did, he promptly marched his Legion through the abandoned center of the Indian country, heading for Grand Glaize, his objective on the Maumee River. In a week he had speeded safely across seventy-seven miles, and on August 8 took the town without firing a single shot. In another week's time he had erected sturdy defense there, and tauntingly named it Fort Defiance.

THE END OF AN ERA

Forty odd miles on down the Maumee near present-day Toledo was the British post Fort Miamis. While he reasoned correctly that the next assemblage of the Indians would be at a point near that stout-walled citadel, he badly underestimated their probable numbers, and also their willingness to fight. But he moved quickly downstream and set up temporary Fort Deposit to shelter his supplies at a point well above Miamis. From there his scouts beat the riverbanks and back country, but without locating any large contingents of the savages. Perhaps he would have to move on to Miamis to find them.

August 20, 1794, dawned in a round of drenching thundershowers, and it was eight o'clock, rather than daylight, before the troops moved forward from little Deposit, keeping along the high north bank above the Maumee. There were signs of Indians lurking about, but nothing approaching an "army" of them. If savages in force could not be encountered, it seemed certain the British garrison below might offer a challenge, so let that be the objective.

Wayne's three-week-old injuries still made him so uncomfortable that he could barely sit a horse. Yet he had been hoisted aboard one, and with teeth tight-clenched against the pain was, with the cavalry and foot soldiers, picking his way gingerly through the everlasting snarl of fallen and half-rotted tree trunks which a prairie "twister" some years before had thrown down to beset their path. It was heavy going, and required close attention and the careful calculation of almost every step, making progress slow.

The Legion had not advanced too far when a burst of shots rang out of the tall grass picking off a number of the mounted Kentucky volunteers. As the remainder of this group swung their horses to avoid a second volley, they charged into the van of the infantry column and threatened to throw the whole party into a rout.

Mad Anthony tore the impeding bandages from his limbs, struck spurs to his horse, and dashing from one group to another, began to shout out a stream of staccato orders punctuated with blistering oaths. He was just bidding the hesitant Wilkinson be about his business of searching out a possible ambush in the thick brush in the ravine along the river when a second round of shots turned back the regrouped cavalry attempting to clear native sharpshooters from the tall grass. Always at his best in the midst of a melee, the commander, his aches now forgotten, quickly reorganized his forces, but not before the Indians had had time to seek shelter in the woods behind and form new lines. With hardly a shot fired in retaliation, the engagement to become historic as the Battle of Fallen Timbers was so far going all in favor of the enemy.

Suddenly the main body of the Indians was discovered at the edge of the forest into which their sharpshooters had fled. Wayne promptly ordered an advance, and also a flanking movement to get at the rear of the savages. As the Legion, massed in close order, drove in among the trees their hours of drill and mock warfare began to pay off. Able to load as well as fire as they advanced, they shot at least two rounds for each returned by their opponents. Then, when they came close at hand and fixed their bayonets, the three thin waves of savages were unable to withstand the tornado-like charge. Taking to their heels, they fled down the valley toward hoped for refuge at Fort Miamis. From a bad beginning, the indomitable Wayne had brought order out of near chaos, and in no more than forty minutes had won a decisive victory.

The stricken red men, terror doubling their speed, arrived at the British post only to find its gates locked tightly against them. Its commandant, Major Campbell, had thought it prudent not to give his American adversary, who had risen materially in his estimation since daybreak, too abundant provocation for battle. Thus he had denied his recent friends sanctuary in their time of greatest need; and thereby doubly beaten, the disillusioned savages scattered to the woods.

Wayne marched his Legion up to the very gates of the fort, and he and the Britisher insulted each other roundly in strained but polite diplomatic language. The Americans even camped beneath its guns for a week trying to prevail upon its defenders to come out and fight. Yet neither officer quite dared hazard the overt act which might well have precipitated a war destined to be delayed for another eighteen years.

On the twenty-sixth of August the American forces returned to

Grand Glaize, continuing there until the middle of September, strengthening its fortifications. The end of an era had arrived, for the Indians had learned two stern lessons: they were no match for well-trained soldiery; and their adopted "father," the king of England, could not be depended upon in a pinch.

Their control of this section of the Northwest Territory was badly shaken by the "Tornado," as they now christened Wayne; and he had no difficulty making a most favorable treaty with them the following year, which opened up large reaches of Ohio to immediate settlement. There would be further Indian difficulties on to the west in the years just ahead, and particularly in the south during the next generation. Then far into the oncoming century there would be a succession of bitter encounters beyond the Mississippi. But this valuable area north of the Ohio now began to open up, the Indians would not again be so considerable a threat, and the new West would touch off developments and changes beyond the wildest dreams of pre-Revolutionary days.

By 1798 the Territory had filled in sufficiently so that it was electing a general assembly. Its meetings in Cincinnati would indicate the distance this frontier had gone in seven short years, and also the will of the people who made up its population. In 1799, William Henry Harrison would become its sole representative in the federal Congress, just then winding up its affairs in Philadelphia, and migrating to Washington as its permanent home. But before this exodus, it would pass an act setting off Ohio as a separate entity and start it on its way to statehood in 1803.

XIV

The West Nurtures Democracy

It is to be regretted that the rich and powerful too often bend the acts of government to their selfish purposes. Distinctions in society will always exist under every just government. Equality of talents, of education, or of wealth can not be produced by human institutions. In the full enjoyment of the gifts of Heaven and the fruits of superior industry, economy, and virtue, every man is equally entitled to protection by law; but when the laws undertake to add to these natural and just advantages artificial distinctions, to grant titles, gratuities, and exclusive privileges, to make the rich richer and the potent more powerful, the humbler members of society—the farmers, mechanics, and laborers—who have neither the time nor the means of securing like favors to themselves, have a right to complain of the injustice of their Government. There are no necessary evils in government. Its evils exist only in its abuses.—Excerpt from Andrew Jackson's *Bank Veto Message*, July 10, 1832.

T HE exploratory journey of Governor Spotswood and his gentleman companions over into the Shenandoah Valley in 1716 was one of the first positive steps in our settlement of the West. This took place some eighteen years before Daniel Boone's birth at the upper end of the corridor that led down through the Piedmont plateau, and by the time he was a young man, settlers were flowing down into this higher country well back from tidewater. Dr. Thomas Walker, an enterprising Virginian, investigated the possibilities in the lower reaches of this great interior valley, and on April 13, 1750, came to the slit in the rock-ribbed hills through which Boone, twenty-five years later, would blaze his Wilderness Road. Kentucky would draw people rather rapidly, even during the war years, and by 1792 had sufficient population to become the first state lying west of the mountains to join the Union.

All the settlers pushing out into the lower Shenandoah Valley, however, would not move up through Cumberland Gap into the

Kentucky country. By the time the Battle of the Alamance was fought, a group that had pushed over the divide to the headwaters of streams flowing west into the great Tennessee River Valley had decreed themselves a free and independent people. It is thought that their numbers were swelled somewhat by the discontented among the North Carolina Regulators following that sad encounter. There were small forts and some cabins along the Holston River, but in 1769 William Bean built his "station" on Boone's Creek near its junction with the Watauga River, and is credited with being the first permanent white settler in what is today Tennessee. Within three years, he and his neighbors had signed the famed Articles of the Watauga Association, and the Reverend Charles Cummings, the fiery backwoods preacher, was at work among them, translating Scotch-Presbyterian theology into practical democracy.

It was from this hill country to the west of the Piedmont that the men in coonskin hats had descended to give battle to Major Pat Ferguson at King's Mountain and turn the tables against Lord Cornwallis. Following the Revolution, they directed their attention away from the valleys of the rivers flowing east and began to explore the regions toward the Mississippi, being quite willing to trade their rolling, stony fields for any of greater promise.

Those in other areas were also sizing up the prospects in the middle reaches of the Cumberland and Tennessee rivers. One such was the Kentucky trapper, Thomas Sharpe Spencer, who made several sallies down from the north into the Cumberland country, liked what he saw there, and in 1778 talked several companions into coming along with him, their expressed purpose being to "plant a small field of corn." The site they chose is highly illuminating, for it indicates a need of the pioneers—a controlling factor in their enterprises—almost lost sight of today. They came upon a salt lick in the Castalian Springs country, a place where natural salt is found on the surface of the ground, and where animals go to lick it up. They knew that it would attract plenty of game, and they also had a source of salt, indispensable not only in their frugal diets, but in preserving meats.

Although they made a brave attempt at planting a small clearing, the enterprising Spencer's companions were without his enthusiasm, soon became fed up, drifted away, and left him alone. By the time his corn was harvested, winter was upon him, and he had no time to construct a cabin. So he took up residence in a gigantic hollow sycamore tree, and managed very well until spring. During the cold months it became abundantly evident to him that it would take concerted action to settle this land; and he, too, headed back into Kentucky.

THE CRUISE OF THE "ADVENTURE"

Colonel James Robertson, working west from the Watauga and Holston settlements at about this same time, also explored the Cumberland Valley. He, like Spencer, discovered another salt lick a few miles further west, and realized how valuable an adjunct it would be close by a proposed settlement. Pressing back home again, he described the area which he had visited so ardently that he set off one of the most remarkable argosies in our history. Preparations were soon under way for an exodus to this promised land the following spring, the journey to be made aboard a great flatboat, the *Adventure*.

Never was a craft more deserving of its name. It and several smaller vessels were constructed, and launched in the Holston River. The party to be transported was selected, and with the coming of higher water from melting snows, was ready to set off.

Its leader, Colonel John Donelson, a Virginia surveyor, had brought his family out from Pittsylvania County some years before. Among his children was a daughter, Rachel, who would one day die of a broken heart, one of the most maligned women in our history. When the party and their meager belongings had been loaded aboard, the little fleet headed down toward the larger Tennessee. There it followed the arching course of this great river as it swings far to the south, shooting its rapids, bumping over its bars, hazarding its whirlpools, and ever at the mercy of the many sunken logs, liable, without warning, to lurch up and tear the bottom from the none too sturdy craft.

Then the Tennessee swings to the north, and they crossed both the state later to be named for this river, and also the broad waist of Kentucky. Arriving at last at the Ohio, the still undaunted band poled and hauled their boats against its current to the mouth of the Cumberland, and then worked their way several hundred miles up its curving reaches until contact was made with the Robertson party, which had gone overland through the trackless wilderness. There, by the salt licks, they set up Fort Nashborough.

As this frontier station expanded, Donelson and his family prospered moderately, the colonel accumulating land, cattle, and slaves, to become one of the settlement's leading citizens. Still it was not all smooth going, for a drought and lean years forced him, like Abraham of old, to seek new pastures and security in another land. He fled up into Kentucky to weather this period of blight, and it was there that his daughter Rachel married one Lewis Robards.

As conditions improved, the Donelsons, minus their married daughter, returned to the settlement soon to be incorporated as Nashville. There the colonel was in much demand as a surveyor, and it was while he was absent on such business in the surrounding wilderness that he was slain. Whether the bullets came from rifles carried by men whose skin was white or red has never been determined. Frontier Tennessee then, and for several years to come, was as wild and woolly a West as any area in all the American story, and its annals are crammed with incidents that make some of our more generally known history tame reading indeed.

The widow Donelson, a woman of stout heart and real ability, soon had her married daughter at home with her. Rachel and Robards had been estranged because of the latter's insane and completely unfounded jealousy of his handsome wife. Her brother had gone to Kentucky and fetched her back, but a reconciliation soon brought Robards to Nashville to be the man in the home. It was perhaps because his mother-in-law had some reservations as to his ability to fill the role that she prudently rented a small cabin, hard by the larger house, to two acceptable young boarders. Indian attacks were not unknown in this outlying settlement in the later 1780s, and two more able-bodied men at hand would surely not be amiss.

With their presence, Robards' mistrust now had something quite tangible on which to build. One in particular of these youngish gentlemen, who had found a somewhat less intimate place at the hearthside, became the object of his especial resentment. The situation promptly drew taut, and to relieve the brittle tension, the totally innocent victim of unfounded suspicions and his companion found lodgings elsewhere. But this was not accomplished until after he had had a few pointed words with the needlessly aggrieved husband. Tradition, while not always fully reliable, stoutly maintains he offered to slice the stupid man's ears from his head with the knife he often wore in his belt.

Whatever form the conversation may have taken, the outraged Robards decamped for Kentucky in a burst of accusations; and, so it was reported, promptly entered a plea with the legislature there for a divorce from his wife. Somewhat garbled word of his actions seeped down to the Nashville area, and Mrs. Robards thought it best to make her home for a time with a married sister in another community.

She had developed into a comely, good-natured, thoroughgoing pioneer woman, having inherited fine attributes from both her parents. She was thus highly desirable in an area which depended as much upon the ability and resolution of its women as upon its menfolk. Few, if any, of her sex in the slowly forming Territory were more deserving, or more worthy, of a man of her own fine stature. She was one day to find such a mate. So it might be well to seek him out and learn something about his origin and development.

THE MAN HEWED FROM A HICKORY LOG

No, he was no carved wooden statue, for he had a birthplace, although it has never been located to the complete satisfaction of the two states anxious to claim the site. It was somewhere in the Waxhaws, a region which lay in the Catawba River Valley, along the debated line that then divided the two Carolinas, and perhaps twenty miles east of Brattonsville, which has been visited. But the man himself in later years contended he was a South Carolinian, so probably he was.

His parents had recently arrived from the north of Ireland, and the severity of that first year of clearing the land, erecting a cabin, and making a crop had carried off the father but a few days before this third son was born in 1767. But it was to this youngest child, however, that his name, Andrew, was given by the widowed mother.

He was hardly more than a slip of a boy when he would see this mother of his, with others willing to resist any trifling with their new-found freedom, marched off to British prison ships at Charleston, and from which she never returned. Thus he was fatherless at birth, and an orphan probably before he ever wore a pair of shoes. He would know the rigors of war by some small participation in the Revolution, and to the end of his life carry the jagged scar of a head wound inflicted by the sword of an arrogant British officer, whose boots he refused either to polish or to lick.

Born among the dispossessed, and matured in the hurly-burly of the frontier, the blows rained on him in his formative years would have dulled and frustrated most. But they managed to shape his hickory core into the leader and champion of a freedom-loving people. That is not to say that the stout hickory trunk was completely without knots and blemishes. There were indeed cracks and deep checks in it, some of which helped to make his life a stormy one. But on the whole the timber of which he was formed was overwhelmingly sound and lasting.

From chores on the small farms of his mother's relatives, he turned first to the trade of saddle making. But his forte lay in dealing with people, not with materials. Next he taught school for a time, hoping to improve himself, for he had no special training for such an undertaking. Then he apprenticed himself to the law in an office in Salisbury, North Carolina, managed admittance to the bar, and to celebrate the occasion, chose to make a trip back through the hills to the west to look over the new settlements there.

These communities along the Watauga and Holston had for a time been the state of Franklin, but that premature government had collapsed, and was now Washington County, again under North Carolina jurisdiction. The twenty-one-year-old Andrew Jackson was somewhat astonished to be offered the post of county solicitor, or prosecuting attorney. It was a man-size job in this rough-and-tumble community; but he took it, and the hickory cudgel he had become seemed equal to the occasion.

The tumultuous, yeasty life appealed to the rusty-haired, gangling, horse-faced young man, and he waded into it with gusto. His quick, brusque, determined ways were well fitted to the time and place, and his cool bravery, native intelligence, and complete honesty soon made him a marked man. It was a nose-twisting, ear-biting, eye-gouging period, when every man depended upon his own wits, strength, subtlety, and determination. It was surely no place for a "Milquetoast," and in the broad assortment of manhood encompassed in the thirty-six thousand inhabitants of the Territory of the United States of America South of the Ohio, Jackson was about as hard-baked and heavily spiced a "cookie" as you might encounter.

On the physical side, he could quite handily butt an opponent in the stomach with the "pint" of a rail, if need be, before the other man knew what was happening. But while he never avoided physical contest, as his years of soldiering in middle life so abundantly testify, his truly great achievements lay in the realm of other methods of approach. There would be another Tennesseean of the next generation who would gain fame by being "first with the most." While this may not have been true as far as Jackson's legal knowledge was concerned, it did pretty well picture him as respects personality and his resolve to see justice done. But whether his choice at any mo-

ment was fists, pistols, or words, he had a most formidable weapon
in his dazzling dark blue eyes. These pointed up the man's inherent
purpose and integrity, and they could flash chilling storm warnings
when he was aroused, which was not infrequently.

As was the custom in those days, the court, and the bevy of
attorneys dependent upon it for their fees, rode circuit and appeared
at all sessions as they were held in rotation in the more populous
communities or county seats. This, of course, brought him to Nashville, and, as an erstwhile boarder in the Donelson household, into
circumstances which were to profoundly affect his future.

As must be apparent by now, it was he to whom the unstable
Robards took such violent exception, and then made tracks to Kentucky, presumably to obtain permanent separation from his wife.

Although Jackson prospered from sizable fees as the chief counsel for local land and mercantile interests, this flurry over a woman
was probably to have far deeper bearing on his later life. Although
he was no longer a paying guest in the Donelson home and Rachel
had gone to live at her sister's, he did not feel that he had been freed
of responsibilities in the matter. The man had a penchant all his life
for righting wrongs; and it was quite likely that it was from this side
of his nature, rather than from any sentimental reaches it may have
had, that he at first continued to be involved.

It should perhaps be explained that though he was never one
to quail before another man, this unbending hickory rod became
something of a willow wand where the female sex was concerned.
He could be starched courtliness itself, but he did not have "a way"
with the ladies, being rather ill at ease where they were concerned,
especially in his younger years.

Surely there is not the slightest indication that the up-and-coming barrister pressed his suit on the desirable Rachel while she was in
temporary seclusion from her mother's home. However, when an opportunity came for her to go to live at some considerable distance
to the south in the Mississippi Territory, Jackson began to edge in
closer to developments.

This move involved a trip of about five hundred fifty miles down
the Natchez Trace, a series of Indian paths slowly evolving into a
pack trail, over which she would travel with a Colonel Stark. It was
a dangerous journey, and the young lawyer was genuinely concerned. True, Stark was of an age which would have pretty much
put him out of the running as a contender for the hand of his lovely
charge. But by this same token, or so Jackson seems to have reasoned,

he was also too old to qualify as her guardian and defender. So, whatever his motives were, he attached himself to the party and saw Rachel to her destination at the sturdy old plantation house, Springfield, still standing outside Natchez.

WOOED AT LEISURE AND MARRIED IN HASTE

Perhaps love flowered as their saddle train plodded along down the Trace, for it was then a trip far longer in days than it now is in hours. Still the hard-bitten young Andy left her there and returned to his circuit riding. It was not too many months, however, before the grapevine fed word down from Kentucky that Robards had *received* a divorce. Quite naturally this momentous word was hurried on to Natchez.

Bear in mind that the postal service did not then reach into Tennessee, and would not until statehood was achieved. Communication was largely by word of mouth carried by the very infrequent travelers through the wilderness spaces that lay between communities perhaps hundreds of miles apart. To have checked Kentucky law, or its rumor mills, would have entailed both time and effort. The word, as received, seemed probable, and in the fall of 1791 the impetuous young man set off for Mississippi. In November he married his Rachel there, and brought her back to Nashville. Then, not too long afterward, the fat was indeed in the fire. Robards, so it developed, had merely received permission to *sue* for divorce, and when he brought his suit to the Kentucky courts in 1793 he had a perfect case. His wife was indeed living with another man.

This time the divorce was speedily granted; but while Nashville received this further word in stride, it did breed a host of ugly implications. The young attorney had slipped up on a point of law. About the only thing for him to do was obtain another permit and remarry, which he promptly did. But quite conscious of what the eager gossips of both sexes could do with this tricky situation, he readied a pair of pistols for use on the first man indiscreet enough to give the matter any awkward or falacious twists. These pistols would be close at hand for most of the remainder of his life.

It had been in the previous year that Jackson received his first rather modest military appointment. The Indian wars had then blazed up again. But in the following year, that in which he had been rewed to Rachel, the natives were pretty well subdued and the Territory of Tennessee began to shape up. A road was then being hacked out of the forest wastes across the Cumberland plateau, and with its completion came a further great influx of settlers.

By 1796, Tennessee was ready for statehood. This was also a signal year in Jackson's career, for it was then that his name would begin to be heard, even if faintly at the outset, on the national scene. He had been chosen the state's sole representative in Congress, there to come face to face with forces with which he would contend over the years ahead. The rude, untamed, and rather boisterous West was already coming into conflict with the conservative East, and the forces of democracy and nationalism taking shape beyond the Alleghenies eventually came to rule the Republic largely through the person of Andrew Jackson. In the next year, 1797, he was appointed United States senator. But he served for a year only, resigning to take his place upon the bench of the Tennessee Supreme Court.

Following service there would come the military experiences. But the hickory log was still to be further carved and shaped along the frontier, where it was not until 1804 that a three-room cabin was built in the wilderness that would eventually develop into "The Hermitage," now a national shrine. Here he and Rachel spent many happy years developing their plantation.

The brace of pistols was called into use on several occasions, once even threatening no less heroic a figure than John Sevier, hero of King's Mountain, and at a time when he was governor of the state, but a political foe. His careless insinuation at a heated moment brought a sharp retort and a flying ball that fortunately did not find its mark, but gave evidence that the hasty act of years before was still not to be treated by innuendo.

As Jackson's name and fame spread, his detractors, largely out of pistol range, found the unfortunate matrimonial flaw in the rugged timber a convenient target. This was particularly so when, as champion of the so-called "democrats" of the new West, he began to loom as a dire threat to vested interests back East. With surprising thoroughness, and by every means at its disposal, this threatened group turned loose a continuing barrage of the most contemptible abuse, aimed at him, but falling principally upon his wife.

Whatever highly glossed social graces Rachel Jackson may have lacked by the foppish standards of a somewhat decadent society in high places along the seaboard, she was an abundant expression of the constructive forces that were planting civilization in the wilderness areas of the West. Her own contributions to what had been achieved locally since, as a girl, she had made the hazardous river journey to Nashville were sufficient by contrast with the life experiences of the great majority of her detractors to put the latter to abject shame. But their avalanche of slander was her undoing, and largely responsible for her death in 1828.

While she was not to be by the side of her husband in his hours of supreme triumph as he took his place in the White House, she was still very much in his mind and heart. To him the slings and arrows of outrageous fortune which had mortally wounded her were typical of the thinking and purposes of a spent and outmoded Republicanism. He would do his best to herd its supporters from the national scene, and the driving force to accomplish the task drew much of its fire and vehemence from his reaction to the despicable drive his opponents had centered about an unfortunate episode in private lives.

This is not to say that Jackson's influence upon the American scene would have been materially less profound if shorn of this Robards matter. By birth and upbringing he was very much the product of the frontier, and of an area which would have an intense influence upon subsequent national developments. Attention from here on must focus primarily beyond the Appalachians, for the West was a dominant factor in American affairs throughout the nineteenth century, and the age of Jackson forecast what sort of impress that huge area promised to leave upon the country's future.

AN IMPORTANT EARLY HIGHWAY

Communication was bound to play a large part in the winning of the transmountain section, and while it is close at hand a brief look at the famous Natchez Trace might be of interest. More and more frequent use made it into a well-traveled highway. By 1796 mail was being carried over it to the city at its lower extremity on the shores of the Mississippi, then our southern outpost, poised above the Spanish in uncertain control of New Orleans.

John L. Sweeny rode the mail as often as his services were required during an eight-year period up to 1804, allowing three weeks of hard riding to complete the eleven-hundred-mile round trip from Nashville to Natchez and return. Beside letters and documents in his saddle pouch, he "toted" provisions, a blanket, and a raucous tin trumpet. The latter not only permitted him to give ample warning of his approach, but also to scare the living daylights out of the unsuspecting and unprepared.

The Trace was for many years to come the pathway over which the flatboat crews made their way back from the end of their water journey at New Orleans. This was the backwoodsman's thrill of a lifetime, and one of his few probable contacts with civilization. But as he plodded his way north through mile after mile of wilderness, the gold and silver coins received from the sale of his cargo made him the likely subject for the ministrations of river pirates turned road agents, who came to infest this lonely trail. In fact it was the hangout of one of the most notorious racketeers of the early 1800s, "Ma" Murrell's boy John, born in sordid surroundings in the river town of Memphis. His gangster combine, the Mystic Brotherhood, traveled up and down it to terrorize the whole lower Mississippi Valley over many years.

Jackson often used it, and perhaps one of the most notable passages over it was to carry out his orders. His victory over the British at New Orleans, won without knowledge on his part that a peace treaty had been signed the previous Christmas Eve, seemed so decisive that he wished word of it to reach President Madison in Washington at the earliest possible moment. The dispatch was handed to a youngish colonel, the second of the three Wade Hamptons, and father of the Civil War hero, and the urgency of his mission impressed upon him.

Choosing three horses, one to bear their provisions and meager gear, and the others to ride, the colonel and his Negro servant slid into the saddles and set out at a gallop up the road to Natchez, and then on up the Trace. Ten days later, and twelve hundred miles farther along, the message of the defeat of the British forces was handed into the White House. Even the Mongol tribesmen of old could have done no better.

Soon there will be another courier, this one dashing south over this same Trace, bearing an important presidential proclamation.

XV

We Begin to Reach toward the Pacific

I sincerely wish you may find it convenient to come here. The pleasure of the trip will be less than you expect but the utility greater. It will make you adore your own country, it's soil, it's climate, it's equality, liberty, laws, people & manners. My God! How little do my country men know what precious blessings they are in possession of, and which no other people on earth enjoy. I confess I had no idea of it myself. While we shall see multiplied instances of Europeans going to live in America, I will venture to say no man now living will ever see an instance of an American removing to Europe & continuing there. Come then & see the proofs of this, and on your return add your testimony to that of every thinking American, in order to satisfy our countrymen how much it is their interest to preserve uninfected by contagion those peculiarities in their government & manners to which they are indebted for these blessings.—Letter of Thomas Jefferson *To James Monroe,* Paris, June 17, 1785.

AS HE galloped into western Pennsylvania to take command of the Legion and train it for the subduing of the Indians in the Northwest Territory, Anthony Wayne encountered early resistance that finally grew into open insurrection and bloodshed as the "Whiskey Rebellion." It, together with controversies stemming from Kentucky, was a manifestation of men shut off from markets. Spain, in possession of New Orleans, had turned the key and barred the way to the open sea down the great river courses of the Ohio and the Mississippi.

While the immediate cause of the uprising across the mountains in Pennsylvania may have been the imposition of an excise tax, it was basically a protest over this throttle hold on cheap water transportation and access to markets. Grain, which could not flow out from the back country at a profit when packed on horse- or muleback, could be advantageously so handled when distilled as liquor. But as soon as a tax was levied upon it, the profits were wiped out, the settlers were deprived of a market for their grain, and promptly rebelled. It took the eloquence of Albert Gallatin to turn the tide of feeling and stop civil strife, and in the West the attempt to collect the tax was looked upon as a test of federal strength. There was dissatisfaction and even disaffection there, which Citizen Genêt had hoped to use to further his purposes, and it would continue to simmer for a number of years.

Further on along the left bank of the Ohio the Kentuckians were tense because of this same situation. The youngest of the states had filled in quite rapidly, and there was pressing need to turn excess products into money to meet payments on land bought at speculators' prices. Transportation being what it then was, their sole hope of reaching a market was via New Orleans, and with that port closed to them, they were in sore straits. When the new government, then centered in Philadelphia, could provide them with no relief, they began to conduct their own international relations, guided by necessity rather than blind loyalty. In fact "loyalty" would be a bit tenuous and considerably opportunist throughout much of the newly settled country in the Mississippi basin for the next decade.

The situation brings Wayne's detractor and disloyal second-in-command, James Wilkinson, back into the picture, and requires a quick look at some of his earlier enterprises. Following the Revolution, he had drifted out into Kentucky, and at twenty-seven set himself up at storekeeping at Lexington. After about two years he shifted some twenty miles up the trail toward Louisville, founded Frankfort, and carried on his trading business from there. Soon he, too, was in the deadening grip of the Spaniards far down the river. When he heard something could be done about it by a few exchanges beneath the table, he decided to try his fine conspiratorial hand at the game.

Loading a flatboat with surplus merchandise, he headed toward New Orleans. Arriving there, he promptly sized up the situation, and found it simple. You merely crossed the right palms with silver, and presto, the bars were down and your goods were admitted to trade in local markets. This sort of thing was just his dish of tea, and once in the confidence of the easygoing Spaniards, his native charm, backed by boundless audacity, quickly opened a roadway to easy money. Not only were his personal concerns fairly well solved, but he took it upon himself to become the chosen vessel by which certain of Kentucky's vexing problems might be lightened.

By the time the group of earnest men were laboring over the

Constitution in Philadelphia in the summer of 1787, he was having his own way with the representatives of proud Spain, and eager to play for bigger stakes. Silver in itchy palms did wonders, but why not give this matter another twist? Fear is quite a motivation, if you can exercise it; so he set out to give the powers-that-be at New Orleans a bad case of the jitters. He stoutly maintained he could round up enough frontiersmen with long rifles to descend the river and hurl Spain's borders far to the west along the Gulf. In fact the Kentuckians were ready and anxious to do just that, looked to him for leadership, and he would provide it unless the Spaniards were willing to play ball with him.

He soon had a deal worked out. Presumably he was to stand as a bulwark between them and the hotheaded men back up in the interior. For this supposed service he was most certainly on some sort of retainer for many years, and in return gave little by way of an earnest of his intents beyond furtively accepting citizenship in New Spain.

Between profitable blockade running and a kickback from the Spanish, it would seem that he should have become wealthy. But his extravagant ways soon had him in financial difficulties. His business foundered, and like Anthony Wayne, he accepted a commission in the Army primarily because of the salary and possible side money that went with it. Also as an officer of the United States Army, he was in an even better position to connive with the grandees down in the Crescent City.

AMERICA'S GIGANTIC MARCH ACROSS THE MISSISSIPPI

Then came a rapid shift in the whole picture. Napoleon had risen to power in France in 1799, and with a characteristic imperial gesture, had soon taken back Louisiana from Spain and made certain moves which looked convincingly as though he intended to restore New France to the position it held when Montcalm went down to defeat on the Plains of Abraham in front of Quebec some forty years before.

Immediately the outlook for the interior settlements turned even darker, and there was a clamor for roads to take the place of inadequate pack trails. Since there was then reasonable doubt whether the federal government was empowered to engage in such enterprises, Jefferson, as he assumed office, made another type of approach to this vexatious problem. Soon after his inauguration, he dispatched Robert Livingston as ambassador to France, providing him with two million dollars to buy New Orleans and the Floridas.

The envoy did his best through several months, but without results. Thinking to strengthen his hand, Jefferson then sent over his neighbor and close friend, James Monroe. This second gentleman was hardly ashore when he and Livingston were confronted with a bewildering proposition. The first consul would sell them not only New Orleans, but that city plus the whole huge Louisiana territory for fifteen million dollars, providing they acted at once. Bonaparte, confronted with war against England, needed cash, and further preferred not to have this overseas possession fall to the British while he was struggling with them closer at home.

It was a tough nut to crack. The envoys had nothing approaching the necessary authorization. Yet in the eight weeks or more needed to get word home and a reply back, the Little Corsican might well change his mind, or make other arrangements. Facing charges up to and including treason, the two gentlemen gambled with destiny and closed the deal.

Word of what they had undertaken is said to have given the strict legalist in the White House some of his most disturbed moments in official life. Yet we wonder. Within but a few days of dispatching Monroe to assist Livingston, he had made a quiet appeal to the Congress for funds for a reconnoissance of the Missouri Valley, to be conducted by army men, and at a time when that area was still securely in French hands. What his real purpose in this enterprise may have been has not been disclosed. He had long mistrusted French ambitions, particularly after Genêt's intentions became apparent, had envisioned America being forced into the British orbit as an alternative to becoming a French pawn, and may have felt the need of military knowledge of an area which might soon have to be seized to preserve our nationalism. Also, at the time Genêt was functioning, Jefferson had organized a scientific exploration under the auspices of the American Philosophical Society, to be conducted by André Michaux, the French botanist. This was to have been a transcontinental affair, but the scientist had been welded into the Genêt escapade. While Jefferson's intentions are a bit cloudy, he seemingly felt that Louisiana *should* be ours, and was preparing for such an eventuality.

Before the funds for an exploring party were made available, the news of the remarkable transaction at the French court broke.

Public astonishment knew no bounds when it was first realized we had acquired this immense stretch of "howling wilderness." By and large the East was aligned against ratification of the purchase, but the South, and especially the West, lined up behind it, the deal received congressional sanction, and turned out to be one of the greatest blessings ever to befall our land.

Now that we owned the whole midsection of the continent back to the spurs of the Rockies, the logical thing to do was find out what we had bought. Thus Congress dutifully gave the President the exploration fund he had requested while the matter was still in the crystal-ball stage.

LEWIS AND CLARK HEAD FOR THE PACIFIC

Peter Jefferson, pioneer surveyor and father of Thomas, had penetrated much uncharted Virginia territory in his day, and the unsatisfied urge of the explorer seems to have been lodged in his eldest son. Curiosity in regard to the wilderness was very much a tradition in Albemarle County, and it welled up especially in Meriwether Lewis, born just across the southwestern mountains from Shadwell, Tom Jefferson's boyhood home.

The man destined to become our third President knew his neighbors well, and although thirty-one years the senior, had his eye on young Lewis as he was going through his formative years. Of him, he later wrote: "He . . . was remarkable even in his infancy for enterprise, boldness, and discretion. When only eight years of age, he habitually went out, in the dead of night, alone with his dogs, into the forest to hunt raccoon and opossum, which, seeking their food in the night, can then only be taken. In this exercise no season or circumstance could obstruct his purpose, plunging through the winter's snows and frozen streams in pursuit of his object."

Perhaps, too, like Jefferson's own grandson, Lewis had worn neither hat nor shoes until he was ten. In either event, here we have a thumbnail sketch of a true pioneer. A volunteer during the Whiskey Rebellion, an army ensign in 1795, and a captain by 1800, young Lewis was called to the White House by his favorably impressed mentor, and became secretary to the President in 1801.

In that less hurried era there would have been room for extended conversations about the great untracked area extending from the western reaches of Virginia, Pennsylvania, and New York clear through to the western ocean. How natural then, now that Louisiana had been purchased and Congress had authorized its exploration, that Jefferson should have chosen Meriwether Lewis to be one of the leaders of the exploring party. But it was a hazardous journey, and evil might befall it, so the command was split.

Quite as naturally, too, the choice of the co-leader fell on William Clark, an army lieutenant, also born to the Albemarle tradition, and the redheaded brother of George Rogers Clark, with whom Jefferson had worked so closely during the Revolution. The plans were perfected in Washington by June of 1803. Equipment exclusive of the boats was assembled at the old Schuylkill Arsenal, still in active operation in Philadelphia, where a record of these properties is still on file. The President was a stickler for detail and records, and he saw to it that every member of the party was provided with a journal and notebooks, with waterproof containers to keep them from ruin when a boat or canoe suddenly overturned.

The weak spot in all this was that while he sent competent woodsmen, there were no members chosen with sufficient scientific background to properly interpret data they were bound to encounter. Considering Jefferson's close association with scientific bodies of his day, it would seem that this phase would have had better attention, providing it was to be something more than merely a military survey.

The party was mobilized at Pittsburgh, and proceeded down the Ohio and up the Mississippi to St. Louis, where it arrived in December 1803. It was the intention to start on up the Missouri at once, but the way was barred. The French had not bothered to send over colonial personnel during the brief period they had again had possession of the area, retaining instead the Spaniards who had previously held the posts. And since no official word of the transfer had been received by the commandant at St. Louis, he refused to permit Lewis and Clark to advance. They were thus forced to make winter quarters on the east side of the great river, opposite the Missouri's mouth.

Their main party consisted of nine young Kentuckians, fourteen soldiers from the regular army who had volunteered for the trip, two French boatmen, an interpreter, a hunter, and a black servant of Captain Clark's. There was also a corporal, six additional soldiers, and nine more boatmen who were to accompany them as far as the Mandan nation, and so through what was presumed to be the more dangerous of the Indian country.

Beside their essential tools, arms, ammunition, and food, they carried no less than fourteen bales of presents for the Indians, including gaudy uniform coats, medals, flags, knives, and tomahawks for the more important chiefs, and looking glasses, scarves, beads, trinkets and gewgaws in great demand by all the native peoples. These goods, their stores, and the members of the party were to occupy three boats.

The largest was fifty-three feet long, drew but three feet of water when loaded, had a mast and sail, as well as places for twenty-two oarsmen. It was decked for about ten feet at bow and stern to form shelter for bunks, while the sides between these decks were lined with lockers which might be raised to form a shield behind which riflemen could find protection during an attack. The two smaller craft carried in one six oarsmen, in the other seven. Two horsemen were to pace the vessels, riding along the banks, to be on guard, or ready to canter off in search of game as needed.

Word of the holdup was, of course, relayed to Washington, and in March, Lewis was made the agent of the government to receive the transfer of Louisiana at St. Louis. Our friend General Wilkinson would be one of those on hand downstream at New Orleans to go through the formalities at that crucial spot.

Finally, on the afternoon of May 14, 1804, the expedition crossed the Mississippi, entered the Missouri, and headed up that stream. Its mission was to explore it to its source, then cross the height of land, make contact with western-flowing rivers and follow them to the Pacific. What a journey it was to be, the detailed daily account of its manifold experiences forming one of the great travel books of all time. Keen observers both, beside being intelligent and judicial men, its leaders described for the first time a wonderland previously seen, except for the Indians, by a very limited number of trappers and Hudson's Bay Company men. It was not a scientific report, but it was an interesting and exciting account. Clark was the map maker, and on his reliable charts the party can be followed across a number of our northwestern states.

The first winter was spent in the Mandan villages in North Dakota among the interesting Indians with whom the remnant of the Norsemen, if not the mythical Welsh party, may well have joined. New Year's Day 1805 was celebrated there in 30 degree below zero temperatures by a stirring buffalo dance. The sacks of presents were already being put to good use.

By mid-March they were rebuilding and adding to their fleet of boats and having a little trouble with their French-Canadian interpreter, Toussaint Charbonneau, who had signed to go through to the

Pacific with them. British traders, still trying to hamper American
efforts, did their best to dissuade him. Finally the two leaders got
the man straightened around, and while he himself proved to be no
prize, it was through him that the expedition was to find the one
person who, with the exception of its leaders, was to contribute most
heavily to its success.

THE LITTLE BIRD WOMAN

Not only were the Indians adept at kidnaping engaging young
squaws, but they also acquired them as prisoners in their frequent
encounters. Thus a girl of the Shoshone Indians to the west had
been captured some years since by the Minnetarees, and sold as a
slave to this Charbonneau, and become one of his wives. Her name
was Sacajawea—meaning "Bird Woman"—and she and her two-
month-old baby accompanied the party as it started up river again
on April 7. During the next twenty months she would cover no less
than five thousand miles as one of its members. This small personable woman alone among thirty hard-bitten soldiers and woodsmen
might well have bred trouble. The interpreter husband, however,
seemed essential, and Lewis and Clark were taking the soldier's
"calculated risk."

By mid-June of 1805 they were making the tiring eighteen-mile-
portage around the site of present-day Great Falls, Montana; and in
July were passing through the deep gorge of the Missouri, just south
of Cascade. They were now using eight canoes and seeing their first
Rocky Mountain big-horn sheep gambol up and down canyon walls
so sheer there seemingly could be no footholds for the nimble creatures. By the end of the month they were at the triple forks of the
great river, and coming closer to the country where Sacajawea had
been taken captive as a girl.

Since they were near the top of the Continental Divide, the
going was rougher and more arduous. They must soon abandon their
canoes and find their way across to the headwaters of streams flowing
toward that limitless western lake into which the Indians thought
the sun plunged each night. They would need horses, which the
natives had; and so they split the party to seek out Shoshone camps,
in whose country they now were.

It was Sunday, August 11, that Captain Lewis made the first
fleeting contact with them, and two days later before he could per-
suade them to meet face to face. Then, with moccasins and boots

stripped off, a small circle formed of white and red men solemnly passed the pipe of peace between them. While this tribal group seemed disposed to be friendly, there were traces of suspicion which lasted through the following week.

Then on Saturday morning, when Captain Clark and his party, which included Charbonneau and his wife, Sacajawea, landed near by, the Indians again became apprehensive. But hardly was the little birdlike woman ashore than she began to squeal and dance with joy, running her fingers into her mouth as a sign the several Indians approaching were of her own tribe. Then as some of the squaws found courage to follow along, the tiny creature let out a whoop of joy, and with her papoose bouncing on her back, dashed to one of the younger women and threw her arms about her. They had been childhood companions and taken prisoner on the same day a few years before, but the other had managed to escape and rejoin her own people.

Clark, welcomed by Lewis, was taken by him to meet with the chiefs in a council. Realizing that little Sacajawea would be indispensable as an interpreter, they quickly sent for her. As she approached, all eyes turned toward her, while her own swept over the dark-skinned male faces in the gathered circle. Once again there was a shriek of joy, and she ran and threw her blanket over young chief Cameahwait—"The One Who Never Walks"—embracing him and weeping profusely. He was none other than her own brother.

After they had conversed briefly, the short parley got under way, the Indian woman hardly able to speak or to contain herself because of her great joy. The canoes having been brought up to the site of the joint camp, they were unloaded and a canopy made of the sails stretched between four great trees. There, about four that afternoon, a more formal council assembled in its shade, and the Indians were delighted when it was proposed to open a trade route to stretch from the Mississippi through their lands to the western ocean. While they were in so pleasant a frame of mind, the need for horses to carry the party over the hills was broached. With a little less enthusiasm they promised to see what they could do, especially since the mounts furnished would be paid for in goods.

Presents were then distributed, and the explorers' own stores and equipment shown and explained to the savages. Perhaps nothing among the latter caught their fancy more than an air rifle. It was, to their way of thinking, a gift direct from the Great Spirit, and, having no need for precious powder, "great medicine" indeed.

Although relations had become much more cordial, it is improbable that the necessary horses would have been caught and brought in had not Sacajawea been present at the meeting and left in camp to stimulate their collection, while advance parties scouted out the route just ahead. Good faith kept with the Indians by the leaders on all occasions no doubt played its part, too, for the Clark brothers, George Rogers and William, were among the most effective Indian envoys this country ever produced. But the whole success of this promising enterprise might have been badly delayed, or unfortunately modified at this juncture, had it not been for the fortunate train of circumstances that placed the little Bird Woman among them.

In August they were on their way west again, and in three months had pressed down to tidewater near the mouth of the mighty Columbia. The waters of the lower river were wrapped in dense fogs, and as they made their way cautiously toward the ocean the thought was ever with them that their inconsiderate government had failed to send a ship to bear them home by sea. This fact compounded by the chill November dampness was highly depressing. At home they had actually been given up as dead, and had they realized it, their spirits would have gone even lower.

But at last the sun broke out, and Clark penned one of his few jubilant lines in his journal—"Ocian in view! O! the joy." So there they wintered, evaporating a store of salt from the sea water, and resting against the hard drive back upstream and over the mountains. It was July of 1806 before they were in the Montana country once again. Little Sacajawea was now guiding Clark over the old buffalo trail, through what was later to be called Bozeman Pass, as he explored the Yellowstone River. Lewis, with the remainder of the party, was returning along a branch of the Missouri.

It was at this time that the latter encountered one of the most unfortunate episodes of the whole expedition. He and three of his men were near where Dupuyer stands today, when they fell in with eight Indians of the Gros Ventre, or "Big Belly," tribe. The natives seemed friendly, so they camped with them during the night. In the morning, however, the tricky savages tried to make off with the explorers' guns and horses, and in the ensuing encounter two of the Indians were killed entirely in self-defense. Let it be said to the everlasting credit of both of these renowned leaders that this was the only instance of the spilling of human blood during nearly three years in this vast wilderness.

Meanwhile Clark was meeting with rather less trying experiences. Several days' search along the Yellowstone had failed to turn up cottonwood trees as large as he would have liked for canoes. So two smaller craft were hewed out, and planks placed between them to form a catamaran. Over the planks was lashed a decking of buffalo hides. The seven men then loaded on their implements and meager supplies, together with Sacajawea and tiny Baptiste, her papoose, and climbing aboard themselves, shot the rapids down that crooked stream, joining Captain Lewis at its mouth on August 12.

By the twenty-third of September in 1806, the expedition was back at St. Louis, where General Wilkinson was now in command, and ordering a bit of exploring done on his own. There it broke up and Charbonneau was paid off, receiving five hundred dollars for his somewhat inconspicuous services. But his little slave wife, Sacajawea, who had been well-nigh indispensable, received nothing, not even her freedom. The proud Shoshones now honor her in the tribal cemetery on the Wind River Reservation in Wyoming. Tradition among them says that an aged woman, who had accompanied Lewis and Clark so many years before, died and was buried there in 1884. A monument not only marks her grave, but also that of her son Baptiste, who grew up to be a reputable guide, and as recompense for courtesies shown a German prince making a trip through the West early in the nineteenth century, was taken as the latter's companion on an extensive tour of Europe.

Sacajawea has a statue in her memory on the capitol grounds at Bismarck, North Dakota, about two score miles from the point where she joined the historic expedition, while her contributions to its success are most interestingly recorded on the novel historical markers in Montana. She is also finding a secure place in the hearts of American children through several entertaining books of which she is the heroine. And few women in our history are more deserving of their affection.

XVI

Our Frontiers are Further Explored

For a hundred years after Jefferson, the real history of the U. S. was the settlement of the land between the Appalachians and the Pacific Ocean. It was one of the greatest migrations in human history. It went in waves: the Kentucky fever, the Oregon and Texas fevers, the Gold Rush, the Kansas fever. Zebulon Pike announced in 1810 that a large part of America was hopeless desert, but by 1850 this, too, had yielded to Mormon resolution and irrigation and long-horned steer. It all happened so fast that neither the Mexicans, who lost the empty half of their country to the infiltrators of "manifest destiny," nor the bison, which were reduced from an ocean to a curio in three human generations, quite knew what hit them. And where the settlers went, the "civilizers"—women, preachers, scribes, gamblers, speculators, tradesmen, schoolmarms and men of business—went too. The tempo was such that Kit Carson, in October, 1849, while trying to rescue a Mrs. White from some Apaches in the Southwest, found near Mrs. White's still-warm corpse in the abandoned Indian camp a novel published that year in Boston called *Kit Carson, Prince of the Gold Hunters.* He was duly touched and embarrassed by the find.—"The American Experience," from *Life's Picture History of Western Man.*

I T   W I L L be recalled that Mr. Penn and Lord Baltimore had found themselves involved in a long drawn out wrangle that had had its inception in the very indifferent maps available at that time. Even a hundred years later, when the negotiations for peace between England and her former colonies were in progress, the charts on which some of the boundaries were to be based were very faulty. This was particularly so as respects the division between the thirteen states and Canada. In the West, the Mississippi River was a most convenient line of demarcation, and a basing point for arbitrary bounds. At least it was for as much of its course as was reasonably well known, but little that was definite was known of it much above the mouth of the Wisconsin, where the French had long ago established a post at Prairie du Chien. Trappers and voyageurs were using the narrowing stream, and there were even Hudson's Bay posts on its far upper reaches, but no one could say for certain where this mighty watercourse had its origin, just how far to the north it extended. In a day when virtually every gasoline filling station has its rack of free but dependable maps, this is hard to understand, nonetheless, it was so.

The matter had come up in 1803 in an attempt to more exactly locate the common boundary between this country and Canada, when it had a bearing on what we had acquired by the Louisiana Purchase. Since our relations with England then seemed to be going from bad to worse, the commandant of the upper Louisiana Territory, General Wilkinson, felt it might be well to know the very point at which this important landmark truly began.

While Lewis and Clark were moving down the Columbia toward the Pacific, he chose one of his young officers with the resounding name of Zebulon Montgomery Pike and put him in charge of twenty men in keelboats. On August 9, 1805, he dispatched them upstream on this quest. It was several months too late in the year for the start of such a venture, for by November 1 the party was frozen in on the west bank of the river in what is now Morrison County, Minnesota, near the beginning of the lake country.

A blockhouse was erected, in which the men settled down, while Pike started off on a sledge journey in early December for a preliminary look at a country deep in snow and with its streams icebound. He managed to work his way up about as far as present-day Pine River, and was then forced to return.

Hardly was he back in camp again when a fire destroyed the tents and threatened to blow up their ammunition. But he had a job to do, and at the head of his dispirited men mounted on snowshoes and packing their remaining supplies on their backs, he pushed off to the north. This man Pike was about to prove himself a brute for punishment.

On February 1 they reached Leech Lake thoroughly exhausted. The young lieutenant was certain this was the great river's main source. Two weeks later, at what is now known as Lake Cass, he was inclined to concede that this body of water might be an *upper* source.

He parleyed with the local Indians, who decided that since his men were neither French nor British they must be "white Indians." To the savages his questions in regard to where the river had its beginning seemed a bit academic, but in return for his telling them about the new kind of Great White Father they had recently acquired in Washington, they were as helpful as they could be in a vague sort of way.

By early March he was back at the remains of the blockhouse; and when the river thawed, he headed down toward St. Louis, where he arrived after nearly nine months of the most rigorous kind of exploring. The information which he had brought was largely speculation and hearsay, and it would still be a number of years before the question would be satisfactorily answered. However, if he thought he deserved a furlough, or at least a long breathing spell after his exertions, he was to be disappointed. Wilkinson needed him for another little jaunt, and in quite a different direction.

PIKE'S JOURNEY INTO THE SOUTHWEST

This one was seemingly based on Wilkinson's own needs, or so it would appear, for there is doubt that it had authorization from Washington. However, some fifty odd Indian chiefs were just about due on their way back to their lodges and hogans from a powwow with Jefferson in the nation's capital. A military escort for them to their points of origin could serve as a convenient pretext for its beginning, and some justifiable reason would surely crop up for its continuance. There were other rivers beside the Missouri which fed into the Mississippi from the west, and perhaps it would be well to investigate their sources as well.

So another group was assembled for the twenty-seven-year-old lieutenant to command, and readied for the trip. It consisted of Wilkinson's own son as its other commissioned officer, together with a surgeon, a sergeant, and sixteen privates. Thus it was not at all a formidable party, but no doubt the governor of upper Louisiana knew what he was about. He usually did.

By the middle of July the Indian chiefs had put in an appearance, and on the fifteenth of that month, in the year 1806, Pike was once more on his way to high adventure. Leaving from St. Louis, he, this time, started up the Missouri, heading for the Osage villages. From them he took off overland and entered Kansas somewhere in the Fort Scott area. Then, bearing to the northwest, he visited the Pawnee towns along the Republican River in what would in a few years be southern Nebraska.

On this latter march he encountered something that gave him

a few moments of grave concern. A large detachment of Mexican cavalry had passed through but so short a time before that the grass was still heavily matted from the passage of the horses' hoofs. Fortunately the party seemed to be headed toward home. It had been a narrow miss, but so far a clean one; for had the two parties clashed, his chance to examine the countryside could very well have terminated here deep in what would not be unmistakably American territory until after the treaty of 1819.

The distances were considerable, and progress on foot was necessarily slow. This journey had not been furnished with funds by a willing Congress, and neither had a President and his secretary planned it, so that it was very much on its own. The middle of September had rolled around by the time it was ready to leave the Pawnee villages behind.

Since the Spanish colonial forces seemed to have moved on, and in the direction in which he chose to travel, Pike set off in their wake, headed southwest. The Spaniards had been roaming this country since the time of Coronado nearly three hundred years before. Now the Americans were to have a look at what they believed they had lately purchased from Napoleon.

Like the far better equipped party just closing its magnificent journey further to the north, Pike also carried a small supply of presents. Melgares, captain of the Spanish cavalry company preceding him, had been busy leaving the flag of Spain in all the Indian camps along his route, so the young American officer saw to it that they had the Stars and Stripes as well. He had found Indian villages flying the British flag on the previous trip; and so, if flags would help, he would court allegiance to the United States. But just what the Indians themselves thought of all this is not known. No doubt they were of the opinion the white men had some strange pastimes of their own.

Near the center of Kansas the party came upon the Arkansas River where that stream's arching course is testified to by the name of present-day Great Bend. Keeping along its north bank, Pike was now traversing a route which in a few years would be one of the most famous trails of the Old West, and which the report he was already compiling as he moved along would help to bring into being. Since the country was alive with buffalo, food was no problem. The Indians were not too great a threat either; so when his potential enemies on horseback gave evidence they were heading into New Mexico to winter, he felt safe in dividing his party.

Young Wilkinson, with several companions, was headed back downstream toward headquarters to make a preliminary report, while Pike and his reduced force continued on up the Arkansas. Already they could see the high mountains to the west, their peaks a dazzling blue in the clear, crisp fall air, and they headed toward them.

By mid-November the party was near Las Animas in Colorado, where the Arkansas is joined by a number of streams flowing into it from the face of the mountain wall that rises abruptly from the boundless eastern plains. Surely the air was already crisp with frost, so it was perhaps with more courage than sound judgment that he plunged on into the high Sierras. He had lived through the past harsh winter, but none of its experiences was as devastating as the weeks just ahead would prove. As the elevation increased, the snows grew deeper and the cold more intense. But perhaps urgent need to get this not entirely official excursion out of the way as soon as possible drove him forward.

Still following along the general course of the Arkansas, but through heavily broken country, he passed by, but could not ascend, the "Grand Peak" which today bears his name. Almost at once he began to bog down under the force of the elements.

By Christmas Day 1806, he was near what is now Salida, at seven thousand feet elevation and in sore distress. Zero temperatures, deep snow, and complete lack of game had put him and his men in a most perilous state. Struggling in mountainous snowbanks as best they could, they arranged shelter of sorts, but they ached from cold and exhaustion, and faced prostration and starvation. Pikes Peak, fifty miles to the east of them now, could easily have become a mighty tombstone for the whole group.

By the middle of January they were totally without food, and had been so for four days. The jig was pretty nearly up, and as it was too late to measure consequences, Pike and a few of those in better condition determined to sally forth and either find something to eat or freeze to death in the snowbanks.

But a kind providence had other plans. A small "gang of buffalo" slogging through the snow appeared, were fallen upon, and there was meat to eat once again. Still it was only a stopgap, and four days later the larder was empty and they were once more face to face with starvation. Talk as glibly as he would about families and friends back home, the young commander could not turn the minds of his companions away from their hunger and utter misery.

Then what seems a heartless plan, but which was perhaps the only logical one under their straitened circumstances, was worked out. Pike would leave the seemingly doomed men behind, and with those fit for the journey, try to beat his way out of the mountain fastness to hoped for succor for them all. After seven days of grueling struggle, he and ten companions came to a river which proved to be the headwaters of the Rio Grande, near what is now the southern border of Colorado.

Although he had some considerable knowledge of the lay of the land and he had been heading due south from a point far up in the western mountains, he claimed he was certain he had come out on the Red River. This belief, which he stoutly maintained for the remainder of his short life, has always given some of his readers the feeling he was perhaps closer to Wilkinson and certain traitorous plans than one might like to think. However, he was free from the strangulation of the mountains, so he erected a small "fort" and began to make moves which would tend to indicate he knew much better where he was than he dared to admit.

FRIJOLES, FANDANGOS, AND FROLIC

Among those who had escaped the clutches of the higher hills was the surgeon from Illinois, Dr. John Robinson. Back at home, a merchant in Kaskaskia had made a request of him. If the medic's duties ever chanced to take him to the Spanish town of Santa Fe, would he do his best to locate a French trader thought to be there? This man had absconded with goods consigned to him, and papers to prove his deceitful ways had been entrusted to Robinson in hope he might make the contact, and perhaps effect restitution or payment. Since the doctor was a civilian, this looked to his superior like an excellent pretext behind which he might be sent on to Santa Fe, a matter of a hundred miles, and get in a little fancy spying at that outpost. So Pike bid him godspeed and started him on his way.

Evidence that he arrived safely came rather promptly when a dragoon and Indian companion dropped by the little fort on what had the appearance of a chance visit. To their artless questions, Pike managed confusing answers. Then there was another call a little later on by two French trappers, which was also perhaps not as casual as it seemed. February was rapidly slipping by, and the stricken men who had been left behind might by now be on the verge of cannibalism, or even frozen corpses. But suddenly a Spanish cavalryman, one Don

Bartholomew Fernandez, at the head of a hundred mounted men, moved in sight. While Pike's nine remaining companions were for shooting it out, their leader very evidently had specific instructions to cover such an occason. He was, it seems, to be very chary about giving offense under any circumstances to our Spanish neighbors. That may have been military caution, or it could have been that Wilkinson was still on a retainer. So Pike promptly surrendered, which action proved a wise decision.

As the Spanish commander began to gently shepherd his little band of captives toward Santa Fe, he left sufficient men behind with instructions to drive back into the hills and bring out such Americans as were still alive among those who had been left to their fate in that outsized icebox. By the greatest of good fortune all had survived, and were returned to civilization. Still two among them would be cripples to the end of their lives from frostbitten feet; and this was at a time when there was no such thing as extra combat pay, and no indemnification for service disabilities.

What had recently looked like the end for the whole party back there in the hills near Salida began now to appear but the beginning of a jubilant Cook's Tour. There were many little towns tucked along the banks of the Rio Grande as it flowed south through the full depth of New Mexico, and each tried to outdo the one before it by way of entertainment. There was a long round of dinners, fandangos, and other festivities. But these were as nothing when compared with the beautiful, warmhearted, soft-spoken, amorous Spanish girls with which each town abounded.

For a soldier's report, Pike really pulled all the stops and played up the señoritas in a grand and surging crescendo. The extravagant description to which he treated them was perhaps born principally of welcome relief from the rather somber weeks and months just passed through, but his winged and gilded words were to have a profound effect upon a coming generation. Among the more sober notes which he sounded were some realistic trade facts. These, too, were to exert a strong pull among those whose hands fairly itched at the thought of Spanish silver coins trickling through their fingers.

His first meeting with the governor at Santa Fe was a little on the cool side. But relations were much less frigid after that grandee got possession of the detailed journal Pike had been penning along the line of march. Also Pike soon found it would be a waste of time trying to delude this gentleman about the real reasons for his presence at the edge of his bailiwick, for Dr. Robinson had been plied with questions very much to the governor's profit before the lieutenant had arrived on the scene.

Still Pike and his companions were not to consider themselves prisoners. Their captor went to great lengths to make this clear, so why couldn't they be friends? The whole party would, of course, have to appear before the governor farther to the south at Chihuahua, in *Old* Mexico, but that was merely a formality.

Looking over the young American commander's garments, the governor decided that the term "seedy" would be a gross understatement for his present appearance. So this well-disposed host, anxious that his charge make the best possible impression at his next official encounter, pressed upon him a brand-, spanking-new shirt and silk neckcloth, made by the governor's own sister, and sent out to him from Spain. Surely the Spaniards were leaning far over backward to be hospitable and make a favorable impression.

Pike, now clad in his new finery, was once more feasted, and then started to his next appointment at the trading center far to the south. Captain Melgares, whose cavalry he had so narrowly avoided back on the Kansas plains, was in charge of the armed escort. He quickly became as boon a companion as had Fernandez, sending messengers ahead to announce their arrival in the long succession of towns, so that there might be more fandangos, more dinner parties, and of course more dark-haired and flashing-eyed señoritas to make life merry.

After relief from death in the frigid mountain fastness and other trying ordeals in the Minnesota country, spring in Mexico was a healing and exhilarating balm. Subject to kind ministrations beyond his wildest hopes, Pike responded by further rhapsodizing of the Spanish countryside and its gentle, friendly citizens, injecting just enough down-to-earth trade information to give his account double-barreled potency, storing his experience temporarily in his memory. It was not only a land of fandangos and conviviality, but also one filled with commercial possibilities; and it was fortunate this young American was able to see so much of it and to describe it so graphically.

Their route lay on down the Rio Grande Valley through Albuquerque and other tranquil little towns to El Paso. There they left the river and moved overland to Chihuahua. The reception at this capital was warm and satisfying, except that Pike found his confiscated records were definitely not to be returned to him. They would be passed up through military channels, and gather dust in archives in Mexico City for near a hundred years before being uncovered by an American scholar.

After the party had again been roundly entertained, it was started toward home via Texas, and made its way over the Rio Grande, and on to San Antonio de Bexar. There, in surroundings with which Moses Austin and his son Stephen would be highly familiar fifteen years hence, the Spanish governor gave them a banquet at which toasts were drunk to President Jefferson, the king of Spain, and none other than General Wilkinson.

Pike was again scribbling notes as fast as he could make them, and secreting them in the muzzles of his men's weapons, which they still carried. While the Spanish authorities believed they would be attacked by American forces, and soon, they were doing their best to assure a favorable report at the hands of this young officer. Perhaps they were fully aware of these copious notes he was now making, for a challenge to a little target practice would have blown them from their hiding places. But he managed to keep hold of his second batch.

San Antonio was the last headquarters where they must appear, and the festivities being over there, he and his men were speeded on their way east. It was the first day of July, 1807, when the party arrived at Fort Natchitoches in western Louisiana, fifty weeks after its departure from St. Louis. What an excursion it had turned out to be.

Taking his notes from the rifle barrels of the party after fear of their confiscation had passed, Pike had quite a time sorting them out and piecing the parts together. But he managed to turn out his *Account of Expeditions to the Sources of the Mississippi and through the Western Parts of Louisiana,* which, when published, became virtually required reading. As a soldier's report it was perhaps not so intended, but it managed to set fire to both romance and cupidity. It thus gave strong emphasis to the Spanish Southwest, which included Texas, and was one of the forces which helped to open up the fabled Santa Fe Trail in the years just ahead.

Since the French had not reoccupied Louisiana, but had left it in the hands of Spanish administrators, there had been no lengthy break in Wilkinson's undercover relations with these people. They had now been forced to withdraw beyond the bounds of this great territory, but those bounds were not yet well established, and there was perhaps ample reason for continuing this American officer on his retainer. On his part, he probably justified its acceptance as he realized that the purchase had not concurrently managed to procure undivided loyalty from many important people in the very areas which it was hoped the acquisition might particularly benefit.

Such defection, and it ran to high places, was due soon for a thorough overhauling. In fact even before the young officer who had been sent on this totally unauthorized mission had been set free by his Spanish custodians, there were happenings which gave the intrepid and presumptuous Wilkinson real pause. To bring the occasion into focus, it will be necessary to drop back and pick up the threads of a parallel incident.

XVII

Nationalism Takes a Firmer Hold

This grandson of Jonathan Edwards had risen early to high place.
Like Hamilton, his rival, he had been one of Washington's aides, and,
as a brilliant New York lawyer, he cherished Napoleonic ambitions,
which he attempted a few years later. He hoped to be emperor of
Mexico, as he wrote to Theodosia, and she, with her beauty, was
to adorn the court, where her son was to be heir apparent; and he
had prepared her for some such role when she was a girl of fourteen
who already presided at his table. As courtly as Talleyrand, and
as devious also, with something serpentine in his gifts of enchantment,
the charming, lively, high-spirited Burr was a lover of style and ideas
alike, with a passion for books and for pictures and especially sculp-
ture. . . . In revolt against a Puritan past, [he] had pondered the
gospel of Chesterfield at the expense of the Scriptures.—Van Wyck
Brooks, *The World of Washington Irving.*

THE minister's son, born in the parsonage by the banks of the
Passaic in Newark, New Jersey, and brought up in its dour
atmosphere, as well as that in the home of his formidable
grandparent Jonathan Edwards, the Puritan theologian, had graduated in 1772 from the small college his father had worked so hard
to found and advance. Soon thereafter he was caught up in the
toils of the Revolution, and being able, personable, well liked, and
of excellent connections, he was quite naturally commissioned an
officer and advanced to a lieutenant colonelcy, and was one of Washington's many aides before the war was over.

Out of uniform, this younger Aaron Burr turned to the practice
of the law, and by 1789 had become attorney general of the state of
New York, and its United States senator two years later. Such progress indicated great acumen in the realms of politics, and he was
indeed one of the founders and the leader of the Society of St.
Tammany, famous—and at times infamous—political club, named,

it is claimed, for a Delaware Indian chief whose wigwam once stood on the grounds on which Princeton's Nassau Hall was erected.

As he wrapped his senatorial toga about him in Washington when the government was being moved there, he began to shine forth on the national scene, where, politically speaking, things were far from sweetness and light. The Union was by no means a foregone conclusion, but still held together by relatively slender strands. Certain of the states, notably Kentucky, were advocating the right to nullify acts of the federal government thought to run counter to the state's immediate interests. Advantages over the near view inclined to outweigh ultimate benefits, and in the newer communities over the mountains loyalty and nationalism were neither ingrained or as yet particularly deep-seated. The preponderant political power lay in the states along the seaboard, to which there was little intention of knuckling under, and the attitude in this respect was in no small degree an outgrowth of past generations' feelings toward absentee landlords.

Even the East had been divided within itself, and the three major sections, northern, southern, and middle states, had found sharp cleavages and the need for frequent compromise as the Constitution had been slowly forged in 1787. Contrary political philosophies still at work were aligning followers into well-defined political parties. The result would not necessarily be an alignment of East against West, nor yet of archconservative against rampant radicalism, despite the attitude of one group toward the other. One realm of thinking found leadership under Hamilton as Washington retired from public life, while the other lined up behind Jefferson.

Aaron Burr, Jr., had already become a leading force in the Jefferson contingent in New York State, and thus was brought into continual collision with his opposite, the austere but purposeful Hamilton. At times they had worked together when a mutual advantage might be served; but after Washington's steadying hand had been removed and the new government hobbled forward under the direction of tough old John Adams, the growing animosity between Burr and Hamilton began to get out of hand. Ultimately it reached that unfortunate point where in those days "gentlemen" felt it could be resolved only by methods which would soon prove outmoded in the popular mind.

While this intense hatred had been growing up, Burr had become a sufficient drawing card so that he was selected as Jefferson's running mate in 1800. The machinery which the Constitution had at first provided for the election of the chief executive was a bit indecisive in spots, and soon had to be clarified by an amendment. An indication of its deficiencies came with this election. Although the party was reasonably assured of carrying Jefferson into the White House, the electors of the Democratic-Republican party pledged to him voted not only for Jefferson, but for Burr as well. The result was a tie for first honors, with no near contenders. It took the Congress many days and some thirty odd ballots to resolve the deadlock and install Jefferson as President and Burr as Vice-President.

While the latter was fully aware that this final result had been the intent of the overzealous electors, he did his utmost to capture the top spot for himself. His underhanded attempts among his friends—and he had many—merely confirmed Hamilton's opinion of the man. As opposed as he was to Jefferson, the final victor, his contempt for Burr now knew no bounds. His remark that while Jefferson was a man of *bad* principles, Burr had *none* opened the breach between them to a yawning chasm.

It would be four years after this contested election, however, before Burr issued his ill-advised challenge to Hamilton. While the latter realized what was at stake beyond the lives of the contestants and sought a way out of this duel in keeping with the code of honor, he was finally forced to take himself across the Hudson to Weehawken, New Jersey, which had long been a favored spot for such encounters.

The fatal shot from Burr's gun figuratively ricocheted, streaked back, and hit the man who had fired it a tremendous blow. Almost from the moment he was politically a "dead duck." Any appeal dueling may ever have had seemed suddenly to have vanished, and the Vice-President soon found himself facing indictments for murder in both his adopted state of New York and in the state of his birth, New Jersey. Taking shelter under the immunity his office afforded, he returned to Washington and completed his term. Quite obviously he did not stand with Jefferson for re-election.

He was but forty-nine when he found himself again in civil life, still in his prime, and very much in need of new pastures in which to graze. They would be more comfortable the further removed they were from the strongholds of the Federalists, of which party his victim had been the guiding spirit. But it appears he had not waited for his immunity to run out before laying plans for his future.

COULD THIS BE TREASON?

The British minister at Washington at the time, Anthony Merry, was a venturesome but not particularly astute person. However, Mr. Burr decided it would be to his advantage to turn his blandishments and scheming ways upon the man. To the gentleman's amazement he was soon in possession of startling information. The dismemberment of the Union, it appeared, was under way, actually well advanced. In view of the contemptuous view taken of these United States by the Foreign Office back home, Merry was certain he would be furnishing it welcome news.

As he bent a willing ear to further details, he was gratified to find that in return for a relatively modest sum of money, say a half million dollars, and the brief loan of a few fighting ships to operate at New Orleans, England might have a hand in the establishment of a friendly, even obedient "federation," somewhat nebulous as to its components, but quite likely comprising Spanish possessions, including Mexico, the recently acquired Louisiana, and even disaffected areas to the east of the Mississippi and along the Ohio. Burr could be as grandiose as he was treacherous and "serpentine." The accounts of proposed enterprises showered upon the ambassador were almost too good to be believed, and he at once communicated a detailed report of the matter to his superiors in London, counseling them to give him authority to back this undertaking of Aaron Burr's. What the latter's personal promises to Merry may have been are not known, a dukedom perhaps, for Burr could be lavish in that respect.

But the Foreign Office craftily hedged this move by playing the other side of the street at the same time. To the Spanish envoy at Washington came fabulous rumors, purported to be from the very lips of the Vice-President himself. Preparations were being made and were about completed for an attack on New Orleans and New Spain. But Mr. Burr, so the emissary assured, was in a position to stop such an enterprise, even if it required the kidnaping of President Jefferson.

Is there any wonder then that the Spaniards were apprehensive, had troops of cavalry patrolling the western plains, and leaned over backward to make a suitable impression on Pike? What indeed was this volatile and unpredictable Yankee government up to anyway, what was it not quite capable of? Spain was accustomed to intrigue, but these Americans were inscrutable and beyond compre-

hension. The best thing the Spaniards could do was brace themselves for an onslaught while they tried to remain calm. But they no
doubt asked their pensioner, General Wilkinson, some rather searching questions. The English, too, seemed to be quite willing to await
further developments.

BURR DESCENDS THE MISSISSIPPI

By the summer of 1805 Burr had decamped from Washington
and was headed down the Ohio toward New Orleans, in which city
he maintained he had considered settling. He was, nonetheless,
looking carefully along the way for a place where his somewhat
spurious talents might be employed, or where his schemes might
be hatched. Not far below Marietta on the Ohio his sensitive nose
caught the scent of promising quarry.

On an island in the river, one Harman Blennerhassett had built
himself a virtual barony. The man was wealthy, and he was also
gullible. Here was a fortress from which to move out to conquest. So
the archplotter sold Blennerhassett "up to the hilt" on his wily
schemes, promising him a part in rich spoils, and even a place as
ambassador at one of the lustrous European courts, representing the
new nation soon to be born.

Burr also stopped by to work on Henry Clay, the mouthpiece of
Kentucky. He did his bit, too, by William Henry Harrison, very much
a power in the affairs of the Indiana Territory. At Nashville he was
the welcome guest of Andrew Jackson for a time at the log cabin that
preceded "The Hermitage." He had, of course, not failed to visit
Wilkinson at St. Louis. While the others may have discounted the
true purposes of the man and decided he was no more than a military
adventurer, a sort of freebooter, the governor of the upper Louisiana
Territory was enough of the same stamp to have no delusions of his
visitor's intents. That he was to have a hand in the scheme, but at
his own good time, is quite probable.

Since so much of Burr's maneuvering was by word of mouth,
too little has come down to us to indicate clearly all he may have had
in mind. Some contend that both his objectives and his methods were
out-and-out treason. Others are ready to insist they did not go that
far, at least by the thinking of men beyond the mountains, who had
moments in which they strongly questioned the benefits of the Union,
and whether it was principally a device by which the "interests" in
the East might keep the struggling frontier in subjection.

However, this much is certain. The long-practiced British Foreign Office in 1806 made it convenient for its ambassador, who had lent his ear to Aaron Burr, to plead ill-health, leave for home, and be replaced by a more discerning representative. Merry's recently received dispatches were heavily bound with red tape, plastered with sizable wads of wax to seal them up, and prudently hidden away for several generations. The whole proceeding had a distinctly rancid odor to the keen noses of British officialdom.

Burr continued on his mischievous way as far as New Orleans, and returned by ship to New York, which he was again free to enter, at the end of 1805. There he went resolutely to work making preparations for his sortie. But he chose his emissaries none too wisely, for they were much less circumspect with their words than he had learned to be. By the next year when he started off to the west to set the machinery in motion, he was a bit embarrassed to find his name and project a frequent matter of conversation by altogether too many people.

He had thought it prudent to call on Colonel George Morgan, the noted Indian trader, agent, and fighting man at his home at "Morganza," a few miles below Pittsburgh. This stalwart pioneer was a far better patriot, too, than Burr had bargained for, and the fur-hatted colonel soon had word of the conspiracy speeding down to the national capital. There seems to be substantial evidence that Morgan was the first to tip off Jefferson to what was afoot to the west over the Alleghenies.

Kentucky promptly called him and his scheme to account. But with Clay as his counsel, a righteous aura was soon restored to both the man and his activities. Jackson, too, found no grievous faults in him; and this despite the fact he must have been fully conscious of the fleet of flatboats being built for the adventurer almost in his own side yard at Clover Bottom on nearby Stone River. When these vessels had been added to others supplied at yards on up the Ohio, the fleet set off for the lower reaches of the Mississippi.

Pike at the moment was plodding along toward the west, and his superior at St. Louis was beginning to get a bit doubtful as to whether there was enough in this Burr scheme for him to risk his position by either involvement, or even by seeming to sanction it through failure to report it to Washington. After casting up both sides of the matter, he decided upon a virtuous course, flashed word to Jefferson, and hurried down to New Orleans to pose as its protector.

As information seeped into the national capital, Jefferson, who had become a thoroughgoing nationalist since entering the presidency, set up the cry of "treason." A proclamation ordering all conspirators and participants to disband was readied, handed to a courier, and galloped across Virginia and Tennessee, and then down the Trace to Natchez. There it caught up with Burr in January 1807, deep in his plotting beneath the vaulted ceiling of Connelly's Tavern on Ellicott's Hill. At once the jig was up. New Orleans was prepared for his onslaught, and to proceed would be merely to waste lives fruitlessly. The ex-Vice-President turned soldier of fortune promptly deserted his followers and sought to flee.

This presidential proclamation had put quite a different complexion on the whole matter, and involvement with a treasonable character was not something to be lightly hazarded. Burr was soon captured, and taken to face trial at Washington, a town some six miles east of Natchez, and then the capital of Mississippi Territory. So great was the interest in the proceedings that the small courthouse was inadequate and the tribunal found accommodations beneath the huge live oaks which still stand before the college later named Jefferson for Burr's accuser.

While he was ultimately cleared and acquitted by no less than John Marshall, Chief Justice of the Supreme Court, the man was through and done. He tried feverishly for a number of years to find backing in Europe for his questionable schemes, only to wind up his days in straitened circumstances practicing law in New York. He did live to be eighty years old, which length of life would seemingly have been better employed by his father.

Wilkinson once again managed to slip through the fire without being badly singed. Still the Spanish ambassador lent a piquant touch to the business by accusing the governor of upper Louisiana of tacit complicity, or at least of "treasonable desire." Yet no harm had been done the apprehensive Spaniards, and war in the Southwest would be delayed for a number of years.

The defect in the loyalty of the western frontier areas, however, was from then on replaced with a more simon-pure brand of allegiance. It would be fifty years before a cancerous growth now catching hold would finally be sufficient to split the nation asunder.

XVIII

Frontier Life and Justice

Come, all you young men, who have a mind to range,
Into the Western country, your station for to change;
For seeking some new pleasure we'll altogether go,
Come along, lively lads, and we'll altogether go
And we'll settle on the banks of the pleasant Ohio.

The land it is good, boys, and you need not to fear
'Tis a garden of Eden in North America.
Come along, my lively lads, and we'll altogether go
And we'll settle on the banks of the pleasant Ohio.

Girls, if you'll card, knit, and spin, we'll plough,
      reap and sow,
And we'll fold you in our arms while the stormy wind
      doth blow.

From *The Forget-Me-Not Songster*, a Collection of Old
Ballads, Philadelphia, c. 1842.

ALTHOUGH the excerpts above do not seem to have found their way into print until some years after the incident that follows took place, the song, or surely the sentiments it expressed, had long been common. The eastern reaches of the Northwest Territory had filled in rapidly enough following Wayne's treaty with the savages at Greene Ville in 1795 so that Ohio was admitted as a state in 1803. The remainder was for a time called Indiana Territory, and it, too, began to fill with settlers at a rate that gave new and deep concern to the native peoples.

Its eastern bounds began just far enough beyond Cincinnati to give that thriving Ohio settlement elbowroom. From there it swept west to the Mississippi. Still it was not an entirely virgin area, since the French had penetrated it long ago, setting up Post Vincennes on the Wabash as early as 1727, by the side of Indian trails that reached from western Florida to Detroit.

But this small settlement had tended to keep within its stockaded town and the common lands immediately surrounding it. Its habitants were not the itchy, spreading out sort of creatures the far-ranging Americans who had filtered in since the end of the Revolution proved to be. The French settlers had given their Indian neighbors little concern, and had been no threat in the overrunning and eviction of the natives.

But now with more and more shipyards springing up about Pittsburgh, Wheeling, and places along the upper reaches of the Ohio and Monongahela, and the former river coming alive with flatboats, the savages realized that the few passive French would soon be swallowed up by this virile horde descending upon them. The situation as in Ohio would be repeated, and they would most certainly be elbowed aside and out of the way.

Congress, badly in need of revenue, had long since put up the public lands in this Northwest Territory for settlement. But at first the blocks had been too large and the prices too steep for the lean pocketbooks of the settlers. Thus speculation had caught hold, and while the laws had been modified and terms made less severe, there were not a few who merely barged in, staked out homesteads, and filed on and paid for their claims only when eviction threatened. That one should be excluded from unoccupied land just because some absentee owner or authority claimed possession had been counter to pioneer opinion for nearly two centuries. Indiana's settlers were under control of old habits in a new environment. Even though uncouth by some standards, the land-hungry had some sense of the proprieties. It was not their intent to *shoot* the tax collector, merely to *evade* him, and a graphic picture of the pioneers along this frontier may help to make the matter clearer.

The citizenry with which Governor William Henry Harrison was working was made up largely of units, usually a young married couple, although a few of them were well into middle age or beyond, for the frontier became an obsession with some. Daniel Boone's reactions are well known, and the seizures he always had when the neighbors' chimneys were "too close." The single man, like Spencer in Tennessee, was not able to function successfully. The farm was one part of the enterprise, the cabin quite another, and it took two to plod along together through the heavy going and drudgery of wilderness life. The bachelor ever had one eye cocked for a worthwhile helpmate, and the spinster preserved her single "blessedness" only by insistent struggle.

This family unit was almost entirely self-sustaining. Consequently it was highly independent. It knew how to be co-operative when common dangers threatened, and it truly ached for social contacts and interchanges beyond its own limited membership. But the unit needs came first—they had to—and then those of the group. Once he felt reasonably secure, the settler looked outward and began to help foster churches, schools, and also take a lively interest in government. This latter was mostly at the local level, for he entertained a lively suspicion of any restraint exerted from a distance.

The core of his life was his clearing, his cabin, and what went on within its limits. His log house was fixed, and not as portable as the Indian's tepee or hogan. When he moved in, he had come to stay, at least by decided contrast with the roving savages. With roots down, crops planted, and the forest cover being cleared back, the settlers knew that either they persisted and drove off the "Injuns" or the latter would finally eject them. It was this threat that gave them their principal reason for subscribing to government, to which, they well knew, they must cede some of their rights for benefits in return.

Within three years of the setup of the territory a sufficient number of the more independent-minded settlers of Anglo-Saxon extraction had appeared upon the scene to demand a representative form of government to attack and deal with their common concerns. Their first general assembly gathered at Vincennes in July 1805.

For the next six years the superintendence of Indian affairs would in itself be nearly enough to keep the governor well occupied. There was a famous team of Indian triplets, two brothers of whom, Tecumseh and the Prophet, were just then at the height of their influence. They would be a thorn in his side until he blunted the power of the fanatical Prophet in the battle that gave Harrison his latter political designation of "Tippecanoe." Thus the area which would one day be brought into the Union as the state of Indiana was dangerous ground until after this encounter in 1811.

However, the Indians were not the only threat to tranquility. There was a white element that floated about on the borders of the wilderness that was second only to the frustrated natives as a source of concern. While it had been dealt with on an individual basis up to now, the police power of government had come into being in the community, and under the encouragement of the respected governor, there was a willingness to give it a try. The great bulk of the people were inherently in favor of rule by law rather than by men. Still it would be men who would enforce the laws if this rule were to abide. What sort of men were called for under such circumstances? It just so happens that Indiana, then approaching statehood, provides an admirable example.

APPROVED FRONTIER JUSTICE

People along the frontier grew old from two causes. One was physical, the result of hard work and great privations. The other was mental, the frustrations of dashed hopes, but particularly the tenseness under which they must live. One never knew when a shot out of a clump of grass, or a tomahawk swung from behind a tree, might snuff out a life. A journey through the back country—and it was mostly back country—was no relaxing Sunday-afternoon stroll. If an Indian did not try his skill in finishing one off, it could well be a highwayman or a plundering horse thief.

These latter were a particular scourge in a country where a horse was hard to come by, and almost indispensable once you owned it. While ten dollars, which was the going price at that time, may not seem a large amount today, it was a considerable sum in those times. This meant that the replacement of a strayed or stolen animal entailed real sacrifice, for the loss could be a threat to one's well-being, and perhaps to that of his whole family as well.

Not only were the Indians very light-fingered as respects horses, but there was also a predatory fringe in the population that considered theft an easier road to riches than the more approved forms of employment. Such gentry were by no means a new phenomenon, for their depredations had been known in the older communities since horses first began to appear in the colonies. The laws against them were always severe, and in Indiana Territory it was provided they were to receive thirty-nine lashes on the bare back—and not with thistledown—for the first offense, while death followed a second conviction.

In earlier days the aggrieved citizenry had merely hoisted the thieves clear of the ground by means of a rope tossed over the most convenient tree limb. It had proved thoroughly effective. Then Governor Harrison began appealing for wider application of the new territorial law. Whip these felons, yes, but give them a chance to reform. There was widespread doubt as to the efficacy of this method, but finally by common consent it would have another trial.

It seems that not long since an immature young prosecuting

attorney had drawn a series of indictments so faulty that a whole jailful of culprits, despite convictions before a jury, had managed to walk out of the court free men because of the technicalities dug up by defending counsel. The populace, which had suffered measurably at the hands of these varmints, was dumfounded at this clumsy exposition of what the law was supposed to achieve for them. They set up such a hullabaloo that the judge who had heard the cases promptly resigned. This left an awkward void on the bench, and the governor was forced to look about for a more effective successor.

He could not well have overlooked him, if mere size was all that counted, for the man who was to prove ideally equipped to remedy this want of forthrightness was one of the finest physical specimens in the whole territory. Broad-shouldered, well muscled, and a full six feet without his moccasins, he was a superior type of frontiersman. Born in the backwoods of Kentucky, he had a native sagacity and keen discernment that completely made up for the manner in which he was forced to spell out and sound the words in such Bible passages as he often chose to read. With a good stout quill, well dipped in pokeberry ink, he could sign his name in letters large enough to have been the envy of no less a person than John Hancock himself.

But no one ever seemed anxious to try to push him about, and none was ever for stepping on his toes a second time. Blunt and sometimes as rough as cast iron in his approach, he had been a general in the Kentucky militia, and it was said that he could lick fully twice his weight in wildcats. His name, by the way, was Marston G. Clark, and being a cousin of General George Rogers Clark, he thus came well recommended.

Harrison chose him to fill the vacancy, and this choice received popular acclaim. The jailhouse was full at the moment as the result of another roundup of horse thieves, so his work was cut out for him. As court day approached, Vincennes began to fill up for a look at this new upholder of the law in action. A grand jury had been impaneled, and it was to be hoped its indictments had been more carefully drawn.

The not too large log courthouse was filled to capacity with witnesses and spectators as the new judge, clad as usual in hunting shirt, leather pants, and foxskin cap, strode in and took his place on the slightly raised platform along one side of the room. His long black hair was drawn into a queue and hung down the back of his neck with as much solemnity as did similar queues still worn in those days by Justices on the Supreme bench in Washington.

As his keen eyes ran over the crowd, conversation quickly died away. He had already been over the indictments, and seeing no need for further formalities, opened the session by barking out, "We'll try John Long first. He seems to be the leader in this business. Bring him into court."

"There he is," responded the sheriff, jerking a thumb toward the man beside him. "I brought him along with me." Then, in a bellicose tone, he ordered, "John Long, stand up."

As the indictment was being read, the judge eyed the prisoner thoroughly through the hairy fringe of the foxskin cap still on his head. Hardly was the reading finished when he demanded, "You're indicted of stealing an Indian pony. Are you guilty, or not guilty?"

Before there could be an answer, the defendant's counsel bounced to his feet to interpose this objection: "May it please the court, we plead in abatement that his name is John *H.* Long."

It was noticeable that this quibbling did not sit at all well with the rustic jurist, and he barked back, "That makes no difference. I know the man, and that's quite sufficient."

The young attorney winced a bit, but with a fee dangling before him, and until this new judge's legal know-how had been further tested, he determined on a broadside attack, adding hurriedly, "We then move to quash the indictment before he pleads."

"State your objections," came in tones that made it more of an order than a granted privilege.

"First," continued the counsel somewhat warily, but hoping he was being firm enough to carry conviction, "there is no value laid upon the horse. Second, it is charged in the indictment to have been a horse, when it was actually a gelding, and . . ."

Annoyed, as though by a buzzing fly, the quick retort was, "I know that an Indian pony is worth ten dollars, and I'll consider that a gelding is a horse. Motion overruled!"

The defense counsel suddenly came to the conclusion that it would be fruitless to try to lead this judge up any blind alleys. Still, if his fee was to be earned, he better get on with the case, plead *not* guilty, and hope the witnesses could be tripped up or confused. He would, however, hold back one more item he had discovered, just in case such a course failed him.

So a plea was entered, a jury was chosen, and the trial got under way. But the testimony was thoroughly conclusive, Long was guilty in the eyes of his peers, and promptly so pronounced. He faced thirty-nine lashes across his naked back, dealt out by a willing and heavy-handed sheriff.

At this crucial point the convicted man's counsel summoned up his courage and played his last card, hoping it was a trump. A noticeable frown passed across Clark's customarily stoical face as he realized there was to be more legal haggling. Yet he paid the young man the compliment of seeming to listen attentively as he protested, "We move arrest in judgment, and on the ground that it is not specifically charged in the indictment that the horse was stolen in the Territory of Indiana."

"Hmm!" exclaimed the judge, apparently very much taken back; but while it appeared that he was reflecting this objection soberly, he was in reality deciding to take full care of two matters. First of all, he was going to shake up the prosecutor, or whoever it was that was drawing indictments with flaws in them big enough to ride a horse through. Also it might be well to teach some of these whippersnapper legal lights that this court was more interested in justice than in finagling and obstruction.

Leaning forward, and in a surprisingly moderate voice, he remarked, "I consider this a much more serious objection than any you have yet made. I-I want to consider it until morning." Then turning to the sheriff, he ordered, "Adjourn the court, and keep the prisoner safe until we need him again."

As the stuffy courthouse cleared, there was some reasonable speculation as to whether this new judge was really the Solomon they had hoped he might be. For some reason, too, he stayed on in the now empty cabin. When the sheriff reappeared, slammed the open door, and came up close to the bench, the foxskin cap bent over close to the upturned ear, and Judge Clark gave the following instructions: The officer and his deputy were to take the prisoner at midnight back out of earshot of the town, bind him to a tree, and lay on the lashes. Then they were to bring him back to the jail, produce him in court in the morning, *and say nothing about the matter to any person.*

One did not trifle with this judge's orders, so they were carried out to the very letter, and court opened early the following morning without the defense counsel having felt the need to contact his client. When the crowd had again quieted down, Clark bent forward slightly, and addressing the attorney with a touch of deference, explained, "I have been thinking about your motion in arrest in the case against Long. I have some doubts that the evidence as given actually proved he did steal the horse in *this* territory. But I do not think I should sustain a motion that, as I understand, will merely discharge the prisoner after he has been found guilty by this jury. So, I feel bound to grant him a *new* trial."

There was a loud shriek, and the prisoner painfully hauled himself to his feet to cry out, "For heaven's sake NO! I've been whipped almost to death already! I want to discharge my attorney and withdraw any such motion!"

Slowly the spectators sensed what must have taken place, and they began to howl, clap each other on the back, and stamp their feet. Slapping the bench beside him a resounding whack with the palm of one of his huge hands, the stern-faced judge barked out an order to be quiet. Then turning to the clerk, he ordered, "Enter the judgment, and mark it satisfied."

In tense silence the spectators watched as the other prisoners were brought before the bar of justice. The machinery was now functioning more smoothly, and convictions soundly based on evidence followed in rather rapid succession. No further motions to quash or to stay judgment were entered. One by one, as convicted, the thieves were roundly flogged and turned loose to spread the word abroad that the homespun justice in Judge Clark's court was not to be tampered with—better still, it was not to be encountered. Horse thieves and other wayward characters began to give the area wide berth.

While he may not have been quite as picturesque as Roy Bean, who professed at a later time to be "law west of the Pecos" down Texas way, he was no figment of the imagination either. The above court scene was written down in pretty much these words by one of Clark's contemporaries, Oliver H. Smith, who was himself a rugged searcher after justice in the same territory in these very times. It was men like Clark, both on and off the bench, who helped to remodel a long succession of frontiers and slowly make them places where life could be lived more safely and with greater security and satisfaction.

XIX

Building the Cumberland Road

SPRINGFIELD, O., September 20, 1818—Citizens and visitors to this city have started a great celebration here with the completion of the National Pike (Cumberland Road) to its terminus at this town. It was announced that the United States mail is now using the road from its eastern terminus to Wheeling. This road was first projected sixteen years ago when the Ohio Constitutional Convention provided a fund from the sale of land for the building of roads. When it was found that the estimated cost of the road exceeded the appropriation, the Government was petitioned to build it. Seeing its value lay in its continuation to the Eastern seaboard, it was considered an Interstate project . . . Traversing three states, and tapping several more, the road is considered an important factor in developing the nation.—A speculative news item from Hoffman & Grattan's *News of the Nation.*

I N A N age when a growing number of us hesitate to build garages for cars which we wear out too fast, it is a little difficult to think of this country without roads. Yet at the first there were but two means of transportation beyond human equipment: the ship and the horse. The role of the navigable river was almost paramount, and may well be responsible for the dominant part Virginia came to play among the thirteen colonies. Her settlers were not only able to push settlements well inland, but once established there, to conveniently float their crops and merchantable products out to market. The importance of the Potomac, the Rappahannock, the James, and the York in this respect are too frequently overlooked.

It had been the navigable streams in the more advanced European countries that had given them precedence in trade and development, and the saddle horse, the pack animal, and the oxcart or horse-drawn wagon supplemented and enlarged upon bulk transportation, which flowed primarily by water. A problem which had been Europe's transplanted itself in the beginning to the frontier on the American continent.

In the homelands there were some remnants of the stone-surfaced highways laid down by Roman military engineers before the onset of the Dark Ages. All else were cart paths, passable in the drier seasons, but axle-deep in mud when the rainy season took over, and gouged and crevassed by ruts and washouts much of the time. Travel was looked upon as an enervating endeavor, and it was.

On this side of the ocean by the close of the Revolution the former Indian paths, which had broadened into pack trails and wagon ways, were further cleared and prepared for stagecoach travel, especially between the larger towns and cities along the seaboard. Still they remained crude and hazardous roads, and as late as 1802 it required a day and a half under the most favorable circumstances, and a fare of five dollars, to make the stage trip of one hundred miles between New York and Philadelphia.

If you turned west from the latter point, a series of stages would land you, weary and perhaps bruised, at Shippensburg, a hundred fifty miles away, in three more days. But if you were headed for the Forks of the Ohio at Pittsburgh, you were forced to finish your adventurous trip on foot or horseback over the mountain trails. There is the record of a man walking the three hundred odd miles from Philadelphia to Pittsburgh in 1807 in twenty-seven days and feeling he had done himself proud.

America's majestic distances were difficult to negotiate, and a distinct deterrent to the progress for which our forefathers were now ready. The pioneer and homesteader, driven west by his hunger for land, made the best of such rough going. Yet it was not long, as has become apparent, before he had a surplus of goods and needed better means by which to move them to market.

As the 1800s began to roll by there was a shrill demand for roads over which far greater loads could be hauled more profitably than they could be borne on the backs of pack animals. The technical answer to such demands fortunately began to appear in England, where the industrial revolution now gripping the British Isles set off a similar demand for more dependable transport. The result there had been the development of so-called "artificial" roads, perfected by two Scottish engineers, Telford and McAdam.

The first developed a type with a heavy stone base, the expense of which was easier stood over the shorter distances encountered in England and Scotland. But the latter, who had been brought here as a boy, had made a comfortable fortune as agent in the sale of war prizes during the Revolution, and then returned home, had a solution better adapted to our needs. He advocated surfacing with crushed stone over a relatively stable subsurface provided with plenty of good drainage. When his ideas were adapted to the Lancaster Pike, a privately constructed toll road from Philadelphia to the Susquehanna, it became the first true highway in the land, and the model for other much needed betterments of this kind.

The financial portion of the problem found its answer in the enabling act drawn in 1802 to admit Ohio as a state. It had included a provision that one twentieth of the monies received from the sale of public lands within its bounds were to be impounded and applied to the construction of roads. Three fifths of these proceeds were to be made available for local roadways within the state, while the remainder was to go toward construction of a national road to connect this first state north of the Ohio with tidewater along the Atlantic coast.

Cautious Jefferson doubted that the Constitution vested the central government with the power to undertake such "internal improvements." But his enterprising Secretary of the Treasury, Albert Gallatin, a Pennsylvanian from the section bound to be benefited by such a road, helped him to overcome his scruples. The postal provision in the Constitution set forth the need for post roads to expedite the transport of the mails. Also, there was the necessity of tightening the bonds of Union. Consequently the western states and territories were very much in favor of the move. While the Congress divided rather evenly on the subject of such public improvements, it did appropriate thirty thousand dollars in 1811, and soon parties of surveyors were searching out a practicable route.

INTERNAL IMPROVEMENTS AND LOCAL POLITICS

Just where should such a road be built? Although he had not been too adept in Indian tactics, the otherwise able Britisher, General Braddock, had followed a logical course with the military path he had caused to be hacked through the woods in 1755 when he had attempted to succor the colonial forces held by the French at Fort Duquesne. While this need not be slavishly followed, it would give the general course of the route, which would thus run from the upper reaches of the Potomac near Fort Cumberland well out in

Maryland, across western Pennsylvania, to a spot on the Ohio somewhere near or below Pittsburgh.

At once the southwestern corner of the Keystone State was in
turmoil. Every community within the area girded for battle, mar-
shaled its respective merits and political influence, and began to
bawl lustily that the "improvement" run through its midst. The
choice of the site for the national capital had set off no such competitive dither as the location of this roadway.

As early as 1806 the President had been authorized to appoint
a board of three commissioners to lay out the road, one from each
of the states whose territory it would cross. Those from Maryland
and Virginia were soon named; but with all this agitation going on,
Pennsylvania withheld participation until the contending towns and
hamlets had been made to see the light and a rational route, based
upon existing circumstances, agreed upon. All this bickering took
time, and it was thus five years before the right of way could be
plotted and the first contracts let for a construction enterprise, which
was, as far as America was concerned, the biggest yet attempted.

Those who have driven west over U.S. Route 40 between the
Potomac and the Ohio will have passed over the course selected
for the Cumberland, or National, Road. From what was then Fort
Cumberland, it worked its way west a bit through Maryland and
crossed over to Uniontown in Pennsylvania. It next pushed up to
Brownsville to make contact with the Monongahela River, an important waterway, as it still is today. Leaving there, it swung up to
the what Pittsburghers now call "Little Washington" to differentiate
it from the national capital, but which inland town in those days was
a threat to the metropolis to the north as a manufacturing center.
After passing through this town on the hilltops, the roadway turned
to the southwest, passed across the shoestring strip of Virginia one
day to be a part of a new state, and ended at Wheeling. There had
been a sharp contest over the terminus here rather than at Steuben-
ville, but since Wheeling lay across the river from the beginning of
the famous Zane's Trace through southern Ohio, it won out.

THE NATURE OF OUR FIRST IMPROVED ROADS

What was to be the nature of this superior highway? The law
prescribed that the right of way be four rods, or sixty-six feet wide,
and cleared of all trees and brush. In the middle of this strip was
to be built a raised carriageway, sufficiently elevated so there

would be suitable drainage to the ditches on either side. Hills, where they required such treatment, were to be pared down until the course of the road rose or fell no more than five feet in every one hundred traveled. These were reasonable grades by the standards of the time.

Wages set for the men of the preparatory parties may be of interest. The year, remember, was 1806, and the regulatory act specified the following daily rates of pay: for the commissioners, four dollars apiece; for each surveyor, three dollars; while the chainmen and markers had to be content with a dollar. This was probably the going scale at the time, but hardly seems excessive by today's standards.

The report of the commissioners respecting the road's surfacing is similarly interesting. Bear in mind that heretofore roads had been merely wider paths cleared through the woods or across country, and from there on maintenance had been left largely in nature's indifferent hands. Thus the traveler was forced to fervently hope during rainy weather that there was a bottom, at some depth, to the mud, and that the driver of the stage would navigate the not infrequent ten- and twelve-foot gullies, washed by succeeding storms, without spilling his passengers out through the windows.

To avoid such contingencies, the report counseled: "As a common road cannot remove the difficulties which always exist in deep ground, and particularly in wet seasons, and as nothing short of a firm, well-formed, stone-capped road can remove the causes which led to the measure of improvement, or render the institution as commodious as a great and growing intercourse appears to require, the expense of such a road becomes the next subject of inquiry."

What were their recommendations? An artificial roadway, that is one with a macadamized surface, for a binder of asphalt was of course as yet undreamed of. The neighboring mountains were solid rock, so why not crush it up and cap the road with layers of this crushed stone as the competent Scot had advocated. The Lancaster, together with the more recent Baltimore and Frederick pikes were proving the practicable type of construction for all-weather, lasting main highways.

Such treatment would cost money, a great deal of money, as was later discovered. But the excessive expense encountered in this earliest of major public works can in part be laid to loosely drawn contracts. However, prospective contractors were each required to furnish a wooden box containing samples of the crushed stone the bidder proposed to use; and these were retained as standards by which to judge whether the materials that went into actual construction were up to par. The work got under way in the eastern reaches of the project in 1811, sections being built by local people having the necessary capital and facilities, for the "undertakers," from whom the contracting firms of today came into being, were then limited in size and number. With the onset of the War of 1812, construction lagged somewhat.

But as section after section was opened up, its use was far above expectations. After peace returned toward the end of 1814, work was again speeded up, and by 1817 the whole of this first segment was opened as far as Wheeling. Then came trouble, and political tension. Traffic was so heavy that the eastern part of the road was wearing out almost before the western end began to echo to the wheels of wagons and stagecoaches. What was to be done with regard to repairs?

Those areas on the east coast not directly benefited had been cool to the project from its outset, especially since revenues from land sales in Ohio had far from equaled the considerable sums poured into the enterprise. They took a jaundiced view of the matter, loudly proclaiming that since more and more money was ostensibly to be sunk in bogholes, in leveling mountains, and bridging streams so that, in the final result, a few tavern keepers along the way might get rich, the whole national wealth would be jeopardized.

The vision of America in the ultimate was still the possession of but a very few in those days. There was perhaps a better sensing of it in the West, where Henry Clay went eloquent in a big way. To combat the conservative elements, there arose an insistent demand not only for repairs to the completed portions, but extension by new sections on to the West, eventually to the Missouri, while some, then judged to be no more than crackpots, even advocated that it reach to the Pacific.

There being no tax money available, tollgates were suggested. Such measures would permit the traffic directly benefited to stand the expense of operation and maintenance. At once the "state's righters" became highly vocal and welded all opposing forces together. The fear of the federal government encroaching upon the privileges of the states downed slowly, especially in this area, where benefits would be widely spread. Congress passed enabling legislation, but it was promptly vetoed to satisfy those who felt this federal body was becoming too autocratic.

In 1819 the Supreme Court pointed a way out of the difficulty, yet it was five years before Congress mustered the necessary courage to again tackle this matter. The tollgates went in, but under state auspices, and the National Road was slowly pushed west from Wheeling, eventually to reach by way of Columbus to Vandalia, then capital of Illinois.

LIMITING INFLUENCES ALREADY AT WORK

The heyday of this National Road came in the 1830s. By then great wagon trains were plodding over it to and from eastern markets and numerous settlers were traversing it to the Ohio Valley and lands beyond. Mail and passengers were being galloped along this artery by stage lines whose names were household terms for speed in homes throughout the land. Yet its importance in the realm of transportation was of limited duration.

Forty odd years before, while the Constitution was being drawn, John Fitch had had a steam-propelled ferry plying the Delaware River to points above and below Philadelphia. While he had been twenty year ahead of his time and died a frustrated man, the developments he had advocated had been taken in hand by others, and by the time the Cumberland Road was at its zenith more and more steamboats were navigating more and more American waterways. Not only were such great rivers as the Mississippi and Ohio being conquered by them, but they were being pushed up smaller streams far into the interior, and once again proving that water transport was cheaper and more satisfactory for bulk merchandise.

In New York State, "Clinton's ditch," the Erie Canal, had shown the way to more flexible waterways, and to more direct ones than nature had in many cases provided. There was a perfect rash of canal building, which facilities, together with the rivers, were to make improved roads a local concern for the better part of the next century. While the role of the canal was somewhat temporary, the railroad which took its place rapidly in the late 1840s would obviate the need for interstate highway systems until the advent of motor vehicles in volume some years after the frontier disappeared.

Yet the National Road served its purpose. It helped to weld East and West into one nation, provided contact between the two sections until better facilities could be perfected, and laid the foundation and gave the pattern for a later public works program which added materially to America's greatness.

XX

An Early Fling at Foreign Trade

Santa Fe is seven thousand feet up, and a newcomer has to gasp
for breath the first few days. It gets very cold in winter and there
is snow. But in summer it's cool . . . It is the second oldest city in the
United States, next to St. Augustine, Florida. Coronado came from
Mexico and roamed all around in 1540. The whole Rio Grande valley
drips with history and with ancient Spanish and Indian culture. And
I don't know of a town in America that has such astonishingly long
unfoldings of nature as you see just outside Santa Fe. The town
lies in a wide valley, close to mountains on the east. They are not
the high, sinister mountains of the northern Rockies; they seem more
like neighbors. But sometimes you can stand in the bright sunshine
in Santa Fe and see not five miles away an ominous blackish-gray
snowstorm swirling down upon the mountain ridge . . . As for the
town itself, there isn't anything else in America that looks like Santa
Fe.—Ernie Pyle, *Home Country*.

THE Spanish had established a fort at St. Louis well back in the
1700s for better control of the fur trade that originated in
the upper Mississippi and Missouri valleys. A few trappers and
traders had added their cabins and modest homes to the structures
of the post, but the town was still rather an inconsequential place
when Wilkinson dispatched Pike from there on his two journeys, or
when Lewis and Clark disbanded their party at this strategic river
port after their return from the Pacific.

Life in the little town, however, picked up materially during
the next fifteen years. First the flatboats, and then the steamboats,
brought enough people to the Missouri Territory so that by 1821 it
had become a state, and the booming community on the Mississippi,
named for France's sanctified thirteenth-century king, was about to
incorporate as a city.

River traffic, however, did not terminate there, but was thrusting on up the Missouri and feeding towns that threatened for a num-

ber of years to outdo St. Louis with its head start. Such towns were serving not only the back country, rapidly being settled, but for quite a period they would be the jumping-off place for a profitable volume of foreign trade.

It was a dozen years after Pike returned from Mexico before the southern boundary of the Louisiana Purchase was clarified. By a treaty signed with Spain in 1819 we had taken over Florida, but relinquished any claims we may have felt we had to Texas. Then two years later Mexico had revolted, gained its independence, and some of the enterprising felt more secure in investigating the stories Pike and the fur trappers had been telling about the pot of gold that lay beneath the other end of a rainbow stretching eight hundred miles down into the Southwest.

While the season was pretty well advanced by the time this latter bit of news filtered into western Missouri, it made a strong appeal to Captain William Becknell, and he fairly itched to be on his way. His friends did their best to dissuade him, but his mind was made up. So he gathered whatever goods he could lay his hands on locally, assembled a small party, packed his animals, and set off on September 1, 1821, for "out yonder."

He left from Arrow Rock, east along the Missouri from present-day Kansas City, and perhaps just to confuse the issue a bit, he let it appear that the Indians in the Rockies were his objective. The fur trade was thriving, and if the neighbors below the border were still not willing to receive visitors, he could easily dispose of his wares.

He, like Pike on that historic journey some years before, struck out for the great bend of the Arkansas and then made his way up that stream. But near Las Animas, whether by mistake or design is not quite clear, he took its left-hand fork, which is the Purgatoire, or "Picketwire," and was soon bogged down in famous Raton Pass on the northern border of New Mexico.

There he experienced several days of exhausting effort getting the pack train through this defile; but the party made it, encountered some Mexican troops who encouraged them to keep on to the south, and finally reached Santa Fe on November 16. The season was indeed growing short. But the goods they had brought were in great demand, trading soon cleared out their stock, and by early December they had set their faces for home. With winter upon them they needed little further stimulation to hurry, and they managed to cover the eight hundred and more miles in forty-eight days without mishap.

And what thrilling news they had to tell! There was gold in "them thar hills"—or silver, to be more exact, as their bags of Spanish coins readily testified. There were people down in the Santa Fe country thirsty for cloth, cutlery, notions, small tools, even for needles and thread. It was a rigorous trip, and a "fur piece," as they say in the Ozarks; but Becknell was most certainly going to start on another trip in about four months, or just as soon as spring opened up.

So there must have been a mad scramble during the next few weeks in the trading centers up and down the Missouri in a search for goods which could be carried to Santa Fe and sold there at a profit. The word had gotten around that a sixty-dollar-investment in this pioneer trading undertaking had paid out as high as nine hundred dollars. This was far above the average profit which trade over the trail yielded. Still that glowing report gave the urge to no less than sixty proprietors, who set out with some fifteen thousand dollars' worth of goods in the early months of 1822.

This larger attempt during the second year proved the practicality of such trade. Although there were fewer traders and a smaller volume of goods in 1823, both numbers and quantity shot up the fourth year, and continued at a high level for many seasons.

The steamboat, now in common use, brought goods from Pittsburgh, Wheeling, New Orleans, and other centers up the Missouri to the towns near that stream's great bend. Blacksmiths, wagon builders, and outfitting stores began to appear and round out a business which gave promise of becoming permanent. As volume increased, pack animals gave way to wagon trains, employing vehicles of the sturdy Conestoga type, or adaptations of it.

THE SANTA FE TRAIL

There were distinct dangers along the way, and prudence counseled the independent parties to travel together over most of the route. Since there were virtually no threats to safety in its first hundred fifty miles, Council Grove, at the edge of the hardwood belt and the beginning of the open plains, became the rallying point. When all the units electing to make the trip had gathered there in May and a leader was chosen and the positions of each group decided upon, the great caravan of many wagons moved off. Pictures show them in four parallel lines, each vehicle drawn by three or four pairs of horses, mules, or cattle, with additional animals in reserve.

Cattle do not seem to have proved as practical for motive power for these early prairie schooners, and were far outnumbered by other creatures generally thought more temperamental.

The drivers customarily rode astride the nigh horse or ox of the pair hitched to the whiffletree, and maneuvered their teams with a long cracking whip, and spicy, shouted commands. While some of the "bullwhackers" rode, many of them trudged along beside their oxen, pouring out to their beasts an almost constant flow of either cajoling or goading words. Since much of the ensuing trade was by barter, great numbers of jacks, jennies, and mules were soon being driven home from New Mexico. This was the beginning of the long-famous Missouri mule.

If danger threatened during the day, but especially when camp was made at night, the four lines were promptly swung about until the wagons formed the sides of a hollow square as a shield against attack. The Indians soon learned to respect the protection this arrangement afforded, and so tried to stage surprise raids which would stampede the party before the protective square could be formed to shelter both men and beasts.

What was to become known as the Santa Fe Trail was more a general direction of travel within fairly narrow limits than a deeply rutted single-track way, as were the caravan routes of the ancient world. It struck off to the southwest by the most direct route seasonal conditions afforded, heading always for the great bend of the Arkansas. From there it usually followed along the northern bank to near where Fort Dodge and the fabulous Dodge City were later to appear. At that point lay a choice.

The river could be forded, and a shorter, more direct route taken through the dry lands on the upper reaches of the Cimarron and Canadian rivers directly into Las Vegas. The alternate led west along the Arkansas over the track that had been laid down in the first year of trading by Becknell. It, too, came first to Las Vegas; and from there into Santa Fe it was always a free-for-all, each party hoping to be first on the scene of trading to capture the cream of the market.

Soon romantic stories of this seasonal trade began to flow back East, and attracted, among others, a rank tenderfoot, one Josiah Gregg. He appeared on the scene in 1831, made a number of journeys with the annual caravan, and became the trail's outstanding historian. His account, titled *Commerce of the Prairies, or the Journal of a Santa Fe Trader,* is still exciting reading.

As early as 1825 this increasing trade had found a live champion in Thomas Hart Benton, the North Carolina boy raised in Tennessee, and now the very vocal senator from Missouri. Largely at his insistence, the United States Government surveyed the route, and there was later a flurry of agitation to build a fixed roadway over its course to hook up ultimately with the National Road now thrusting west from Wheeling.

A survey party did set up earth and broken stone cairns to indicate its direction across trackless grasslands, but these markers soon disappeared through the action of wind, rain, and frost. Some further government recognition was accorded this enterprise as federal cavalry accompanied the parties to and from the Mexican border. But these protective measures were limited to two or three seasons, for by and large the groups that rolled down the trail were quite competent to care for themselves. While some surrendered their lives to the variety of hazards along the way, their total number is far less than one might gather from the motion picture and other fictional accounts based on its operation.

It was well into the 1830s before the trade over "Benton's Road," as it was sometimes called, began to hit its stride. The bulk of the trading at the other end took place in Santa Fe, although a few parties, perhaps late arrivals, pushed on down the Rio Grande, some as far as Chihuahua. During about fifteen years this trade thrived, which is not to say that its volume was impressive, for it was but a drop in the bucket as compared with the total import and export business of the growing young country as a whole. In the year of its peak traffic it involved no more than thirty traders as principals, some three hundred fifty men in all, and the two hundred fifty wagons used bore goods with a total value of but $450,000. Nonetheless, the trail exerted influences quite out of proportion to the number who journeyed over it, or the value of what they carried outward bound.

It covered a far greater distance than the National Road would traverse, and ran through country of a new and quite different type. It thus began to stimulate the thinking and preparations soon called upon to take men and women over still longer trails to the Pacific coast. It increased the flow of eastern goods into the West, and gave quite an impetus to the swelling frontier. Before it began to taper off in the middle and late 1840s, it would exert other influences, some immediate, others spread over a longer period. Then as interest in it began to die down, the attention it had fostered transferred to other avenues of travel to far places.

In Missouri, where it originated, it brought several marked benefits. It laid the foundation of the substantial community which now centers in Kansas City, and, closer to its own times, the military establishments which began to thrust out from Fort Leavenworth. Not only did the mules driven home from Mexico give us a new draft animal accustomed to a diet of corn, which was to be a staple crop of the central valleys, but the silver coins also brought back played their conspicuous part. It was not quite after the manner of the contribution made by the pirates a hundred years or more before, but an instance of the effect this precious metal had may be illuminating.

Even after Jackson started us on the way toward a specie currency, the banking business operated on a none too secure basis. In a moment of stringency in 1839, suspicion was directed at the Bank of Missouri. This brought on a run which threatened both that institution and the solvency of the entire state. But the homeward-bound traders suddenly dumped some $45,000 of hard money into its coffers, and this quick transfusion into the financial bloodstream staved off disaster. By the following year it could be conservatively reported that "the State of Missouri is as this day the soundest in the union in her monetary affairs. She is filled with specie; and the interior Mexican states have supplied it."

But apart from Missouri's own concerns, this traffic over the Santa Fe Trail exerted a most beneficial influence in breaking down a totally unfounded belief. Pike, Lewis and Clark, and other observers had pronounced the huge treeless plains between the Missouri and the Rockies as a totally worthless stretch, unfit for habitation by any except the Indians. They had been compared with the steppes of Tartary, with the Sahara in Africa, and came to bear the opprobrious designation of the great American desert.

This opinion and attitude had carried up to the White House itself, and Monroe, while President, had based an Indian policy upon it, which would prove difficult to carry out and vexatious in adjustment as these boundless plains were later opened up for settlement. It would take much crossing and recrossing of these seemingly limitless open spaces by countless travelers before the true value of the plains country would be fully realized, and the Santa Fe, and later the trails to Oregon, California, and Utah, would play their part in reassessing a mighty frontier, destined to become one of the nation's great assets and heritages.

XXI

A Frontier Contribution to Science

. . . Thus then ye meate being chaw'd in ye mouth receives ye first tincture from ye spittle, and going through ye oesophagus is imbued with ye same, till in ye fundus of ye stomach it lyes in a liquor of ye same nature but greater activity, & being encompassed about by the coate of ye stomach, it lyes in that watery bed as in its proper menstrum: & receiving by little & little this piercing and searching liquor into all its parts and ferments, and so dissolves into a kind of mash, from which ye nutrimentall parts of life of ye meate are now become separable and faeculent. Which being done, ye stomach having performed its proper worke, by ye compression of itself sends it forth through ye Pylorus into ye guts, leaving a small quantity still as ye remaining ferment.—Manuscript notes of *Lectures on Medicine*, delivered at Oxford University in the seventeenth century.

As MAN and the animals on which he was dependent for his food moved north with the retreating glaciers, the fur of the creatures whose flesh he consumed became a prime necessity as well. Their hides amplified his own thin skin in the contest with the weather during the colder seasons. And long after he had lost much of the protective outer layer of fat with which nature had endowed him and he had become a little soft, and vainer, he satisfied his latent conceit by adding fur to his clothing of leather or rude textiles. It not only aided in keeping him physically warm, but set his ego pleasantly aglow as well.

Thus fur was probably among the earliest articles of exchange, and the pelts peeled from the various animals came to have a wide range of values, much as they have today. By their relative scarcity or difficulty of capture certain pelts, such as those of the sable, ermine, mink, or beaver, long ago found themselves a well-elevated niche in man's estimation. By contrast the hides of the deer, bear, buffalo, and the larger and more common creatures commanded less respect and value. But there was continuing demand, and the fur trade in Europe was brisk and well organized when

Columbus headed west; and it was not long before shipments from America were doubtless disturbing this European market, and quite likely stimulating new vogues and trends among couturiers and hat-makers.

The elation of the Dutch traders was very real when one of their first ships to return from New Amsterdam carried a furry cargo running to thousands of guilders, and there would be endless bales and hogsheads crammed full of hides and pelts on ship after ship out of American ports through the years to come. There had been keen competition, between the Swedes and Dutch and other groups, throughout the colonial period, and the rivalry between the Americans and the British out of Canada following the Revolution was acute and intensely bitter. As we moved into the 1800s, the new government was determined that our nationals get their full share of this trapping and trade, even to fostering something of a monopoly if need be to effect it. This heightened interest tended to bring to the fore one of the best known names in the American fur business, John Jacob Astor, the immigrant boy held up to several earlier generations as the "self-made man" worthy of emulation.

He had left Germany and gained some business experience in England producing and selling musical instruments before arriving here, primed for fame and fortune, in 1784. Choosing the fur trade as his province, he organized the legendary American Fur Company in 1808, and became the largest factor in this storied business. He would have pitted against him at many points along our still uncertain northern border another famous organization. As early as 1670 the king of England had chartered the *Governor and Company of Adventurers of England, Trading into Hudson Bay*. Later it would be known as the Hudson's Bay Company; and after Canada fell to the British this, and other smaller concerns based upon Montreal, pushed their efforts out through the Great Lakes region and on to the Pacific coast.

Thus the fur frontier ranged over much of the country, and one very promising area was the unsettled Pacific Northwest. To service it, Astor established a post at the mouth of the Columbia River just in time to have it seized by the British at the onset of the War of 1812. When that contest was out of the way, he began to move into another equally promising area about the Great Lakes. There is an island where Michigan and Huron mix their waters, and close by the passage through to Superior, called Mackinac. There, in 1817, Astor centered his American Fur Company, with headquarters close by the United States border fort. Within five years the concern was receiving some three million dollars' worth of pelts each spring, brought in by as many as two thousand voyageurs, principally Frenchmen, who scoured not only the nearby forests, but the headwaters of the Mississippi and the shores of Lake Superior.

In a business in which almost anything could happen, and usually did, perhaps the most novel, far-reaching, and in certain respects most beneficial occurence in the varied experiences of the fur traffic took place at this Mackinac Island post. This springboard into the wilderness would seem the most unlikely place in which to discover a budding scientist, but so it was.

MEDICAL PRACTICE IN THE EARLY 1800S

The man who had a major part in the development of this rare phenomenon, and who played "I spy" with our digestive processes to the everlasting benefit of succeeding generations, was a doctor named William Beaumont. Let it be emphasized, too, that he was of quite a different sort than were many of the medical quacks then streaming out into the frontier communities.

His forebears had come from England as early as 1635, and had settled in Connecticut. There he was born in 1785, and we know little of his childhood except that he was the type of youngster ready and willing to accept a dare. In winning one, he had stood too close to a cannon being fired, and suffered some impairment in his hearing in later life, presumably as a result.

By the time he was twenty-one he had saved up a hundred dollars, then a considerable sum; and hitching his horse to a light sleigh, and with a barrel of hard cider to keep him company, set off to the north in search of an education and livelihood. Settling in Champlain, a small community in New York State near the Canadian border, he taught school there for three years. Then he apprenticed himself to a local physician, and by 1812 the medical society in neighboring Vermont granted him his license to practice. Almost at once he found himself in the Army as a surgeon's mate.

At the end of the War of 1812, he and another ex-army surgeon started a joint practice in Plattsburg, and, as was not too uncommon in older days, opened a store in which to sell drugs and medicines, gradually branching out into groceries as well. But storekeeping was uncertain and the Army had its compensations. So he applied for a commission, received one signed by President Monroe in March 1820, and was ordered to Fort Mackinac to be associated there with his former commandant. Taking a "delay en route," he visited his family in Connecticut, and was then off on his adventures.

From Albany, he traveled out by way of the Erie Canal as far as that project had been completed, to a point just beyond Auburn. To him it seemed fraught with tremendous benefits to coming generations. From there he went on to Buffalo by stage. After a very brief side trip to view Niagara, he went aboard the steamboat *Walk-in-the-Water*, a tiny side-wheeler, which hugged the south shore of Lake Erie, and gave him a chance to view the beginnings of Cleveland and Sandusky as he chugged along to Detroit.

There he was forced to lay over about two weeks, meeting a few acquaintances, but considering the place somewhat "indifferent." To while away one long Sunday, he attended a Presbyterian service in the morning, and one at a Catholic church in the afternoon. But on June 14 he was again aboard the *Walk-in-the-Water*, which worked its way up along the shore, first of Lake St. Clair, and then of Lake Huron toward the post where he was to serve.

He thus came to Fort Mackinac at the very height of its busy season, when the island's beaches would be lined with the tents of a transient population of perhaps as many as five thousand and great bundles of furs were being traded by the Indians and French voyageurs, who had come in from the woods from all directions. Such rendezvous were always tumultuous affairs, and the resulting dances, parties, and an almost continual round of festivities, punctuated frequently by fights and brawls, made it a jubilant place for seven or eight weeks. Then, as the trappers left for the back country, it quieted down again. Still it was new, exciting, and thrilling far beyond the placid life in the towns along the western shore of Lake Champlain which he had recently forsaken.

But young Dr. Beaumont had left his heart back there in those staid surroundings, and in 1821 he took a leave sufficient to get him back to Plattsburg, where he was married. He and his young bride were soon on their way back to the lively atmosphere at the fort by the junction of the two great lakes. The following winter passed with nothing more thrilling than the birth of a daughter. Then as late spring rolled around, the settlement began to fill in again with added people, color, and clamor.

THE MAN WITH THE LID ON HIS STOMACH

It was on June 6 that a tragic accident occurred, which, while not too unusual in itself, was destined to become medical history of the first order. In a scuffle outside the company's store, a twenty-nine-year-old French voyageur, Alexis St. Martin, received a nasty gunshot wound in his upper abdomen, which left a hole large enough so that a man might thrust his fist into it. A messenger was speeded to the neighboring fort, and within a few minutes Beaumont was bending over the prostrate man stretched upon a cot.

Deftly he picked shot and pieces of flesh and clothing from the huge hole in the unfortunate's mid-section. He did all that he could at the moment; but as he rose from beside the desperately injured one, he gave it as his opinion that the voyageur could not possibly last until the next day. Adding a few brief instructions, he hurried over to the army post to tend to matters there. When he was back again within an hour or two, he was astonished to find the young man showing signs of rallying.

As soon as the patient could be moved, he was carried to the hospital at the fort. There, as his wound was further cleaned, hope began to mount for his recovery. A hospital record which was to run for more than two years and cover many pages was started. One of its early entries shows that the still open orifice was of a size so that the doctor could readily look through it into the stomach of the living man, and also watch the action of one lung as the breath was drawn in and exhaled. It was a situation to excite a serious-minded physician, and was to prove the chance not of one, but of many lifetimes.

By the end of ten days, the gaping wound was beginning to heal satisfactorily along its edges. The man was sustained first by injections, and then by introducing food and drink directly into his stomach, the hole being capped until it absorbed nutriment from the charge. This went on for three weeks, the patient manifesting rather normal appetite as healing also continued.

But this latter aspect posed a problem. Despite all that could be done to stimulate them to do so, the edges of the wound stubbornly resisted fusing together. What remained was an open cleft, nearly three inches across. For five months more the doctor did his best to try to close up this direct opening to the stomach.

Finally a year had elapsed. The man was on his feet once again, able to be about, and even to chop wood. But he had suddenly become a pauper through his misfortunes, for the county refused to furnish further assistance in this case. Still he was in no condition to be discharged and take to the woods again. It was perhaps a difficult choice at first, but there seemed to be nothing for Beaumont to do but to adopt the patient into his own family. His salary as a post surgeon was but forty dollars a month, plus quarters and part rations for him and his wife, and with a baby to provide for. But he accepted the responsibility, and beyond the rewards of charity, the now thirty-eight-year-old physician began to envision other compensations. Said he in his diary:

This case affords excellent opportunity for experimenting upon the gastric fluids and processes of digestion. It would give no pain, nor cause the least uneasiness, to extract a gill of fluid every two or three days . . . Various kinds of digestible substances might be introduced into the stomach, and then examined during the whole process of digestion. I may, therefore, be able henceforth to give some interesting experiments on these subjects.

Far better than a "hole in the head," this man had one in his stomach. This made him more than a mere guinea pig, for he was actually a complete, living, gastric laboratory. Was the subject ready to play such a role? Was he willing to become an experimental workshop? It seems he was not exactly enthusiastic about it.

First he felt himself to be the unfortunate object of charity. But beyond that, while some people stirred up trouble over him with other members of his family, many of them just persisted in pointing him out, and behind his back whispered with a smile and annoying implications, "There's the man with the lid on his stomach!" This did not set well with a proud young Frenchman, a voyageur by birth and by inclination, who would much rather push off in his canoe with his traps, and again search the streams for beaver. But the inconvenient doorway into his inner regions was a severe handicap to the active life of a woodsman. So he agreed to stay on, and by early 1825 had found a niche in medical history along side that of his deliverer, when a detailed article based on the progressing experiments appeared in the reputable *Medical Recorder*.

Deciding the distant outpost was not conducive to further study and research, Dr. Beaumont managed to have himself shifted a shade closer in toward civilization. Taking his family, and his ward, he transferred to Fort Niagara, outside growing Buffalo, now the lake port of the completed canal. But it proved an unfortunate move, for Alexis St. Martin, close to the borders of his native Canada, took french leave, disappeared, and the experiments came to a sudden termination.

Then there were several rather lean years for the doctor, punctuated by difficulties between him and the Army, resulting in some sharp words for President Adams and his transfer back into the Michigan country to Fort Howard, and then on into Wisconsin to Fort Crawford at Prairie du Chien. But he was a thoroughgoing practitioner, gained repute in the medical fraternity, and finally managed to get back to civilization and into touch with men who could aid him in the advanced research he had long planned.

Also, good fortune suddenly smiled upon him again. His mobile laboratory was recovered; and at Plattsburg, where he was presently recruiting officer, he began again the long-delayed experiments on Alexis St. Martin's open-front stomach. There were several series of these, and in 1833 their results were set forth in permanent form in *Experiments and Observations on the Gastric Juice and the Physiology of Digestion*, by William Beaumont, M.D., Surgeon, U.S.A.

This frontier army physician had made a lasting name for himself, for, as the famous Dr. William Osler said of him, "His experiments settled finally the chemical nature of the digestive process . . . The man was greater than his work. The pioneer physiologist of the United States and *the first to make a contribution of enduring value*, that work remains a model of patient, persevering research." So much for the good doctor, whose place in the scheme of things was reasonably secure.

But how about, as Osler refers to him, "that old fistulous Alexis"? He was a marked man, and for some time as much in demand as though he had two heads, four arms, or ten fingers on each hand. Medical colleges and learned societies up and down the land all wanted to have a peek through the gastric fistula—for a consideration of course. There had been one or two other hazily recorded examples of the same rarity in medical history, but here was one in the flesh; and for a time he was a seven-day wonder. He had married, had four children, and as he began to slip back into the limbo, he made his home in Cavendish, Vermont, supporting his family chopping cordwood. Finally in extreme old age and penury he fled back to Canada again, and died there in 1880, at the age of eighty-three.

Oh, there were other highly interesting things that happened in upper Michigan and elsewhere in the fur trade in those early days. But none of them set off quite such a remarkable train of circumstances as did a nervous finger pressed against a long-rifle trigger that momentous day in 1822. Still the fur trade played so considerable a part in the winning of the West that other phases of it deserve attention, and necessitate a journey far beyond the Mississippi.

XXII

The Fur Trade Pioneers the Far West

It was the roving trader and solitary trapper who first sought out these inhospitable wilds, traced the streams to their sources, scaled the mountain passes, and explored a boundless expanse of territory where the foot of the white man had never trodden before. The Far West became a field of romantic adventure, and developed a class of men who loved the wandering career of the native inhabitant rather than the toilsome lot of the industrious colonist. The type of life that thus developed, though essentially evanescent, and not representing any profound national movement, was a distinct and necessary phase in the growth of this new country.—Hiram Martin Chittenden, *Fur Trade of the Far West.*

O NE of the great fur-producing areas was the Missouri Valley, and beyond it the whole great mountain backbone of the continent stretching from Canada to Mexico, with an extension at its northern end to the mouth of the Columbia in the Oregon country. French trappers had no doubt camped on the site of St. Louis years before the Spaniards had erected their fort there. Although it was on the Mississippi, it was but about a dozen miles below the mouth of the Missouri, and thus at a natural gateway to the fur country to the north, and especially to the west. It was destined to become the center of that trade, which would produce a greater dollar volume than any other "crop" harvested beyond the Mississippi for many years to come.

The pelts and hides that flowed through this market place fell into two main divisions: the *fine* furs being principally beaver, otter, mink, fox and a relatively few others; while the more common types were buffalo, deer, antelope, and bear. Some meat, especially buffalo and bear tallow, together with a few other items, formed less consequential by-products. But for years the beavers' downy covering held top spot in importance, and did not yield it until the human male altered his preference to high hats fashioned from silk.

Beyond the Indians, who continued to furnish a large portion of the total take of skins, there were "free" hunters and trappers who staked themselves, operated where they chose, and traded their catch with whomever they pleased. They customarily took in return tobacco, powder, shot, and a few prime necessities, not overlooking one of somewhat dubious value—liquor. These free-lance operators were apparently outnumbered by those who were employed by one or another of the organized fur companies, to whom they were *supposed* to turn over their entire catch at some appointed trading post. Their wages were paid similarly in kind. By and large the trappers, whether free or hirelings, led an exciting, far-ranging life, but without the monetary returns that went to the traders and factors. Still these latter faced a gamble which could put them "in clover" or in the poorhouse with about equal speed and facility.

While no single enterprise operating from St. Louis may have achieved the volume of Astor's great company, several of them managed to encompass in their operations a wide number of men who wrote their names indelibly into the story of the West. One group in particular included a dozen or more personalities who roved together for a number of years, and then went on to other accomplishments severally or in smaller parties, and whose varied exploits fill a whole shelf of highly readable books.

Some of their undertakings while they were still together as novices do give a clear picture of the life which bred a race of stalwarts who began the certain winning of the West for the generations to follow. They centered about a Virginian named William Ashley, who had drifted out into the great valley some years after the Revolution, had done well in land speculation and the manufacture of gunpowder, and as Missouri approached statehood, was a contender for political honors with no less a local hero than Thomas Hart Benton.

Ashley's first partner was Andrew Henry, who had made his way west from Pennsylvania, had had a relatively brief fling at trapping, and then taken up lead mining to his profit. Early in 1822 both he and Ashley had managed to obtain government licenses to trade on the upper Missouri, and had decided to make it a joint endeavor. With spring about to break, they caused the following ad to appear in the Missouri *Republican*. The date was March 20, and it read:

TO ENTERPRISING YOUNG MEN. The subscriber wishes to engage one hundred young men to ascend the Missouri river to its
source, there to be employed one, two, or three years. For particulars
enquire of Major Henry, near the lead mines in the county of Washington, who will ascend with, and command, the party; or of the
subscriber, near St. Louis.—William H. Ashley.

With a nice dash of uncertainty in it, the advertisement developed pulling power and brought a host of inquirers. But the real
"clincher" quite likely was the assurance given in person to those
who presented themselves that the party was to tap a new area, on
both sides of the mountains, where the fur catch would be "richer
than the mines of Peru." Also the party intended to push on across
the divide and descend to the very mouth of the Columbia itself on
the alluring Pacific coast.

Blacksmiths' apprentices dropped their hammers. Billiard-parlor
operators hurriedly sold out. Old hands at the fur trade volunteered,
so did consumptives in search of bracing mountain air, and even
tenderfeet fresh from back East. From among the many applicants,
a likely appearing party was assembled. While a few of its members
eventually turned yellow, others bloomed into heroes; and the group,
with Andy Henry at its head, made off up the Missouri in two large
keelboats on April 15, 1822.

THE BREEDING AND NURTURE OF FUR TRAPPERS

In the very area where Santa Fe traders were about to
center their eastern bases, one craft hit a submerged snag and sank
so suddenly that all its contents were lost, while many of its passengers narrowly escaped drowning. It was an unfortunate beginning; but still this was the risky fur business, and a profit usually
had to be earned in one way or another before it was firmly in hand.

Crowded together now in one boat, with a portion of the party
following along the shore, they managed to push on up as far as Great
Falls. There a brush with the Assiniboin Indians stopped them in
their tracks, and they fell back to the mouth of the Yellowstone River,
establishing a post there, from which they hunted and trapped the
area during the winter ahead.

Back in St. Louis, Ashley had recruited another group of one
hundred, picked up two more keelboats, and set off with them on
March 23, 1823. His intentions were to join Henry at the triple forks
of the Missouri in western Montana, and with the combined parties

really comb the pelts out of that wilderness region. By the end of April he had reached the Arikara villages near the present lower border of South Dakota. This tribe appears to have allowed Henry to pass the year before without incident. But while they were highly unpredictable, Ashley badly needed horses, and risked stopping to trade with them when it appeared they might be friendly.

The trade was completed, and while a group of the men were left behind to guard the horses on the beach below the breastworks standing before one of the savages' palisaded towns, Ashley went back to the keelboats anchored well out in the river to pass the night. His interpreter had warned him the savages' affability was all on the surface, but he went to sleep without a qualm.

Indian rifles began barking at daylight, and within fifteen or twenty minutes the party was in a bad way, had to hastily pick up what wounded it could, and beat a hasty retreat downstream to a wooded island to catch its breath. It had been a gruesome business, but it quickly separated the wheat from the chaff, since the latter promptly mutinied and refused to try another run past the well-fortified Indian camp.

Their leader had no choice but to load his wounded and the timorous into one of the boats and send them back down river to St. Louis. Yes, there were supposedly high profits in this business, but none had been sighted thus far.

Thirty men from among the hundred starters volunteered to go on. But word had been dispatched to the Indian agent, and also to General Atkinson, asking for a military escort, so it seemed prudent to wait and see whether such aid would be forthcoming. In the meanwhile, however, it would be necessary to contact Henry, far on up the Missouri and daily expecting the arrival of reinforcements.

Ashley then did some quick thinking involving this whole upper Missouri country as a field of operations. Next he called for a volunteer courier, and the first to step forward was young Jedediah Smith, born of a good family not too many years before in New York State. There he had received an excellent education, and almost at the moment of his arrival in St. Louis had joined the expedition. Something about him made a strong appeal to Ashley, so he was dispatched, along with a Canadian voyageur as companion, on the perilous journey. And he proved an excellent choice, for he made a successful trip, and lived to become Ashley's partner and one of the most intrepid and respected members of this spectacular business, before finally losing his life in the Santa Fe trade when crossing the dangerous Cimarron country in 1831.

ASHLEY MOVES HIS TRAPPING OPERATIONS
TO THE WEST

When word reached Henry, he descended the river, slipped past the Arikara villages, and joined Ashley near the site of present-day Pierre, South Dakota. Dropping down to the mouth of the Teton River, they had the good fortune to meet there with troops sent out for their protection. When horses had been found, Henry took his own and the remainder of Ashley's men and struck out overland for the Yellowstone River.

But there was a third clash with the Indians, two more men were lost, and many horses had to be replaced. They were by now entering the Powder River country, where prospects for their primary business of trapping were more promising. Here, too, it seemed safe to split the party, Henry taking the larger group north to establish a new post at the junction of the Big Horn and Yellowstone, while a smaller number, under the leadership of the experienced Etienne Provost, headed southwest.

This latter contingent still managed to embrace its share of men who would make "grass roots" history. Pressing across South Pass, through which the famous Oregon Trail would soon run, they moved on into what is now Utah. Just how far beyond the Wasatch Mountains they then went is not certain, but it seems likely they came to know something of the central part of that state. It would appear they ultimately followed up the Bear River, which runs toward the north along the eastern edge of the mountain ridge that lies in back of the present-day capital of Utah, and they seem to have found rich hunting grounds.

Ashley, after comparing notes with Henry, decided to change the whole scheme of operations. Maintenance of outposts at considerable distances from St. Louis was expensive and hazardous. Also the growing competition in that area counseled abandonment of efforts in the upper Missouri Valley. From now on they would depend upon catches by itinerant parties, working promising localities to the west rather than to the north, with regular points for the pickup in the late spring.

He had been interested in politics, so he made a hurried trip back to the river port to run for governor of the state. But his defeat

at the polls turned him back toward the hills again, to give his fur
enterprise his chief interest. In the late fall of 1824 he was on his way,
passing through Council Bluffs on November 1. This time he moved
out along the Platte River, finally taking its south fork, and went on
to winter in the spacious Green River Valley in southwestern Wyoming.

A STARTLING DISCOVERY

About this same time the Provost party was digging in for the
winter along the Bear River, probably near where that stream, now
turned to the south, crosses back from its excursion into Wyoming to
Utah, where it originates. It has a most erratic course, and this fact
very likely set the group to wondering about its eventual outflow.
The argument must have waxed hot, for a group wager seems to
have developed, and one of their number was selected to look into
the matter and report back with his findings.

The choice fell on twenty-year-old Jim Bridger, another Virginia
boy, but a Missourian since about 1812. Plodding down along the
stream as it meanders through a lovely valley, he must have gotten
a real thrill when at last he saw a huge patch of shimmering blue
ahead. What could it be? It was not so much this fairly large bay
immediately before him, for through its narrow entrance at the south
the distant horizon still rested on waves white capped by the early
winter winds. He was certain, too, that it stretched off further than
the eye could see beyond the great promontory to the west. This was
a find indeed, so he hurried to where the river emptied out into
this great expanse of vivid blue water.

At the shore at last, he walked along the sandy beach away from
the river's mouth. Then dropping to his knees, he tasted the water
brought in by the lapping waves. It was salt! Very salty! That settled
it. The haphazard Bear River evidently emptied into an arm of the
mighty Pacific, there seemed little doubt of it. This was news of
great import, and he hurried back upstream to his companions.
Whether the word he brought settled the bet or not is beside the
point, but this discovery was very likely the talk of the camp for the
remainder of the winter.

It was spring, however, before the find could be thoroughly investigated. Then four men, using skin boats, crept about its shores,
moving on until at last they had covered its entire ·circumference
without finding the least trace of an outlet. It was very baffling, but

actually two great discoveries had been made. The whole party had found its way into that expansive area running into several states whose landlocked bounds keep all water within its confines and gain for it the designation of the Great Basin. And the bright blue sea glistening before them in the spring sunlight was the remains of a once much vaster body of water, but still the mighty Great Salt Lake. Perhaps other white men had seen it before Jim Bridger happened upon it, but if so, we have no record of their having done it.

Across the mountains to the east, at about the time this salty sea was being disproved an arm of the Pacific, Ashley was starting off on further adventures of his own. There was then some doubt as to the course of the sizable Green River. So in April of 1825 he started down its tortuous course, passing through mile after long mile of deep canyon, only to come to grief in the plunging cascade near the mouth of the stream that now bears his name as it pitches down from the Uinta Mountains to add its waters to the Green. His vessel was wrecked, and forty years later some of its contents were picked up along the banks by a geological survey party. It was wild country, seldom traversed, and still is. Pushing on down as far as Desolation Canyon, he there abandoned further search.

Turning north over the mountains, he sought contact with his other party, but was forced to move up into what is now Wyoming before he joined with them. It was here on Burnt Fork, in July 1824, that the first of a long series of great rendezvous, or fur-trading fairs, was held in the Sierras, which would be annual events for many years.

It was about this same time also that the profit phase of the business began to come to the surface, and it provided Ashley with the stake that encouraged him to retire and leave the field to younger men. Just how he came into possession of them is still not entirely clear, but he soon was the owner of one hundred packs of fine furs, variously reported to have been worth from seventy-five thousand to a quarter million dollars. One theory is that he stumbled upon the cache of the famed Canadian, Peter Skene Ogden, who would later give his name to Ogden, Utah, and also succor the hard-pressed Whitman Party bound for Oregon. There being manifest ill will toward these intruders from above the border, it could have been within the moral concepts of the frontier to take possession of this rich haul.

However, such a solution is hardly in keeping with Ashley's other dealings, and thus favors the contention that Ogden, in straitened circumstances and in need of immediate cash, sold out at ruinously low prices. But whatever the truth of the matter, the new owner was soon on his way back to the States to convert the take into ready money.

Returning to the mountains again early in 1826, he attended the annual rendezvous held that year on the site of present-day Ogden, and was now ready to relinquish the reins. Jedediah Smith had already taken Henry's place, and Ashley sold out his remaining interest to two other members of the party, William Sublette and David Jackson. This latter managed to have one of the most majestic bits of scenery in the whole United States named for him, the Jackson Hole country at the foot of the Tetons in Wyoming. Sublette and his partner, Robert Campbell, built a log fort over in Wyoming in 1834 which ultimately became the well-known Fort Laramie.

Jim Bridger went on to become probably the most restless mountain man the country ever produced, for there were few valleys from border to border west of the Mississippi through which he had not wandered. He never did learn to read or write in the ordinary manner. But he only had to see a bit of country once to always remember it, which ability made of him the most famous guide of his time. Later he had a fort of his own on Black's Fork of the Green River, which became the most celebrated post between the Father of Waters farther east and the Pacific coast beyond the mountains. Still he was but a notch or two above many others who graduated from this same rigorous fur-trapping school.

That the West would have ultimately been tamed without men tempered in this harsh educational establishment—the Rocky Mountain College—is probable; but that it could have been accomplished as rapidly, or as well, is open to serious question. Quite naturally some of these and also other outstanding characters who played a part in the fur business must of necessity be encountered again as interest in the frontier moves on toward the Pacific, into the Northwest, and ultimately encompasses the Great Plains.

XXIII

The Perplexing Indian Problem

THE INDIAN AND THE BUFFALO. The buffalo was the department store of the Plains Indian. The flesh was food, the blood was drink, skins furnished wigwams, robes made blankets and beds, dressed hides supplied moccasins and clothing, hair was twisted into ropes, rawhide bound tools to handles, green hides made pots for cooking over buffalo-chip fires, hides from bulls' necks made shields that would turn arrows, ribs were runners for dog-drawn sleds, small bones were awls and needles, from hooves came glue for feathering arrows, from sinews came thread and bowstrings, from horns came bowls, cups and spoons, and even from gall stones a *medicine* paint was made. When the millions of buffalo that roamed the prairies were exterminated the Plains Tribes were starved into submittion.—Text of a historical marker, on U.S. Route 50S at Garden City, Finney County, Kansas.

CORONADO and his party, pressing toward Quivira, had been the first white men to encounter the Great Plains. They and others whose lot was cast upon them came to know the grimness of these boundless flat lands, and their forbidding aspects translated them in men's imagination into the great American desert. One of their great redeeming features was the grazing they provided for countless herds of buffalo, yet the bison was but one among many animals with which these plains abounded, and upon which the Indians lived, and, by their lights, lived fairly well.

Why not then reserve this "desert" area, as King George had earlier attempted to reserve all lands beyond the Alleghenies, and leave it unmolested as the home of the native peoples, even moving to it the remnants of displaced eastern tribes standing in the way of progress? President Monroe, who developed the Doctrine for all America, set up an Indian policy based upon such lines of thought. Out of it grew the Indian reservations, some vestiges of which remain to this day.

Had he and his successors been able to freeze conditions as they obtained in the forepart of the 1800s, had our population remained relatively stationary, and the American people been content to stay largely east of the Mississippi and confine their energies, these western plains might today still be primarily the home of the savages. But the pressure of altering circumstances was against such plans.

However, in 1825 the government began to establish what it hoped would be a permanent Indian frontier. It began in Wisconsin, swung out into Minnesota, then down the western bank of the Mississippi, dropping back from that stream through eastern Iowa, ran west along the northern border of Missouri, then south again on its western border and that of the Arkansas Territory to the Red River. West and northwest of this line many of the Indians were to find a new home.

The task of removing the natives and getting them bedded down in their new preserves would take more than one volume to recount. But perhaps the forced migration of the Cherokees and the Seminoles attracted more general attention than that of the other tribes. The former were beginning to acquire some visible signs of civilization from their white neighbors in the Southeast, and one episode out of this experience is worth recounting. Caught up in their exodus was one of the most remarkable characters among the American Indians, whose story has been pretty much overlooked by present generations. His brethren had a most descriptive name for him, which makes an appropriate caption for the brief tale of his experiences.

THE MAN WITH THE TALKING LEAVES

His father, George Gist, seems to have crept into Georgia among one of the waves of reputable Saltburgers who founded the now "lost" town of Ebenezer. But he was a restless good-for-nothing, a wanderer, and finally took up unlicensed trading with the Cherokees in the mountains to the west. There, sometime about 1768, or perhaps in the following year, he made the best trade of his life. For a few trinkets he purchased an Indian maid, who became his slave wife.

It is said she built their hogan, apart a little from the tribal village, furnished it, grew the crops, waited upon her husband hand and foot, and did her best to make his new life sheltered and satisfying—but to no lasting avail. Before too many moons had passed, he rode off, presumably on a trading mission, and vanished completely and permanently. But his loss proved endurable, particularly when his son was born not too long afterward in the humble home thatched with branches.

The maternal grandfather, so tradition runs, visited his daughter and her offspring, grunted a qualified approval of the half-breed child when he was assured it was a male, but apparently thereafter left it pretty much to the mother's ministrations. By tribal customs this was *her* home, and in it she now ruled supreme. Perhaps, though, there had been a fleeting trace of approval on the otherwise immobile face to accompany the grunt when the child's sex had been disclosed. Or it may be the mother reasoned the preferred gender should have prompted satisfaction, for she chose the name *Se-quo-yah*, which, in Cherokee, meant "he *guessed* it."

This youngster of diverse backgrounds, born in the year 1770, grew up as an Indian. Yet one gets the impression that he developed just a trifle apart from the mainstream of Cherokee life. However, he played the games of other Indian boys, spoke only their tongue, accepted their beliefs, and was reckoned one of the community.

His mother proved to be a most industrious person, perhaps over and above the standards for her sex among her own people. Quite a few of the Indians were slowly beginning to accept certain of the white man's ways of life, and perhaps her brief intimate association gave her even greater incentive in this direction. To her other farming activities she willingly added the keeping of cows; and her son, somewhat contrary to the male customs of his kind, helped with their care. More significant still, he began to demonstrate mechanical skill by making creamery utensils adapted from those he saw in use by white neighbors in the settlements.

His mother, too, seems to have engaged in trading between the whites and her own people. This the son took up as he grew older, so that his contacts outside the tribe broadened, although he does not seem to have acquired any proficiency in any other language than Cherokee. Some of his enterprises brought in coined money, and this silver he learned to fashion into ornaments, until he became a fairly competent, self-taught silversmith.

As this latter business increased, he felt the need of a trade-mark. Some of his compatriots were anglicizing their names, and recalling that of his own father, Sequoyah approached a friend and asked him to print it for him. The man labored over the task, and in place of Gist managed to spell it *Guess*. But this was quite satisfactory to the young half-breed; so he sunk the letters in a steel punch and began to stamp his wares with this designation. This accounts for his dual name, for he is often spoken of as "George Guess."

From work in silver, he moved on to blacksmithing, and followed that trade for a number of years in the mountain community of which he was more and more a part. He had learned this handcraft by watching the white smiths in the settlements, and there would have been many occasions when, had he been able to phrase them, he could have asked questions to his great advantage. It was perhaps this direct need for a means of communication that set him to work at the project that was years later to make him famous.

His contacts in the settlement, and now with the missionaries beginning to visit and live among the tribe, had made him conscious of the white man's books and written documents. By these "talking leaves" ideas could be both transmitted and stored up. It was no doubt this inner urge, not yet fully understood, that set him next to drawing. His first attempts were pitiably crude, but persisting, he became a reasonable artist.

He had bargained for and purchased himself a wife out of his tribe, and had managed to pick a woman as resolute and industrious as his mother. For a time there was harmony, but it eventually gave place to discord. She was primarily a worker, while her mild, pensive husband, listening to inner voices, was fast becoming a dreamer. The idea of "talking leaves" for the benefit of his own people was taking firm possession of him. While he was nagged at home, the tribesmen at first tended to accept his philosophical ways as evidence of mystic powers.

To his wife's great disgust, he began to neglect his business to frequent the Moravian Mission School. He was too old to be a regular pupil, but the talking leaves in use there would give him no peace. Even an English spelling book, given him no doubt to stay his everlasting questions, was of no aid, and just another goad, for he could not make use of a single character in it. It was suggested that he learn English, but this was not the solution he sought.

All Indians, by the nature of their lives, were forced to employ keen discrimination with regard to sound. Thus Sequoyah had been able from boyhood to quickly recognize the many different noises which he heard all about him. He found he had been sorting them out automatically. Now that he grasped what he had been doing and brought the matter up into conscious thought, the basic idea he was seeking began to be more apparent.

Spoken words, too, were a continuing and varying pattern of distinct sounds. If these were carefully chosen and ordered, they made sense and conveyed thought. How then could he *picture* a train of the disjointed, separate sounds so that the record "talked" and could be employed to carry one's thoughts to another, perhaps miles away? The white men had such a method. Could he devise one for his people? Would pictures do it? Ah, perhaps they would!

So he was soon drawing pictographs by the dozen on bark with berry ink. But he found he was trying to capture whole thoughts, and their number and variety seemed endless. Still it took him some months to realize that by such an approach he was building a picture gallery which it would take a lifetime to commit to memory. It was a blind alley, and he had to withdraw from it.

Back once again in the realm of pure sounds, he may quite likely at first have taken his own name apart and discovered it had three syllables, made up in turn of a number of basic sounds. Quickly he began picking apart other Cherokee words, noting down each distinct sound he encountered. As he worked on he came to the conclusion that their final number would not be unreasonable. So he kept listing them, avidly listening to his own voice and to those of others about him.

By this time his wife had pretty much abandoned her visionary husband, who slighted everyday affairs, moved about in deep reverie, sometimes staring fixedly at the lips of a speaker, only to stop the person and have him mouth certain words over and over. His formerly engaging face was now sober and preoccupied. Members of his tribe began to look askance at him. He was placid and harmless, but the word got about that he was not quite right. His daughter seems to have been the only one who kept faith in him throughout this devouring search.

Try as he would to explain to others what he was attempting, about the best he received in response was either blank stares, or, not infrequently, open jeers. Even the teachers at the mission schools sought to dissuade him. The English language was available, they assured him, replete with its own "talking leaves," so why not adopt it and be done with this fleeting figment of his clouded imagination?

To one whose nation was being hard pressed by those who spoke and issued orders in their own strange language, such a suggestion could have been little short of insult. There was very evidently no help in that quarter, so he avoided the schools and fell back on his own resources. He consoled himself that it would be just a little while longer now. Then, when he was certain he had caught and recorded every needed sound, he would be able to prove to his *own* people the benefit of what he had labored so hard to achieve for them.

He had been thirty-nine when he began serious work on this project. Now he was nearly fifty, and for the last three years he had seldom left his home. But each passing day cut down the possibility that any needed factor had been neglected. Repeated tests on his daughter showed clearly that he, too, could make leaves *talk*, and in the Cherokee language.

THE INVENTION OF AN ALPHABET

It was in 1821 that he finally displayed his finished work—an alphabet of eighty-five characters. He had settled on six musical sounds, the vowels; plus twelve dividing sounds, the consonants. These, in combination with a few needed additions, provided all that ever would be required. Proudly he presented the results of a dozen years of concentrated effort, only to have his people look with suspicion on what he had wrought. His brain child had been stillborn as far as their reaction was concerned. Somewhat crushed, he went back to his sedentary, retiring ways.

Two years later Sequoyah elected to join with those groups that were heeding the government orders and moving out into western Arkansas, in the area later to become the Indian Territory, and eventually Oklahoma. The home which he built near Sallisaw is now maintained as a museum to his memory. But even in this new land he was at first held somewhat in derision. His tribesmen were finding it hard to give credence to anything offered by one whom they had come to believe a bit crazy.

Slowly, however, it dawned on their headmen what a boon it might be if this alphabet would do for them what its inventor claimed for it. The need was sufficient so they pocketed their pride and put the whole matter on trial, permitting their own sons to be the objects of experiment. After a period of intensive instruction at Sequoyah's hands, exhaustive tests were held. Actually their sons had been taught to *read*. Some of the man's loudest detractors, to their own amazement, found that they, too, could read easily after only three days of tutoring. This was indeed something to be treasured and put to immediate use.

A written correspondence could now be carried on between the two segments of the nation, separated by some five hundred miles. The word of what had happened was hurried back East, and there a medal was struck to honor Sequoyah and dispatched to him. But it would be another four years before this mighty contribution came into its own.

The headquarters of the Cherokee Council was still at Echota, in Georgia. There, on February 21, 1828, great excitement reigned. A new and improved printing press was being delivered. With it were chases and other furniture for a complete printing plant, but more important still were the fonts of Sequoyah's new Cherokee alphabet, together with others of English type. Then began the publication of the *Cherokee Phoenix,* first native newspaper on the continent, edited by Elias Boudinot, a full-blooded Cherokee, who had attended the mission school in Cornwall, Connecticut, and married one of the most popular young ladies in that town.

It is claimed that within less than a year after the *Phoenix* was first published fully three quarters of the entire Cherokee nation had not only learned to read but also to write by means of this wondrous new alphabet. To few men has come the opportunity to serve so many so well during their own life span. Also it is said that this was but the sixth time in all history that a totally new alphabet had been devised.

Although his own, and the four neighboring tribes, were finally moved to new homes in the West, they managed remarkable accomplishments there. Contrary to the beliefs of Monroe and his immediate successors in the White House, they achieved civilization beyond former hope, and to their everlasting credit.

And the man who gave one of these tribes talking leaves in their native tongue was to be honored by far beyond his own tribe's gratitude. His statue, which stands in our National Capitol, may be in his likeness; but the mighty redwood trees—the majestic Sequoias—named for him, are in better keeping with the magnitude of his genius.

DEAD BUFFALOES AND BLOOD-RED WHEAT

The quote at the head of this chapter is by no means an exaggeration, but a simple statement of the plains Indians' almost complete dependence upon the buffalo for livelihood. In the earliest days a few herds had lived to the east of the Mississippi, and had ranged well up to the headwaters of the streams that drain the

western slopes of the Appalachian highlands. But the last remnants
of them disappeared rapidly as white settlers began to penetrate to
the interior. To the west of the great river, however, they were a
major factor in the maintenance of the tribes native to that area,
and other tribes herded there from the regions now being intensively
settled. At last there came the day when the trans-Mississippi plains
were needed to contain the expanding population and the white man
needed the buffaloes' meat and hides and their range pastures for
homestead plots. From then on the red man was in jeopardy, and
rights granted to him by treaties under the Indian policy were threatened and abrogated.

The several tribes, of which Sequoyah's Cherokees were one,
that had been able to adjust to the cultural ways of their white neighbors, became the Five Civilized Tribes, living for many years as
independent nations in the Indian Territory, and were slowly absorbed into the mainstream of American life. The section in which
they had been settled proved to be anything but "desert," and
ultimately became the state of Oklahoma.

Neighboring tribes to the north and south, who were unable to
adapt to an agricultural life, did not fare nearly so well. Below, in
Texas, buffaloes were slaughtered for quick profits, but basically to
take over their range pastures for the raising of cattle. Above, in
Kansas, there was this same slaughter, but in one respect for a different purpose worth noting, and the ultimate use of land there has
its interesting phases.

In the strife over the extension of slavery these Kansas plains
would be bathed in human blood in the years before the outbreak
of the War between the States. At a time when the first settlers were
crowding in, a small boy, born in the Iowa country, was brought
there by his parents. By 1857, and the time he was eleven years old,
William Frederick Cody had lost his father in the border warfare
then raging and his mother was forced to depend upon her young
son to add to the family income.

He had become adept in the handling of a rifle, and also an
accomplished horseman, and when fourteen joined the short-lived
pony express, where he hung up a most remarkable record of three
hundred twenty miles covered on horseback in less than twenty-
two hours.

But when the express was terminated within less than two
years, he was for a time something of a protege of "Wild Bill" Hickok,
when that two-gun marshal was riding herd on the stampeding boom

town of Hays. The Kansas Pacific Railroad was pushing its tracks west through the land of the Jayhawkers, and decided to create a little local good will by staging a buffalo-hunting contest. When young Bill Cody, butt of many a joke by local bully boys, won the affair hands down, he was on his way to fame and fortune. The first step in that direction was a contract to provide meat for the railroad.

There were twelve hundred tracklayers in the gang, and his bogey was set at twelve carcasses a day. For such production he was to receive the almost unheard of salary of five hundred dollars per month; and stimulated by it, he went to work with a will. Within the next eighteen months he killed no less than 4,280 of these great shaggy creatures. There had been millions of them at the beginning, but in the face of wholesale slaughter at the hands of such men as "Buffalo Bill" Cody of Kansas, or Billy Dixon of Texas, their days were limited. The plains of Kansas were receiving a second blood bath, this time from the bison, and there would be a third, but of more peaceable kind.

A great change came in the status of the plains country with the passage of the Homestead Act in 1862. This provided a quarter section—160 acres—from the unappropriated portions of the public domain to the head of a family, or to any male citizen, or intended citizen, twenty-one years old or older. He had only to live upon the claim for five years, cultivate it and make certain improvements, then it was his. The thirst for land was still unslaked, and the prospect of free homesteads pulled settlers not only from the East, but from Europe as well.

Among the latter was a group of Dutch Mennonites who had fled to Russia in 1790, taken over fields in the Crimea, planted them to wheat, and prospered there for some eighty years, enjoying freedom of worship, and freedom from military service as well. When this latter right was threatened, they sought a new haven, and found it in Kansas, where the state legislature, anxious to obtain such substantial settlers, arranged military exemption for these conscientious objectors. Preparations for the mass migration were made well in advance back on the Russian steppes. Their children were put to work laboriously hand-gathering the very best of the hard red-gold kernels of the wheat they had raised so successfully in the lands just north of the Black Sea.

Within a month of their landing in New York in 1874, advance parties were sowing this precious seed in the Kansas soil. That fall saw the harvest of the first crop in this country of the famous turkey red wheat that would swell to a three-hundred-mile wide ocean of the waving grain, and make the Sunflower State the granary of the nation.

The buffaloes were gone, and in their place were wheat fields; and Indians, for the greater part little suited to becoming farmers, were becoming government wards instead.

XXIV

Breaking and Reaping the Prairies

We cross the prairie as of old
    The pilgrims crossed the sea,
To make the West, as they the East,
    The homestead of the free!

We're flowing from our native hills
    As our free rivers flow:
The blessing of our Mother-land
    Is on us as we go.

We go to plant her common schools
    On distant prairie swells,
And give the sabbaths of the wild
    The music of her bells.

—John Greenleaf Whittier, 1856, *The Kansas Emigrants.*

WHILE the song above, echoed by the voices that sang it on the westward trail, clearly indicated the good intents of the hordes of settlers, the prairies which they sought posed a number of problems in addition to those involving the dispossession of the buffalo and the Indians. These other concerns did not act as a deterrent, but they were and had been very real for the past several generations, and now called for adjustment. They revolved about the use of land, and man's tools with which to work and cultivate it.

The reaping hook, lodged over Mrs. Bratton's neck in the closing years of the Revolution, was very much like the bronze sickles wielded by the reapers behind whom Ruth gleaned in the fields of Boaz more than three thousand years before. As we gained our freedom, grain was still being leveled by this same crude device, and then thrashed with flails older than written history. In the back country, corn and wheat were cracked and crushed into a coarse meal or flour by pounding the grains in a mortar gouged from the top of a tree stump. There were some stone mills, driven by wind or water power, but life and living were still a rugged experience for the great majority as America turned into the nineteenth century.

The bulk of the population was dependent upon agriculture, and farming with the aid only of such crude tools as were then available, powered largely by the strength lodged in the arms, legs, and backs of the farmer and the members of his family, made that phase of life something of a frontier within itself, and subject to radical improvement.

Food, which had been man's continuing concern down the long centuries, was still a primary consideration, but the situation was altering markedly. Where, in colonial days, virtually every American was directly tied to the land, the census of 1830 showed that one out of each four inhabitants lived in a city or town. The farmer, who had once produced for his own family alone, now had other mouths to feed as well.

Interest continued to center in the production of grain, the most easily stored and transported of foodstuffs. Although corn had been taken over from the Indians, and was an important crop, it was the cereal grasses, wheat, oats, rye, and barley, and especially the first, that went into human consumption. But the raising of them still embraced a lot of drudgery and backbreaking toil. Clearing new land had probably been the cause of Andy Jackson and many another pioneer child being without a father at birth, for the acres opened up to the plow levied their human toll. Even after the land was cleared, broken up, and the crop in, the annual harvest by hand methods was a demanding period.

The sickle had given place to the scythe, a long blade fitted to the end of a shaft, by which means a man might stand erect and cut a wider swath through the standing grain more effectively and with less effort. Then a series of bows had been added to this scythe, which cradled the severed stalks and allowed them to be deposited in neat windrows, so they might be more readily gathered, bundled, and shocked. Some improvements in tools had been made, permitting larger yields for the man power expended, which aided in preventing famine, that dread evil which, since the earliest days, had never stalked the American countryside. However, still greater demands were being laid upon the farmers as population mounted, and land use and its cultivation called for greater efficiency.

The difficulty was that the fields were not always one unbroken series of tiny shafts standing bolt upright. Rain, hail, or tearing winds often broke them over and snarled them into a mat. Still the crop when ripe must be promptly cut and salvaged of all that it could be made to yield, even if only by the most exhausting effort. While the harvest season had long been a time of celebration, embodying sincere thanksgiving for the food it provided, its more jovial phases were surely a commemoration of the fact that its frustrating toil was over for another year.

However, the grain *had* to be reaped, and in making the best of the situation, the task itself had become highly competitive. It thus developed those in each area who displayed great skill with the tools at hand. Men prided themselves on the acreage they could cut and cradle, or bind and shock, between sunup and darkness. Yet it was a wearisome business, and beyond those with swollen pride in their abilities, there was a far greater number who would have welcomed relief from the burden of these tasks—but how?

Science was then not only being invited, but even strongly urged to come to the aid of a wide range of human activities. It had made one vitalizing contribution to agriculture through the person of Eli Whitney, whose cotton gin had sent the cultivation of that crop spiraling upward at a dizzying rate. What might it do in the realm of wheat production, the limit of which was not set by the acreage that could be planted, but by what could be harvested and saved? Ingenious men began to coax science in this respect, the efforts in one instance beginning as early as the closing years of the Revolution.

Then suddenly one among them did "crack" the problem, and invented a machine that would satisfactorily cut standing grain. Also he managed the feat in little more than two short, although very full, months, and eventually succeeded in making his name nationally famous to this day. But tradition held back progress at the outset, and despite his machine's huge potential, it required still another mechanical development before its production and sale began to gather momentum. Each of these accomplishments was in reality a greater contribution to human welfare than the cotton gin, and deserve attention in the order of their perfection.

MORE POWER TO THE FARMERS

Rockbridge County, well down the Shenandoah Valley, took in its first permanent settler about 1737. It was pleasant, promising country, along a natural route to the South, and later to Kentucky and Tennessee, so it filled in rather rapidly. The land was cleared, and its fields were soon pushed well up onto the sides of its rolling hills. Too far north for cotton, it proved excellent grain country.

At about this time, Ulster expelled a party of sturdy Scotch-Irish Presbyterians, who sought refuge in America. Among them was one Thomas McCormick, who stayed briefly in Pennsylvania, but moved on to join a group of these outcasts down in Virginia; and there began to contribute his part in opening up this new area. They were a sober, thrifty, hard-working lot, and did well by themselves, especially the McCormick family. By the time Thomas' grandson, Robert, was himself raising a family, he was rated a pretty substantial citizen. He owned considerable land, farmed, had saw and grist-mills, and a distillery, and a very well-equipped blacksmith shop.

Robert had been married in 1808, and the following year chose as the given name for his newborn son that of the great empire builder of the Medes and Persians, Cyrus. To this was added the name of the child's mother's family, Hall. A kind providence had arranged an excellent choice of parents, and set the birthdate but three days after that of the Kentucky boy born over the mountains to the west, who would come to be known as the Great Emancipator.

Since young Cyrus' father was so much in and about the farm blacksmith shop, it was quite natural that his own mechanical ability should have been stimulated. Just how old he was when he first saw his father wrestling with the problem of a machine reaper is not known. Quite likely it was rather early in his boyhood, for grain fields stretched in all directions, and that whole section of the valley was hard put each summer to find enough man power to get the crop down and safely shocked once it began to ripen.

The older McCormick developed some definite ideas, which he started to work out in tangible form. What he had in mind was a device on wheels which could be pushed ahead of a pair of horses, thus keeping them from trampling the stalks. Across its front, and raised somewhat above the level of the roots, would be fixed a series of curved blades. Then from the turning wheels on which the frame was mounted, he would take power to whirl beaters that would press the stems against the sharp cutters, sever the stalks, and let the straw fall onto a platform, from which it could be gathered and bundled.

One difficulty was the condition of the grain to be cut. Sometimes it was uniformly ripe, dry, and brittle, and responded favorably. But, if it was still green in spots, it then tended to be damp and stringy and failed to shear off. There were moments when the cumbersome machine performed fairly well, but more often it would leave the reaped area a shambles of broken, tangled straw, with the precious grain spilled from the ears and widely scattered.

How many times it was pushed back to the shop, dismantled, and reworked for further testing is not known. Evidently this had been going on through at least a dozen, and perhaps even as many as twenty, years. The Scotch-Irish have a reputation for being stubborn and persistent, and the need for the machine was becoming more and more pressing.

Just how much young Cyrus worked with his father on this project is not known either. He managed some schooling, but that was never in harvest season, when, like all boys of that time, he would have been expected to contribute his share in the work to be done. But being handy with tools, he no doubt saw much of this sustained attempt.

That he put in time in the harvest fields himself is certain, for at fifteen he constructed a cradle better fitted to his size and strength at the time than the larger standard tools. Within the next two or three years he also developed a practical sidehill plow. He would some day inherit these acres, so he was quite naturally interested in better equipment. Thus it seems reasonable that he lived pretty close to the ups and downs of his father's efforts with a reaper.

But by 1831 the older man was still baffled, and he at last laid aside his own machine with a finality that clearly left the field open to Cyrus. The earliest grain, ripe by the beginning of May, had not yielded to the father's latest improvements. The last of the crop would be out of the way by the time August appeared. If a test of an entirely new approach, which the son advocated, was to be tried that year, he would have to move fast.

So the twenty-two-year-old Cyrus McCormick went to work, the only helper who could be spared him being his able young slave Jo Anderson. Since a new principle was involved, they would have to start from scratch; and apparently his father left him to his own devices. There was, fortunately, enough wood and metal on hand for his needs.

In place of stationary curved blades, his would be a single straight blade, and move back and forth to give a shearing action. Its production, and the gears and cams to work it, took time. A frame and platform different from that used before had to be built, and following it a device for dividing the grain and pressing it back against the cutter bar. Long days were put in, master and slave working like a team and sharing the work.

Finally, after six hectic weeks, what seemed like a suitable solution had been completed. Rather secretly, it was wheeled out into a field hard by the shop. But while Cyrus was evidently on the right track, its performance was still far short of what it should be. So back it went for alterations. The two men thought they had worked long hours before, but now they really stepped up the pace.

The straight-edged, traveling cutter was an improvement, but there was a need for deep notches along this blade to seize the stalks. So it was given a saw-tooth edge, which proved highly practical. The scheme for dividing the standing grain was remodeled, and a reel added to hold it against the jiggling, serrated, cutting edge.

The month of July had nearly run out by the time everything was reassembled and in working order. No doubt the father had looked in occasionally on the work, but this attempt was the son's, and he respected that fact. Now that it seemed safe to hazard a trial in public, he no doubt helped pass the word along as to when and where it would be held. And on a hot afternoon in late July the horse was hitched between the shafts and the still somewhat crude reaper rolled out to a neighboring field.

As it clattered into sight, the hand mowers lowered their cradles, leaned their weight on the long handles, and with the "catchers," who had paused in their binding of sheaves, were prepared to be highly critical of this second generation of McCormicks, attempting to prove that a machine could ever be built to do such highly skilled work. Quite unconscious of this apathetic audience, the two men who had struggled with this involved contrivance for eight straight weeks ran critical eyes once again over its every last part.

Then, with Cyrus driving and Jo running along beside to draw the cut grain from the gathering board into a windrow, they started into the standing stalks. The onlookers stood tense, as the spinning reel pressed back the grain and the chattering knife cleanly severed it. There was no lack of interest now, for after a long series of defeats, this new model, by a second generation, did the job. It worked!

Few men had ever spent a more profitable eight weeks. But we must remember, too, that no one else at that time had had the opportunity to profit by so long a series of trials and errors. A determined man had salvaged his father's unrewarding experiences, and had given a needy world a most valuable tool. Cyrus Hall McCormick had brought machinery to agriculture, where still more of it was badly needed.

Strangely enough it was actually ten years before Cyrus McCormick sold his first reaper—he was that much ahead of his time.

THE PRAIRIES ARE FORCED TO YIELD

But in those ten years the population would increase by a third, and a tight spot might well be developing at another point along this still uncertain pathway to more abundant food supply. There was distinct need for additional ground to be cleared and broken, but that was killing toil.

It is true that the bent sticks first used had given place to better formed wooden plows still in general use, but they had many defects. Men had wrestled with this problem, too, but not very effectively as yet. Thomas Jefferson is reputed to have figured just how the plowshare should be curved to do the work intended to the best advantage. In fact he was awarded a gold medal by the French for his advanced and effective design. Then, when Cyrus McCormick was but ten years old, Jethro Wood had cast the first iron shares, but they were excessively heavy, awkward, and not particularly popular.

Also there had long been the prevailing idea in the West that the open prairies, since they did not produce trees, would not grow a crop. A few hardy souls had been willing to risk a trial, but the tough buffalo sod which covered the plains broke wooden plows almost as fast as they began to turn a furrow. Even when cast-iron plows were brought in, they were nearly as useless. While they did not break so readily, the sticky loam would not shear away from the face of the share. It merely formed into a ball or wad and threw the plow clear of the furrow. For a time it looked as though the men down in Washington were not far wrong and these open plains were indeed a sort of "desert."

But a Vermont-born Yankee had headed west about six years after Cyrus McCormick had completed his reaper. He, too, was a blacksmith, named John Deere, and he set himself up in a shop in the hamlet of Grand Detour in Illinois. Almost at once he ran head on into this problem of breaking new land which, between wet and dry seasons, was either "too thick to drink, or too wet to plow." After a little reflection on the subject, he dug out a piece of a broken saw blade stowed away in his shop. Over a wooden form which he worked out, he shaped this steel into a smooth, properly curved share. To it he affixed a forged landside, and bolted the assembly to a stout wooden frame.

Recalling adverse comments about the weight of cast-iron plows, he tossed his own creation up onto his ample shoulders and strode off across the flatlands looking for possible customers. As often as he could find a settler willing to risk a test, he had a live prospect; for this steel share cut cleanly through the wiry turf, brought up the rich loam beneath, and laid it right on top of the now buried clods.

He was soon in the plow business, and expanded it into a factory in Moline in 1847. By the end of ten years the prairie farmers were buying his improved tools at the rate of ten thousand a year. The way was being paved for far greater stretches of land under cultivation, and proved to be a potent factor in the ensuing Mississippi Valley boom.

John Deere, however, had one advantage over McCormick. The latter could not just toss his reaper up onto his shoulder and set out to beat the countryside for customers. He was an ardent missionary, however, and finally in 1841 he managed to sell two of his reaping machines for a hundred dollars each. The next year he sold seven, and by 1844 his output reached fifty.

The fact that eight of the orders received that year had come from Cincinnati alone gave Cyrus McCormick real pause. He realized that he was located back in the somewhat staid and conservative East, and a full hundred miles from the nearest of the railroads then being built. The printed descriptions he had been sending out were beginning to bring in orders. What could be accomplished if he got out and talked to more and more people face to face?

So he set off on horseback, and spent two years covering New York State, Ohio, Illinois, Missouri, and Wisconsin. The sales frontier received some much needed attention, and paid off in a big way. Improved plows were opening up acreage to grain faster than it could be reaped by hand methods. During his two-year sales trip he took in orders for two hundred forty grain cutters. The blacksmith shop back in the Shenandoah Valley was now definitely outgrown. So, in 1847, McCormick also built a factory. Where? In Chicago, already a distribution point for the great heart land then booming. Before the war years arrived, the demand for better tools to attack and tame the agricultural frontier had his production of power reapers running at thousands of units annually.

Things were really happening down on the farm during the second quarter of the nineteenth century, and the year 1831 stands out as something of a landmark. An agricultural revolution was under way, and the names McCormick, Deere, Oliver, and those of other pioneers who were trail blazers in this important part of our national life deserve to be recalled and respected.

XXV

Texas Unfurls the Lone Star Flag

The Texans conducted their revolution after the pattern which their fathers had used sixty years earlier. They formed local committees of safety and correspondence, and by August, 1835, every municipality, precinct, or jurisdiction had such a committee. Through these committees, a call was issued for a general convention, or *consultation*. An election was called for October 5 to elect delegates to a general consultation on October 15. Events were moving so rapidly that before the general consultation met, war was inevitable. Austin had returned from his long imprisonment in Mexico converted to the cause of war. He took charge of the local committee at his capital, San Felipe, and assumed direction of the revolutionary movement.
—Walter Prescott Webb, *The Texas Rangers*.

THERE was a brief period in 1819 when it looked as though the United States had achieved its final territorial growth. Deliberate expansion had never been a part of American policy, although its nationals have forced its hand in this respect at times. In the above year the little that was known about the country beyond the Mississippi was discouraging, the fallacious impression that it was principally "desert" was well ingrained, and in the treaty made with Spain it seemed prudent to acquire Florida and forget about remote Texas. But one lone Connecticut Yankee, without benefit of the politicos in Washington, set the country on a new course, and quite without out realization of the ultimate effects of his acts.

Old Moses Austin, while born in Connecticut, had acquired a competence from trade in Philadelphia, wasted it at lead mining in Virginia, became a Spanish citizen, and built a considerable fortune in the early days in the Missouri country. Then he had suddenly become one of the many victims of the depression of 1818–19. Broken financially, but not in spirit, he stomped away from his vanished millions in that territory, which was just about to attain statehood, and headed for a new "promised land." He had educated his Virginia-born son, Stephen, as a gentleman, and had established him in the neighboring Arkansas Territory. So the fifty-nine-year-old father made his way to Little Rock on foot.

The second great wave in the long flood of western migration was then building up and, like Boone and his followers heading into Kentucky two generations before, a few hardy souls were filtering through Louisiana and Arkansas into the uncertain reaches of Spain's vast domain to the west and southwest. The hold which the Spanish had upon the area was even less secure than when Pike had visited in these parts, and this weakness offered a challenge to men of daring and determination. The infiltration was by a frontier breed possessing these characteristics to a remarkable degree, and the Spaniards soon realized that men who needed little more than a musket and a poke of cornmeal to make their way would be hard indeed to resist.

From his son, Moses Austin borrowed a horse, a mule, a Negro servant named Richmond, and fifty dollars in cash. With his former Spanish passport in his pocket, he and the slave man set out on the perilous seven-hundred-fifty mile journey to San Antonio de Bexar. In strong contrast to Pike's reception there, Austin's was distinctly frosty. In fact Governor Martínez would have no part of the man, even refusing to so much as speak to him. Despite the American's fiery, determined ways, it looked as though his exhausting jaunt had been in vain.

A less daring gambler with destiny might readily have given up when he found himself faced with an ultimatum to get back to wherever he came from, and promptly, too, or be thrown into jail. But the now elderly man was still most resourceful, improved an opportunity to exert a little influence, was soon closeted with the reluctant governor, and had a deal arranged. Permission would be sought from the powers higher up for Austin to settle three hundred families on Texas soil.

Certain his petition would be granted, he started the long return trip to Arkansas. There he would make preparations that would permit him to be back the following May with the first settlers. But the effort proved too great for him. His health broke, and although he lingered until the next June, death terminated his attempt to find a place for the land-hungry in Texas. Confirmation of his plea had been received in January, and after the father had been buried, young Stephen took up the project.

As tough of purpose and of fiber as his sire, but far more adaptable, he had settlers moving into the Spanish Southwest in 1822, and was getting real co-operation from Martínez. Actually the whole picture had shifted since the older man's first approach—Mexico had won its independence from Spain. So Austin worked himself into the good graces of the new government in Mexico City and wrote a liberal immigration law for it. By 1831 there were nearly six thousand Americans in Texas, most of whom had come in under his auspices.

Such an influx had been more than either the Spaniards or then the Mexicans had anticipated. Such numbers could be a distinct threat, for the men who made it up—and their womenfolk, too—were a resolute lot. They were no herd of docile peons; and the inevitable clash came in 1835, when the American settlers revolted.

Mexico was then dominated by the grand schemer Antonio López de Santa Anna. He resolved to make short work of these rebels, and as he swept up out of Mexico with a sizable army, it began to look as though he might succeed. But the stubborn Americans refused to be cowered by this show of force, and were determined to stand up, and die if need be, for their rights.

The first major encounter came at San Antonio, where Santa Anna managed to surround less than two hundred of the men, with quite a number of their women and children, in a mission church on its central square. Certain he could blast them out in no time at all, he attacked, only to have this steadfast band sell its lives so dearly that it cost him heavily both in men and in shaken confidence. This historic Battle of the Alamo, in February 1836, was the beginning of Mexican losses beyond all expectation.

Gathering his depleted forces, the Mexican commander hoped again for a quick decision. He did gain a point, but slaughtered so many Americans in doing so that the trigger fingers of the remainder itched almost beyond endurance. Then, on April 21, Santa Anna, encountered Sam Houston, with about one quarter as many men, at San Jacinto, near the upper shores of Galveston Bay. Yet what the Texans lacked in numbers they more than made up for in firmness of purpose. Within half an hour it was all over. Santa Anna's forces were devastated and Texas was free.

For fifteen years the younger Austin had given unstintedly of himself, even to a long imprisonment in Mexico. He had been so busy, in fact, that he had never gotten around to building a home of his own. There had been periods from 1835 into this epic year of 1836 when it seemed certain that the torch which he had grasped from

his father's faltering hand must surely be snuffed out. Then, after
Houston's success, it glowed brightly, and the Lone Star Republic
was brought into being. But the forty-three-year-old man had also
given his all, and as the year ended, so did his closely packed life.

FRONTIER DEVELOPMENTS IN TEXAS

When Mexico had terminated further immigration into Texas
in 1830, there was immediate sentiment in favor of separation. The
settlers were from the same stock that had threatened the Spanish
officials at New Orleans, driven the Indians from areas in which they
wished to make clearings and build cabins back in Kentucky and
Tennessee, and whose parents and grandparents had not been above
defying the United States Government on occasion. They were
Americans, and not Latins. Their forebears had fought for and won
their liberty and an autonomous government, and their descendants
were now determined upon the same course. As the quote at the
head of this chapter indicates, they made their preparations for resistance to the same pattern that had worked sixty years before. Also
they held their consultation at Austin in October of 1835, and there
they framed a constitution for themselves. The following March they
held another conclave, and adopted their declaration of independence. This was to have been the first step toward incorporation in
the United States, and agents soon departed for Washington to demand their acceptance into the Union. But politics intervened, 1836
being an election year. Texas' entry would logically be as a slave
state, and Jackson, then President, was in a bit of a dilemma and
could not see his way clear to act in Texas' behalf. By the following
year financial panic had seized the country, and any expansionist
tendencies were displaced by the need to curtail and restore the
solvency of what we possessed. Until 1845 Texas would be forced
to go its own way as an independent republic.

While its history for some years to come would be relatively
turbulent, there was innate desire and striving for democratic processes and the resolution of problems and dangers by law and order.
Here was a huge frontier, some of whose Red River settlements
were as close to Chicago and Lake Michigan as they were to the faraway areas about El Paso on the Rio Grande. Texas had a huge
West of its own to win, and to help gather it into the fold, it set up
one of the most romantic of service organizations, the Texas Rangers.

This body of men first came into being as early as 1835, during the days when separation was being considered, and before the revolution actually got under way. Irregular companies were then set up to range to the frontier, and protect the settlements from Indian attack, now that a clash with Mexican forces seemed inevitable. After freedom had been won and the republic established, they were called up for limited service whenever danger threatened. As soon as it subsided, they disbanded and rode off home to more peaceful pursuits. They were not yet a formal, permanent organization, but the pattern later to be adopted when they were given permanent status was evolving.

Like the first Americans to enter Texas, they always traveled light. Since distances were great, that fact necessitated they be mounted. Most of them were young, for it was an active, vigorous, demanding duty. They had to be cool in the face of danger, totally unfamiliar with fear, and their selection in that respect was so carefully made that no Ranger down the years was ever accused of cowardice. The role they played called for a certain amount of pride in their ability, with the consequence that they were a "mite" particular about weapons and mounts.

For a time the former had been the old long rifles that had gained such a reputation during several generations when lodged in the hands of proficient men. But they were unwieldy and cumbersome to load, handle, and shoot, particularly from horseback. Quite naturally when the revolver came along the Rangers latched onto it and made it their weapon. With a Colt Walker—named for one of the service's captains, who specified its design—slung in a holster on either hip, a Ranger was better able to compete with the Indian with a quiver filled with poisoned arrows. Between his pair of "six guns," he had twelve hard-hitting blows which he could deliver in rapid succession, and from the back of a running horse almost as effectively as when on foot.

The loosely organized companies of Rangers were among the first Texans to volunteer for the War with Mexico in 1846. Then, after that struggle was over, they went home again and stood by, a little impatiently at times no doubt, while the soldiers of the United States Army attempted to guard their frontier. But the wily Comanche natives managed to slip by the men in uniform. At one full moon after another they staged their raids, growing bolder and bolder, and playing havoc with the outlying settlements. "Minute companies" of Rangers were drafted to stave off these depredations, and Governor Runnels' patience began to wear thin as federal protection became less and less effective. Texas was now a state, and quite capable of taking care of her own. So the governor decided to make the Rangers a permanent organization.

Calling on old Rip Ford, he made this indomitable character Captain of Rangers, and recruited a force of a hundred to serve under him, together with an equal number of friendly Shawnee and Tonkawa Indians. Ford's instructions were fairly sweeping—clean out all troublemakers. So Rip headed up into the Canadian River country in search of the leader of the renegade natives. There he met the Comanche chief, Iron Jacket, who took his name from the ancient coat of chain armor, perhaps seized by his ancestors in battle in the days of Coronado. But his metallic waistcoat was incapable of stopping the hard-hitting balls from Ranger rifles, and he was soon among his ancestors in the happy hunting ground, and his warriors completely routed. The Rangers as an established group proved their worth from the very beginning.

It was not too many months before they were forcing their mounts a thousand miles to the south to answer a call down near the mouth of the Rio Grande. A Spanish adventurer, Juan Cortinas, as fiery as his own red hair, had seized Brownsville, disposed of some of his enemies, stolen the cannon from the local fort, and dug in some distance up the river, determined to have his way along the border. Federal troops were already on hand, as was a volunteer company of Rangers from the vicinity. So old Rip joined with them, marched to Rio Grande City, and waded into the ensuing fight. Since his own men had now been equipped with six-shooters, they were better able to take the in-fighting, and bore the brunt of the affair. With a gun in either hand, they stormed the Mexicans and promptly ran them off. After the fracas was over a count disclosed some sixteen wounded Rangers, sixty dead Mexicans, but not a single one of the federal troops had been a casualty. And no wonder! The battle was pretty much over before they had gotten into it.

Then came lean times. First there was the War between the States, in which the Rangers volunteered and had a part as regular soldiers. When that struggle was over, there were the uncertain years of Reconstruction when the state, like many another, was in political turmoil. The Rangers were abolished, and a state police force inaugurated that was in sorry contrast to the earlier organization, and merely added to the confusion through which the Texans were being dragged by "carpetbag" administrations. It was not until 1874 that the people again managed to get control of their own affairs and elect a representative legislature. One of its first acts was to disband the ineffectual police and bring the Ranger forces back to life.

Two groups were then organized. One was the fabled Frontier Battalion, commanded by the resourceful Major John B. Jones. There was also the so-called Special Force, headed by Captain L. H. McNelly. Both commanders had learned the value of stern discipline in their own experiences in the Confederate Army. Picking their men with the greatest of care, they soon built one of the finest law-enforcement organizations that has ever existed. The Indians, the desperadoes, the murderers, the thieves, and the lawless began to have abiding respect for the fearless men who were proud to be counted among its members.

Hard-hitting Rip Ford had long maintained that "a Texas Ranger can ride like a Mexican, trail like an Indian, shoot like a Tennesseean, and fight like the devil." Such proficiency became a tradition of the organization, and the Rangers lived up to it to a man. Occasionally they made mistakes, for when real trouble threatened they customarily shot first and asked questions later on. There were occasions, but mighty few of them, when they were poorly led. Eventually there came a time when they operated singly in most instances, and could indeed be "one-man armies" at troubled spots. They were adept at slipping into a ticklish situation where trouble was brewing, a pair of guns in shoulder holsters well concealed by an outsized vest, and looking about as inoffensive as the jay birds perched along neighboring barbed-wire fences. Quick of eye, and spare of words, they could soon worm their way to the center of the difficulty, and at an appropriate moment unlimber two vicious weapons and take command of a desperate situation coolly, effectively, and single-handedly.

There is the old classic out of the bulging files of Ranger accomplishments that clearly illustrates the spirit in which such activities were carried out. A town threatened with a riot had put in a hurried call to the governor of the state for help. Since the telegraph reply had been to the effect that the *help* would be aboard the afternoon train, the jittery mayor was naturally on hand to welcome it. To his utter astonishment, just one man descended from the cars, clad in the inevitable Stetson and high-heeled boots, but no guns showing. His eyes fairly popping, and madder than a hornet, His Honor accosted this placid character and demanded to know if the governor of the state had sent only *one* man to quell a riot!

The Ranger, adjusted his cud, spat reflectively, and then turning a pair of icy blue eyes on his questioner, observed quite dispassionately, "There hain't but one riot is there?"

Men equipped with such magnificent confidence were capable of writing real history, and they did, and in abundance. Still the Rangers were never a large force, and by no means dominated the state's many achievements. It has had its full complement of resourceful men down the years, big in heart, in vision, and in courage.

XXVI

At the End of the Oregon Trail

Last spring, 1846, was a busy season in the city of St. Louis. Not only were emigrants from every part of the country preparing for the journey to Oregon and California, but an unusual number of traders were making ready their wagons and outfits for Santa Fe. Many of the emigrants, especially those bound for California, were persons of wealth and standing. The hotels were crowded, and the gunsmiths and saddlers were kept constantly at work in providing arms and equipment for different parties of travelers. Almost every day steamboats were leaving the levee and passing up the Missouri, crowded with passengers on their way to the frontier.—Francis Parkman, *The California and Oregon Trail.*

S CENES such as the young Boston Brahman, Francis Parkman, described at St. Louis shortly before the mid-century had characterized the spring season there, and at other Missouri towns, for the past dozen years or more. Had he been, say, at Independence, some miles up the Missouri River and near its great bend in the early months of 1832, he would have witnessed preparations there on the part of no less than three major groups bent on trying out the shorter route to the Columbia River country pioneered by Ashley's band of trappers years before.

The first of these was headed by a French-born officer of the United States Army, Captain B. L. E. Bonneville, who had been provided a leave of absence so he might lead a private party over the mountains and, without giving our British cousins grounds on which to mistrust his purposes, assess the military problems liable to be encountered in the Rockies and in the Northwest. Jim Bridger, "Old Gabe," was an important member of this party, one of the chief purposes of which was to test the use of wagons in place of pack animals. William Sublette, another Ashley alumnus, had found them highly practicable two years before along the Platte Valley, and their merits would now be measured over the mountain sections of the long trail.

Bill was on hand to offer suggestions, for he and his brother Milton were putting together the second of the three parties, which would head far back into the hills to collect the fur catch of the past winter. The third outfit was, in western parlance, something of a "doozie." Its leading spirit was no mountaineer, but a well-to-do iceman from Cambridge, Massachusetts, bent on becoming a big-time entrepreneur in this new land being opened up in the Columbia Valley. He had enthused a group of followers to go there under his direction, and to properly prepare for so strenuous a journey, he had conducted a rigorous training program on an island in Boston Harbor. Then he had shepherded his flock, with considerable fanfare, this far on the way. He personified the enterprise which would be needed in this new section, as well as the public relations efforts which would be required to fill it and the other areas on the western rim of the continent with settlers.

The Spanish had long since explored the rivers and bays of this upper Pacific coast country, and had named the section about the mouth of the mighty Columbia Oregon, after the wild marjoram that grew there. But California had satisfied their needs, and they paid little or no attention to the land above. British and American vessels had later touched along these shores, claiming certain rights, and Astor had attempted to found a base at the river's mouth, only to be thrust out by the British at the onset of the War of 1812. The Russians had worked it over for a time, even establishing posts as far south as San Francisco Bay, but they had finally been eased to the north beyond the base of the Alaska Peninsula by the British. Spanish, and later Mexican, interests terminated at the 46th parallel, and Oregon was thus a rough trapezoid, reaching from there up to a point at 54° 40′ of north latitude, beyond which the Russian interlopers had been thrust, and clearly bounded on the west by the Pacific, but with its eastern extremities back in the Rockies less definitely marked.

Since 1827 there had been a treaty permitting joint occupancy by the United States and Britain, which served well enough as long as the chief interest there was the fur trade. The Hudson's Bay Company had managed a strong foothold, and the graduates of the "Rocky Mountain College," once a trail had been blazed by Lewis and Clark, were soon sidling in and out of the area in the pursuit of their profession.

Since this gentry fought shy of the settlements, the encouraging stories its members could have related did not at first get into wide circulation. Contacts by sea began to pick up, however, and the word soon got around that the Indians in the Columbia River area were of a superior type, and fit recipients for a portion of the intense missionary zeal then gripping the country.

Despite their wooden axles and other shortcomings, Bonneville's wagons managed to negotiate the mountain trails, and the success of this enterprise quickly filtered back to the East. By 1834 the Oregon natives had suddenly become a matter of great concern to the Methodists, and the Presbyterians were also on the scene the following year surveying the situation. Then in 1836 the pioneer missionary Dr. Marcus Whitman made history by taking his stately blonde bride, Narcissa, over the Rockies in a wagon—surely one of the most robust honeymoons imaginable. Her well-glossed eastern veneer would warp and check a bit under the rigors of the frontier life, but she and other resolute wives of the missionaries would be a tremendous influence for good in the communities they would help to open up.

Whitman established his mission in the country where the waters of the Snake mingle with those of the Columbia, and encountered tribal customs and observances which forced something of an oblique attack, to which the ladies were able to make a potent contribution. The practical approach was model homesteads, and the savages eventually succumbed. There was soon a community filling in about neighboring Fort Walla Walla, and others far downstream about Fort Vancouver, across the Columbia from present-day Portland, Dr. John McLoughlin, chief factor for Hudson's Bay Company in this whole immense area, was delighted with what was being accomplished, and became a staunch friend and supporter of the efforts.

Delighted, too, with the progress they were making, and with the country in which their lot had been cast, the missionaries began sending home highly enthusiastic letters. Naturally these had wide circulation in both the secular and religious press, and stimulated interest in Oregon. Thus the three parties preparing to leave Independence in 1832 had been no more than the advance agents of a new migration getting under way. The panic of 1837 would be a strong deterrent for a time, but as its effects wore off and the country moved into the "Roaring Forties," the discontented from Maine to Florida and west to the Mississippi began to itch. With the setting up of an Indian Agency out there in 1842, the trek was on in earnest.

As demanding as had been the entries into Kentucky and Tennessee and through the Forks of the Ohio into the old Northwest Territory, the trip to this newer Northwest was a far more exacting endeavor. It helped write determination indelibly on the American character, and even when Francis Parkman made his own historic journey there after the trail was fairly well founded, it was still an extreme test of human endurance. Yet thousands were willing to make the efforts and sacrifices involved.

As Parkman observed, many of the parties were composed of substantial citizens, adequately financed and equipped, yet as he got well out along the trail, his reactions then indicated that such were perhaps in the minority. Some employed the older avenue of approach, taking boats up the Missouri as far as high water in spring and early summer permitted navigation. But by far the greater number outfitted in towns along the river's lower reaches, greased up the axles of their linchpin wagons, stowed Ma and the kids and their gear aboard, and when everything was set, took off on what could be anywhere from a four- to an eight-month jaunt.

TURN RIGHT FOR OREGON

Two famous trails were but one as they left Independence. Then they shortly came to a parting of the ways near where Gardner, Kansas, stands today. Those parties that heeded the sign pointing to the left were headed down the Santa Fe Trail to the Mexican towns along the Rio Grande; while those who observed the rough board by the right fork, reading "Road to Oregon," were bound for even greater adventures. A historical marker at the spot today records the witty comment of an earlier age: "So simple a sign never before announced so long a journey."

It was a full two thousand miles, some of it rugged enough to quickly weed out the weaklings, yet most of its worst stretches were still days and weeks ahead. The first objective was the Platte River, over the prairies and across a handful of smaller streams to the north. Then for a long distance the plains rose no more rapidly than the bed of that fairly lazy stream. Still their intense sunlight began to play upon the eyes, their distances upon the soul, and their extreme dryness upon the wheels of the wagons. Felloes and spokes soon began to loosen, tires to roll off, and drivers had to seek the bed of the river and hazard its quicksands, so that its trickle of water, almost thick enough to plow, might soak them tight again. Potable water was becoming fairly scarce, and, even when boiled, brought on dysentery. The cattles' hoofs became tender, and heavy loads and none too easy going began to sap their strength.

About sixty miles beyond Fort Kearney, built in 1846, the river forked, and those heading for Oregon kept along its northern branch, passing famed Scotts Bluff, and heading toward the second major objective, Fort Laramie. This had at first been a fur post, had passed through several hands, been rebuilt a short distance farther up Laramie Creek, and was one of the trail's most important appendages. A party of Sioux, or one from another of the local tribes, was almost certain to be encamped near by in spring and summer, and the wagon trains turned in here for a breather, many of them for a bit of carousing within the great hollow square of buildings before tackling the mountains, now in full view. A little later it would become a military post.

Here would be found traders from Taos, down in New Mexico, the first of the really wild and woolly western towns, with herds of mules, and stocks of flour, tobacco, powder, other trade goods, and especially raw alcohol, which, in the mountain country, passed for whiskey, and at about fifty cents a gallon. The Indians, too, were on hand to trade, or pilfer, as the opportunity warranted. But with the mountains before them and the realization that days had already been lost by unanticipated eventualities, the trail parties were soon under way again.

The plaguy mosquitoes of the prairies now began to give place to the annoyance of alkaline dust. There was a rough bit of country in the stretch beyond Laramie, past Independence Rock, and on into the Sweetwater country, where the road mounted up to the ridgepole of the continent. The graves along its sides were more frequent, and where the grades became stiffer, a wide assortment of goods littered the trail, jettisoned to lighten loads.

The wagon tracks pushed on through famous South Pass in the Wind River Mountains, eased down to and across the Green River to Jim Bridger's fort, which lay some miles west of that stream. Then it swung north along the eastern edge of the Wasatch ridge, picked up the Bear River and followed it to Soda Springs, where it pressed through the hills to Fort Hall on the westbound Snake River. Moving along with that curving stream for nearly two hundred miles where it bordered the lava plains, the route then left the river, and, cutting across one of its long arcs, made directly for Fort Boise. Just beyond there were another few miles beside the twisting river, but where it swung off on a long detour to the north, the trail held its north-westerly direction to and across the Blue Mountains.

At this latter ridge it branched. By keeping to the right, one came to Whitman's Mission, where the circuitous Snake joined the Columbia just above the latter's sharp curve to the west. The left-hand trail hit the larger stream below this mighty bend, passed along its southern bank for many miles, past the Dalles and on to Fort William, where the Willamette River, flowing north through the broad and fertile valley between the Cascade and Coast ranges, meets the Columbia. This latter area was the principal objective of the westward-bound. The journey to it had been a grueling expe-rience, but what those who had braved it found after their arrival was sufficiently attractive so that they were persuaded to stay.

ONE OF OREGON'S MOST COLORFUL CHARACTERS

Those who have read the classic account which Parkman gave of his own trip there in 1846, and which he called *The California and Oregon Trail*, will recall his vivid descriptions of the characters en-countered along it, and at the trail's end. They were a colorful lot, but perhaps none among them more so than he of the most decep-tive name—Joe Meek. He had grown up in the plantation country in the South, from which he had set forth at fourteen, heading west, and into the lively fur trade.

Operating as a free trader, or at times under the banner of one or another of the companies, he had been the erstwhile companion of Kit Carson, Bridger, the Sublettes, and most of its other greats and near greats, as well, too, as of some of the varmints and rascals of that lusty business. He had ranged the mountain country from Montana to Lower California, from Vancouver to Mexico, husbanded several squaws, cut a wide swath and a fabulous series of didoes, and after the infiltration of settlers had grown heavy enough so that the joint occupation with Britain was terminated and the United States set up Oregon Territory, he became the upholder of the law in the land at the end of the famous trail.

He had been matured at the hands of the desert sun, of icy moun-tain streams, vengeful Indians, and by not infrequent periods on short rations. He could recount occasions when he had been forced to subsist on the pulp of black locusts, and at other times on ants. He had had innumerable encounters with animals and savages, and liked to boast that a wax-figure group in a St. Louis museum pictured none other than he, a ferocious she-bear, and her "passel" of cubs, in a strenuous workout. Had the Rocky Mountain College in which he had long been matriculated issued formal diplomas, his would surely have been given *summa cum laude*.

Such Spartan training had been quite foreign to that of the missionary folk Joe now encountered with greater frequency. The taming process which they began to introduce into Oregon nettled him at first, but later intrigued him, and he took to dropping by occasionally, and even sitting in at revival meetings.

In preparation for one held along the Bear River, the women-folk had labored through a whole day concocting delicacies to tempt the Indians to the evening get-together. The baking fumes had reached to Joe's sensitive nose, and set up a nostalgic train of thought. So he was on hand on the mission grounds as darkness fell, but held just a bit apart so that his show of interest would not be misunderstood. The savages approached the affair with fewer scruples, entered into the services being conducted, and one venturesome brave even stood up boldly and sang a song. For this zealous display he was immediately rewarded with a crisp, brown, hot biscuit.

As he disappeared behind a convenient bush to munch it without hindrance, a heavy hand descended upon his shoulder, and a crisp voice close by his ear imparted a few succinct instructions. Gulping down the remainder of the morsel, the young buck was promptly back in the midst of the meeting, the campfire lighting up his face as he trilled a second verse of his song. As he returned with another similar donation, a hand from the shadows appropriated it, and Joe Meek had his first taste of white bread in many a year. It was little things like that that broke down his resistance.

There were moments, however, when these "do-gooders" and their womenfolk continued to plague him no end, dampening and limiting his soaring spirits in his lighter moments. Thus he was not above aping their ways when he could do so to his advantage. Currently he was badly in need of another squaw to take the place of Mountain Lamb, the fetching little Snake girl whom he had been careless enough to have with him at the time of a clash with a party of Bannocks, and the chief's tomahawk had dispatched the winsome "Mrs." Meek. He had pondered the subject, come to the conclusion the Nez Percé women made good, reliable wives, and, a tribe of them being handy, the missionaries' activities gave him an idea. Meek suddenly visted the tribe, and in the guise of an evangelist.

It nearly bowled the natives over, but the man had a way with him, the Indians were patient, and he had garnered quite a tidy sum by way of freewill offerings before he felt constrained to broach the true purpose of his visitation. He finally explained to them at a well-attended session that it would be highly gratifying if they should choose to present him with a wife. At once there was tension and the makings of trouble. The partly Christianized members of this tribal group had been carefully instructed by others who had labored with them in respect to the great merits of strict monogomy. This Joe Meek already had a wife—somewhere! Here he was demanding another.

Now Joe was neither meek, nor one to lay down a project as lost until he had given it his best. He had taught himself to read during long days and nights in snowbound cabins, and the Bible being a complete library within a single cover, he always had one by him. Hauling it forth, he thumbed through to the books of Samuel and First Kings, and went to work expounding the benefits which had flowed first to David, and then to his son Solomon when the marital establishments of both were as thick with wives as a holly shrub with jay birds. It took some days of strenuous exegesis on his part, but eventually he won his point and his squaw.

But let it be emphasized that these Christian people, and especially their womenfolk, make a signal contribution among the natives, despite Whitman's death at their hands in 1847. At first it came more readily via the squaws, who were more mobile. Steel needles, well-spun thread, scissors, flap-jack turners, combs, buttons, and a host of other wondrous items and gear for homemaking and improving the amenities of life won them over, and they in turn went to work on their more recalcitrant husbands.

Beyond the savages, there was influence, too, on the mountain men, and later on the more effervescent of the settlers. Among the former it revived memories of half-forgotten things, and they probably kicked themselves at first for being "sissies," but they soon got to trooping up and down before Narcissa Whitman's cabin in the hope she would rush out and hand them a religious tract and give them a few civil words and an animating whiff of wholesome womanhood. They yielded slowly and reluctantly for the most part, but the civilizing influence of the home missionaries along our frontiers was a priceless contribution, too often overlooked today.

FIRST AID, MOUNTAIN STYLE

Poor Joe Meek was soon again in the midst of wife trouble. He had taken his Nez Percé consort over onto the eastern slopes of the

Rockies to attend the trappers' rendezvous in the spring of 1838. There a matrimonial storm broke, and the self-reliant woman rounded up her own ponies, tossed her meager gear aboard, and set off for home at a gallop. The word of her defection was a trifle delayed in getting to her husband, and to blunt the keen edge of his first burst of anguish and chagrin, he tanked up heavily. Then sensing the husbandly duty convention imposed upon him, he rounded up his own horse and pack mules, tethered a good big canteen of fiery "mountain dew" to his saddle horn, and took off in pursuit, fueling up as he hurried along.

Thus propelled, he made his way down the Sweetwater and up into South Pass, where he paused to spend the night and let his "biler" cool down. Up and off again at daybreak, his thinking machinery seemed lodged on dead center, and the self-induced heat waves before his eye clouded his vision a trifle. Almost before he knew it, he was close by two standing horses, and the distraught figure of a woman bending over that of a man prone on the ground. "Drat all Injuns," he thought to himself as he jogged along closer; but the scene, although not too unusual, had certain vestiges which quickly cleared the burning haze from his head.

The male member of this twosome was definitely a missionary, and he loudly professed to be dying of thirst. His wife begged water of Joe, her own tongue pretty well swollen by the same lack, as her frenzied but thickened words indicated. Still just enough off the beam so that he failed to recall the abstention practiced by the other characters in this bit of drama, he hauled loose and thrust forward his nearly empty canteen of alcohol. One quick whiff, and it was promptly thrust back at him again. The prostrate man would sooner die than taste of it—and the Reverend Mr. Smith meant precisely that.

Unaccustomed to such saintly forebearance, the Meek one tarnished the desert air with a string of double-jointed curses. "Why the cowardly, white-livered, such-and-such," he pointedly observed, and went on to explain to the expiring creature that he had better die and be done with it before an imaginary band of Indians, which he maintained had been hot on his trail, arrived and got their scalpitchy hands on him. The poor wife was horrified, the more so when, despite her violent protests, this rude creature who had suddenly appeared out of the desert wastes began to hoist her up into the saddle of her own horse, profanely explaining that there was no good reason why she should be scalped as well. Before she could resist, he had vaulted into his own saddle, screamed a command at his pack animals, and the whole troop galloped off down the trail, the poor woman gripped by horror.

After a brisk canter of perhaps a half mile, her captor swung off into the brush, grinned at her rather discomfortingly, but whirled about in his saddle, and looked back. His little ruse had worked. Asa Smith was now on his feet, trying to climb aboard his own horse, whose reins had snagged on a stone, and was soon taking after them. Meek finally let him catch up that afternoon well down the trail at Frank Ermatinger's temporary camp. The poor missionary was by then nearly frantic for water, which was fed to him slowly; but he had learned a valuable lesson—never say die while there is still breath in your body. Joe was by now as sober as a judge, and his runaway squaw no longer a prime concern. So he got the reverend gentleman and his good wife straightened around and ready for the trail again, and then piloted them as far as Fort Hall, near present-day Pocatello. He proved a serviceable guardian angel, even if a bit rough in manner and approach.

THE AMBASSADOR FROM OREGON

As early as 1843 the incoming settlers had thrust aside the benevolently despotic powers formerly exercised by Dr. McLoughlin of the Hudson's Bay Company and loudly demanded that the area be taken over by the United States. They finally gathered that same year at now forgotten Champoeg and set up a local government patterned after that in the Iowa Territory. But it was unsatisfactory, and provided little in the way of enforceable laws, land titles, or rights. Still such activities were much in the American tradition, and the settlers continued to stream in.

The expansionists were exerting more and more pressure in Congress, and in that "year of decision," 1846, voted to terminate joint occupancy with Britain, and the United States soon took sole possession of the Oregon country up to the 49th parallel. A territory was established, and President Polk would sign the bill bringing it into being in Washington in August of 1848. This would be done in the presence of at least two men who would have to uphold the new laws which it provided. One was an Indianian, General Joseph Lane, who had made a name for himself in the recently completed War with Mexico, and had been appointed governor. The other was a cousin by marriage of the President, and who had now termed himself "envoy extraordinary and minister plenipotentiary from the Republic of Oregon to the Court of the United States." He was to be the first territorial marshal, and his name was Joseph L. Meek.

There were suitable funds for his junket East, and Joe used them liberally. Great strides had been made in many phases of life since he had taken refuge in the hills as a youth, and there was precious little this self-styled ambassador missed. Obviously, he had to try out that new national pride and joy, the steam railroads, and he was aboard the cars just as soon as he came to the first railhead.

Now in the West, and in those areas where civilization had not gotten too firm a foothold, you clambered aboard a wagon, or up onto the vacant back of a horse or mule, joined the passing party, and paid your way in any convenient and helpful manner. Certainly no one ever accosted you and demanded your "ticket." Thus when the conductor came through the cars picking them up, there were a few confused moments, for Joe had neglected to buy one. The lordly gentleman in the aisle was courteous but firm, and then firm, but not so courteous, while the jackanapes in the seat hid behind a perplexed look and muddied up the waters by jabbering away in the Snake Indian dialect.

The life he had led had had its full complement of bluff and bluster, and he put his mastery of both to work, on the way and after he reached Washington. There he headed for the city's best hotel, and, as he maintained, "ragged, dirty, and lousy," ensconced himself in a suite. He would enjoy the prerogatives of an ambassador even if he could not quite muster the customary bland and polished manners.

With his old bosom pal, Kit Carson, the pair managed to do the town up brown. They were lionized quite a bit, but without its drawing the spring-steel temper of either. Finally when the gaiety began to wear down, Joe and the general headed back for the West. Up the Missouri at Fort Leavenworth they were accorded a military escort as befitted their stations, and set out on the trail on September 10, but headed toward Santa Fe and California, rather than over the northern route where snow would soon begin to fall. It was six months later, March 2, 1849, before they were home in Oregon again; and along the way every blessed soldier in the escort party, save one, had gone AWOL. The West had attractions for all kinds and conditions of men in those days, even at the risk of life, liberty or what not.

XXVII

The Acquisition of California

Oh, don't you remember sweet Betsy from Pike,
Who crossed the big mountains with her lover, Ike,
With two yokes of cattle, a large yellow dog—
A tall Shanghi rooster and one spotted hog?

They soon reached the desert, where Betsy gave out,
And down in the sand she lay rolling about,
While Ike, half distracted, looked on in surprise,
Saying, "Betsy, get up, you'll get sand in your eyes."

Sweet Betsy got up in a great deal of pain,
Declared she'd go back to Pike County again,
But Ike gave a sigh, and they fondly embraced,
And they traveled along with his arm 'round her waist.

—Stanzas from *Sweet Betsy from Pike*, appearing
in *Put's Golden Songster*, San Francisco, 1858.

THE financial panic that had been the immediate heritage of the Jackson administration was a most severe one, but the inherent vigor and growth of the country pushed up through the wrecked confidence it bred, and by the mid-forties exciting things were again happening. The Harrison-Tyler term had fallen on uncertain times and amid political turmoil, and the Democrats, wary of sectional differences but determined to win the election in the fall of 1844, ran the first "dark horse" candidate. They not only chose a winner, but in James K. Polk selected perhaps the man best equipped for the years just ahead.

Texas, broken away first from the Spanish domains and then from the uncertain grasp of shifting power politics in Mexico, had won its freedom, if not a place in the Union. Mexico was still determined to recapture this fat province, and to forestall such a move the Texans appeared ready to enter the British orbit, or accept other

European backing, rather than revert to their former status. There were, in addition, two other former Spanish provinces now loosely held by the country below the Rio Grande—New Mexico and California—which needed stabilizing, and which the expansionist element in the Congress felt, along with Oregon, should be parts of the United States. The Texans had tried to extend sovereignty out along the Rio Grande into the Santa Fe country, and had sent an ill-fated expeditionary force there for the purpose. The area was far removed from Mexico City, and seemed destined soon to be separated from its control.

California, and particularly the southern half of that huge province, was a storybook land, peopled by a feudal society as bland and unchangeable as the climate in which it lived. It was visited occasionally by American ships plying the hide trade, and sailors often slipped over the side and found some means of livelihood in this gracious land. There were "Betsys from Pike," who, with their husbands and families, were stealing in from over the mountains, more and more of them pushing due west rather than northwest into Oregon, and establishing ranches without bothering to clear their titles with the local government. Their numbers in total were not great, but sufficient to set up a threat. Also they sang the land's praises, sent glowing word home by any means available, and promoted still more emigration. Soon the expansionists who demanded that Oregon be annexed were not above taking over California if it could be done peacefully, even by connivance.

The leading light among them was Old Bullion, Senator Thomas Hart Benton of Missouri, patron of the Santa Fe Trail, who was determined to carry the United States to the Pacific, and beyond, if the situation warranted. By an unexpected train of circumstances, he found at his disposal a young man well fitted to help carry through certain of his plans. His name was John Charles Frémont, a Savannah boy, educated at Charleston, and an instructor in mathematics in the Navy for a time, followed by a year or two of surveying ashore before he was finally commissioned a lieutenant in the Topographical Corps.

As a member of one of its parties, he ascended the Missouri River in 1839, and had his first hand-to-hand encounter with the Great West. This area was definitely to be his dish of tea for the next several years. There was, however, a brief stint at a desk job in Washington, during which he secretly married Senator Benton's able daughter Jessie. The incident temporarily threw the statesman's toga heavily askew, but he perhaps recognized usable abilities in the at first unwanted son-in-law, and young Frémont was soon in command of an exploration party sent to chart new trails over the Sierras and on to the west. The accurate and readable report he compiled, with his wife's help, went into wide circulation, and in the following year, 1843, he set off at the head of another party. Visiting the Salt Lake area, he moved up into Oregon, carefully described the trail to that land, and on his return managed to traverse nearly the whole length of Spanish California. The report of this journey when issued became almost required reading by the westward-bound, and provided the occasion for a third journey, undertaken in 1845.

FRÉMONT HEADS FOR CALIFORNIA

In the spring of that year he was actively recruiting his party in St. Louis. The golden age of the fur trade had passed, or at least its more romantic days were over, and he had his pick of the mountain men. The over-all purpose of the trip was a bit hazy, but purportedly to determine the shortest practicable route through to the Pacific, with possibly an easier link with Oregon. Polk was moving into the presidency, and greedy eyes were beginning to be leveled at California.

Kit Carson had been out there as early as 1830, so his services were sought, and he was encouraged to leave the ranch he had established near wide-open Taos to act as chief scout. He not only came himself, but brought along his able partner, Dick Owens, as well. The party set off over the Santa Fe Trail, heading for the great trading citadel on the Arkansas at the edge of Colorado, Bent's Fort. Here, where the road Becknell had laid out years before turned to the south, this group pushed on to the north and west over the mountains into the Salt Lake Valley.

The intimation of opening up a shorter or less arduous trail into Oregon could still hold good, but it would evidently be found through California, for the party headed due west from the great body of brackish water Jim Bridger had stumbled upon. The Indians were more than a little incredulous, for they were certain the endless alkaline flats of the Great Basin just to the west were virtually impassable. Still Frémont's band managed to locate food and water along the way and opened up a new avenue of travel which would resound to heavy traffic within but a few years. However, it was a hazardous venture, for it was late November by the time they had crossed Nevada, and the higher hills beyond Lake Tahoe were already white with snow.

For a second time the group was broken up into two units in an attempt to plunge through passes which it was hoped might be negotiated before the drifts were too deep. The larger contingent was piloted by Jim Walker, who had been with Bonneville's first wagon train to Oregon, and also included Carson and Owens. They kept to the south, working their way slowly over the summit through a pass which still bears Carson's name. Frémont, with fewer numbers, drove directly west, probably through Truckee Valley, on over what was later called Emigrant Pass, and found far easier going.

By the ninth of December, 1835, he was at New Helvetia, Colonel Sutter's famous fort at the edge of present-day Sacramento. The able, kindly, affable Swiss, who had long been a Mexican citizen and official, as well as a large landholder and power in the community, received Frémont and the fragment of his party most kindly. Despite the suspicions which the American's presence had raised among the native authorities as he had passed down through the land some months before, the colonel was hospitable and helpful.

Actually the situation had altered somewhat since this previous visit. Mexican control had come to an end, and the province was now autonomous, and ruled by local forces from Los Angeles and Monterey. Between these two centers though there was enough cleavage to foster possible civil strife. The young officer with the Byronesque touch listened avidly to his host, and plied him with questions in an attempt to become fully oriented to the situation. Possibly destiny was about to open great opportunities before him. Still he must not overplay his hand.

The fort was flea-infested, but it provided a spot in which to catch one's breath after the mad dash through the snowy hills. So Frémont sat and cogitated a few days, recalling the tension brewing between the United States and Mexico, and conscious as well that the keen-minded merchant, Thomas O. Larkin, had been installed at Monterey as American consul with instructions to wet-nurse any revolutionary activities which might play into American hands. Also, it was readily evident that the settlers who had stolen into the upper reaches of this land and gone to ranching were apprehensive and girding for trouble.

It would be well for him to appear before the proper authorities at Monterey and attempt to explain his sudden reappearance within their bailiwick, and also to check with Consul Larkin. So trusting that the balance of the party were perfectly competent to make their way through the mountains safely, he set off for what was then the most important town in California, beautifully situated on a sightly bay, about midway along the coast.

There he turned on the charm, added a pinch of firmness, and a liberal dash of duplicity. He even went so far as to claim he had *left* the bulk of his party beyond the borders of the province. Seemingly convinced that he was harmless, his hosts permitted the intruder to buy mounts and place orders for goods and stores, and he, of course, managed long conversations with Larkin. Making his way back to Sutter's Fort, he was at last joined by the remainder of his party, and stayed on there until late in February of 1846, playing for time and confident from day to day that there would be some indication of the part he was certain he was to play in great affairs.

As he and the forty men set out for Monterey to pick up the horses and supplies, an ontoward incident occurred. There had been difficulty between some of the Walker contingent and one of the Spanish dons in the great valley, and other incidents that had nettled Sutter, so it could not have been totally unexpected. Just as the group were nearing Salinas, a Mexican officer reined in before Frémont and thrust a curtly worded order into his hands. He had his choice—either leave California immediately or be seized and thrown into prison.

Was this the call to action? In a blaze of indignation the American informed the courier in biting tones that he might inform his superiors that this peaceful group would take its own good time in removing from the province and that was that! As the officer swung his horse toward Monterey to report, the exploring party spurred their own beasts in the same direction, galloping to the top of Hawk's Peak in the Gabilan range behind the town. There they threw up hurried fortifications and raised the Stars and Stripes.

Fortunately this very brash gesture was responded to in somewhat dilatory fashion by the Mexican commandant. Frémont was definitely on insecure ground, might embarrass Washington when there was still hope of taking over this huge coastal province by peaceful means, and discretion soon overcame valor, and he retired, swung to the north, and headed for Oregon at the head of a disgruntled band of men. They had had no intention of stopping with this nose-thumbing episode, but their leader encouraged them on their way. In April they were well up to the north, having a preliminary look at the Cascade Mountains, when a spring snowfall gave the party pause. Also it provided Frémont an excuse to pull back toward the stage on which he still expected the curtain would soon rise and he would pick up his cue and make a proper entrance.

Early in May a group of mounted men suddenly charged into the camp. They were American ranchers accompanying a marine corps lieutenant, Archibald Gillespie, bearing dispatches for Frémont. He had been sent via Vera Cruz and Mexico City, been forced to flee that land, and had committed the contents of the messages he bore to memory before destroying the papers. At last aboard an American sloop at the west coast port of Mazatlán, he journeyed from there via the Hawaiian Islands. Thus the word he brought was a trifle stale and his news now obsolete. After contacting Larkin, he had been hurried up the valley in search of the retreating Frémont.

While what he imparted may have been a bit inconclusive, it at least firmed the humiliated American's resolve, and the conversations between them lasted until far into the night. For the second time in his long career, "The Pathfinder" thoughtlessly neglected to post a proper guard, and toward morning there was a visitation by the Klamath Indians. It was a bloody affair, and while it cost the life of but one of the party, who could now ill be spared, it whetted the remainder's thirst for action. Also it was a straw in an evil wind soon to be made apparent. The neighboring tribal village was burned to the ground, and its inhabitants widely scattered before the party headed south again.

Arriving at the famous Lassen Ranch on May 24, Frémont was quickly shown a recent order over the signature of the Mexican commandant warning all non-Mexican settlers to vacate immediately. He was also informed that to help implement this order the authorities were inciting the savages to attack any and all interlopers. The purpose behind the raid by the Klamaths now became all too apparent, and the American ranchers were for immediately seizing the initiative.

Representatives from among them demanded what Frémont proposed to do. Still convinced that word of actual war could not long be delayed but hesitant to pit his limited strength against heavy odds, or to outrage Washington by a precipitate act, the military man masquerading as a surveyor was impaled on the horns of a dilemma. Heroes have been made down through the ages by playing the long chance at such moments. Still a continent of equal size could probably be assembled from those who have gone down to defeat and ignominy when the circumstances were not sufficiently favorable.

There were manifold occasions when it seemed that this gentleman's number would be drawn and he would be added to the select circle of the immortals. But each time there was a narrow but distinct miss, and in this instance caution counseled a continuation of the program of "watchful waiting."

ANOTHER LONE STAR FLAG IS UNFURLED

By now the ranchers were thoroughly disgusted with such "pussyfooting," and evidently planned to force his hand. Falling upon a party of Mexican hostlers herding government horses to the south, they stampeded the *vaqueros* and drove off the animals. With this rash act, the die was cast.

Under Frémont's encouragement, if not with his direct participation, another party of twenty-three of the ranchers thundered into the sleepy little mission town of Sonoma on June 14, seized a reasonable quantity of needed military stores, and a much larger prize in the person of General Vallejo. This retired commandant, although friendly to the Americans, was still a powerful figure in native California affairs.

There was no side-stepping the situation any longer, so Frémont puffed out his chest, took over plunder and prisoner, and hurried both to Sutter's Fort. There was a brief, sharp verbal encounter between the American brevet captain and the Swiss colonel long since a Mexican judge. But Cincinnatus had named himself dictator at last in California, and in short order the stockade became an American outpost, and Sutter was soon afterward impressed into the forces of the United States as a lieutenant of dragoons at fifty dollars per month.

Back in Sonoma, the ranchers had been busy launching the Republic of California. This took place on the very day the town was seized, and perhaps its most colorful incident was the hoisting of another flag on which a lone star had a prominent place. One William L. Todd, whose aunt was the still not too widely known wife of a downstate Illinois politician, A. Lincoln, played the part of a west coast Betsy Ross. He had in his possession a piece of brownish cloth about five feet long. While a rather indifferent artist, that fact did not deter him in the least, and he set to work, probably with pokeberry juice.

First he drew a five-pointed star in the upper right-hand corner. Opposite it, at the upper left, he sketched in what passed for a grizzly bear. And then, so that there might be no trace of doubt as to what was symbolized, he lettered below CALIFORNIA REPUBLIC. Texas now had its counterpart out beyond the mountains, and the date of its nativity was June 14, 1846.

Back in Washington but two days before, and quite without an inkling of what was transpiring a continent away, the Congress voted to terminate the joint occupancy of Oregon, which land would soon be part of the United States. At about this same moment a band of Mormons, some sixteen thousand strong, and with one of the ablest of all American leaders, Brigham Young, at its head, was bound for Utah. War with Mexico was actually just a month old. It was a year of decision indeed, and the number of stars later to appear in the blue field of Old Glory that were at that moment in the making was far greater than these widely scattered incidents would have then clearly indicated.

Frémont had no difficulty in enlisting enough additional men to raise his forces to about one hundred fifty. He was just preparing to leave Sutter's Fort with this augmented group when word reached him that war with Mexico was under way. Since this justified the course he had finally taken, he started off with greater resolve. By June 25 he was at Sonoma, and a week later had his small army ferried over the neighboring great bay to seize the unimposing fort that stood well up toward the inner end of the long peninsula that all but closes off the bay waters from those of the Pacific. This tiny Mexican post was soon his, and in an exultant mood, he named the nearby rock-bound channel joining bay and ocean the Golden Gate.

With Vallejo his prisoner of war and Sutter brought over to the American cause, the scattered native elements in the northern portion of the province were no longer a primary concern. What conditions farther south would be like remained to be seen. Frémont was back at Sonoma by the Fourth of July, taking part in the formation of the California Battalion, two hundred fifty men strong. The spirits of this relatively small contingent were quickly heightened when word was brought that federal support was at hand. Commodore Sloat, an elderly and overcautious naval commander, had seized Monterey on July 7, a few days before a British landing there could be brought off. Two days later the American ships sailed into San Francisco Bay, only to find peace and quiet there, too.

THE OCCUPATION BY AMERICAN FORCES

By the middle of this same month Frémont headed for Monterey, taking about one hundred fifty picked men with him. Once there, he visited Sloat aboard his ship, but found the man still a bit dazed by what had happened, uncertain of the part he was expected to play, and hesitant about co-operation. Thus it was something of a relief when he soon sailed away, leaving the remainder of the squadron in command of the more aggressive Commodore Stockton.

Since the conversations with Sloat had brought out the fact that he was acting quite without authority, Frémont willingly accepted a place for himself and his followers in a service unit called the Navy Battalion of Mounted Horsemen. Presumably it was navy, although it may have been the original Horse Marines, but whatever it was that Stockton offered, it won "The Pathfinder" a boost in rank to major, and gave him the feeling that he was now "legitimate" in intents and purposes.

He and his new superior cooked up plans for action, and since the north was relatively quiet, the landmen and their *remuda* and gear were loaded aboard ship and taken to San Diego. Poor Kit Carson experienced his first, and last, case of seasickness. But their warm reception at the hands of the people in this first founded of the California pueblos soon helped to put their land legs beneath them again. After ten days of festivities, much like those Pike had experienced years before in New Mexico, some forty men were left to garrison the town, and the remainder, together with Frémont, started overland for Los Angeles.

Moving up the coast as far as San Pedro without unpleasant incident, the party was augmented here by some three hundred sixty seamen and marines and a few pieces of mobile artillery put ashore by Stockton. To oppose such a force, the local Mexican commanders had no more than two hundred fifty. Since the outcome of any clash seemed foreordained, the native soldiery took to its heels, and the Americans marched into the City of Our Lady the Queen of the Angels unopposed on August 12.

By Stockton's proclamation, California was now a part of the United States, and little Los Angeles declared the capital of this new territory. The city had not had the forethought to take over the shoestring strip which now connects it with its harbor, the naval commodore was, for those days at least, a bit too far inland for his ships to be of much aid to him, and a surprise attack on September 22 put the pueblo back in Mexican possession, and guerrilla troops continued to hold it.

Frémont had been returned to the northern part of the province to be certain that order was maintained there, and also to muster another striking force. It took considerable effort, but by late November he had assembled better than four hundred men, and left with them for San Luis Obispo, intending to move as rapidly as possible down along the coast. But the "high fog" blowing in from off the ocean proved to be rain clouds, and they poured down their supersaturated contents day after day. And as though the weather alone were not enough, the countryside had been pretty well stripped of beef cattle and horses, so that food was none too plentiful and replacement of mounts and pack animals almost impossible.

Soon the trails were deep in mud, and unshod horses slipped and slithered about, often plunging into swollen arroyos, where the floodwater swept them away together with saddles and gear. By Christmas Day of 1846 the party had advanced no farther than the mountains behind Santa Barbara. Taking his spent forces into the almost deserted town, Frémont rested there a whole week. Then he pushed on down the ocean front for a way, meeting up with a courier bearing word that Los Angeles was again in American hands.

General Stephen Watts Kearney had led the frontier-trained First Dragoons, plus a hastily recruited regiment of Missouri volunteers, from Fort Leavenworth down the Santa Fe Trail, and taken over the New Mexico area. Since his orders had permitted him to move on to California if such seemed to him to be a calculated risk, he had started in that direction with a limited force at about the time Stockton had returned Frémont to the north to recruit more Horse Marines, and headed Kit Carson for Washington bearing dispatches. Kearney had encountered the latter almost within gunshot of his home in Taos, had countermanded his orders, and taken him over as guide for the fast-moving dragoon company with which the general was to undertake a dash to California.

The troopers had arrived on the outskirts of San Diego before they encountered resistance. Carson had been convinced the partisan band would not fight, but it did, and came within an ace of cutting the American party to ribbons. But Kearney finally managed to hook up with Stockton at this southern port, and early in January 1847, their combined forces were sufficient to give them possession of Los Angeles once more.

However, while the sleepy little town clustered about its plaza was again firmly in American hands, the back country was still the hide-out of armed resistance. Frémont, whose movement inland through the Santa Paula Valley may have made it appear that he was bent on clearing out pockets of insurgents, was destined to terminate the hostilities. As he was about to pitch camp hard by San Fernando Mission in the late afternoon of January 12, 1847, a Mexican courier put in a sudden appearance. He had been hurriedly dispatched by Don Andres Pico, leader of the partisan remnant, who badly wanted to surrender to someone, just as long as he was an American.

The authority to receive such a capitulation was perhaps Stockton's—or had it transferred to Kearney? Such things as rank, responsibility, precedence, and military protocol had gotten badly snarled up, and Frémont was eventually court-martialed in connection with happenings that took place as the curtain was falling on this conquest, which, in many of its aspects, proved to be out-and-out *opéra bouffe.*

The important fact is that resistance ceased entirely by early January of 1847, and California was American, and perhaps had been since the Bear Flag was unfurled the previous June. There seems to be a prevalent impression, particularly among easterners, that the acquisition of what was to become the second-largest state was in some way contingent upon the discovery of gold there. That followed, quite independently and unexpectedly, and something over a year after Pico surrendered to Frémont.

Within a few weeks more than a year great things had indeed happened. It was only about three days before the close of 1845 that Texas formally became a part of the United States by annexation. Toward the end of April 1846, war was under way with Mexico, and so declared by resolution the following month. Before this momentous month was over and done, the President had forwarded the notice of the termination of joint occupancy of Oregon to London, and from that time this great chunk of the Northwest was to all intents and purposes a part of the United States. By late August, Kearney had occupied Santa Fe, and New Mexico was due to become American territory. The fate of California was pretty well established by the early summer of that same year, although perhaps not conclusively until the following January. Within a matter of months the still young United States had burst its seams, expanded violently across mountains and deserts, and was within a few square miles of its ultimate continental limits. A huge new frontier had been opened up that would now begin to fill in with such startling rapidity that within another half century the American frontier itself would be no more.

XXVIII

Socialism and Communism are Tested

The character and conduct of our own population in the United States show conclusively that nothing so stimulates intelligence in the poor, and at the same time nothing so well enables them to bear the inconvenience of their lot, as a reasonable prospect that with industry and economy they may raise themselves out of the condition of hired laborers into that of independent employees of their own labor . . . Hitherto, our cheap and fertile lands have acted as an important safety-valve for the enterprise and discontent of our non-capitalist population . . . Any circumstances, as the exhaustion of these lands, which should materially impair this opportunity for independence would be, I believe, a serious calamity to our country.—Charles Nordhoff, *Communistic Societies in the United States*, London, 1875.

THERE had been a period of intense emotionalism in the 1820s. Jacksonian democracy was its political expression, while its religious, economic, and social aspects came to find many forms and outlets, such as Mormonism, Unitarianism, anti-Masonry, and a wide array of experiments in group living. These latter had their inception for the most part in Europe, which had long been wracked by war, famine, pestilence, and persecution, and from which unfortunate conditions many sought escape.

Among the first to give the communal form of life a trial in this country were the Shakers, whose high priestess was Mother Ann Lee, who came to this country in 1774. Their earliest society was founded in 1787 at Mount Lebanon, New York, and during the years ahead their many settlements would be widely scattered across the country. Both communism and celibacy were practiced; and despite this last injunction, sufficient converts continued to be brought in so that some of the communities persisted until into the early 1900s.

Perhaps the most widely publicized of such attempts was the famous Brook Farm Institute of Agriculture and Education, at West

Roxbury in Massachusetts, established in 1841. To it such celebrated men as Hawthorne, Emerson, and Horace Greeley lent their names and support. The godfather of the project had been a French social- ist, François Fourier, and it started off with a great fanfare. But waning enthusiasm, plus a disastrous fire, wound up its affairs by 1846. Another colony along very similar lines, and also based upon Fourier's formulas, was tried out at Red Bank, New Jersey, but was short-lived.

One of our well-known trade names of today saw its inception in the Oneida Community, established to the pattern proposed by J. H. Noyes in 1848. Communism there, following Plato's scheme, was to embrace not only tangible property, but sex relationships as well, the latter being tied in some manner to a professed belief in the dual sex attributes of God. The colony's neighbors were outraged from the start, there was internal strife as well, and it ultimately wound up manufacturing mousetraps, and then, as a joint stock ven- ture, launched into the production of silverware.

There were, in addition, among the more prominent attempts of this sort made during the first three quarters of the last century the Harmonists at Economy, Ohio; the Separatists of Zoar, near by in the same state; the Wallingford Perfectionists in Connecticut; the Au- rora Community in Oregon, and another of this same persuasion at Bethel in Missouri; the Bishop Hill Commune in Illinois; little Social Freedom Community down in Virginia; Cedar Vale on the Kansas plains; and the Icarians at Corning, Iowa. Larger perhaps than any of the foregoing, with the possible exception of the Shakers, was a group that took more permanent root in Iowa, and into whose ac- tivities it might be interesting to take a detailed look.

It should be mentioned, however, that there were other com- munities that were *not* primarily communistic located at Anaheim, California, Vineland, New Jersey, and the Silkville Prairie home in Kansas. Thus these escapists and socially elite were scattered all over the map. They came and they went, only two among them all show- ing even a small measure of endurance.

TO AMERICA AND FREEDOM—OF SORTS

The assemblage deserving consideration was no new johnny- come-lately sect when it first appeared in America. It had been drawn together slowly as the "True Inspiration Congregations" back in Germany early in the 1700s. Its leaders were "instruments," spiritual mouthpieces selected from among the membership because of their godly attributes. At various times in the homeland they had included such lowly vessels as a stocking weaver, a carpenter, and an illiterate serving-maid. The followers were thus humble folk, but frugal, industrious, thrifty, and determined.

When an exodus to a more promising land was ordained, the then current "instrument," Christian Metz, and four associates financed by the group, sailed for New York in 1842. Starting their search, they moved out the Erie Canal, and came to the booming metropolis at its western terminus. On its outskirts they decided to locate their American "Land of Canaan." Accustomed to relatively stationary communities at home, they bought a sizable parcel of land at the edge of, but pleasantly apart from, sprawling Buffalo. They named it, as other hopefuls had named similarly conceived settlements in this new land, Ebenezer, "Stone of Help."

Hastening back home, they selected some three hundred fifty persons willing to try life in the "wilderness," and were back at the site they had selected early in the next year. More than two hundred others would follow in 1844, and with further accruals during ensuing years, they soon had better than one thousand settled in their three plain, trim, well-ordered villages—Upper, Lower, and Middle Ebenezer. Each was complete with homes, church, shops, and storehouses. Funds from savings had been sufficient so that money had not been too great a concern, and a completely communistic arrangement was not this sect's first intent, either before emigrating, or after establishment here.

But the membership came face to face with two sobering problems. The first was the realization that not all of their members were either accustomed to or interested in centering their efforts on agriculture, which was to have been the main form of employment. Such singleness of purpose, it was thought, would permit them to give greater attention to the spiritual side of life. But this temporal matter was threatening to wreck the colony, so factories were set up to retain the loyalty of those not cut out to be farmers. They thought this and other attendant problems through with true German thoroughness, and finally came up with a communal arrangement as the best solution. And under it the colony began to thrive.

But so, too, did neighboring Buffalo. Soon it was reaching out and out, and closer and closer, until there was less than sufficient insulating space left between the True Inspirationists and their not so pious and circumscribed neighbors. The worldliness with which they were being surrounded was catching; and within a dozen years escape was again in order. So, like Joshua, Caleb, and the other ten of old, emissaries were sent to spy out the remainder of the land. Their reconnoissance finally ended in Iowa. There the prospects seemed most promising, and land was cheap; so they bought, eventually, from a dozen to fifteen square miles of it and erected no less than seven villages.

Still there was to be no crossing of the Red Sea in a body. They were prudent enough to remove slowly over a period of years, beginning in 1855. They had made quite a substantial investment in Ebenezer, and their eight-thousand-acre tract was disposed of piecemeal, families being moved west only as their places were sold at a profit. By such an orderly transfer they were able to sustain the cost of a new and far larger homesite, together with all the attendant moving expense. Evidently they were not entirely what you might term visionaries. In fact their leaders often proved to be hard men with a dollar.

THE AMANA COMMUNITIES

What did they call their new hideaway? A passage from the fourth chapter of the Song of Solomon had given them an inspiration. It read: "Come with me from Lebanon, my spouse, with me from Lebanon: look from the top of Amana . . ." There was a tricky bit of symbolism involved, but suffice it to say that Amana meant in the Hebrew something fixed, as by a solemn treaty, an unfailing portion, perpetual security.

By comparison with the life experiences of a Joe Meek, a Jim Bridger, or many another among the stalwarts along the frontier, life in the Amana Communities might seem flat, stale, and uninteresting. Yet it was far from sterile in the minds of its inhabitants, who looked for glory in something beside heroics and bold adventure. No one there was ever forced to subsist on a diet of locusts or ants, and while there were no Bacchanalian spring rendezvous either, the little towns had their decided merits and attractive aspects. In visiting there, one had a choice among East, Middle, West, or South Amana, Amana-near-the-Hill; Homestead, or Amana proper. It would make little difference which, for the seven were about as alike as the blooms of the wild roses that grew in profusion along their fences, about the sole difference in fact being that Middle Amana had the distinction of having the printing office.

Each of them was separated from its neighbor by about a mile and a half, and along its single, straggling street were the homes, together with the church, the schoolhouse, a general store at which the farmers from beyond the communities themselves came to trade, an inn or tavern at which the public was accommodated in keeping with the thought in Hebrews 13:2, and its shoemaker, carpenter, and tailor shops. Beyond these structures were the barns, mills, factories, and other work and storage buildings, for each of the seven communities was virtually self-sufficient.

The homes were of brick, stone, or wood, very plain, severe, and purposely devoid of paint. The churches were merely larger houses, and totally without adornment, especially as respects steeples, which, like the Quakers, this sect abhorred. Their barns were ample and well arranged, and usually there was a cluster of houses at the outskirts to accommodate nonmembers hired from time to time to plump out the labor supply.

What, to the unpracticed eye, might look like larger homes proved to be cookhouses or prayerhouses. Feeding was on a communistic basis, but limited to about thirty to each of the common dining rooms. The younger women, under the direction of their elders, prepared and served the meals, which were announced by the ringing of a large bell. The sexes sat at separate tables, and the children were also segregated, such deployment serving "to prevent silly conversation and trifling conduct." Life was real, life was earnest, and heaven alone was its goal.

Food came from the common stores; and those too ill to attend at the cookhouses had their meals carried to them in baskets provided for the purpose. For those who did respond to the clattering bell, there was a moment of silence followed by grace before sitting down to eat, and another brief prayer before they separated. The bare-topped tables groaned under abundant supplies, and the food was polished off rapidly by hearty appetites. Breakfast was at six or six-thirty, fluctuating with the seasons, dinner at eleven-thirty, and supper at six or seven. You were entitled to pick up a midmorning snack of bread, with either beer or wine to wash it down. And, if your girth would tolerate it, there could be another of bread, butter, and coffee in midafternoon.

Where did the money come from? From work—and still it was in no sense slavery. Each village had its foreman, and these seven leaders met every evening to decide upon needs and the labor assignments for the next day. If you did not have a regular place in one of the factories, you received a ticket telling you where to report, and for what duties. But even the factory hands could be shifted about to care for peak loads.

THE PATTERN OF COMMUNAL LIFE

As preparation for their life work, the members received a fair schooling, but only in the three *Rs*, plus liberal drill in Bible and catechism. However, the scholars went directly from breakfast to school, where lessons lasted from seven until nine-thirty, under a male teacher who tolerated no straying from the straight and narrow path of rectitude and discipline. Then—boys and girls alike—picked up their knitting and clicked the needles dextrously and without pause until the dinner bell rang.

By one o'clock all were back on the benches again for a go at more lessons until three. After that knitting was the order of the day again, and no one dared drop a stitch until four-thirty. Why all this knitting, and for boys, too? Just to keep little hands out of mischief? No, rather to develop habits of industry, for the socks, mittens, and other items produced sold well in the community stores. Also it was good discipline, and an excellent preparation for the beehive type of life of the commune. The membership didn't question, it merely complied. Yet surprisingly enough the great bulk of the membership took it, and liked it, throughout long lifetimes. The whole planned and well-ordered regimen was one to engender a strong feeling of shelter and security.

If the houses were plain and unpainted, so, too, was the appearance of their occupants. Whatever they wore was produced locally, and for utility rather than adornment. As a member, you had a yearly allowance for your personal needs; but you were supposed to save enough from it to make reasonable contributions to charitable purposes. You had charge accounts at the store, the tailor's, the shoemaker's, and with the other artisans. But you lived within them, for they could not be overdrawn.

People from the outside accepted as members were so thoroughly scrutinized that there was little falling from grace, and few withdrawals. Persistence was truly remarkable, and obtained despite the fact there were countless rules which could be easily broken merely through neglect, and some regulations by which you lost standing through the commission of the most natural and inevitable human acts. Take marriage as an example of these latter, the permissible age for men being twenty-four.

Both bride and groom might have led most exemplary lives, climbing slowly up to the third or highest of the grades or castes into which the members were divided on the basis of their individual piety and spirituality. One or the other of the pair could even have achieved that exalted state of being an "instrument." But immediately upon marrying both husband and wife were unceremoniously cast down to the children's, or beginners', class. Strive as you would, it still took several years before you could struggle back up the steep ladder into the higher realms.

And the tying of the hymeneal knot was an experience to make one cringe. The ceremony was limited to the pair being joined, their parents, and three stodgy "elders." There was no Lohengrin, bridesmaids, best man, bouquets, trains, or doodads. Instead there was a day-long session, the elders hammering into the minds of the young couple the scope of their duties to one another, and the variety and extent of the pitfalls of domestic and married life. After such topics had been labored and belabored through many hours, as was customary, being broken on the rack or an appearance before the Spanish Inquisition would have seemed merely routine.

The men were permitted to carry watches, but the ownership of jewelry or other gewgaws by either sex was strictly *verboten*. While boys and girls sat in the same room in school, there was no passing of notes, no monkey business. To and from school you walked along soberly, boys with boys, and girls with girls. Saturdays you went to school. Oh yes, there were Sunday afternoons when the long church service was at last over and one might walk in the fields. But the boys went in one direction—by custom and ordinance—and the girls in another.

What, no dating? And how about courtship? Either or both were managed only by the utmost in stealth and furtiveness. What a life! Still the young people "fell in love," managed to get their feelings exchanged, and probably enjoyed the more such clandestine courtship as they could contrive. They married, had families, and kept the seven neighboring villages steaming ahead for many years.

Surprisingly enough the governing board of the Amana Communities was pestered to death by candidates wanting to join the sect. And it was not so much just casual inquirers and applicants as it was those who wrote that they had sold their worldly goods, were setting out tomorrow, and be sure to have a place ready for them on their arrival a week from Tuesday. Such as were accepted came principally from the old country, being German, or Swiss, with a few from Bohemia. These were carefully screened, had to be vouched for back home, for passage money was sent from this end when required.

When the move to Iowa was made in the mid-forties, this section was then the Far West, and for years to come these communities would be a considerable distance from the more populous East, and much farther from Europe. Still its members kept in touch with communicants back in the homelands, could always fill its ranks from there; and it is supposed that Anton Dvořák, great Czech composer, found inspiration for certain themes in his *New World Symphony* during long visits among friends at Amana, when he spent three years in this country as director of the National Conservatory in New York.

Basically these congregations were a religious society. The industrial phase of their common life was subservient to this principal purpose, and was intended to yield plenteous sustenance rather than a profit. While life in Amana might seem static and barren by today's standards, the contrast with that of the common people during much of the last century could, in many respects, have been in favor of these communities. Surely when laid alongside that of the poorer classes in Europe it was overflowing abundance. In fact, during many years its membership could have been increased to a point where its land holdings would have been totally inadequate.

However, this segregated, unprogressive type of life began to lose certain of its advantages. It was secure and stable, but it was drab and ascetic, too. Also it was tied to an economy rapidly being outmoded, and as we barged into the booming twentieth century, the balance that had fostered loyalty began to tip away. As an older generation that had known little of any other manner of existence passed from the scene, the end was in sight.

Brook Farm, the expression largely of a group of intellectuals, had managed to hold together only five years. Oneida Community ran for thirty-odd before it succumbed, and became a straight business enterprise. Most of the other social experiments were of far shorter duration than either of the above. Only the Shakers and Amana among the communistic ventures outlived the 1800s, and they but briefly. As the American way of life expanded and brought greater benefits to ever greater numbers, the over-all climate was not conducive to these sequestered enterprises in communal living.

Nonetheless, it is well to recall that communism has been tried out in the past in our own country, not once, but many times, and found wanting.

XXIX

The Frontier of the Miners

Placer gold deposits have been formed by the disintegration of the gold bearing rocks and the carrying down of their contents into the beds of streams. Here the steady action of running water separates the gold from the lighter materials associated with it and, because of their lower specific gravity, carries them away faster than the heavier gold. The gold freed from the enclosing rock, which has been swept along by the force of the current, is frequently found in large quantities at the bars and riffles of the stream. It is also found scattered finely through the sands which form the beds of these streams. In this way, in every country where gold is found, nature has, to a large extent, anticipated the miner's work, and has left the precious metal in such form that it can be easily and quickly obtained.—Edward Sherwood Mead, *The Story of Gold.*

CHANTED the poet Thomas Hood, "Gold! Gold! Gold! Gold! Bright and yellow, hard and cold." These and other sentiments must have throbbed in the hearts of men from the day the first European set foot on this continent. The thoughts of it had played on the disordered minds of Cabeza de Vaca and his companions, and touched off the ill-starred Coronado expedition. Hope of encountering it in great quantities had stimulated De Soto, and even the English were responsive to gold's appeal, for the failure to uncover mines was, along with the savage winter frost, a major reason for the default of the Popham colonists.

While the yearning was for gold, the first metal found here in usable quantities was, of course, iron. It is claimed that the earliest crude mill and furnace for its reclamation built in the English colonies stood on a small creek in Chesterfield County, Virginia, just south of present-day Richmond, where it was erected as early as 1619. This would have been only a dozen years after the first landing on the James, while the Indians were still a menace, and it appears the savages destroyed it in its third year of operation.

It would be almost a hundred years thereafter before there was anything like a fully equipped iron furnace, and again Virginia could claim a "first." This one was placed in operation by Governor Spotswood in 1716, a few miles west of Fredericksburg, while there was a second built five years later, about four miles from the Washington homestead at Wakefield. This latter was no doubt in operation at the time the "Father of His Country" was born near by.

Where the earliest such facilities were established in New England would be hard to say, for in that area for years to come iron would be fished from the bottoms of the hundreds of marshy ponds and shallow lakes left as the result of glacial activity rather than mined from the earth. Such bog iron could be brought to the surface with rakes and tongs, and was still being recovered in considerable quantities well past the middle of the last century. It took little refining before it was ready to be cast, and the early smiths are said to have used it for light forgings, especially nails.

There were lead outcroppings at many points, and the great ease with which this metal could be smelted, plus a considerable demand for its use in a wide range of products, especially for rifle balls, encouraged the wide attention it received. There is evidence that the colonies were entirely self-sufficient in this respect at the outset of the Revolution, and that a considerable quantity of this ductile metal was stock-piled. During the war years British prisoners manned some of the mines, and in the years immediately after the war supplies held at some of the numerous shot towers were released and drawn into tubing. Many a farm home during the next century and a half enjoyed running water, piped in from a spring through a conduit formed from metal originally intended for bullets.

It was lead that took Moses Austin first to Wythe County in the lower Shenandoah, and later to Missouri while that country was still Spanish. There he pioneered the mining area behind Ste. Genevieve, and from this activity laid the foundation of the sizable fortune later lost in land speculation. It was from neighboring pits during the next few years that Andrew Henry acquired the stake that made him a partner of General Ashley in the fur trade.

As Pike was on his way north to investigate the source of the Mississippi, he stopped at the workings of Julien Dubuque on that river's western bank, where the city named for the pioneer miner now stands. Many of the fortunes accumulated in the early days in the great river valley had their inception in the lead country, which sprawled out from Iowa into Illinois and Wisconsin. In 1829 some twelve million pounds would be recovered from this area alone, and the output would increase in subsequent years, and furnish, among other products, the ball and shot used to win and tame the north-western frontier.

Coal, one of the most valuable substances which we take from the earth, managed a rather late start. There was ample wood, which could be resolved into charcoal for special uses; and it was not until the advent of the canal boats, followed rapidly by the railroads, that the mineral fuel began to be shipped. The stories to the effect that no one quite knew what to do with this rocklike substance when it first appeared on the market are surely much overdrawn. Actually coal was being mined along the James River in Virginia as early as 1750. As soon as facilities to burn it were perfected and it could be readily shipped, it came into wide use. And it proved most fortunate indeed that the iron-bearing areas in many parts of the country also had substantial seams of coal near by. Coal has its story, and it is an important one, too. But it is hardly of the frontier flavor, with the possible exception of the Molly Maguires, the organization patterned after an Irish secret society, which opposed the coal mine operators in rural Pennsylvania for more than twenty years. The long series of crimes perpetrated there was in the best tradition of the Plummer gang that held sway a couple of years later in the Montana gold fields.

Copper had been worked to a very limited extent in colonial days, and there are instances of copper as well as lead mines being operated by prisoners of war during the Revolution. Yet until after the middle of the last century the demand for this metal was rather moderate, and it played no such conspicuous part in frontier affairs as did iron, lead, or even gold.

THE CALIFORNIA GOLD RUSH

North of Mexico the Indians had not advanced to the stage of development where gold was used as prodigally as it had been in that country, and also farther south in Peru. If the natives above the Rio Grande knew of the free gold in the placer deposits, they had made but inconsequential use of it. This is perhaps in part accounted for by the fact that some of the very richest of such deposits ever discovered within the United States lay in an area inhabited by the most backward of all the tribes.

For this same reason it was pretty well out of reach of the Eu-

ropean interlopers until well into the 1800s. There had been traces
of the precious metal discovered in the southern highlands in the
early days, but it was well into the nineteenth century before any of
these discoveries were worked on a commercial basis. Once again
Virginia takes precedence, and by 1835 there was considerable activity about Dillwyn in Buckingham County, some fifty miles west of
Richmond. From then until the discovery in California, this was the
principal gold-mining region in the country, but it dwindled away
rapidly as huge amounts began to be recovered from western
streams.

It was the chance discovery of colors in the tailrace of a sawmill
built to supply lumber for growing San Francisco that set fire to
the avarice pent up in America since the days of Ponce de León
and Hernando de Soto. The resulting descent upon California that
began in 1848, but reached huge proportions the following year, was
probably the most fabulous single happening in our long history.
Surely it was the most colorful.

Not only did it attract the customary flotsam and jetsam of the
frontier, but many substantial citizens also succumbed to the lure of
gold. Doctors, lawyers, successful merchants, and skilled craftsmen
joined with every Tom, Dick, and Harry not staked down, and set
off overland by wagon, on horseback, or afoot. Others made the long
journey by boat to Panama, then across the isthmus, and again by
boat up the Pacific shore, while some went by ship down and about
Cape Horn.

Many of the big killings were made by those close at hand,
who were able to get up into the hills in back of Coloma in the
summer months immediately following Marshall's remarkable find.
It was then that a chap named Hudson is said to have taken some
twenty thousand dollars from a small canyon in about two weeks.
Close by a half-grown boy recovered some seventy-seven ounces during the first day he worked a "small hole," and ninety ounces on the
following day. Better than thirty-three hundred dollars for a two-
day effort by a fuzzy-chinned youngster was not at all bad.

Rich gravels were ultimately proved up along the west-flowing
streams and their side canyons over a distance of more than two
hundred miles, from the foothills of Mount Lassen on the north down
into Mariposa County. But perhaps the richest single stretch uncovered was along the Middle Fork of the American River. This stream
and its tributaries had cut through a whole ganglion of ancient

glacial river courses that had originally stripped the gold from the virgin rock untold eons before, and whose intersected beds of gravel had in turn been despoiled by the American.

Gold, nineteen times as heavy as water, naturally tends not only to sink, but to burrow into each crack and cranny in the bedrock over which streams flow. But surging floodwaters, aboil with sand and light gravel, tend to dislodge the colors and small nuggets, drive them on downstream, often pocketing both in the bars that form in slack water, especially as the June freshets subside. Several such bars along the Middle Fork yielded from one to more than three million dollars each.

However, such heavy cream, either exposed or easily come by along the water courses large and small, was soon skimmed off, and the unfortunate outnumbered the successful in this quest by huge odds. Some few pockets remained hidden for later years; and long after the white men had abandoned creek after creek as having been completely "cleaned up," the patient Chinese worked them over again, and often took out enough treasure to buy themselves ease and plenty in their older years back in the homeland. The banks of many a California stream in the placer country are still littered with broken bits of novel, round, brown clay wine jugs, which in the past had been tossed when empty against the rocks by some tireless Chinaman, extracting the last color and trace from the creek and its banks.

Hard-rock mining then slowly took hold, while many a gravel deposit would yield its quota of dust as drifts were sunk into its exposed face. But of the more than a billion dollars' worth of gold recovered from the California placers during a little more than fifty years following discovery, the lion's share was taken by hydraulicking.

Gravel deposits, sometimes two, three, or more hundred feet deep, often lay well up on the side of a canyon far deeper. Where a suitable volume of water could be brought to a point high enough above such a deposit so that its fall would build up a considerable pressure, the gravel could be torn loose, worked over, and then moved out of the way after its golden content had been recovered, and this profitable processing carried on at a minimum cost. It took substantial capital to arrange water rights and deliver a sufficient volume of it to a reservoir, sometimes through miles of canals, or by expensive flumes built across numerous canyons. Then there was added outlay for piping and sluice boxes. But once the installation was properly made, its upkeep and operation were nominal in contrast to the returns.

Water taken from the reservoir, many feet above the workings, was brought down in pipes to immense traversing nozzles called Monitors, or giants. Some hurled four-, five-, or even nine-inch streams of water under very high pressure. These readily undercut the bank of gravel, which collapsed and washed down. The larger boulders were picked out by a derrick or trundled off on a stoneboat, and the remainder was washed, or better shot through long lines of sluice boxes ahead of the compelling stream from the giant.

The sluices, whose bottoms were lined with riffle bars or blocks, tended to trap the bulk of the gold particles, while the spent gravel was unceremoniously driven out the far end into the canyon dumping ground. There it was intended that the early summer high water would carry it on down and out of the operator's way. And it did just that to the extent that after a few years the larger streams were carrying a heavy burden of fines, sand, and smaller gravel far down toward San Francisco Bay and spreading ruin over hundreds and thousands of acres of excellent farm land.

Soon the agricultural communities were up in arms, but to little avail, for the powerful mining interests were very much in ascendance at Sacramento. The louder the growing number of farmers shouted, the heavier the load of strangulating sediment sent down with the next year's floodwaters. Had there been a tendency to compromise this evil situation and some reasonable precautions taken, far more of the golden horde might have been recovered. But by the 1880s agriculture was slowly capturing the balance of political power. Then in 1884 came an act that virtually put a stop to all hydraulic mining. The federal government was becoming alarmed. The spoil carried on and on as river courses silted up was at last threatening to fill in the channel to the Mare Island Navy Yard.

There was a bit of relief in 1893, but it was short-lived. Dredging was resorted to in some areas, and drift mining in others. It is estimated that there is as much as a billion dollars' worth of recoverable gold still hidden in the gravels on the western slopes of the mountains in California. But much of it is very liable to remain there during the foreseeable future. It can no longer be profitably extracted by the use of water that today is far more valuable for other and less spectacular purposes.

THE REBOUND SETS IN

What happened to the army of men who flocked into the Golden State after the word of Marshall's chance discovery? Many of them stayed on to furnish the man power and the will power badly needed to tame that huge area. The adventurous drifted off in response to flights of fancy or wild rumors, combing the hills and valleys of Oregon and Washington. In search of still another bonanza, some of them even pushed up into the Fraser River country in British Columbia, only to bounce back when fortune again evaded them.

By 1858 there was a strike in Colorado, and a stampede touched off by the discoveries of the Russell party from Georgia, which had come upon placer gold in the vicinity of present-day Denver. Distance not only lends enchantment, but where the yellow metal is concerned, almost always breeds exaggeration. By the time word had been carried back East, or had thrust through to the Pacific coast, it had grown to such proportions that it built up another robust pilgrimage of the fancy-free Argonauts. Many climbed back over the mountains, while new thousands tromped in the other direction across the plains, some even trundling handcarts and wheelbarrows as they chanted the spirited tocsin "Pikes Peak, or Bust!" But the sands along Cherry Creek were not exactly yellow with gold; and once more the unfortunates and disillusioned began to turn elsewhere, this time relieving their pent up emotions with the newer cry of "Pikes Peak? Humbug!"

This, together with indifferent mining success in the Pacific Northwest, tended to develop a new phenomenon. The frontier in previous times had continuously exerted its pull toward the west, but before the war years a countercurrent had begun to set in. Hardrock mining in Colorado, as in California, would hold a certain number to this laborious effort; but the floating population still bent an ear to the earth, listening for the call of promising placers.

It came next from the Idaho country, deep in mountains which shut it in, and left the happenings there without much in the way of written records of what transpired. That it was lurid was evident, and it was equally certain that for most it was disappointing. Rumors began floating about that the *real* riches lay on to the east in Montana. A French half-breed, François Finlay, better known as *Be-net-see*, had panned out some colors as early as 1852 at the mouth of a

tiny creek emptying into Deer Lodge River on the northern slope
of Lone Tree Hill, in the western part of the state. Six years later
the Stuart boys, together with some companions, confirmed this find;
and the word soon reached the frustrated Pikes Peakers and the
ambulatory forty-niners still holed up in Idaho or beyond to the west.
From then on Montana was to have its wild and woolly era.

Soon there were hordes swarming into such camps as Confederate Gulch and Diamond City, where pay dirt in the famous Montana
Bar was *said* to run as high as two thousand dollars a pan. There were
also Prickly Pear Creek, Alder, Orofino, Grizzly, and Last Chance
gulches. The remains of the last three lie beneath present-day Hel-
ena, where gold colors still occasionally appear in the city's gutters
after a heavy rain.

But of all the camps, perhaps the most rambunctious was Bannack, on Grasshopper Creek in the southwestern corner of the
territory. Gold-bearing sand was discovered in the vicinity in the
summer of 1862, and the camp filled in so rapidly that it became
the first capital of Montana. But among its other acquisitions was
one Henry Plummer, by contrast with whom characters like the
James brothers were little more than wayward boys.

To signal his arrival in town, he bowed to the best traditions of
western films and promptly slew a man. Then, to give evidence of
his histrionic abilities, he pleaded his own case before the miners'
court and won on grounds of self-defense. With his facile tongue, he
soon sweet-talked himself into the sheriff's job, where he became the
directing head of a band of cutthroats and road agents. For a time,
and until Plummer was taken in hand by the vigilantes and summarily strung up in 1864, Bannack was about as lawless a community as
ever festered in this fair land.

While his rule was in progress, the gold fever had transferred to
Virginia City, fifty miles to the east, and eventually drew the territorial capital along with it. In this latter place fortunes mounted
rapidly, and gave sleepless nights and worried days to their posses-
sors. There was virtually no way of getting one's riches out to civilization and safekeeping without word reaching the outlaws who
infested every trail. The outbound parties were thus forced to resort
to the most ingenious devices to defeat these despoilers. One group
even spent days hollowing out a pocket in the tongue of their prairie
schooner, which they successfully used as a safety deposit box in
which to carry their colors, nuggets, and amalgam.

THE LAST OF THE GOLD RUSHES

There was another Virginia City to the south, in what was at first the Utah Territory, and later Nevada. Silver had been found there on the eastern slopes of Mount Davidson, with considerable gold associated with it. Soon the Washoe mining district was in operation, and people flocked in, the majority heading back east from California. Yet it received little attention until the discovery of the Comstock Lode in the spring of 1859. Before fall the miners about Carson City had organized a government, and the result was that the Nevada Territory was soon set up. A young Missourian named Clemens was the private secretary of the territorial secretary, arriving on the scene in 1861. Under his pen name, Mark Twain, he made this cluster of Nevada mining camps famous. Carson City went on to become the territorial and then the state capital, while Virginia City, just over the hills to the north, long a ghost town, is being restored and has become something of a resort, doing its best to preserve the flavor of its more flamboyant days.

Between the hordes of settlers still streaming west and the mining booms which fostered settlement in areas which had previously looked most unpromising for human occupancy, Indian hostilities mounted rapidly. Much of the difficulty was due to lack of a sound legal system to deal with them, and also to an Indian service riddled with the contaminating influences of the "spoils system." By 1867 the conclusion had been reached that the natives could no longer be tolerated as roving tribes, and the northern groups were invited to a big powwow at Fort Laramie in September of that year.

But the Indians failed to heed the summons. Instead, Red Cloud of the potent Sioux sent in word that there could only be peace when the United States stopped building roads through the Indian country, garrisoning them with troops, and thus interfering with the savages' unhampered enjoyment of areas which had been granted to them in solemn treaties. It took six months to pacify the tribesmen, and the conclave was finally held in April of the following year, at which the Sioux agreed to keep within a permanent reserve set up for them in the southwest corner of the Dakota Territory.

For several years the tension was relieved, and although the federal troops still patrolled the plains country and kept a finger on the pulse of affairs, there were no serious clashes with the natives. Then came a historic incident familiar to every school child, and customarily associated with this touchy Indian situation, but actually more directly the outcome of the last of the major gold rushes.

In 1875 the impetuous George Armstrong Custer was stationed at Fort Laramie. One day one of his scouts burst into the post bearing highly interesting but possibly disturbing news—there had been a sizable gold strike about a hundred fifty miles to the northeast in the Black Hills. The cavalry commander rode over into the area for a look-see, and found the Sioux braves smoldering. The penetration of white prospectors and the customary advance guard of the mining camps was annoying, but the gross dishonesty of the men assigned by the Indian Service to the Red Cloud agency made matters doubly bad. Since the latter situation was not rectified, and the former worsened rapidly as the spring of 1875 brought in a flood tide of miners, the Sioux flowed out of the reservation and scattered across the plains, the warriors spoiling for trouble. When the bands failed to return to their restricted area by the late fall, an order demanding their return was circulated among them early that winter.

But they were still at large and distinctly astir when the spring of 1876 set in. With trouble shaping up, three columns of troops began to penetrate the plains, bent on rounding up these refractory bands. The two on the east were under the command of Generals Terry and Custer, and were actively probing for concentrations of either Sioux or Cheyenne warriors. When one of Custer's scouts picked up a fresh trail along the Rosebud River, the general started in pursuit, coming suddenly into contact with the third column, under command of General Gibbon, moving in from the west.

The two officers held a conference aboard a supply vessel anchored in the river, at which it was decided that Custer would move up that stream, while Gibbon would continue on east and join forces with Terry. They would then move the joint command out to the Little Big Horn River, in which valley they believed their quarry lay hidden.

Custer was to have completed his reconnaissance and joined with the other two commanders on June 26. But he, too, had reached the Little Big Horn on the twenty-fifth, where he came upon a strong, hostile band under Chiefs Gall, Crazy Horse, Two Moons, and that potent medicine man, Sitting Bull. He could very probably have evaded immediate encounter, but although outnumbered by at least ten to one, Custer gave battle, and with the well-known result. He and his brave dragoons died at the hands of savages outraged by the white men's perfidy. Gun-toting, vengeful miners had swarmed into

Deadwood, and thereby broken a treaty solemnly entered into by the benighted Indians. And as though that were not enough, the agents in whose hands their day-to-day destinies were cast were growing rich by fraud, and principally at the natives' expense. This country's Indian policy was long a tragic business.

The twin camps of Deadwood and Lead in the Dakota Territory marked the last unrestrained rush along the mining frontier. There Wild Bill Hickok, Calamity Jane, Deadwood Dick, and numerous unrecorded tenants of the Boot Hill Cemetery wrote the last of the lusty sagas of the mining camps. From then on mining became more and more a commercial enterprise, particularly as placer deposits played out and the various metals, including gold, came chiefly as the result of hard-rock mining. There would still be the occasional "desert rats" searching out the back country, ever hopeful of chancing upon bits of "float" indicating a vein in the neighborhood, or encountering a rich mat of glistening colors on the bedrock of some little visited mountain stream. Some of this gentry came to have an international complexion, since they worked their way across borders and poked inquisitive noses into prospects all the way from Alaska through much of South America.

And a few of them persist to this day, but the odds are that when met up with they would far more probably be packing a Geiger counter than a six gun. Since the government has taken to burying gold beneath the ground, uranium has surplanted it as the most romantic and exotic of the metals.

XXX

The Roving Cowboy is Fenced in at Last

'Twas good to live when all the range
 Without no fence or fuss,
Belonged, in partnership with God,
 To the Government and us.

With skyline bounds from east to west,
 With room to go and come,
I liked my fellow man the best,
 When he was scattered some.

When my old soul hunts range and rest
 Beyond the last divide,
Just plant me on some strip of west
 That's sunny, lone, and wide.

Let cattle rub my headstone 'round,
 And coyottes wail their kin,
Let horses come and paw the mound,
 But don't you fence me in.

—Verses by Badger Clark, Jr., quoted by
 Charles A. Siringo in *Riata and Spurs*.

OTH in the canebrake pastures in the tidewater country, and the pea vine pastures back beyond the fall line, there were cowpens, such as that in South Carolina near which Morgan beat the British Tarleton during the Revolution. The droves assembled at them were taken even in those early days by "cow drives" to Charleston, and later to Philadelphia, and even to New York. By the close of the War of 1812, the Ohio country was filling in rapidly, and herds of as many as a thousand head were driven across the mountains and fattened locally for the eastern Pennsylvania market. Daniel Drew, first of the fabulous stock jobbers, got his start driving cattle to the New York market, where, after a long drink of water to increase their weight, they were sold to Henry Astor, butcher brother of fur-rich John Jacob, and gave rise to the term "watered stock."

Actually it was in the Spanish provinces of the Southwest that our cattle frontier had its real beginning, although the impulse that thrust it into importance came not at the hands of the descendants of those who brought the very first cattle to America, but by the activities of Texas immigrants who had experienced the cow drives from southern and western pastures to eastern markets.

Since the padres who founded the missions hoped to stabilize the conversion of the natives by the introduction of an agricultural economy, Spanish cattle were early introduced. They were chiefly an Andalusian strain, which, by the description of some of the old-timers were "half horns, and the rest bones and hide." They were grayish brown in color, with long slim faces topped by a pair of horns that frequently spread to five or even six feet between the tips. They were of a squarish build, with long straight backs, narrow forequarters, slab sides, and high hipbones that could crush a man's foot or leg, when the fast-moving creatures missed goring a rider or a horse with their spike-like antlers and then brought their hind quarters into play. But it was these immense horns that made them truly murderous. They were bad enough on the open range, but a great hazard when they came to be shipped in cattle cars. It was not unusual then to post men on either side of the loading chutes equipped with hatchets or heavy machetes. As the lanky, agile beasts mounted into the car, the death-dealing horns were lopped off.

Such cattle, in appearance much like the aurochs, the European bison and ancient ancestor of the cow, were running wild from early days in the limitless plains in the south of Texas. Here the climate was mild enough so that newborn calves rarely died of exposure, and the critters multiplied with such rapidity that they had little intrinsic worth. There had been branding irons in America since the days of Hernando Cortés, and although they were used, there were cows enough and to spare, and little quibbling over ownership.

Their meat, lean and almost devoid of fat, served needs close at hand. Then as their numbers increased and there were more and more people in Texas and that area ultimately became separated from Mexico, some attempt was made to drive them to markets beyond the confines of the Lone Star State. Being half wild, they were dangerous to handle or even approach on foot, and this made the horse indispensable.

Here, too, the Spanish, perhaps unwittingly, had made provision for what was ultimately to take place. They had brought in a Moorish type of steed, originally from Arabia. After several generations of these animals had grazed on the sparse grass of the hills of Spain and further generations had foraged the southwestern plains, they had become a hardy breed, and as tough as whiteleather. When settlers from Kentucky and Tennessee followed Austin into this land, they brought with them an excellent riding horse that was fast and tractable. A cross between these two strains gave an ideal mount for "working" cows.

From such sources came the fabled longhorns, as well as the cow pony. Also from Spain had come the glossy-fleeced Merino sheep that would be the basis of the flocks that would bring about the range wars and bloodshed, as the cattlemen and herdsmen fought for the privilege of grazing the open range in the public domain.

Excess cattle were being driven out of Texas in the fifties to the extent that there were well-developed trails to Natchitoches, New Orleans, Missouri, Nebraska, and even into California. The first two points were river ports, but water shipment proved rather impractical. The cattle either had to pick up their own food in transit or be moved rapidly enough so they could be landed at slaughtering points with a minimum of expense for artificial feeding. Thus the other great essential to the expanding of the cattle business was the railroad, and once the rails began to thrust west over the Great Plains, the possibility of getting Texas stock to market at an attractive profit was better assured. Then began the long drives, which would put ever greater numbers of cattle on the same pastures of the Great Plains, which had served the buffalo so abundantly. The Union Pacific was the first to reach to points where "cow towns" would logically spring up; and Abilene, Kansas, would be the earliest among them, getting its start in 1867.

THE GOLDEN AGE OF THE TRAIL DRIVE

Joseph McCoy, a stockman from Illinois, was certain that a sizable market could be found for the millions of cattle roaming the Texas country if they could be brought to one of these railheads. It was he who built the shipping facilities at Abilene and dispatched his agents to the south to encourage the ranchers to round up their stock and start it overland toward transportation. It was he, too, who had the trail laid out from the Red River north to Abilene. At its lower end it connected with one blazed across from the North Canadian River by the half-breed Indian trader Jesse Chisholm, and this Chisholm Trail came for a time to be the most famous road to market in the land.

During the five years following the first drives over it in 1867, more than a million head flowed into Abilene and aboard cattle cars. Soon the little community was a traditional cow town, replete with gambling dens, saloons, and dance halls. Wild Bill Hickok built his reputation there as the deadliest two-gun marshal of the frontier. But equally heroic, even if less well known, was Tom Smith, who had preceded him, depending on his two bare fists to enforce the ordinance against wearing firearms.

By 1872 the Santa Fe had built out to a point further south, beyond the great bend of the Arkansas River, and Dodge City came into being, not only as the "Cowboy Capital," but the staging point for the wagon trains hauling goods into Texas. Old Tascosa, down in Oldham County, and long a heap of adobe ruins, was for some years a southern terminus of these caravans. One of the bullwhackers who regularly made trips between these two points in the old days had a home a bit farther east, facing several acres of meadow in a pocket in the cliffs, where the Big Blue empties into the Canadian. It was a single-room stone house, with five-inch loopholes liberally distributed along its four walls, evidence that danger was never far removed. Often he was away for five to six months at a time, for it was something of a journey up and back over the trail. When asked in his older years how his wife and children managed during his long absences, he looked a bit puzzled by the question, and gruffly replied, "Who Maw? Why all she had to do was to lift down the Sharps rifle, step to the doorway, and she could shoot a buffalo grazing out front without leaving the house."

Perhaps nothing could be more indicative of the fiber of the women who made homes for their menfolk in the early days of the cattle and freighting trade. The male contingent might be bullwhackers, or more likely they were cowhands in one of the outfits driving cattle to northern markets. The average herd ran from two to three thousand, and required from a dozen to fourteen men. On the move there were two veterans who rode point at the head of the long column, fifty feet or so wide. There were two more each at swing and at flank positions further on back. Then at the rear there were three making up the drag, to hold in the strays and urge on the laggards.

There was also the top hand to boss the works, and two horse wranglers to handle the mounts, which ran five to eight per man, since horses were customarily ridden in fairly short relays because of the rigor of the work. Then, of course, there was the old woman, the cook, often a hard-bitten Spaniard, or Negro, male who, perhaps more than any other member, influenced the morale of the whole group. He not only prepared the meals, but drove the chuck wagon, heavy laden with beans and salt pork, pulling up ahead of the mile-long file of driven cattle to search out a logical spot for the next pause where a meal could be prepared, and then as the outfit came abreast, hurriedly taken aboard.

This is not to say that the herd was constantly on the move. There were daytime pauses for grazing, while at night the cattle were bunched in a circle, making it more convenient for the night riders to keep them quiet and contented. There were frequent occasions when the jittery, excitable creatures would stampede during the night, but the worst period was from about two in the morning through to dawn. Cuds had been pretty well chewed by midnight, and the beasts felt the need to move about a bit. Any untoward happening then could end in disaster. It usually took quite a bit of soothing chatter, and even the singing of cowboy dirges or camp meeting hymns to get the herd through this restless period. Once they had gotten their legs uncramped and had rolled over onto their other sides without unnecessarily goring one another, or a cow pony had not whinnied too loudly, or stepped in a gopher or prairie dog hole and frightened himself and the cows, peace might well reign until the sky began to gray in the east.

Fifteen miles a day, or about five hundred a month, was average progress on the trail drive, dependent, of course, on the weather and the luck at avoiding stampedes. These latter might injure men and animals, and hold the herd back for a day, or even far longer, while strays were rounded up. If streams were swollen, it might be necessary to hold fast until the waters lowered sufficiently to test for quicksands and be certain a safe crossing could be made. In the warmer months there was always the hazard of thundershowers, which not only brought flash floods along creeks or rivers, but a blinding bolt of lightning quickly followed by a crash of thunder could send the whole kit and caboodle racing off before the howling wind and pelting rain or hail. Then it took the utmost in clever hard riding to swing the lead cattle, and in ever smaller circles, get them to milling, and finally to a halt.

As a consequence, by the time a cowhand reached Abilene, Dodge City, Wichita, Ogallala, or wherever it was the herd was delivered, he was pretty desperately in need of some relaxation. Usually the competition for it was pretty keen, being sought for in a small town filled with like-minded hunters, trappers, soldiers, railroad workers, bullwhackers, Indians, or thugs. It would be provided at the hands of saloon keepers, gamblers, and dancehall girls adept at giving all comers the full "treatment" in short order. Vice and violence were easily come by in these seething centers; and if one got a bit too far out of hand, he would very likely come under the harsh ministrations of such upholders of the law as Bat Masterson, Wyatt Earp, or Bill Tilghman at Dodge City, or their counterparts elsewhere. The cowboy led a rugged life, both at work and at play.

Still no phase of frontier life in this country has left a more indelible imprint upon a greater number than did the men of this romantic vocation. It is three quarters of a century since the cowboy passed the zenith of this exotic colorfulness. Yet a whole generation of children today pay him affectionate veneration, decked out in his classic habiliments, proudly toting his weapons, and eagerly employing his supposed lingo. Some of our best loved fictional characters have been derived from him, and those with such appeal and endurance as Hopalong Cassidy seem to have been minted from the same metal as the very men who once rode the range.

Who were some of the outstanding figures of the cattle frontier? One of the greatest of them, whose experiences paralleled the best of its traditions down into recent times, was a rugged Texan, who retained his inexhaustible vigor of mind and body until laid low in his ninety-fourth year.

ONE OF THE GREATEST OF THE COWPOKES

His name was Charles Goodnight, and no man was ever more deserving of the title of "colonel." He had been born in 1836 up in Macoupin County, Illinois, thirty odd miles northeast of St. Louis. But his father died when he was quite young, his mother married again, and the new family group moved down into Texas the year after that state was taken into the Union. Settling in Milam County, the ten-year-old Charlie grew up with Indians almost at the cabin door, and came to know them in all their ways.

When he was twenty he launched himself in the cattle business, and the following year, 1857, moved up into Palo Pinto County, in the Red River country west of Fort Worth. Here he was highly active among the independent or minutemen rangers, spent much of his time as a scout and guide in operations against the Indians, and made a reputation for himself in the Pease River fight against the savages in 1860.

When the War between the States broke out, he promptly joined the Frontier Regiment of the Texas Rangers, and became undoubtedly the most able open-country scout in the land. When the war closed, he pushed far out to the southwest and established the first cattle ranch along the Pecos River in southern New Mexico. But within two years he had moved his operations up into Colorado, and by 1870 had located a huge permanent grazing range on the Arkansas River a few miles above Pueblo.

The long drives did not all terminate in Kansas and Nebraska. Cattle were being furnished to its Indian wards by the federal government, there were railroad construction, mining operations, and other activities calling for beef for food, and herds pushed on toward the north, fattening on the buffalo grass, and finally occupied the free ranges that extended through to the Canadian border. Goodnight, with the aid of his partner, Oliver Loving, laid out trails from New Mexico and Texas extending up into Wyoming. Preparations were being made to build a mighty cattle empire back against the western mountains, in the free grasslands that were then the cattlemen's paradise.

But the panic of 1873 that followed the too rapid expansion of railroads in this country left the western range overstocked and forced the colonel back into Texas. Herding some sixteen hundred cows, he drove them across three hundred miles of wilderness and holed up with them in Palo Duro Canyon, a deep gash in the rolling plains at the south edge of the Texas Panhandle.

Soon he was in the midst of turmoil and trouble occasioned by the New Mexican shepherds. They had driven their flocks out into his ranges along the Canadian River, and war immediately broke out. The sharp hoofs of sheep quickly destroy the turf on the plains, and it turns brown, taking months to recuperate. Worst still, or so cattlemen have always staunchly contended, these woolly creatures leave an odor across the grassland and about water holes which cows will not tolerate. The New Mexican shepherds realized their advantages, and were determined to oust the cattlemen from the better ranges.

There was the inevitable clash, when Goodnight's cowhands fell upon the flocks and drove the baaing sheep out across the sand draws and into the sluggish current of the Canadian, drowning some four hundred of them. A court in the New Mexico Territory to the west found for the sheepmen and against the Texans, and a compromise had to be reached. The result was that the sheepherders took over the more desirable Canadian Valley, while the Goodnight cattle remained in the canyon area. Happily it had cost no human lives, as would the later Graham-Tewksbury feud in Arizona, which brought better than thirty cattle- and sheepmen to their deaths before it burned itself out.

But there was soon another deep concern. The buffalo were rapidly being exterminated, professional hunters such as Billy Dixon slaughtering them in huge numbers primarily for their hides. The Texas Indians, their "department store on the hoof" growing scarce, began to rebel and turned to poaching on the range cattle. There had been a short, sharp encounter between the hunters and the Comanche and Kiowa warriors under Quanah Parker at 'Dobe Walls in 1874. This chief, born of a white mother, had refused to settle in the Indian Territory, and although beaten in this fight, continued to make trouble.

Colonel Goodnight was now busy laying out the famous JA Ranch and blazing a trail from it to Dodge City, but maintaining his headquarters in a log home at the bottom of Palo Duro Canyon. With capital from Ireland, he began to improve this great million-acre tract in 1877 until it would eventually run as many as a hundred thousand head of stock.

Then, in 1878, Quanah Parker and his followers began cutting out knots of Goodnight cattle and running them off to their villages. They were frankly hungry, and the rancher, knowing Indians, could see their side of the situation. However, it was perhaps better to have some troops on the scene and see that Quanah's promises to General Nelson A. Miles three years before were kept. As scouts slipped out to summon help, the uninvited guests who had turned up at the ranch headquarters were fed and the colonel went to work upon their chief. By the time troopers reached the canyon the two men had made a peace pact that was never broken. For years there were Indian hands on the home ranch at Goodnight, and it was often said its owner thought more of them than he did of some of his other neighbors. Certainly they lent a tangy flavor to the barbecues for which this ranch became famous, for they usually wound up the festivities by racing across the prairies riding bareback in pursuit of a buffalo calf finally bowled over with bow and arrow.

THE LAST OF THE LONGHORNS

But the next big move was to start a new trend in the cattle business, due by then to undergo a thorough change. A new era had been forecast by a Yankee invention in 1873, barbed wire. This not only doomed the open range, but more objectively it permitted the segregation of cattle within a cow-tight enclosure. Now interbreeding could be controlled, and by crossbreeding, the beef characteristics improved. The days of the longhorns were now numbered, and Colonel Goodnight is credited with starting the serious efforts employed from then on of building into these virile range cattle the more desirable features of the shorthorns and Herefords. Soon his JA Ranch was producing some of the finest beef in the country.

More remarkable still were his attempts to cross Polled Angus cattle with the native bisons to produce a hybrid creature which he called cattalo. He continued to be interested in this enterprise until his death.

While the Indian troubles slacked off after his understanding with Quanah Parker, there were other difficulties aplenty. Undesirable characters were beginning to filter into the cow country, breaking down fence lines, raiding the herds, rustling stock, even stampeding it on the drive to market. Some drifted in from the outside, but many were cowhands gone wrong, and trying to get a ranch of their own started by thieving the necessary cattle from others. There were disputes, too, over the division of the range, continuing friction with the sheepmen, and other common problems. To better attack them, this natural-born leader, who always treated reading and writing with considerable indifference, put together the powerful Panhandle Stockmen's Association. Like similar groups soon organized in other areas, it went to work to rid the plains of the outlaws, systematize range problems and work, police the trails, advance better breeding, and bring some semblance of order into what was becoming a gigantic business.

Its leading spirit in this West Texas country, often referred to as "The Burbank of the Range," was this vigorous, fiery chunk of a man. He had a 50-caliber bullet-like head, set well forward on a pair of rugged shoulders. Trim at the hips, he did display a very bad case of occupational disease, in that his legs were strongly bowed, being sprung to that shape by the hundreds of horses he had ridden. He had a shock of heavy, unruly hair above shaggy eyebrows that shielded a pair of snapping gimlet eyes. He sat a cow pony with consummate ease and grace, and while he was no ballet performer, his bandy legs could propel him across a corral or branding pen at a near canter.

He was never one to quibble over words or situations, meeting both head on and riding fast. He had been in contact with a full complement of liars, thieves, rustlers, and other human types of weed throughout a long active life, and he hated them all consummately. He was equally impatient in the face of hypocrisy and overzealous flattery. His strong dislike of the latter was sharply pointed up in the year he was eighty-three.

JUST TOO MUCH GOODNIGHT

Persuaded that he should "retire," but still anxious that his experiments with cattalo be continued, he made suitable arrangements involving these latter in 1919, and to celebrate the transfer of the home ranch at Goodnight, a huge buffalo barbecue was held there on Labor Day that year. Many of the guests, including several elderly bullwhackers, made it a rare "old-timers' day." There was a lot of gossip swapped about the roasting pits, sunk in the earth between the headquarters house and the horse barns, during the long morning.

Then after the ample noon meal, the several hundred guests collected about the porch at the southwest corner of the home and a banker from nearby Amarillo launched into an oration worthy of so auspicious an occasion. He eulogized the colonel up one side and down the other, until his honeyed words were too many and too rich for the Goodnight appetite. As the speaker paused momentarily for breath, the old man bounded to his feet, crammed his Stetson onto his head, waddled down the steps, and lit out among the picnic tables and barbecue pits, Mis' Molly, his wife, promptly taking off after him.

At this abrupt walkout, the courtly gentleman left behind on the porch failed for words. Slowly Mrs. Goodnight got a rope over her husband and began to work him back toward the house. Somewhat reluctantly he mounted to the second or third step, snatched off his hat, and swung toward the audience, his eyes fairly spitting sparks.

Cooling down a mite, he ran his hand slowly through his hair, and began:

"You have probably heard what this gentleman has been saying. He sure enough meant well; but his remarks remind me of a telegram I tried to send from Fort Worth some years back, when I was held down there by business longer than I had expected to be. As I gave it to the man in the telegraph office, it went something like this, 'Mrs. Charles Goodnight, Goodnight, Texas. Will not be home tonight on the night train. Will come by tomorrow night's train.' And I told him to sign it 'Charles Goodnight.'

"But before I could get out of the place, the operator bawled out that he wouldn't send it. When I asked him why, he told me straight out, 'It's got too damn much Goodnight in it.' And that, my friends, is just what was the matter with that speech."

Plumping his hat back on his head, the old man started again for the barn, while the crowd heehawed and clapped and moved out toward the east pasture. This time he kept going. Perhaps he was just a little concerned as to whether the Indian boys had their bows and arrows ready to bring down the buffalo calf, which event was to climax the day-long program. Actually a visiting airplane had to go aloft and dive at the half-tame critter before he would consent to dash across the big pasture with one of the young braves after him. A single well-placed arrow sank two thirds of its shaft below the hide, reached the creature's heart, and over and over it rolled.

The circumstances surrounding this bit of entertainment that closed the celebration of the transfer of the property that day in 1919 were highly significant. How life on the plains and along the cattle frontier had tamed down from the roistering, hard-hitting days of the trail drives. Long before the colonel's passing in 1929 the range was completely fenced in, not only in Texas, but everywhere that men took any pride in the cows they raised. Sheep might graze in the summer pastures high in the Rockies without benefit of barbed wire, but highly bred beef cattle require such restriction.

How different indeed it was from that day not too many years before when another of the early Texas cattle barons had ridden up the trail with his herds to one of the cow towns, and then had boarded the train of cattle cars and gone on to Kansas City. Parting with the creatures at the slaughterhouse pens, he was driven into town and put up at what was then the newest and best hotel. Shortly he ran afoul of two gadgets that thoroughly stampeded his peace of mind.

On one side of his palatial room was a snarl of pipes, all painted up to make them look like gold, which hissed, chattered, and made an infernal noise while pouring out more heat than that fiery place down yonder run by Satan himself.

The cattleman was anything but mechanically minded, and after tinkering unsuccessfully with the contraption for a while, he turned his attention to one of the two large windows. Almost at once there was a profane protest—some consarned fool had put a strange thingamajig on it, a lock probably, to keep burglars out. He fiddled with it for a minute or two, but tug as he would, he could not budge either sash.

By that time he was as hot as a fighting rooster. So he reared back, histed up one foot, and hauled off his cowboy boot. Getting a firm, two-handed grip on its pull straps, he lashed out and broke a sizable chunk out of the big windowpane. Filling his lungs with God's good, fresh, and much cooler air, he finally swung around, twitched the blankets from the bed, rolled up in them before the gaping window, and was soon peacefully asleep.

America was changing unmistakably, and in many, many respects, as the final quarter of the nineteenth century got under way.

XXXI

Timber-r-r-r-r!

Come all ye sons of Freedom throughout the State of Maine,
Come all ye gallant lumbermen, and listen to my strain,
On the banks of the Penobscot, where the rapid waters flow,
O! We'll range the wild woods over, and a-lumbering we will go;
Come, all ye gallant lumberers, that range the wild woods through,
Where the river flows and the timber grows we're bound with a
    jolly crew;
For the music of the mills is stopped by the binding frost and
    snow;
So we'll take our packs upon our backs, and a-lumbering we will go;
    And a-lumbering we will go,
    So a-lumbering we will go,
O! We'll range the wild woods over, and a-lumbering we will go.

—Various sources, including: Exeter (New Hampshire) *News
Letter*, 1845; and Springer, *Forest Life and Forest Trees*, 1851.

B EYOND the ocean of water which Columbus and the Norsemen
had crossed was another ocean—an ocean of trees. From East-
port down to Key West on the Atlantic coast, back along the
Gulf as far as the Brazos River, and from there north through Arkansas, around Missouri, and up into Minnesota was virgin forest,
hundreds of thousands of square miles of it. To the men and women
who came at first to Jamestown, Plymouth, St. Mary's, and the other
early settlements this almost unbroken stand of trees must have been
little short of appalling. These folk had to eat, and because the woods
were so prevalent, the ax was actually as necessary as the sword or
blunderbuss, and in the end provided the more fruitful conquest.

Time and man power were both at a premium, crops had to be
planted, and in the race with time and available energy these first
plantings had to be made in what later came to be called "deaden-

ings." The trees were girdled, a trick learned from the Indians, and achieved by chopping a circle of bark from about the trunk, which killed some trees, although a deeper cut through the sap wood was required to finish off the hardier sort like the oaks. Corn, rye, beans, and a few other staple foods did reasonably well in the semi-shade, for although there were no leaves to shut off the sunshine, the trunks and branches continued to stand until they rotted and fell or were finally cut down with an ax and burned.

Not only was this the means by which the first clearings were achieved, but similar expedients were used during the next two centuries as the agricultural frontier slowly pushed over the Appalachians and on to the Mississippi, where the dense forests petered out and the open plains began. Even after the land-hungry had broken through to the eastern edge of these treeless plains, men tended to shun them. They provided no logs for a cabin, no rails for fences, few springs and water holes, and consequently the fallacious belief that land unsuited to sustaining forest cover was surely incapable of producing worth-while crops.

While most of the colonists had come from backgrounds where timber was limited and much building was with stone or brick, the needs of shelter here were so pressing and wood was so plentiful that it was rapidly accepted and used. But to frame a house using only an ax, and adz, broad ax, or a pit saw was a slow process, and almost an impossible task for a man working alone. The back country would have filled in much less rapidly had it not been for the Swedes, Finns, and very likely some of the Germans, who brought the log cabin to these shores.

However, lumbering on a local scale began fairly early. The saw is a very old instrument, reaching far back into the Egyptian and Babylonian civilizations, and sawyers were skilled craftsmen in Europe before America was discovered. Here they continued to operate whipsaws, the logs being rolled onto skids above the saw pit and chinked or lashed in place. Then one man stood above on top of the log and guided the saw along a chalked line, while the man in the pit below pulled down, dragging the teeth, which cut only in that one direction, striking off the four outer slabs to form a squared timber, and then perhaps splitting the latter into planks or boards.

Soon water power was being applied to this laborious task, but for generations to come, even though power-driven, it would still be the old fashioned up-and-down type of saw, for lumbering tools changed very little until well into the 1800s.

It is a little difficult, in an age when metals are in such common use, to realize how dependent many phases of life were upon timber three centuries ago. Even as late as the Revolutionary War the British Navy was heavily handicapped by the condition of its ships, and especially their masts and booms, many of which were old enough so that they had lost their flexibility and split and broke up because of their excess brittleness. It had not been the intent of the government back home that such conditions would prevail, however. Naval needs had been building up, and some steps had been taken in the previous century to care for them, but the colonists had pretty much negated any benefits.

When a new charter was granted Massachusetts in 1691, the king had laid claim to all trees more than two feet through when measured at a point one foot above the ground, provided they grew on land not previously granted to private persons. The best of the pines were in this manner reserved for navy masts, and such trees might not be cut without express permission on penalty of a heavy fine. In 1711, during the reign of Queen Anne, an act extended this restriction to all colonies from New Jersey up into Maine. Then royally appointed surveyors began to range the woods, affixing the "broad arrow" blaze to all trees withheld by the crown. This activity was to have a number of well-defined results. It built up disrespect for vested rights in standing timber, which gave sanction to the poaching on government timberlands that lasted through to the end of the 1800s. More immediately it worked hardships in many communities within easy reach of tidewater by appropriating the best trees. It also tended to develop lumbering as a business in the woods of Maine, from which area the associated crafts and traditions would slowly spread during the next two hundred years to all the forest frontiers.

MAINE LED THE WAY

As evidence of the workings of the broad arrow policy of the British Government, take the gracious old Congregational meetinghouse still in use in Farmington, Connecticut. When the Ecclesiastical Society there decided in 1770 that a new and more commodious structure was needed and left the details of its design and erection in the capable hands of Captain Judah Woodruff, this able master builder realized there was not enough unappropriated timber of suitable quality available locally to permit its construction. He was forced to make the long journey to the woods of Maine, in which area His British Majesty had thoughtlessly granted land without retaining a hold on its forests. There the captain was able to select prime trees, get them logged and prepared for shipment to the neighboring river port of Hartford. In 1772 he completed his fine church building from timbers brought a considerable distance, from the Maine woods.

Perhaps the choppers and sawyers along the Penobscot and the Kennebec and the other rivers were already singing these and other of the many verses of the song quoted at the beginning of this chapter. Long before the Revolution lumbering had become primarily a winter activity. At a time when the logs might have to go for months before being sawed into timber and boards, less was lost by decay if cutting was done when there was but little sap in the trees. Also the high water of spring was needed to flush the logs from the woods and on their way to market. This seasonal cast would be handed on and on as lumbering moved west, and had perhaps its most colorful era in the north woods about the Great Lakes during the latter half of the 1800s. By then it was feeling the stimulation of greater demand, and slowly improving tools would help to bring it to fuller stature.

The ax was still the most widely used of all its implements. Local smiths had been able to make themselves famous by forging superior types, and eventually Yankee ingenuity managed to combine the best of these features in one standardized type, uniform in quality. Strangely enough it was not until about 1860 that the double-bitted Yankee ax put in an appearance.

The saw remained pretty primitive until after the War of 1812. It was at about the termination of that conflict that the first circular or buzz saw appeared in this country. It was then four years before it showed up in the lumber camps in the Maine woods, and it is said it did not go into use in some southern areas until just before the outbreak of the War between the States. This rotary disk saw was a distinct advance, but the even more potent band saw was not introduced until the Centennial Exhibition in 1876, and was then some years finding its way into extensive employment.

Operations in the rapidly expanding lumber industry in Michigan in the years just after the close of the Civil War were still highly colorful and reasonably typical. They had not altered too greatly from activities in Maine a century before, and many phases would experience but a minimum of change on into the early years of the present century. A "visit" there during that era will provide perhaps the best picture of what life was like along the lumber frontier.

LIFE IN THE LUMBER CAMPS

The woods of Michigan's Lower Peninsula, like those over the lake in Wisconsin, and on out in Minnesota, were for the most part drained by relatively small and often sluggish streams. Cut logs were transported to the banks of these streams most readily on sledges or low sleds over snow or ice, and from that point they could be moved on to the mill for processing when the melting snows put these streams over their banks in the spring freshets of April. Since snow would be on the ground most years soon after Thanksgiving, the bulk of the work in the woods was thus concentrated in the four colder months.

The timber tracts customarily bordered areas turning to agriculture. This being a nonproductive period down on the farm, and with the prospects of acquiring about a hundred dollars in cash before spring, together with bed and board in the interim, many farmers and villagers were ready and willing to leave home and family and take to the woods. It provided a nice stake in days when access to cash income was limited, which helped out with spring planting or in the reduction of a mortgage.

There was, of course, the other side of the picture as well. Lumbering had long been a craft, although a seasonal one, and many thought of themselves as woodsmen, and turned to farming or other pursuits to carry them through the months between their labors in the forests.

But whatever their motives and ambitions, they lived along the fringe of the frontier, were well used to sustained hard work and to life under rather primitive conditions. By contrast with the routine affairs on the small farm or about the cluster of homes at the crossroads, there was activity and adventure around a logging camp. Among other satisfactions it provided was that basic human desire to *belong*, to be an integral part of worth-while, measurable achievement. Also, it offered ample opportunity for competition with others in respect to strength, skill, and endurance. Consequently along the margin of the backwoods it was the thing to do.

The aspirations of growing boys usually stem from the latent ambitions of any group, and in the north woods in those days most of the young fry wanted to be lumberjacks, river hogs, or raftmen. Many of them did have their chance to serve time at one or all of these activities, while some went on to become foremen, storekeepers, owners, and a few to be "lumber barons" in their own right.

It was necessary to anticipate at least four months' needs, for the "store" operated in connection with most wood camps was a somewhat sketchy affair. Thus it was well to cram a "turkey sack" full of the warmest of clothing before heading back into the forest to the camp of one's choice. There the candidate for a job sought out the wanigan, or headquarters, and looked for the bull of the woods, or foreman. If mutually satisfactory arrangements were made, the ink slinger, or timekeeper, signed the new hand on at the lordly sum of one dollar a day and found—that is bunk and grub. That was about the going rate for those who had brought nothing beyond their own strength and skill. If there was a team of horses or yoke of oxen involved as well, the daily stipend was somewhat higher, but not too much. These preliminaries over with, the next point of call would be the bunkhouse, variously called the shanty, caboose, and on occasions, even more forceful names.

This latter was almost always a long, narrow, and virtually windowless structure, except for skylights in the roof. It was sometimes of logs, but later usually framed, rough sheathing, and with a roof of "shakes," or basswood logs from which the center had been split, and they could then be laid and fitted together like half-round tile. This would be the crowded and cluttered "home" for from twenty-five to fifty men during the next sixteen or more weeks. The doors were at either end, while some of the larger shanties had one fore, or aft, or both, in about the center of the longer walls. Ranged along these latter would be two tiers of bunks, uppers and lowers. The former seemed to be preferred, although it is doubtful if there was really much choice in such a human beehive.

The turkey sack tossed into a bunk was evidence of possession, and the next activity was a trip out to the stack for sufficient hay, straw, or swamp grass to make a mattress over which blankets might be spread. Pillows were not "good form," since a wadded up mackinaw beneath the head served quite as well. These were the sleeping accommodations, and in most camps it was one to a bunk. In the colder areas bunks were often shared so that bodily warmth could be pooled. One thing, however, was distinctly understood—everyone slept in his long knitted woolen underwear. A person could have better hope of wearing a monocle, and getting away with it, than of being caught mounting into a bunk clad in anything as effete as a nightshirt.

By the entrance door was a rack for tools, and the ever present grindstone on which to touch up the bit of one's ax or the point of a peavey. The water that dripped down to dampen the slowly revolving stone dripped from it onto the floor, and there froze during the night, creating a hazard for the unwary in the early morning. About in the center of the long room was a sheet-iron stove, with a pipe running from a coil within it to another in a barrel near by. This inseparable pair supplied heat and hot water. Against a piece of wall, and not always too convenient to the water supply, was a wash bench. There were several basins, a ledge scattered with bars and pieces of wood-ash soap, a concoction of cooking grease and lye, and a roller towel affixed to the wall. Such were the lavatory facilities.

Down the center aisle was a double row of backless benches, known as the deacon seats, on which members of the gang might disport themselves when not in their bunks, in the woods, or at meals. Above these was a maze of lines or poles on which damp clothing or week-end washings might be hung to dry. Ventilation was rather sketchy, and between smoke from the wood stove and coal oil lanterns, steam from sweaty bodies and moist clothing, and tobacco fumes, there were times when suffocation seemed certain. Those on the upper tier of bunks often bored or gouged a hole in the wall near their heads at which they could take in a lungful of clear air from time to time. These emergency vents could be stopped off when not in use with a wadded sock.

All in all this dormitory was a dank, musty, evil-smelling place, with a compound odor strong enough to completely deaden olfactory powers. In every gang, too, there was some unconsciously generous soul who would provide a supply of *other-than-human* occupants. Soon after the camp opened up minute, highly active, and most ravenous little beasties would scatter quickly throughout the bunkhouse. Living under such conditions, none could hope to be free from lice. The living quarters were the responsibility of the bull cook and his helpers, and were livable in proportion to cookie's sense of neatness and cleanliness.

The workday began at three or three-thirty for the teamsters or bullwhackers, so the animals might be fed and cared for before breakfast. The remainder of the gang lolled around in bed for another half hour until the loud beating of a cookpan with a heavy spoon or the raucous voice of one of the cook's helpers made further sleep utterly impossible. Blankets were thrown off, and outer clothing pulled on over already warmed underwear. Then the quickly dressed men filed out into the crisp darkness and over to the cookhouse, which was presided over as a rule by a pretty formidable character. Cookie brooked no interference with his part of the show, since he had to bow only to the will of the bull of the woods himself.

As long as he produced palatable food in fair variety and mountainous quantities, he was highly regarded. But just let him show the least incompetence by the rough standards of the woodsmen, let him scrimp in quantity, or get into a rut so that the same dishes appeared with too great frequency, and there was a mutiny that even a Captain Bligh could not quell. A dissatisfied crew could oust an undesirable cook merely by refusing to leave the shanty for work until he was fired.

The calorie demand upon the old-time logger working in zero weather was not equaled by any other group in his own time or by any industrial class today. His "biler" had to be properly stoked or his employer just did not get a full dollar's worth of effort from him in the period from before dawn until well after darkness. Men who would work in howling blizzards or in icy streams up to their armpits without whimper or complaint were the most temperamental of prima donnas when it came to their chow.

Thus the oilcloth table tops in the cookhouse were always amply laden with a wide assortment of fuel-rich foods as the men plumped down on the surrounding benches for their four-thirty breakfast. It, like other meals, was eaten in stoical silence, a universal tradition of the north woods. This was the time to eat, not to talk. The cook explained the general practice to the uninitiated, and had his methods of enforcing the dictum on any whose garrulous ways upset this established custom.

After the men had taken aboard a great plentitude, and rather hurriedly, they returned to the shanty, picked up their tools, and waited for the old bull himself to kick the door open. This happened just as soon as a man could see his hand before his face, the foreman bellowing out a most insistent invitation that they come out and greet the breaking day. In response to which the still sleepy retinue trooped off into the neighboring woods to whatever their assigned task might be.

WORK IN THE WOODS

Various proficiencies were called for to serve in one or more of several well-defined groups of tasks. For instance the operations began with a standing tree, to which a chopper addressed himself, hacking out a V-shaped kerf, or undercut, which determined the direction in which the trunk would drop, with the least damage to itself and to surrounding trees. In the earlier days the fall was completed by chopping through from the opposite side until the cut met the kerf and severed the trunk. It is surprising to realize that it was about 1880 before the two-man crosscut saw came into general use for this purpose.

As gravity began to take firm hold of the nearly severed trunk, the resounding cry of "Timber-r-r-r!" rang out, and all within the danger zone dropped their tools and took shelter. Once prone on the ground, the branches had to be lopped off, and the long clean stem of the tree bucked into saw logs of approved length. Formerly this was also done with an ax, and not until fairly late in the century was the saw used.

Like the longhorn steer on the Texas plains, the saw log was merchantable only when delivered at a market. The first essential in this respect was a roundup by the banks of the nearest stream down which they might be floated in the spring. By way of preparation, a gang of swampers, or "road monkeys," cleared out and leveled off trails over which great sledge loads of logs could be toted. The best of these tote roads were built of hard-packed snow, dampened, and allowed to form into deep layers of ice, with rutted tracks to hold the runners of the sleds in place. Sand or fine brush had to be scattered over the unavoidable slopes to keep the heavy loads from getting out of control and bashing up both team and driver.

Single logs were snaked to loading points, where deckers with cant hooks deftly rolled them aboard the sledges, carefully balancing the loads and anchoring them firmly in place with skillfully arranged chains. Then the teamsters took over and navigated the high-piled sleds over the slick snow or ice roads. These latter, following another tradition, chose to ride the load rather than walk beside their teams. Thus they had to be swathed in many layers of clothing to keep from freezing. In place of exercise, they either gently coaxed or raucously bellowed at their horses or cattle, the primary purpose being to keep loads moving as fast as possible and on an even keel.

Arriving at the creek or river, the logs were either rolled out onto the ice, or so piled that they could be released and would roll into the swirling current as the downstream drive was ready to get under way in the spring. Here another type of craftsman, the scaler, computed the probable board feet of recoverable lumber in each and every log, called the quantity to a tally boy who recorded it, and then, with a series of notches not unlike cattle brands, he rapidly recorded the ownership and its potential possibilities as a saw log on each.

The ubiquitous foreman kept the various tasks running smoothly from the time the gang hit the firing line until toward midday. About eleven-thirty he picked out a convenient spot, well sheltered in rough weather, had a fire started, the brush cleared back, the snow tramped down, and preparations made for the reception of the cook sled. Loaded back at the cookhouse, the containers of food swathed with blankets in what was usually a vain attempt to keep them warm, the sled's arrival in the woods signaled the noon break.

The teapot was quickly shifted over the crackling fire, and the men of the gang lined up, drew an icy-cold tin plate, knife, fork, spoon, and cup, and filed past the cook's helpers to have liberal servings of bread, stew, pie, and other fare dumped upon their plates. Bailing out steaming cups of boiling tea, they crouched down wherever they could and tried to get as much food aboard as possible before it froze to the plates. Then, to keep it from freezing in their gullets as well, they poured down cups of the scalding brew strong enough to tan an elephant's hide.

This noon meal was tossed off with even greater dispatch than those eaten in the cookshack, and when finished, the men either hugged the fire or stamped around to keep from stiffening up. Soon all were back at work, and kept at it as long as the light held out. Trailing back to the shanty, there was the merest go at "tidying up" before supper, after which there was time for conversation and a smoke or two before rolling up in blankets for the night. Promptly at nine o'clock all lights were out, and usually by then the shanty was already atremble with snoring men. Six days of this, as like as peas in a pod, made up the week. The seventh—Sunday—was given over to washing clothes, mending them, soling shoes, repairing and sharpening tools, or lounging about a bit. Few read extensively, and fewer still wrote much more than their names, so communication with the outside world was somewhat limited.

Such was life and activity in the lumber camps for a stretch of fifteen, sixteen, or more weeks, depending upon when the cold weather set in and how forward or reluctant spring might be. When the streams went over their banks, those who had plowing to attend to at home pocketed their wages and headed in that direction. Others with less secure domestic ties, or in need of a little more cash, stood by for the next and more spectacular chapter in the season's activities.

If the creek or river beside which the saw logs had been piled was small, free logs were driven hurriedly down with the surging waters. If the stream was larger, the water deeper, and there were fewer obstructions, the logs were made up into rafts. Here was work that was thrilling, exciting, and as demanding as a roundup, a branding, or a long drive in the cattle business.

In handling free logs the great hazard was a jam, and when one threatened, or actually piled up, there was a call for skill and daring equal to that required to turn and slow down a stampeding herd. Like the loading pens at Abilene or Dodge City to the cowmen, the objective of the river hog or of the rafter was the sawmill. Once he had turned over his "herd" to the sorters at the great booms in the river or pond above the mill, he pocketed his wages, perhaps cut a few capers in the sawmill town, and then headed for some sort of employment that would take up his time until late fall. Then once more he would stuff his belongings into his "kennebecker," or turkey sack, and again seek out a bunkhouse in the woods.

Wages crept up slowly, camp conditions improved at about the same pace, and the lumber frontier wandered about, across the north woods, down through the South, along the Gulf coast, and finally out into California and the Pacific Northwest. Better transportation in the woods and from the mill to market furnished by the railroad eventually made lumbering a year-round activity. But, like cattle, and to a lesser extent mining, it retained many of its frontier tendencies until long after it had become an important industry.

Since the first census, taken in 1790, there had been a frontier line, which traced the extent of our westward thrust, and at the far edge of which the population dropped below six persons per square mile. As succeeding reports appeared at ten-year intervals, this line continued to advance toward the west, not always uniformly, but usually by geographic regions which altering conditions or discoveries opened up to pioneering and land use of one form or another. The first employment of the tract may not have been for agriculture, but the satisfaction of land hunger had from the very first been the one certain inducement to permanent occupancy.

The report of the census taken in 1880 showed rather clearly that the best farm lands contained in the public domain had already been disposed of. But the movement toward the west was still on, the pressure being markedly increased by immigration from abroad which, during that decade, averaged about a half million people a year. Consequently the plains were receiving more settlers than they could then accommodate, and there was a reaction. The frontier reached its ultimate at sometime between 1885 and 1890, and by 1900 it had actually receded from its line of greatest advance. There were still ample expanses of virtually uninhabited wilderness, and there were continuing frontier conditions in certain areas, but the frontier as a well-defined influence was finished. From the moment the first Europeans had set foot here on this "fresh continent," it had been a powerful factor and made mighty and far-reaching contributions.

Why so? Because "America" soon came to be another name for opportunity. Yet that opportunity hurled down a challenge, and the men who accepted it learned to make more effective use of their human energies than had previously been achieved. The absence of famine, which had plagued even the civilized world for sixty centuries of written history, was but one among many items of proof. Along the American frontier men and women had seized control of their own lives to a greater measure than the majority had ever before dared assume, and under the stimulus of self-interest had been able to achieve superior accomplishments. They had sought freedom, and having found it, had put it to work.

History can be shown to be one long series of challenges and responses, and the frontier that opened here with the visit of the first Norsemen was a continuing challenge. It demanded rugged strength, spiritual as well as physical. Its primitiveness tended to develop a certain coarseness, which inclined toward strength and stability rather than their opposites. Life at the edge of the wilderness forced one to be acute and inquisitive. Just staying alive required full consciousness not only of all that transpired within sight and hearing, but also active concern with what lurked behind every tree, bush, hill, or Indian's dead-pan countenance. The frontiersman had to be sharp, subtle, and mentally awake by habit rather than by conscious effort, as well as curious, questioning, and given to constant inquiry about all his surroundings.

The major anxieties were food and water, with bodily warmth a close third during more than half the year. These, together with safety for family and creatures, were material considerations, and their satisfaction demanded that one be eminently and uninterruptedly practical, inventive, resourceful, and quick to see and grasp expedients. The frontier way of life was heavily littered with physical and material things. Either man dominated them or they dominated him. The choice was clear-cut and desperately certain.

Existence at the edge of the wilds was no bed of roses, but a constant extortion of effort. It tended to stimulation, making men restless, dissatisfied, and hopeful of betterment just over the crest of the next ridge. Thus they learned through compulsion to drive themselves—at first for their own good—and it became a habitual approach to life, redounding to the general benefit.

The need to be self-reliant and self-sustaining developed a dominant individualism. This can run to evil as well as to good, but the tendency was that men who could stand firmly on their own two feet were that much better equipped to lend able hands to common causes for the general welfare. Left to their own devices, these pioneers first perfected their freedom, and then learned to control it by the acceptance of responsibility—for control *is* responsibility. And being free, they approached life with greater buoyancy, optimism, and exuberance.

These are some of the American characteristics which the frontier bred and fostered, and our American democracy is fundamentally the result of life experiences along its borders rather than being a creation by fiat or legislative decree. Its abiding ambition was freedom and well-being for the masses. So impelled, it managed to create a society having a larger proportion of intelligent, if plain, people than had previously been achieved. Freedom had thus brought social abundance, and in turn produced greater and widely disseminated material abundance.

The traditional frontier had served America admirably before it ran its course. It provided a rich heritage, and also a pressing obligation—to conserve and strengthen the democratic institutions and ideals which it had nourished. They are sorely needed today, and will be in the years ahead as Americans move down other types of frontiers that offer their challenge as conclusively as did the frontier just visited.

Through the era of discovery, the long period of colonization, and the first century of American independence it was a frontier of land, habitable land. Once strictly physical, today's frontiers lie in areas that are social, political, and spiritual. Men one hundred and more years ago were land-hungry, and the desire of possession drew them on over uncertain trails to the rainbow's end. Today men are security-hungry, and the craving forces them to march along strange paths through the morasses of industrial and economic complications, beset by the mounting tensions of a rapidly contracting world.

The scenery along today's traces and trails may not look as adventurous and colorful as those of the past appear in retrospect. But quite likely the overemphasized romantic aspects of life about them —such as the "picturesqueness" of the stealthy savage, the "thrill" of stagecoach travel, or the "snugness" of life in a sod-roofed dugout on the plains—may have been utterly lost upon the grandparents who encountered them. The men who rowed the boats which Abe Whipple led that night in the attack on the *Gaspé* hardly looked upon themselves as heroes, and if Mrs. Bratton thought about the matter as she fought to keep from fainting while the reaping hook arched above her neck, she probably felt herself a somewhat insufficient heroine. There were trying and seemingly insurmountable problems rising along the frontiers in America's past, and they were faced up to by men and women a bit confused, and altogether quite humble beneath the touch of bravado needed to keep their courage properly inflated.

Still these Americans of both genders faced up to their tasks with resolution and fortitude. Through their efforts a new world was discovered, a nation born, a continent won, and a civilization given new direction and impetus. From them came the richest of legacies, which must be guarded, enjoyed, profited by, and handed on perfected and augmented.

Said Emerson Hough in recording its passing, "The frontier! There is no word in the English language more stirring . . ." May this be true, and may the frontiers along which current generations are forced to travel stir them to accomplishments equal to those which the challenge of an earlier frontier stimulated in their forebears.

Milestone Events Having a Bearing
on the American Frontier

790

Among the first attempts to press out into the unknown western ocean appear to be those of monks from Ireland in search of religious retreats and new fields for missionary endeavor. They had reached the Faroe Islands over a long expanse of open sea during the seventh century, and pushed on across further leagues of uncharted ocean toward the close of the following century, reaching Iceland in the above year.

874

Norsemen drawn from the same sea-roving stock that had sacked Slav settlements on Russian rivers had set up principalities in that land in past centuries, and even sped down south-flowing rivers to the Black Sea to threaten Constantinople, and were now turning their attention to coastal lands and islands below them along the Atlantic's shores. Groups sailing westward from the fiords of Norway also reached Iceland, and established a New Norway there.

982–85

Eric the Red, an Icelandic nobleman, sailed off into the setting sun to confirm tales of the existence of islands in the ocean to the west, and discovered the great land mass of Greenland, which was rapidly colonized.

1000

Leif Ericsson, a son of Eric the Red, while returning to Greenland from Norway, was caught in a severe storm and blown far to the southwest. His first landfall was a country quite unfamiliar to him, and could have been Nova Scotia, but more probably was New England, since he gave it the name Vinland (Wineland) because of the abundance of wild grapes found there. He evidently reported very favorably on its climate and prospects on his arrival at home in Greenland.

1010–13

Thorfinn Karlsevni, brother-in-law of Leif Ericsson, with a considerable party in three ships, set out to relocate Vinland. This group appear to have spent part of four years along the upper eastern shores of the North American continent, and may have ventured as far south as Long Island Sound, although they left little if any positive evidence of their visit. While Vinland is mentioned in Germanic literature beginning about 1074, detailed records of this particular voyage did not find permanent form until they were incorporated in Norse sagas produced in the fourteenth century. Ever greater credence, however, is now being given these early Norse visitations.

1170

There is the unsubstantiated tradition of a voyage by a party of Welshmen into the Gulf of Mexico at about this time. Some have even claimed that its members penetrated to the interior and are responsible for a stone citadel of undetermined origin in southeastern Tennessee. Others maintain they were absorbed into an Indian tribe far to the north beyond the Mississippi.

1334

The discovery of the Canary Islands off the African coast, which were later to be used as a stepping stone by Columbus on his first voyage.

1362

The date on the Kensington (Rune) Stone, dug from among embracing tree roots in western Minnesota in 1898, and now generally accepted as authentic. It appears to be tangible evidence of a Norse party in this midcontinent area in the middle of the 1300s. The fact that the party was well-nigh wiped out near by, and that the few stragglers who may have found their way back to Norway reached home shortly before the dark ages settled upon that country with the eclipse of Norse literature, may logically account for the scarcity of records concerning this interesting and enterprising exploration.

1410

The translation of Ptolemy's *Geography* into Latin in this year revived the long-held contention the earth was a sphere, helped circulate this belief among navigators, and developed the conviction in some that Asia might be reached by sailing to the west.

1418

Exploration of the Madeira Islands, which, although hazily known before that time, made the existence of land areas over the western horizon a certainty in the minds of people in the south of Europe. Nine years later the Portuguese also explored seven of the Azores Islands.

1448

A map drawn in this year by the cartographer Andrea Biancho included land far to the west in the area occupied by Brazil, from which some infer that South America had already been visited.

1470–74

During these years the Danes, also of Nordic or Viking stock, seem to have dispatched an expedition under command of two Germans far to the west. While there is no direct evidence it penetrated beyond Greenland, certain incidents, such as the following, lead to the conjecture it may also have visited Labrador and Newfoundland.

1474

Joao Vaz Corte-Real was awarded a captaincy of one of the Azores by the Portuguese Government for having completed a voyage to the Land of the Codfish, presumably Newfoundland. Under what auspices this exploit was successfully undertaken is not recorded. Some scholars favor his being a member of the above Danish expedition. Others contend that Basque and Breton fishermen were quite probably already sailing to the Banks off Newfoundland and replenishing their supplies of wood and fresh water on our eastern seaboard. There are indications that great secrecy was imposed on ocean enterprises by the government in Lisbon in the early fifteenth century, and it would also be the natural inclination of the skippers of fishing craft to maintain silence with regard to new and profitable fishing grounds.

1492

The first voyage of Columbus, on which he touched at Watlings Island, one of the Bahamas. He termed this group of islands and his later discoveries the Indies, apparently believing them to lie somewhere off the coast of Asia, and thus gave the name of Indians to the native peoples of America.

1493

Stirred by Columbus's findings, Ferdinand and Isabella encouraged Pope Alexander VI to set up a line of demarcation granting to Spain possession of new lands discovered west of a meridian a hundred leagues beyond the Azores and Cape Verde Islands, and reserving to Portugal new areas to the east of it. By the Treaty of Tordesillas the following year, the two countries agreed to this arrangement, with one important reservation. The Portuguese demanded the line be moved 270 leagues further west, which placed the eastern bulge of South America within their sphere of influence.

The shift was made, and may indicate that Portuguese navigators were already familiar with the shores of Brazil, and perhaps even more of the great southern continent.

It was 1493, the year in which Columbus began his second western voyage, that the scholarly Peter Martyr declared that a New World had been discovered.

1497

The first voyage of John Cabot, an Italian merchant resident in England, who for some years past had been financing expeditions to seek out the source of "Brazil wood" used in dyeing. On his trip he touched at Cape Breton Island and cruised far to the south along the mainland.

1498

Crossing the ocean again the following year in company with his son Sebastian, John Cabot reached Greenland, then Labrador, and continued down past Nova Scotia and New England, and quite likely to the Delaware capes and Bay. England thus claimed prior rights to these northern reaches of the Atlantic coast by discovery.

1499

The Spanish conquistador Alonso de Ojeda, accompanied by Amerigo Vespucci, made a voyage which reached to the mouth of the Amazon River. Vespucci completed a second trip into this area in 1501–2, and so well publicized his exploits that the two continents in the New World were eventually named for him.

1508–11

The conquest of Cuba, and then of Puerto Rico, was completed by the Spanish, who soon used them as convenient bases for sallies onto the mainland.

1513

Juan Ponce de León, governor of Puerto Rico, landed in Florida on Easter Sunday, and claimed it for Spain. On a subsequent expedition, he was wounded in an encounter with the Indians, and died on the return voyage to his capital in San Juan.

1519

Hernando Cortés attacked Mexico, and with such success that by 1521 he had subdued the Aztecs and made Mexico City the capital of the viceroyalty of New Spain, of which he was appointed captain-general and governor.

A reconnoissance of the Gulf coast was made by Alvárez Pineda, who covered it with some thoroughness from Florida west to Vera Cruz. He and his party were probably the first Europeans to visit the mouth of the mighty Mississippi.

1521–25

During these years several Spanish parties explored the Atlantic shore line north from Florida, one of them reaching Nova Scotia.

1524

Giovanni de Verrazzano, an Italian navigator in the employ of the French monarch, Francis I, landed in Albemarle Sound on the coast of North Carolina, proceeded as far north as Maine, touching at New York and Narragansett Bay, and named the whole area New France.

1526–28

A colony planted near present-day Beaufort in South Carolina by the Spanish under Lucas Vásquez de Allyon was finally wiped out by the Indians in retaliation for the impressment into slavery of some of their fellow tribesmen by a De Allyon party from Haiti some years previously.

1534–41

During these years the French navigator Jacques Cartier made three voyages to America, the last under De Roberval's command. The Gaspé coast and the St. Lawrence River as far as the Lachine Rapids at Montreal Island were explored, but no permanent settlements were planted.

1536

Alvaro Nuñez Cabeza de Vaca, shipwrecked with a party en route from Florida to Mexico, together with three companions spent about six years in captivity among the Indians on the Texas coast. Escaping overland, the four men made their way across a portion of our Southwest, and arrived in Compostela, Mexico, in 1536. They told fabulous tales of what they had encountered on this journey, which later touched off an ill-starred expedition into the area in search of cities of gold.

1539

After nearly a year at a base in Cuba perfecting his plans, Hernando de Soto, who had been authorized to plant colonies in the Florida area, landed with about a thousand men on the shore of Tampa Bay, set off up the coast, and wintered near the present site of Tallahassee. Drawn by the hopes of finding gold, he and his dwindling party pressed inland, and during several years wandered through the central South, crossed the Mississippi, and wintered in 1541–42 far out along the Arkansas River. Returning to the former stream in the spring, he was unsuccessful in planting a colony in present Bolivar County, Mississippi. He died shortly afterward, was buried in the muddy bed of the great stream, and it required nearly a year for the remnant of his followers to make their way to the coast of Mexico.

In 1539 the governor of New Spain dispatched a priest, Fray Marcos de Niza, north from Mexico City to verify the tales of seven golden cities in the Zuñi country, in what is now Arizona-New Mexico, recounted by the members of the De Vaca party.

1540–42

Fray Marcos on his return was so certain he, too, had seen the seven cities with walls of gold that an expedition of some magnitude was fitted out and placed under the command of Francisco Vásquez de Coronado, governor of one of the western Mexican provinces. It pressed to the north on a fruitless search which took the main body, or smaller scouting parties from it, into parts of Arizona, New Mexico, Texas, Oklahoma, and Kansas. Although the adventurers were forced to return to Mexico empty-handed, the expedition did result in the first known missionary efforts among the native peoples in what is now the United States, when one of the accompanying priests, Fray Juan de Padilla, returned to the Quivira Indian villages in central Kansas. He was later killed, reportedly when he sought to leave this group to work among other tribes, and thus became the first Christian martyr within the limits of our country.

Hernando de Alarcón, in command of ships sent up the west coast to support the Coronado expedition, ascended the Gulf of California, entered the mouth of the Colorado River, and explored its lower reaches in 1540.

1542–43

At about the time of Coronado's return, Juan Rodriguez Cabrillo explored the Pacific coast, but in some way failed to discover either of the important bays at Monterey and at San Francisco.

1549

Although a Dominican priest, Fray Luis Cancer de Babastro tried to make a peaceful penetration of Florida and work among the Indians there. He was slain, and the effort terminated.

1553

A small octavo volume of 102 leaves printed in England in Gothic letter in this year, and titled *A Treatyse of the Newe India*, is considered to have been the first book on America in the English language.

1559

Tristán de Luna made an unsuccessful attempt to colonize the Carolinas from a base at Pensacola, but was forced to withdraw his forces after two years.

1562–65

Taking advantage of their religious discontent, French authorities somewhat surreptitiously permitted the Huguenots to make three separate efforts to plant colonies in the Carolinas and Florida under the leadership of Jean de Ribaut and René de Laudonnière. The first, on Port Royal Sound at the southern edge of South Carolina, was a signal failure; while the two attempts at the mouth of the St. Johns River in Florida were eventually wiped out by Spanish forces under Pedro Menéndez de Avilés.

The latter commander, after expelling the French, completed the founding of St. Augustine in 1565, making it the oldest permanent settlement within the United States. By his system of military posts and garrisons he secured firm possession of Florida, but was unable to obtain footholds further to the north.

1577–80

Francis Drake, on a world-circling voyage, paused to refit his ships in Drake's Bay behind Point Reyes, thirty miles up the coast from the Golden Gate. He named the area New Albion, and claimed it for England.

1584–86

Sir Walter Raleigh sent a party to found a settlement on our eastern coast. It landed at Roanoke Island, just behind the Outer Banks on the North Carolina ocean front. The name Virginia was given to the area in honor of Queen Elizabeth. But the enterprise quickly foundered and the dissatisfied colonists were returned to England by Sir Francis Drake.

1587

A second party sent out by Raleigh under John White landed in the same locality, and erected cabins. The leader returned to England that same year for supplies and additional recruits, but unsettled conditions there prevented his coming back to America until 1591. On his arrival he found only a few traces of those left behind four years before, but some evidence that they might have moved elsewhere. Search failed to uncover their whereabouts, and the group has since been known as the Lost Colony. The name Virginia Dare, given to a granddaughter of White's born soon after their first arrival, has managed to be perpetuated.

1598–1608

Juan de Oñate subjugated the Indian population of what is today New Mexico, and from bases there in the upper Rio Grande Valley sent parties to explore an area from California east into Kansas. The capital of this new province, Santa Fe, was not established until 1610, two years after Oñate himself had departed.

1602

Unsuccessful attempts were made by the Spaniards under Sebastián Vizcáino to establish settlements at Monterey Bay, and also at a point above San Francisco Bay. The narrow Golden Gate seems to have deceived the earlier explorers, and this landlocked expanse of some three hundred fifty square miles of sheltered anchorage was passed by.

In this same year Mace visited the Carolina coast and brought home a shipload of trading products, while Captains Gosnold and Gilbert explored the Maine and Massachusetts area, and might have planted a colony on the latter shores had any of their men consented to remain behind while a return to England was made for supplies. In 1605 Weymouth visited the Maine coast and carried home several friendly Indians and an enthusiastic report.

1603

Samuel de Champlain sailed from France, and re-explored the shores of the St. Lawrence River to the Lachine Rapids, and also the coast of Nova Scotia, where Poutrincourt was to re-establish Port Royal seven years later. He also investigated the New England coast as far as Cape Cod before returning to France.

1606–7

The London Company sent out three ships and about a hundred twenty colonists under the command of Captain Christopher Newport. They sailed in December, but contrary winds kept the party for six weeks virtually within sight of the English coast. Finally reaching Chesapeake Bay, they selected a site on the north shore of the James River, and in May 1607 the first permanent English colony in America was established at Jamestown.

In this latter year, another group, headed by George Popham, established a fort and base near the mouth of the Kennebec River on the Maine coast. Although progress was made and a ship appeared the following spring with supplies and additional settlers, the disillusioned men chose to return to the homeland.

1608

Champlain returned to the great Canadian waterway, founded Quebec, which was to become the anchor of French hopes of empire in America, and in 1609 visited the long narrow lake between Vermont and New York State which was named after him.

1609

Henry Hudson, an English navigator in the employ of the Dutch, seeking a northwest passage, explored the river which now bears his name, established amicable relations with the natives, and cleared the way for the Hollanders to set up a trading post on Manhattan Island four years later.

1610

Captain Newport, returning to Jamestown with more than four hundred additional settlers and a new governor, Thomas West, Lord de la Warr, gave a new lease of life to the faltering colony. Although De La Warr left the following year, Sir Thomas Dale, who remained in command, brought order out of chaos and succeeded in giving Virginia a stable foundation, on which it soon began to thrive.

1611

Colonization of Ulster in Ireland was undertaken by English and Scottish Protestants. The later expulsions of descendants of these colonists sent to America some of the hardiest of our frontier stock— the Scotch-Irish, many of whom pushed back into the wilderness, and were prominent among those who first crossed the Appalachians and began the conquest of the West.

1612

The cultivation of tobacco was first attempted in Virginia. When the colonists soon learned to cure it for shipment, it provided the chief cash crop, gave needed economic impulse, and even helped to mold that colony's social structure.

In this same year Dutch merchants dispatched a party to the mouth of the Hudson, where a post was established on Manhattan Island in 1613, and in the following year a fort, first called Nassau, and later Orange, was built near the present site of Albany. The coast was explored as far east as Cape Cod, and the foundation laid for a profitable fur trade with the natives.

1614

English colonists from Jamestown, probably in search of codfish, seem to have sent vessels as far north as the Maine coast. There, in 1613, Captain Samuel Argall, in command of some thirteen small craft, discovered the Mission San Savior, set up on Mount Desert Is-

land by two French priests from Port Royal in Nova Scotia, captured
it, and terminated its activities. In the next year, 1614, Captain
John Smith, of Virginia fame, mapped the New England coast in
some detail and renewed the interest in it at home, which had cooled
measurably after the default of the Popham colony in Maine. Smith
was attempting a third voyage to America when he was captured
by pirates. His *Description of New England,* written while imprisoned aboard the pirate vessel, and published in England after his
escape, proved excellent promotional literature for that section of
America.

1619

Arrival of the first of several groups of women at Jamestown,
the first in the colony, who had been selected in England by the
London Company and shipped to America because of their willingness to become wives of the local planters. The French would follow similar procedure in connection with the settlement at New
Orleans more than a hundred years later.

In 1619 some twenty Negroes were set ashore, also at Jamestown, and sold as slaves, the first among the thousands to flow
in ever greater numbers during the next two and a half centuries.

The year also witnessed, on June 30, the first session of a representative assembly meeting in America.

1620

The separatist group known as the Pilgrims obtained a patent
from the London Company to form a second colony in Virginia. But
contrary to the original agreement, they were brought to shore far
to the north of the company's domain and chose a site for their settlement on Cape Cod Bay in Massachusetts, which they named Plymouth. Their Mayflower Compact, drawn up and signed before they
landed, placed control of their affairs in their own hands, and is one
of the first great American documents through which government
by the consent of the governed became the basis of our heritage.

1623–24

During these years the Council for New England managed to plant small colonies at Dover, New Hampshire, at Saco and at Casco Bay in Maine, and on Cape Ann in Massachusetts.

It was in 1624 that the charter of the London Company was revoked and Virginia became a royal colony. Thus began the recapture of colonies in America by the British crown, an effort which would extend well into the next century.

1625

The first settlement made on the island of Barbados, the most easterly of the West Indies. It grew rapidly, several attempts were made by its inhabitants to plant colonies in the Carolinas, and trade and exchange of residents with this island figured prominently in the early history of South Carolina, and of Charleston in particular.

1626

Peter Minuit's New Netherland Company purchased Manhattan Island from the Indians for about twenty-four dollars in trinkets, founded New Amsterdam as a permanent town, and began small outlying settlements in the Hudson Valley, Connecticut, New Jersey, Delaware, and Pennsylvania.

1628

John Endecott and a party of about fifty Puritan colonists sent out from England founded Salem, Massachusetts.

English forces captured Acadia (Nova Scotia) and Quebec during a war with the French, but these and other areas in New France were restored by peace terms four years later.

1629

A new colonial corporation, The Governor and Company of Massachusetts Bay, having been formed, some four hundred additional settlers were sent out to join the group at Salem.

1630

When agreement was reached that governance of the colonies sponsored by this new Massachusetts Bay Company might originate in the colonies rather than in England, several responsible leaders and large numbers of prospective settlers were encouraged to come to America. In this year alone some seventeen ships bearing nearly a thousand colonists arrived in the Bay area, and before the year was out towns that became Boston, Dorchester, Lynn, Mystic, Roxbury, and Watertown had been started. By 1634 a representative system of government was established, and within its first twelve years the Bay community received some sixteen thousand settlers.

1633

The Dutch from New Amsterdam began active trading operations along the Connecticut shore, erected a post at Dutch Point below present-day Hartford, and gave concern to the Massachusetts colonists because of their encroachment.

1634

Jean Nicolet, intrepid French explorer, pressed to the west over the Great Lakes as far as Sault Ste. Marie and Green Bay, Wisconsin. Others carried on his early endeavors, and by 1665 La Pointe Mission had been founded near the far end of Lake Superior.

1634

In March the party dispatched the previous year by Cecil Calvert, Lord Baltimore, arrived in Chesapeake Bay. After a brief call at Jamestown, it landed at the mouth of the Potomac River and founded the first town in the Maryland colony at St. Mary's.

1635-36

In the former year a fort was established at Saybrook, at the mouth of the Connecticut River, by settlers sent out from England under the command of John Winthrop, Jr. The next year the Reverend Thomas Hooker led a group overland from Cambridge in the Bay colony to found Hartford, while a second group from Watertown settled Wethersfield, and others a third town to the north, Windsor.

1636

The general court of the Bay colony, feeling the need for additional ministers to serve the great number of new communities springing up, authorized the formation of a "schoale or colledge" for their training. It was to be located in New Towne, later Cambridge, and four hundred pounds was appropriated for the purpose. In 1637 the Reverend John Harvard came to preach in America, and, dying here the following year, left a somewhat larger sum and his library to the new college, which was given his name in 1639.

In 1636 Roger Williams was banished from the Bay colony because of the liberality of his expressed views. He took refuge among the Narragansett Indians, and formed a colony at Providence in which ecclesiastical and political affairs were to be completely separate.

Anne Hutchinson, banished under similar circumstances two years later, took refuge with supporters on an island near by in Narragansett Bay, later called Rhode Island. Resulting settlements at Portsmouth, and the next year at Newport, when joined with the Williams settlement in 1644, were chartered as the English colony of Rhode Island and Providence Plantations.

1638

Using the organizing ability and experience of the Hollander, Peter Minuit, no longer associated with affairs at New Amsterdam, several groups of Swedish and Finnish settlers journeyed into the Delaware Valley beginning in this year. Fort Christina was erected on the site of present-day Wilmington, Delaware, and farms cleared and homes built along the western shore of the Delaware River as far up as the later site of Philadelphia. One of their log cabins, erected about 1644, is still in use in the area; and it was among these particular settlers that the type of housing which was to characterize the American frontier for well over two hundred years originated.

1639

The first printing office in what was to become the United States was set up at Cambridge, Massachusetts.

1643

A confederation was effected among the four Connecticut colonies and the group about Massachusetts Bay, including Plymouth, for common defense. This was one of the first steps toward group action, and would find its ultimate expression in the United States of America.

1651

The passage in this year of the Navigation Act was the first in a series of laws enacted by the British Parliament in an attempt to control growing colonial trade. The hampering tendencies of such legislation, limiting as it did prized freedom of action on this side of the ocean, accumulated over the next century and played a leading part in widening the breach that finally broke the colonies away from the homeland.

1652

The settlements in Maine as far east as Casco Bay were brought under the jurisdiction of Massachusetts.

1655

The Swedish settlements along the Delaware were taken over by the Dutch under Peter Stuyvesant.

1662

Charles II granted a liberal charter embodying a large measure of home rule, under which the settlements in the Connecticut Valley and at New Haven were joined three years later as the Colony of Connecticut.

1663

A royal grant was made to eight Lords Proprietors covering a strip of land between 31 and 36 degrees north latitude and reaching to the Pacific. This opened up the Carolina area to more intensive settlement. While there was some infiltration of the Albemarle country from Jamestown, and several abortive attempts along the coast, the village established on the south bank of the Ashley River in 1670, called Charles Towne, and moved to its present site in 1680, marked the beginning of real colonization.

In 1663 John Eliot's Bible in an Indian tongue, one of the first major works published in America, was printed at Cambridge.

1664

As an incident in the war between the British and the Dutch, New Amsterdam and other holdings of the Netherlands between Connecticut and Maryland were taken over by the English. The town at the mouth of the Hudson was renamed New York, in honor of the king's brother, the Duke of York, and the upriver fort became Albany. The area between the North and South rivers, or the Hudson and Delaware, to be known henceforth as New Jersey, was granted to Lord Berkeley and Sir George Carteret.

1670

A British joint-stock company, later called Hudson's Bay Company, was chartered in this year by Charles II. It eventually spread a chain of forts and trading posts across Canada from the Atlantic to the Pacific, exercised complete power in the areas in which it operated, and was considered more powerful by the Indians than any government. It was destined to play a conspicuous role in the fur trade along American frontiers from Michigan to Oregon.

1673

The two Jesuit priests, Fathers Jacques Marquette and Louis Joliet, using the almost unbroken waterway formed by the Fox and Wisconsin rivers, passed from Green Bay on Lake Michigan to the Mississippi River, and down that stream to its junction with the Arkansas. By means of this long water passage, formed by the St. Lawrence, the Great Lakes, and the Mississippi and its tributaries, the French had ready access to and a communicating medium by which to control the whole interior of the continent.

In this same year, while England and Holland were again embroiled in war, the Dutch gained temporary control over their lost holdings in the former New Netherland.

1675–76

The Indians of New England, decimated and weak after an epidemic that occurred when colonies were first planted, had gained sufficient power to resist the advancing frontier as the settlers pressed inland. King Philip's War forced the abandonment of or completely destroyed some twenty colonial settlements throughout the area, and cost heavily in lives and property. It was one of the first major evidences of the clash between civilization and savagery that was to extend through the next two centuries, or until the American frontier disappeared.

1676

This Indian unrest extended in these same years to the Virginia colony. Atrocities along its frontier, taken too casually by the royal governor, Sir William Berkeley, brought leading citizens into revolt against his ineffectualness under the leadership of Nathaniel Bacon. Although Bacon's Rebellion was quelled, it left a pattern for more resolute and comprehensive action in the American Revolution a hundred years later.

1679

René de la Salle explored the shores of Lake Michigan, and built Fort Crèvecoeur on the Illinois River, another waterway joining the lake with the Mississippi. Three years later he descended the latter stream to its mouth on the Gulf and claimed the whole great valley it drains for France.

1680

A native revolt in New Mexico drove the Spanish to abandon for sixteen years their settlements in that area.

1681

William Penn was granted a charter to a rectangle of land "beginning [at] the fortieth degree of Northern Latitude," a designation soon to cause many years of litigation, and extending 5 degrees west from the Delaware River. Its eastern border still contained a scattering of Swedish, Finnish, and Dutch settlers when Penn arrived in the following year and began to lay out his "greene countrie towne" at Philadelphia.

1683

The founding of Germantown, Pennsylvania, signaled the beginning about this time of the influx of Palatinate Germans, who, with the Scotch-Irish, pioneered the frontier areas, especially in that

colony, and began the intensive movement of settlers into the transmountain country in the next century.

1684

The Massachusetts charter was annulled due to continuing friction between the colonists and the authorities at home. Two years
later the Dominion of New England was formed, and an attempt
made to consolidate the several colonies between Maine and New
York under the governorship of Sir Edmund Andros, who managed
to assume control only of Plymouth and Rhode Island.

La Salle sailed from France with a large party intending to
plant a colony at the mouth of the Mississippi, but failing to find it,
set up a base on Matagorda Bay well down the Texas coast. From
there he made several vain endeavors to locate the outlet of the great
river, being killed by his companions on the fourth and last attempt.
His little colony was wiped out by the Indians in 1689. It was he
who gave the name Louisiana to a large area in the interior of North
America.

1687

Andros demanded the surrender of Connecticut's charter, but
was foiled when candles in a meeting room were suddenly blown
out and one of the Patriots made off with the document and hid it
in a cavity in the famous Charter Oak at the edge of the Hartford
settlement. The drive to suppress charter governments in other colonies continued during the following year.

1689

It was early in this year that news of the Revolution of 1688,
which displaced James II in favor of William of Orange, reached
Boston. Governor Andros was immediately imprisoned, and charter
government was restored in Massachusetts, Rhode Island, and Connecticut.

1690

The War of the League of Augsburg in Europe had repercussions in America, where it was called King William's War. It resulted chiefly in massacres of settlers by the Indians allied with the French, which occurred in the frontier communities in upper New York and in Maine.

1692

The Puritan excesses reached their zenith in the Salem witch trials.

1693

The college of William and Mary in Virginia, second founded in the colonies, was named in honor of the ruling sovereigns, and thus carried the new names which had been proclaimed four years previously for the colonies of Virginia and Maryland respectively.

1699

Pierre Lemoyne Sieur d'Iberville, born and reared in Quebec, sailed from France hoping to found colonies on the Gulf coast and forestall, or at least compete with, similar hopes on the part of England and Spain. His posts at Biloxi and Mobile managed to maintain precarious footholds.

In the same year French priests founded two mission stations in the Illinois country.

1701

Antoine de la Mothe Cadillac built a fort at a strategic point on the river connecting lakes Erie and St. Clair, where Detroit now stands. It was a thorn in the flesh of the western frontier until firmly in our hands following the War of 1812.

In 1701 a third colonial college was founded in the Connecticut colony at Branford, and later moved to New Haven and named for Elihu Yale.

1702–13

The War of the Spanish Succession, known on this side of the ocean as Queen Anne's War, again brought the struggle between England and France for colonial dominance to open bloodshed. The Connecticut Valley was raided by the French from Canada and their Indian allies in 1704. In 1708 colonial militia was among the forces sent against Montreal and Quebec.

1711–15

The wars with the Tuscaroras and Yamassees raised havoc in the Carolinas, and added evidence of continuing trouble to be expected as the expanding frontier pushed the native peoples from their home areas.

1716

Governor Alexander Spotswood led a party of Virginia gentlemen known as "The Knights of the Golden Horseshoe" on an exploration trip to the west which discovered and soon opened to settlement the Shenandoah Valley, and encouraged the filling in of the Piedmont frontier in the Carolinas.

1717

The first of several attempts during the colonial period to prohibit or restrict the slave trade was made in South Carolina, lasting until 1719. There was strict prohibition of importation of new slaves during the years 1741–44, and the traffic was curbed between 1746 and 1749, and again between 1766 and 1780 by a prohibitive tax, while in the years 1769–70 the trade was restricted by agreement of the nonimport association. There was constant fear that the preponderance of slaves over the scattered white settlers might bring on insurrection and massacres.

1718

A base was established on the banks of the Mississippi some miles above its mouth by Jean Baptiste Bienville, younger brother of D'Iberville, who had founded Biloxi and Mobile. This post gave control of the lower reaches of the great river to France, which later passed to Spain, and eventually forced the Louisiana Purchase.

1720–22

The Spanish during these years managed to get firm possession of the Texas area.

1722

Governor William Burnet carried on negotiations with the Six Nations of Indians at Albany, a step in aligning this powerful confederation of natives on the side of the English in the contest for control of the continent.

1730

Sir Alexander Cuming, a Scottish adventurer recently arrived in the South Carolina colony, undertook a one-man embassy to the towns of the Cherokee tribe as far north as the lower Blue Ridge Mountains, and won from its chiefs a promise to accept and abide by regulations laid down by the English authorities.

1733

Savannah was laid out, and Georgia, the last of the thirteen colonies, opened to settlement under the guidance of James Oglethorpe.

In this same year Parliament passed the Molasses Act in a further attempt to curb the trade of the colonies with other than British interests. It fostered privateering and smuggling, and brought on the hated writs of assistance, which gave British colonial officials virtually unlimited right of search in private premises. These enactments inflamed public opinion, and helped condition a coming generation for the ultimate break with the homeland.

1735

Trial of John Peter Zenger, newspaper publisher in New York, imprisoned the previous year for libel of the governor of the colony. This was probably the most famous court case of the colonial period, and Zenger was defended by the outstanding colonial lawyer Andrew Hamilton, who not only freed the defendant but established the right of freedom of the press and of trial by jury, making them American heritages.

1743–48

The War of the Austrian Succession, known in the colonies as King George's War, was the third European conflict to transmit its influence to this side of the Atlantic. The French lost their stout fortress Louisbourg, in Nova Scotia, to New England volunteers, and the hostilities called forth the great talents of Sir William Johnson and Conrad Weiser in restraining powerful Indian groups from allying with the French.

1749

The organization of the Ohio Company by Virginians focused attention upon the great river valley beyond the mountains, and brought on a contest with the French attempting to gain a foothold there.

1753

To counter the growing interest of the Virginians, the Marquis Duquesne erected Fort Le Boeuf at Presque Isle near the portage on the Venango Trail leading from Lake Erie to the Ohio River. It was here in December of the same year that the youthful George Washington delivered the ultimatum from Governor Dinwiddie of Virginia warning the French they were trespassing on British soil. A year and a half later, and a hundred miles south of this point, Washington was a member of the Braddock party that suffered defeat at the hands of the French and Indians at Fort Duquesne, built just to the east of the present city limits of Pittsburgh.

1754

The growing threat of the French along the western border of the colonies from New England to Virginia prompted the calling of the Albany Congress. Here a plan of union to achieve better common defense was developed by Benjamin Franklin. Although it was rejected by the colonies themselves and received no support in England, it aided in paving the way for the accomplishments of the Continental Congress two decades later.

1755–63

The fourth European conflict, the Seven Years' War, also reached to America, where it was known as the French and Indian War. It became the training ground for a number of military leaders who rose to prominence in the Revolution. By the time of the surrender of Montreal in 1760, the French had irrevocably lost their holdings on this side of the ocean and the British were in position to extend their empire, in which endeavor they determined to exact more aid and more wholesome respect from their American colonies.

1762

American colonization had proved to be so great a financial loss that France ceded the Louisiana area to Spain.

1763

By proclamation issued in this year, George III attempted to limit colonial expansion to a line along the sources of the rivers flowing from the Appalachians into the Atlantic Ocean. The land beyond was to be reserved to the natives, and strict control over trade within this reserved area was established. This act tended to heighten interest in these western lands, and developed many ingenious schemes to by-pass the limitations imposed.

In 1763 and the next two years there were further attempts to tighten control over colonial affairs by the passage of the Sugar, Colonial Currency, Stamp, and Quartering acts. While the most obnox-

ious, the Stamp Act, was promptly repealed, patriotic forces in the
colonies began to solidify, and used these enactments as means of
inflaming public opinion and widening the breach between Britain
and her colonies.

1768

Charles Mason and Jeremiah Dixon, two English astronomers
and mathematicians, closed three generations of litigation between
Baltimore and Penn heirs by an exact survey of the boundaries of
Pennsylvania, Maryland, and Delaware, establishing their famous
Mason-Dixon Line.

At a treaty signed at Fort Stanwix, the Six Nations, made up of
tribes in New York State, ceded to the British crown whatever title
they had to lands between the Ohio and Tennessee rivers. At the
same time they transferred to a private firm of traders with the natives in the Pittsburgh area land that now comprises about one fourth
of the state of West Virginia.

Hardly had the Stanwix treaty been signed when Daniel Boone
left his cabin on the Yadkin River and headed west "in quest of the
country of Kentucke."

1769

José de Gálvez began the occupation of California from Mexico,
establishing settlements at San Diego in that year, Monterey the
following year, San Francisco in 1776, and Los Angeles in 1781.

Far to the east, the Watauga settlement, which had its beginnings in 1769 on one of the headwater streams of the Tennessee
River, not only formed an Association, whose Articles—drafted in
1772—were the first written constitution in America of a free and
independent people, but several of the leaders in this frontier community found conspicuous places in the Revolution, and in the later
perfection of our democracy.

1770

The Boston Massacre, a disastrous brawl brought on by hatred
of the British troops quartered in that city, resulted in deaths of both
soldiers and citizens. It is often accounted the first bloodshed of the
Revolution.

1771

The Battle of the Alamance, in which North Carolina Regulators were shot down, although seeking a parley under a flag of truce, by militia commanded by the fiery royal governor, William Tryon. Many colonists who survived this encounter, and a mass hanging a month following, made their way over the mountains to the Watauga area, and some had their revenge nine years later at the Battle of King's Mountain.

1772

Rhode Island Patriots in the shipping trade, harassed by the virtual blockade of their harbors, burned and sank one of the British revenue cutters, the *Gaspé*, after it had run aground in Narragansett Bay off Bristol.

The tension was now mounting rapidly, and committees of correspondence were soon set up in Massachusetts and Virginia, by means of which leading patriots might keep in touch with each other. Within two years there were similar committees in all colonies except Pennsylvania, where individuals carried on the interchange of letters.

1773

Resistance to the continued tax on tea, which had found expression in one form or another in several ports, reached a crisis in December in the dramatic handling of the matter in the Boston Tea Party.

1774

Spanish explorers made a reconnoissance of the Pacific coast as far north as the Gulf of Alaska, and discovered the mouth of the Columbia River.

By the fall of this year the relations between the colonies and the mother country had grown so grave that the First Continental Congress was assembled at Carpenters' Hall in Philadelphia, with representation of all colonies except Georgia. It adjourned within a few weeks, over the toast "May Britain be wise and America be free," appointing the tenth day of the following May for a second meeting.

1775

On April 19 occurred that "little thing" which produced the "great event," as the "shot heard round the world" echoed in the crisp morning air on Lexington Common. The die was cast, and the Revolutionary War began in earnest.

In this same eventful year the Transylvania Company was formed, which undertook the settlement of Kentucky, transferred the frontier beyond the mountains, and began the winning of the West.

1776

Opinion favoring independence gained strength, and the Virginia Assembly, meeting in May, formed a new government and passed a resolution which its representatives were to read before the reconvened Continental Congress, to the effect that "these United Colonies, are, and of right ought to be, free and independent States." In response to this document a committee was formed in the Congress and Thomas Jefferson assigned the task of drafting a suitable instrument. This was debated, and finally agreed to on July 4, and had a public reading on the eighth, which touched off a tremendous celebration.

Evidence that frontiers beyond the Alleghenies were filling in came with the petition to the Continental Congress of settlers beyond these mountains asking that they be allowed to set up a new province or state, to be known as Westsylvania. This plea came but a short time after the signing of the Declaration.

1777

Articles of Confederation, designed to gather the thirteen states into a union to be known as the United States of America, passed the Congress, and the plan was referred to the assemblies in the several states for consideration.

Sufficient settlers had entered the Kentucky country so that a meeting was called in Harrodsburg about the middle of 1776, which sent George Rogers Clark to the Virginia Assembly with a petition whereby local government might be formed. In the following year, 1777, the assembly organized this "respectable Body of Prime Riflemen" as a Virginia county, having the boundaries of the present state of Kentucky.

1781

The final and decisive engagement of the Revolution was the siege of the British forces under Lord Cornwallis trapped on the peninsula at Yorktown, which began in the last days of September, and was terminated by his surrender on October 19.

1783

It was nearly two full years after the above capitulation before a treaty of peace was signed, on September 3, 1783, between the United Colonies and Great Britain. The delay was attributable to our ally, France, rather than to our late antogonist, anxious now to regain both the trade and good will of her former colonies rather than have them aligned against her by her perennial enemies, the French and Spaniards.

France still smarted from the loss of her colonial empire in Canada and Louisiana, and for some years sought to keep the new United States as a dependent ally, restricted to the area east of the Appalachians, in the hope that our unity might be broken by the mountains, and the western settlements joined to a recaptured Louisiana.

1784–87

A severe depression settled over the land soon after the signing of the peace, the aftermath of the war and particularly its financing, and attributable in no small part to the fact that as an independent nation we were debarred from certain markets which we had enjoyed previously. Shays' Rebellion in western Massachusetts was one of the more marked manifestations of these lean years, which gave impetus to migration into western lands.

1785

On January 27 of this year a typical convention was held at the settlement of Clarksville, on the opposite bank of the Ohio River from Louisville. It was so far removed at that moment from any formal government, being outside the limits of Kentucky, that it called together the "majority of the actual settlers of the town" to draw up laws for their own governance that would be acceptable under the "general laws" of the United States. There would be many such "associations" in outlying areas in the years ahead, as witnessed by the later vigilance committees.

1785–87

This interest in western lands, the pressures set up by an increasing population, and a need to honor bonuses in land granted for military service brought about the formation of a Public Domain by the cession of their claims to territory beyond the mountains by certain of the seaboard states. A land ordinance dealing with its survey and sale was passed, while in 1787 this was amplified by the Northwest Ordinance, providing for government in this area from which a number of new states would be carved, and which provided a whole series of frontiers during the next half century.

1787

The inability of the Articles of Confederation to care for the expanding needs of the still independent states prompted five of them to call a convention at Annapolis in 1786 in the interest of a "more perfect union." This resulted in another meeting in Philadelphia the following year, to which twelve sent representatives, the exception being Rhode Island. After a long series of secret sessions covering more than four months, the draft of a proposed Constitution was signed by the delegates still present on September 17, and copies of the document sent to all the states for hoped for ratification.

1788

Before the end of 1787 three states, Delaware, New Jersey, and Pennsylvania had agreed to the new federal Constitution. Connecticut and Georgia ratified it soon after the turn into 1788, followed by a close decision in Massachusetts in February. By spring Maryland and South Carolina had fallen into line, which made eight, with nine favorable responses needed to place the document in operation. On June 21, New Hampshire gave its consent, Virginia and New York followed shortly afterward, North Carolina in the following year, and Rhode Island not until 1790.

1789

The new Congress elected to serve under the Constitution assembled in New York on March 4, and Washington was inaugurated first President on April 30.

1789–95

Far to the west the Spanish during these years were making rather unsuccessful attempts to colonize the Pacific Northwest as far up as Vancouver Island.

1791

Samuel Slater, in association with Moses Brown, established the first factory in America for machine spinning of cotton yarn on power-driven looms at Pawtucket, Rhode Island.

1792

Kentucky, the first state to be formed from land lying west of the Appalachians, was admitted to the Union.

It was in this same year that a young law student, Eli Whitney, visiting on a Georgia plantation perfected a mechanical cotton gin.

This device popularized the cultivation of short staple cotton, and in but a few years worked profound changes upon life in the South Atlantic and Gulf states. In 1798 Whitney began the manufacture of muskets for the government by a method of interchangeable parts, which was the forerunner of modern mass production, and strongly influenced many other types of manufacture in the century ahead.

1792

The Whiskey Rebellion, centering in western Pennsylvania, was a straw in the wind pointing up the desperate need for better communication between the frontier expanding rapidly to the west beyond the mountains, and the markets on the eastern seaboard and in Europe. Tension continued for two years, and subsided only after Albert Gallatin's eloquence addressed to 226 of the rebels at Whiskey Point on the Monongahela River ended the possibility of bloody civil strife.

1795

General Anthony Wayne, after decisively subduing the Indians at Fallen Timbers in northwestern Ohio in 1794 and making a display of force to British troops still occupying American territory and stimulating their Indian allies to rebellion, signed an effective treaty with the natives at Greenville in 1795. This led to the opening of large tracts in Ohio to settlement, which was sufficiently rapid that the Ohio Territory achieved statehood eight years later.

1796

Tennessee became a state, and but six years after North Carolina had relinquished claims to the area. The frontiersmen in this state, and in Kentucky immediately to the north, developed the "western viewpoint," which in the years ahead strongly offset more conservative attitudes prevailing in the older eastern areas, and materially aided in perfecting our concepts of democracy.

1797

Charles Newbold, an American, patented the cast iron plow, the curvature of whose share is said to have been carefully figured out by Thomas Jefferson.

1800

In the secret Treaty of San Ildefonso, Spain, after thirty-eight years in possession, passed the Louisiana area back to France. Rumors of the exchange filtered through to America, but France did not occupy any of the key defense points, and Spanish officers and soldiers continued in possession of such strategic points as New Orleans and St. Louis.

1803

In a surprise move engineered by Napoleon, the huge but very indefinite Louisiana country beyond the Mississippi River was purchased from France. Since it embraced New Orleans, it gave the United States control of the mighty watercourse, and an unhampered outlet to markets for products of the increasing number of settlers in the great river's tributary valleys. This turned the growing defection of these settlers to staunch loyalty and strengthened our sense of nationalism. It also provided a tremendous new area for expansion and produced a long series of frontiers, which were to have profound influence upon our development.

1804–6

To explore what had been acquired the year before, President Jefferson dispatched a party to the west under the able joint command of Meriwether Lewis and William Clark. They investigated the northern plains, crossed the Rockies, descended the Columbia River to the Pacific Ocean, produced dependable maps and collected valuable information about a completely unknown area, and strengthened our ultimate claim to the Oregon country.

1805-6

A young army officer, Zebulon M. Pike, made an exploratory trip to the headwaters of the Mississippi River in the Minnesota country, and another which took him into the southern Rockies, Mexico, and Texas, extending our knowledge of these areas, soon to become active frontiers.

1807

Robert Fulton, with the backing of Robert R. Livingston, built and perfected the steamboat *Clermont,* which successfully ascended the Hudson from New York to Albany in about thirty-two hours. This development was soon to have a profound influence upon the whole country, furnishing inexpensive transportation wherever there was navigable waters, especially along the Mississippi and its tributaries.

In this same year Aaron Burr, former Vice-President, and an enemy of Jefferson's, hoping to play upon the presumed lack of loyalty to the Union in the West, attempted an unsuccessful organizational scheme in the lower Mississippi Valley, with the evident intention of setting up an independent nation. His plans, however, were frustrated, and although tried for treason, he was acquitted.

1811-12

The stiffening attitude of the Indians toward settlement north of the Ohio River was attributed by many westerners to secret encouragement by the British in Canada. A group called the War Hawks, led by Henry Clay of Kentucky, obtained control of the Congress. With their position strengthened by William Henry Harrison's defeat of native forces in the Battle of Tippecanoe, this belligerent group succeeded in forcing a declaration of war on Britain on June 18, 1812.

1812-14

While American naval vessels scored some brilliant victories at sea and on the Great Lakes, these counted for little in the prosecution of this unpopular war. Reverses ashore were discouraging, and after Britain's release from commitments on the Continent, enough forces were dispatched to this country to make the enemy's efforts highly discouraging. General Andrew Jackson did succeed in crushing the power of the Creek Indians with lasting benefits, but his victory at New Orleans was actually won after peace had been signed.

1814

As the Treaty of Ghent was being prepared for signatures and the ending of this inconclusive war, a group in the New England states, in which the war had been particularly unpopular, called a convention at Hartford. At first this looked like an attempt at secession, and while the final outcome was far from it, it did emphasize the wide divergence of views and the strong sectional bias which plagued the country in its formative years. That these attitudes blended into a short "era of good feeling" and a stronger sense of nationalism in the years just ahead does not mean that sectionalism was not to play a conspicuous role in our national affairs, even until after the turn of the next century.

1818

Although the Treaty of Ghent left many controversial points between Britain and this country unsettled, a convention held in this year satisfactorily adjusted questions in connection with the common boundary between the United States and Canada.

1819

Following the termination of the Seminole War in 1817–18, Spain agreed to cede Florida to the United States, and at the same time clarified the western boundaries of the Louisiana Purchase, opening more of that great area to further investigation and use.

It was in this same year that an American steamship, the *Savannah*, crossed the ocean to Liverpool, dependent in part, however, on sails.

1820

After a brief respite, sectional feeling began again to crystallize, being brought to the fore by the growing contest over extension of slavery, especially into states to be carved from the Louisiana Purchase. Partial yielding by both sides had characterized the Constitutional Convention which had established the Union thirty-three years before. This same pattern was again resorted to in achieving the Missouri Compromise, in which a boundary between slave and free states was agreed upon.

The disposal of the public domain, now grown to a huge area, had been subject to much abuse. A new land law passed in this year was calculated to cut down speculation in public lands and establish a uniform minimum price of $1.25 per acre on land opened to occupancy.

1821

William Becknell of Missouri pioneered the Santa Fe Trail, opening up commerce with the northern provinces of Mexico, and giving stability to the towns growing up along the bend of the Missouri River where it swings to the north at present-day Kansas City. These would long be important outfitting points for western exploration, trade, and settlement.

1825

In this year Robert Owen, a Welshman who had successfully operated spinning mills in Scotland on the basis of co-operative enterprise, established a communistic society at New Harmony, Indiana. This was the first of a number of such experiments extending well through the century, but was shorter lived than some, terminating in 1827.

The completion of the Erie Canal provided water transportation between New York and the Hudson Valley and all points on the shores of the Great Lakes. It thus became an important artery of travel and commerce, and played a conspicuous part in the opening up and development of the tier of states from New York west to Minnesota.

1828

With a fanfare of celebrations on July 4 of this year, construction was begun on the Baltimore and Ohio Railroad, the first major public conveyance system on rails in this country. Although it was introduced just as the canal-building era was getting into full swing, the steam locomotive within the next twenty years would prove its greater flexibility, and make the extensive canal system obsolete for the most part within a few years of its completion.

1829

The defeat of John Quincy Adams for the presidency by Andrew Jackson in the fall of 1828 signaled the end of an era, and ushered in that of the common man with Jackson's inauguration the following spring. A conservatism which had long outlived the Revolution, particularly in political affairs, began to break down. Suffrage reforms, already under way in some of the states, quickly spread, and the democratic spirit and principles forged along the western frontier were enacted into laws. A Workingmen's party was formed in New York that proposed a broad program of social reforms, many of which were adopted in the years immediately ahead.

1830

The organization of the Church of the Latter-Day Saints, and the publication of the *Book of Mormon* both took place in this year. The followers of Joseph Smith were to labor on and encounter persecution along several frontiers, but later made a magnificent contribution in their settlement of the Great Salt Lake area and the fostering of the state of Utah.

In this same year an act was passed creating a Commissioner of Indian Affairs and authorizing the removal of certain tribes to reservations to be established west of the Mississippi River. While this solution did put an end to some of the worst clashes with the native peoples, it still posed many problems, which had to be worked out slowly over the years ahead.

1831

With the establishment in Boston of the anti-slavery publication, the *Liberator*, the abolitionist movement began to shape up and gain in power, increasing the sectional tensions which had to be resolved thirty years later in the War between the States.

1832

This growing sectional strife suddenly came to a head in the reaction in South Carolina to the tariff act passed in this year, resulting in an Ordinance of Nullification, which sought to set aside the federal act's provisions within that state. Despite President Jackson's strong stand in the matter, it took a compromise act promising tariff reductions to prevent an open breach.

1834

Cyrus Hall McCormick received a patent on a reaping machine which he had brought to practical usefulness three years before. It was destined to contribute heavily toward bringing the great prairie country under profitable cultivation.

Far to the west the establishment of a mission station in eastern Oregon paved the way for the great influx of settlers who would be on their way to this new frontier after the panic of 1837 had run its course.

1836

A colonization scheme begun by Moses Austin, and completed by his son Stephen after the father's death, had poured considerable numbers of American colonists into Texas during the 1820s and '30s. Mexico, having freed itself from Spanish domination in 1821, and after some years of internal turmoil, sought to strengthen its hold over Texas and Texan affairs. The American settlers resisted the methods employed, and gained their independence at the Battle of San Jacinto on April 21 of this year. Although an independent nation for nine years, Texas was annexed as a state in 1845, precipitating war with Mexico.

It was in this same year that Samuel Colt received a patent on a multi-shot weapon, later standardized as the six-shooter, which was soon to play its somber part along many a frontier.

1836—37

Two years of poor crops, Jackson's strong-arm policies in regard to financial affairs, and especially his executive order requiring hard-money payments in the purchase of public lands brought about a sharp recession, which, in 1837, became a panic, leaving the West prostrate. Before the area beyond the mountains was well on its feet again, we had pushed through to the Pacific and the country had entered another era in its affairs.

It was just as the panic was settling down that John Deere perfected a steel plow suitable to the heavily turfed and gummy prairie soils. Possibly no other instrument did more toward winning the West, and surely none was more effective in breaking down the reluctance to settle the great treeless plains that occupied so considerable a portion of the interior of our country.

1839

The discovery of a method of vulcanizing rubber by Charles Goodyear made this substance widely useful as waterproof footwear and clothing, but did not reach the zenith of its benefits until the advent of the automobile.

1844

Residents of Spanish extraction living in California succeeded in freeing themselves from Mexican control, and entered upon an independent status, soon to be challenged by the American settlers who had for some years been moving into the area and establishing ranches.

Back on the Atlantic coast a device was being put to practical tests that was to have great influence in annihilating distance, speeding communication, and welding our scattered people together in more perfect union. Although he had developed the first practical telegraph twelve years before, Samuel F. B. Morse had only in this year persuaded a reluctant Congress to build an experimental line, and on May 24 transmitted the first telegraph message at a distance between Washington and Baltimore.

1845

Texas, after nine years as an independent nation under the Lone Star flag, was annexed to the United States under a joint resolution of Congress.

1846

There were strong expansionist advocates in the Congress during the 1840s, determined that our western boundaries should be the shores of the Pacific. Several reconnoissance parties, either with open or tacit government backing, had in recent years been in California or the Oregon country; and in 1846 a treaty was made with Britain setting the northern boundary of the latter area at the 49th parallel. Thus the Columbia Valley and land to the north of it were firmly in our hands and open to intensive exploitation.

At about the same time war was declared against Mexico, an aftermath of the annexation of Texas, and latent in other problems stemming from the Louisiana Purchase. The peace signed at its successful conclusion two years after gave us firm title to the Southwest, excepting a small area later purchased, and to California. Together with the Oregon Treaty, it established our continental boundaries virtually as we know them today, gave us huge additional territory and new resources, which were opened up and developed with great rapidity during the balance of the century.

1847

Famine in Ireland began the extensive emigration from that land to this country. A portion of the influx remained along the eastern seaboard, but great numbers pressed on into the Mississippi Valley, then filling in rapidly.

1848

The discovery of gold at Sutter's mill near Coloma in January of this year, a few days before the signing of peace with Mexico, set off one of the greatest stampedes in the history of the world, for the influence of this news reached far beyond our own shores. During the momentous year 1849, when the gold fever was at its height, enough settlers entered the area so that California was admitted as a state in 1850. Many who suffered discouragement pushed north into Oregon, which territory came to statehood nine years later.

1850

Although the Compromise fought through the Congress in this year emphasized the immense gulf opening up between the major sections of the country, considerable importance should be attached to another piece of federal legislation. It provided substantial land grants to aid construction of new railroads. Rapid communication was highly essential to the expanding and rapidly growing country, and the railroads were destined to provide it.

1854

Immigration in this year ran above four hundred thousand, and together with the nine previous years had totaled just under three million souls. America was impressing itself upon Europe as a land of opportunity, and the tide of newcomers to these shores would, after a setback during the war years ahead, run in the hundreds of thousands, and some years above a million, until 1930.

But the tensions were mounting, and slavery developed bloodshed in Kansas over the question of popular sovereignty raised by the Kansas-Nebraska Act. Out of "bleeding Kansas" were to come such diverse characters as John Brown, the North's "martyr" at Harper's Ferry, and Buffalo Bill Cody, of buffalo killing, pony express, and circus fame.

Beyond our own shores Commodore Matthew Perry negotiated a commercial treaty with Japan, ending that country's isolation and improving the trade prospects of our new ports along the Pacific coast.

1857

The prosperity and excitement of the 1850s came to a sudden close with the onset of a financial crisis in 1857, twenty years following the devastating panic of the Jackson era. Ensuing hard times bred discontent and set men to roving. Some of them discovered gold near Pikes Peak in Colorado in 1858, and by the spring of the next year a great horde set off from Council Bluffs toward the mountains. The gold strike was limited, but the mountain country received a heavy consignment of settlers.

1858

The famous Lincoln-Douglas debates brought the sectional differences between North and South into sharper focus, and forecast the trend of affairs which three years later would result in civil conflict.

1859

The drilling of the first producing oil well at Titusville, Pennsylvania, gave access to new lubricants for the ever greater number of machines with moving parts appearing on the American scene, provided a new means of illumination, the coal-oil lamp, and a powerful, explosive fuel.

In mid-October John Brown, heading a small body of men, seized the federal arsenal at Harper's Ferry, Virginia, in an attempt to capture arms to start a slave insurrection. Loitering in the town, he was captured by marines hurried in under command of Colonel Robt. E. Lee. This madly fanatical enterprise, with its grim termination, unleashed bitter feeling both North and South, and pointedly dramatized the chasm opening between the two great sections of our land.

1860

The election of Abraham Lincoln, followed shortly by South Carolina's blunt protest in the Order of Secession, made open war well-nigh inevitable.

1861

The Act of Secession, eventually subscribed to by ten of the southern states, the firing on the *Star of the West*, formation of the Confederate States of America, and the election of its president and vice-president, were quickly followed by the opening of hostilities on April 12 with the bombardment of Fort Sumter. The high tide of southern hopes began to ebb with the outcome of the battle fought at Gettysburg in the first three days of July 1863; while all action finally terminated with surrender of the last Confederate forces in Louisiana at the end of May 1865. More than a month previously Lincoln had been assassinated, and the country moved into the difficult period of Reconstruction and recovery from this devastating war.

1866

About the middle of this year a successful Atlantic cable was placed in operation linking us with Great Britain and the Continent, speeding up news from America, and increasing immigration, still principally from northern Europe.

1867

Alaska was purchased from the Russians, adding a land area of more than a half million square miles, and a new frontier, which is still to be fully exploited.

1869

One of the great milestones was passed in the opening of the Union Pacific Railroad to traffic, thus connecting the Atlantic and Pacific coasts by rail. George Westinghouse perfected his air brake, which was to make railroad travel safer and more comfortable; while James Oliver's chilled-steel moldboard plow would help to break an ever greater number of virgin acres for cultivation. The first experiments with refrigerated railway cars would pay rich dividends in better living in the years to come.

1870

Exposure of the Tweed Ring in New York politics was followed two years later by the Crédit Mobilier and other scandals which implicated men in high federal positions in the Grant administration.

1871

There was a race riot in California brought about by the wholesale importation of Chinese into that state as contract laborers. By a federal statute of 1882 Chinese labor was barred, and in 1885 another enactment terminated the bringing in of any and all contract labor.

1873

Withdrawal of European capital invested in the United States, occasioned by financial stringency there, brought on a severe panic here. Repercussions along the frontier and generally throughout the West gave impetus to the Granger Movement, which provided the farmers a stronger voice in local and national politics.

In this year, too, the Comstock Lode, rich deposits of silver ores in the Washoe area in Nevada, proved to be the Great Bonanza, and poured out quantities of new wealth.

1876

The Centennial Year, celebrating one hundred years of independent existence, brought the great exposition at Philadelphia, which dramatized the enormous progress that had been made both in material and in social phases of life in these United States. It was in this year also that Glidden and Vaughan patented a machine for production of barbed wire, which would soon fence the plains, stabilize the cattle business, and break the open range up into pastures, ranches, and farms. There was the successful demonstration of voice transmission over telephone wires by Alexander Graham Bell; and General Custer and his command were wiped out by the Sioux

Indians in Montana, the indirect result of a gold strike in the Black Hills of the Dakota Territory.

1877

The Indian war in Idaho was the outcome of further pressure upon the natives by the expanding mining and lumber frontiers. In this same year, too, the Desert Land Act began to give encouragement for the construction of dams and canals to facilitate irrigation in the arid sections of the West.

1881

The surrender and death of Chief Sitting Bull, Sioux Indian medicine man, was but one episode in the determined resistance of the northern Indians to encroachment in the plains country and the loss of reservations promised to them as homes in perpetuity.

1882

The Star-Route Fraud dramatically pointed up the irregularities and graft obtaining in the Post Office Department of the federal government, and indicated that questionable practices might be relatively common among federal officeholders.

1883

After some eighteen years of agitation of the subject by the President and the Congress, the first attempt was made at civil service reform and the divorce of political activities from federal employment.

In this year the second transcontinental railroad, the Northern Pacific, was placed in operation, followed shortly by the Southern Pacific. Within the next ten years three others had penetrated to the Pacific coast.

1885

The letter postage to any point within the continental United States, which had been reduced two years previously from three cents to two cents per half ounce, was again cut in half by dropping it to two cents per full ounce.

1886

The American Federation of Labor was organized, the first lasting grouping of a number of national trade unions. The Haymarket Square Riot in Chicago this same year had so discredited the Knights of Labor that a new consolidating organization was called for.

In October of this same year Bartholdi's Statue of Liberty Enlightening the World, one of our foremost symbols, was unveiled in New York Harbor.

1887

Disturbances among the Indians in the Southwest terminated with the surrender of Geronimo and his Apache warriors to General Nelson A. Miles.

By 1874 the railroads had achieved sufficient interstate status so that some measure of federal control seemed necessary. Certain practices of the carriers in those days were dubious enough to call for the appointment of a congressional investigating committee in 1885. As a result of its hearings, the Interstate Commerce Act was passed in 1887 and a commission to administer it set up.

1889

As though to signal the passing of the American frontier, four states carved from the trans-Mississippi country—North Dakota, South Dakota, Washington, and Montana—achieved statehood in this year. Wyoming and Idaho would follow in the next year, Utah in 1896, Oklahoma in 1907, and New Mexico and Arizona in 1912.

Previously Nevada had been admitted in 1864, Nebraska in 1867, and Colorado in 1876.

The year 1889 also further marked the demise of the frontier by the opening of unassigned portions of the Indian Territory (Oklahoma) to settlement.

The first census, taken in 1790, showed our population then to be 3,929,214. Thirteen years later, as the West was slowly opening up and that fact was being employed to justify the Louisiana Purchase, Jefferson expressed the opinion that it might conceivably be two hundred years before there were cities of consequence beyond the Mississippi River.

But the eleventh census, taken in 1890, indicated that during our first century under the Constitution we had grown to a nation of 62,947,714 people, an increase of nearly sixteenfold. There were cities of size and importance from coast to coast, and from the Canadian border to the Gulf—but the frontier, that habitable area having an average of less than two inhabitants per square mile, had vanished. It had indeed been a remarkable hundred years.

Index